MEMOIRS OF A BENGAL CIVILIAN

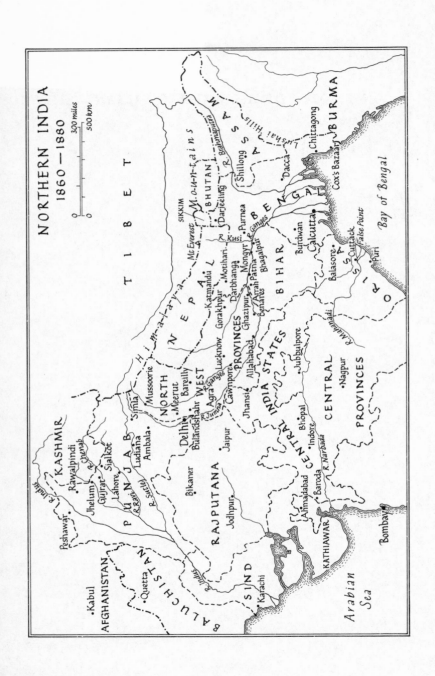

NORTHERN INDIA
1860 — 1880

300 miles
500 km

T I B E T

H i m a l a y a

NEPAL

N A G A

L u s h a i   H i l l s

BURMA

Chittagong

Shillong

Dacca

BHUTAN

Darjeeling

SIKKIM

Mt Everest

R. Kusi

Purnea

BENGAL

Cox's Bazaar

Bay of Bengal

False Point

Calcutta

Burdwan

Bhagalpur

Monghyr

Patna

Benares

Ghazipur

Arrah

BIHAR

Balasore

Cuttack

Puri

ORISSA

R. Ganges

R. Brahmaputra

Darbhanga

Motihari

Karmandi

Gorakhpur

NORTH

WEST

PROVINCES

Lucknow

Cawnpore

Allahabad

Agra

R. Ganges

R. Jumna

Meerut

Bareilly

Mussoorie

Simla

Bulandshahr

Delhi

Ambala

Ludiana

Lahore

Sialkot

Gujrat

R. Chenab

Jhelum

R. Jhelum

Rawalpindi

KASHMIR

Peshawar

R. Indus

Kabul

AFGHANISTAN

Quetta

BALUCHISTAN

R. Indus

Karachi

SIND

KATHIAWAR

Ahmadabad

Baroda

Bombay

Arabian
Sea

Bikaner

Jodhpur

RAJPUTANA

Jaipur

Jhansi

CENTRAL INDIA STATES

Bhopal

Indore

R. Narbada

CENTRAL

PROVINCES

Jubbulpore

Nagpur

R. Mahanadi

John Beames, aged about 21, on the eve of his departure for India

MEMOIRS OF A
BENGAL
CIVILIAN

JOHN BEAMES

The lively narrative of a Victorian district-officer

ELAND BOOKS

Published by
ELAND BOOKS
53 Eland Road London SW11 5JX

This edition first published by
Chatto & Windus 1961

ISBN 0 907871 75 5
First issued in this paperback edition 1984
©Chatto & Windus 1961

Printed and bound in Great Britain
by Redwood Burn Ltd, Trowbridge, Wiltshire

CONTENTS

INTRODUCTION

By Philip Mason

SOME years ago, as a preliminary to writing a book about the Indian Civil Service, I asked a wide circle for diaries, sketches, letters, and all kinds of unpublished material which might help. A good deal of what came in I found tedious reading; some was trivial, some technical, and some not general enough in its application. But the account of his own life written by John Beames was quite another matter. I found it a pleasure to read and quoted from it freely; I kept wishing I could quote more.

Beames's life is the work of an individualist if ever there was one, but at the same time it is representative; the things that happened to Beames were the kind of things that happened to all of us in India, not only in the years after the Mutiny but seventy years later, and he looked on his work and on his seniors in just the kind of way that the good District Officer of a certain kind always did. With all this he might be a bore, but in fact he is a delight to read because he seems, naturally and without effort, to understand some of the secrets of good writing. He has a clear mind, he knows what he wants to say, and he says it without hesitation. Like Trollope, he has trained himself to write swiftly, not pausing to 'gaze out of the window and nibble the end of his pen'. He seldom allows himself to be side-tracked by digressions and qualifications; he is never pompous or self conscious or timid. These are negative virtues—though it is the lack of them that is responsible for a great deal of bad writing—and they would not be enough without an observant eye, a well-stocked mind, strong likes and dislikes, positive opinions. The result is a plain lively English that not many men wrote in the age of Carlyle and Ruskin; it is nearer to the English of Swift and Defoe or of our own time than to what we think of as Victorian English. What we think is, incidentally, a little unfair to the Victorians; there is plenty of nervous English in Trollope and Surtees and in many Indian state papers and district gazetteers. It disappears with self-consciousness and comes to the surface when the writer is more concerned with matter than with manner.

Beames did not write for publication but to amuse his family, not, one feels, that it would have made much difference if he had known that his story would be published. It is the essence of his attraction that he never conceals an opinion or pretends to be anything but himself. Indeed, he was always in trouble for being too outspoken. He had, for instance, a poor opinion of soldiers and remarks that the Indian Government 'acted on the assumption that military men were fit for any duties and were apparently not required with their regiments. . . .' Since civil and staff pay were much better than regimental, there was no doubt a good deal of truth in his belief that some regimental soldiers had gone to some trouble to catch the eye of a superior and get a civil appointment. And sometimes, no doubt, there were cases like that of 'Delilah Aberystwith and that bad Ulysses Gunn' and others exposed in 'Departmental Ditties'—not, of course, only among soldiers. But it was sweeping of Beames to think that all soldiers in civil employment had had to fawn and intrigue to get their appointments; it was unwise to tell the ex-soldier who was head of his district that he felt like St Paul before the chief captain who 'with a great sum obtained this freedom'. 'But I,' Beames continued, 'was free born.'

This was not the behaviour of a man likely to win special promotion. He thought little of Lieutenant-Governors in general and of almost every specimen of the class he met. John Lawrence he considered 'a rough coarse man, in appearance more like a navvy than a gentleman . . .' who tried to turn his officers into 'homeless vagrant governing-machines . . .' But his special dislike was for Sir Richard Temple, who was Lieutenant-Governor of three provinces in succession. Beames was always scathing about Temple, and particularly about his views on the famine which in 1874 seemed likely in Bihar. 'In his usual theatrical way,' wrote Beames of Sir Richard, 'he rode at the rate of fifty or sixty miles a day through the districts, forming as he said an opinion on the condition of the people and the state of the crops. He would sit down at night after one of these wild scampers and write a vainglorious minute. . . .'

Beames was not alone in regarding this brilliant man as something of a showman, and he was entirely representative in his attitude to authority. He wrote on one occasion: 'I was in fact called upon to act and not to act at the same time, a false position in which Government is fond of placing officers by way of shuffling off its own responsibility, a regular Secretariat trick.' Here he echoes the cry of every district officer and every Colonial Governor, blamed for weakness if he does not act and for harshness if he does. Of course it is unfair; the razor-edge which the administration has to walk is not created by the Secretariat (or by

'Whitehall', or the Colonial Office, or whatever is the bugbear of the moment); it is inherent in the situation, in Nyasaland today, in India yesterday. That he does not see this is Beames's limitation as an officer but his strength as a writer and he is more amusing to read than many a man who is more prudent, tactful and balanced.

You might call him intellectually arrogant; when he was appointed to Champaran, one of the few districts in India where planters were strong, he determined to be master in his own district, not, as he says, 'from mere lust for power . . . but because the district was a sacred trust delivered to me by Government and I was bound to be faithful to that charge. I should have been very base had I from love of ease or wish for popularity sat idly by and let others usurp my place and duties. Ruling men is not a task that can be performed by *le premier venu* and though I was young at it, still I had five years' training and experience prefaced by a liberal education, while these ex-mates of merchant ships and *ci devant* clerks in counting-houses had had neither'. There *is* arrogance here, but with it went a noble determination to do what was just to the peasant whatever the cost. Here in Champaran he supported a peasant against the tyranny of a rich planter; later in Orissa he challenged the Government and its laws on behalf of an old woman who was prosecuted for picking up the salt that was delivered by the sea free of tax at the door of her hut. After a number of reprimands, he won his case and the law was changed.

Beames is still remembered in India by a small circle as a scholar, a grammarian, and a philologist; this was a game with the left hand, as the Hindustani phrase goes, a hobby. He was an accomplished and industrious linguist. But to scores who cannot follow him into such realms he will give pleasure by his sketches of an India that had changed but not wholly disappeared two generations later. Let me give one sample only; he is describing an old-fashioned police officer before the reforms of 1861. The man he chooses is: 'a tall, portly Mohammedan, grey-bearded, with a smooth sleek look, crafty as a fox, extremely polished in manner, deferential to his superiors, but haughty and tyrannical to his inferiors. With his huge scarlet turban laced with gold, his sword hung from a gold embroidered baldric, spotless white clothes and long riding boots, he bestrode a gaunt roan horse with grey eyes, a pink nose and a long flowing tail. . . .' His book is full of such pictures and conveys most vividly the atmosphere of the East India Company's College at Haileybury, of life in Calcutta just after the Mutiny, of the Punjab and Lawrence, and later of both Bihar and Orissa. And it is worth pausing to think of the life led by his young bride when she came to join him in the

Punjab, and of their first meeting after two years' separation, after the long voyage to India, after the three weeks' journey from Calcutta by pony-cart, all accomplished among strangers. It is our good fortune that Beames was so outspoken a critic of his superiors; he was several times in trouble and transferred as a result and he therefore saw more of India than most of us.

I do not think that Beames can have been an easy man to get on with; I suspect that if he had been my District Officer I should often have smarted under criticism the more painful because it was deserved. But I feel sure that if I had known him I should have respected him and I shall certainly think much less well of anyone who does not end his book with a liking for this obstinate, faithful man, so just, so lively in his interests, so plain and downright in his judgements, above all so honest with himself and with everyone he met.

Publisher's Note

The first few dull pages about ancestors should not deter the reader from continuing with this otherwise remarkable and entertaining book.

PREFACE

THIS narrative was begun at Cuttack, where I was Magistrate and Collector, in 1875, and was continued at intervals till 1878 when, owing to my being transferred to Chittagong, and to other causes, it was discontinued. I tried to go on with it in 1880 at Chinsurah but I then found a curious thing. I could not remember recent events so clearly as I did those which had occurred long ago. As I had brought down my narrative to the year 1870 it was necessary to wait till the subsequent events had receded further into the past so that I might recollect them better. The manuscript was therefore laid aside, and by degrees forgotten. Now in the year 1896, having retired from the Civil Service, and returned to England, I take it up again, and as on reading it over I see many things which I should now prefer to describe differently, as well as some which are incorrect, it seems better to write it from the beginning.

If it should be asked why so obscure a person should think it worth his while to write the story of his life at all I reply that it is precisely because I am an obscure person—an average, ordinary, middle-class Englishman—that I write it. There is an abundance of biographies of eminent and illustrious men, but the very fact that they were eminent takes them out of the category of ordinary mortals. Their lives, therefore, though deeply interesting on account of their great deeds, are different from the general run of men who were their contemporaries. It will I think be interesting to posterity—or at any rate to my descendants—to read the account of how an ordinary, average Englishman lived in the reign of Queen Victoria. Such as my life has been, such has been that of thousands of other men in this period of time. And as India, where I spent so large a portion of my life, is already changing and many institutions and conditions of existence which were in my day, are passing away, the Indian part of my life may be perhaps useful as a record of a state of things which has ceased to be. Finally my descendants if they ever read these pages may be interested in learning what manner of men their forefathers were. And even if no one should care to read these pages, it amuses me to write them, which is perhaps as good a reason for writing them as any other.

Netherclay House
Bishop's Hull near Taunton,
Somersetshire.

JOHN BEAMES
12 October 1896

CHAPTER I
ANCESTORS

BEFORE I begin to write about myself I ought, I think, to give some account of my ancestors. These, as far as we know about them, may be divided into two groups, one beginning in the eleventh and stretching down to the fifteenth century, the other beginning at the end of the seventeenth century and descending in an unbroken line to the present day. With the first group our connexion is, if not doubtful, at any rate not clearly traceable, so I shall merely mention a few of the best established facts concerning them.

Of course they 'came over with the Conqueror', like all respectable English families. It is the fashion to laugh at this claim, as a mere idle boast. But it is true in our case, at least if we are really descended from this family. In the Roll of Battle Abbey among the names of Duke William's followers occurs the name Belemis. It is also spelt Belmeys, Beaumeis, Bealum, and in various other ways. Spelling in those times was not subject to any rules. There were three brothers of this name in the Norman Army—William, Richard and Walter. They came according to one account from Beaumez near Alençon, according to another from Les Beaumes near Avignon. They were attached to the service of Roger de Montgomeri, Earl of Shrewsbury, and obtained the manors of Tong and Donington in Shropshire, as also Ashby in Derbyshire. Richard was a priest and rose to be Bishop of London in 1108, and Warden of the Welsh Marches. He devoted all his episcopal income to the rebuilding of St Paul's Cathedral. His nephew, also called Richard, became Bishop of London about 1145. The Tong and Donington lines died out, the first in 1200, the second in 1329, but there was a third line settled in Lincolnshire represented by Henry de Belemis of Limberg Magna, and another at Sawtree Beaumes in Huntingdonshire. A de Beaumys also held lands in Sussex and near Reading, where there is still a ruined moat called Beaumys Castle.

About the year 1450 the last of various scattered notices of persons of this name is found. The family appears to have sunk into obscurity in the Wars of the Roses. Besides the identity of name, there is also the fact that their crest and coat of arms were the same as those we now bear, to support the supposition that we are descended from them.

If so, it is most probably from the branch settled near Reading that we are derived, for about two centuries later the name Beaumes or Beames is found to be tolerably common in Berkshire and North Wiltshire, and some of them were bankers of Chippenham.

It was probably to this line that the John Beames belonged who, in or about 1728, married Sarah, daughter of the Revd John Power of Clifton near Bristol. This John Beames is sometimes called Roger Beames (by my grandfather in some notes of his which I have) I do not know why. He is said to have been born in 1695 and may be regarded as the founder of the present family. The Revd John Power by his will dated 26 March 1743 bequeathed all his property at Clifton to his grandson John Beames, son of his daughter Sarah. This property remained in the family for several generations, in fact, a portion of it is in their possession still. Although the social position of John I, alias Roger, does not seem to have been very exalted, he was evidently of gentle birth, he was an *armiger*, and I have in my possession two silver shields of his or his son's bearing, *azure* six garbs *or*, 3, 2 and 1, crest a garb *or*; the same coat and crest as that of the old Norman de Beaumys.

I know nothing more about John I, except that he had two sons, John II and George. In an affidavit sworn at the Guildhall, London, by this George on the 2nd December 1786 before the celebrated Wilkes, Lord Mayor, John II is described as 'late of St Mary Overy's Churchyard in the parish of St Saviour's Southwark in the County of Surrey, victualler, deceased' and George himself is described as a butcher of Oxford Street. The descendants of the Norman Barons had come down in the world, but not more so than those of many others whose names are in the Roll of Battle Abbey. These ancient names, as the Duchess of Cleveland shows, survive very largely among the peasantry when they have died out among the noble and gentle families.

In 1749 John II married Sarah Halliday, and had two sons and two daughters. His eldest son died in a terrible manner when an infant thirteen months old. The father had been out and returning home stood for a while on his doorstep talking to a friend. The nurse, who was at an upper window, seeing him below held out the baby to see its father. The child in its eagerness to reach its father sprung forwards, slipped out of the nurse's arms, fell and was dashed to pieces on the doorstep before its father's feet! His second son John III was born in 1754 and baptized at St James's Church, Piccadilly, where the baptismal certificate was found a hundred years later by my father when he was Assistant Preacher of that church. The two daughters were named Sarah and Mary. The latter is said to have married one Connop, but beyond this, I have no information about them.

John III appears to have been at first in business for in the affidavit above-mentioned he is said to have been 'of Thames Street, London, but now of Clifton near the Hotwells, Bristol'. He evidently succeeded to the Clifton estates on the death of his father. The house in which he lived—Hillfield House—is still in existence at the lower end of Granby Hill just above the Hotwells. It must have been a fine old house then, though it is now divided into two and part of it is let out as a shop. Its gardens covered the whole hillside, and the fields surrounding it were long known as Beames's hill fields. They and most of the garden have now been built over. At Hillfield my great grandfather lived till his death. He married a widow, Sarah Reeves (they all seem to have married Sarahs) whose maiden name was Ivyleafe, a strong-minded, clever woman.[1] He himself led a life of dissipation, drinking and gambling. Dreadful stories are told of his conduct. He belonged to a club in Bristol where play ran high and he gambled away the greater part of the Clifton property. Clifton was then a rural village, but it soon after became a fashionable watering place, and the land he gambled away became very valuable. As my cousin, old Benjamin Burroughs, from whom I have derived much of the information I am now recording, and who knows every inch of Clifton, often says with a sigh we might have been million-aires if it had not been for this great-grandfather. The unhappy man eventually became insane and died in 1789. He left two children, and two sons had died before him in infancy; they were named George and Samuel.

The two surviving children were my grandfather John IV, born 16 May 1781, and Sarah, born in 1783. She married Benjamin Gustavus Burroughs, a physician of Bristol by whom she had a family of four sons and two daughters, of whom I shall frequently have occasion to make mention hereafter.

My great-grandmother thus left a widow devoted herself to the task of saving and managing what was left of the Clifton property. She was very successful and contrived to build up a very respectable income. She married for the third time, a Captain Powell (whether R.N. or Merchant Service I do not know—but he was a sailor of some kind), whom she survived, eventually dying on 19 March 1840 aged 84. Ben Burroughs tells me she wanted to marry a fourth time after Powell's death, and was with difficulty dissuaded by her children and grandchildren. As all the property was left to her, she was well-off and kept up a good state at Hillfield House. She was fond of society and loved to give large parties; she held a prominent position in Clifton society. I have heard her

[1] I have a likeness of her copied from a miniature.

described as a tall, rather masculine woman—'a grenadier in petticoats' my father used to call her.

She sent her son, my grandfather, to the Grammar School at Sherborne in Dorsetshire whence in due course he proceeded to Exeter College, Oxford. After a time however he changed to Lincoln College. It was here that he displayed the first signs of his perverse and passionate character. The examinations for the B.A. degree had hitherto been held at each College separately, but about this time a new regulation was introduced under which the examinations were held by the University and the power of conferring degrees was taken away from the College authorities and transferred to those of the University. This change was strenuously opposed by the Heads of several Colleges, prominent among whom was Dr Tatham, Rector of Lincoln. A rumour was spread abroad that men from the recalcitrant Colleges would be unfavourably regarded by the Examiners and this roused much ill-feeling. My grandfather characteristically excited himself very much on this account and he went into the Schools bristling with irritation and prepared beforehand to see injustice in everything that was done. In the examination for Honours in Classics, he was put on in Aristotle, an author whom he had, as he often asserted in later life, completely mastered. The Examiners had, it appears, fixed certain parts of Aristotle's works as the tests, and when he had passed satisfactorily in those, he was put on in some part not included in the test. This he thought was done in the hope of plucking him, because he was a Lincoln man. So he refused to go on, flung the book at the heads of the Examiners, and stalked out of the hall pouring forth a volley of curses. This at least is how he used to tell the story. It did not transpire what, if any, punishment he incurred for this conduct but in the class lists for 1806 his name appears as Second Class in Literæ Humaniores, and he always asserted that though he was superior to Sir Robert Peel and other subsequently distinguished men who took Firsts in that year, he was refused a First on account of his outbreak. My father has told me that the story was well known at the time, and was confirmed by several of my grandfather's contemporaries whom he had asked about it. After this he went to Lincoln's Inn and was in due course called to the Bar in 1811. He rose rapidly in his profession, being a man of brilliant intellect, and indefatigable industry, marred however by the most violent temper. He was eminent as an equity draftsman and chamber counsel; as a pleader his success was not so great, his rudeness and violence of language making him unpopular with Judges. He gained in fact the sobriquet of 'Cross Beames', and there is an excellent caricature of him by the celebrated HB (John Doyle) standing in wig and gown under some crossed beams of the scaffolding of the new Hall of Lincoln's Inn which was then being built, with the words 'Cross Beames' underneath. He was rather proud of this picture and had it hung up in his house! He used to spend his vacations at Hillfield House with his mother, or whenever he had a quarrel with her, an event of frequent occurrence, at Cowslip Lodge, a small house and estate near Wrington in Somersetshire, some twelve miles south of Bristol. It was part of the Clifton property and is still in our family. He was an officer of the Royal Bristol Volunteers. The great European war was then in full progress and Volunteer corps were formed in all parts of the Kingdom. It must have been not later than 1811 that he married his first wife, Mary Collins. I am told that she was a very beautiful woman, and deeply attached to him. She was, however, very delicate, and being fond of society and amusement did not take enough care of her health. Her brother-in-law Dr Burroughs often, it is said, warned her that she was exerting herself too much, and going to too many balls and parties, but neither she nor her mother-in-law Mrs Powell, with whom she spent most of her time, paid any attention to the warning. One evening at a party at Hillfield House she broke a blood-vessel, was carried to bed, and died in a few hours. She had been married only a little more than a year, and left no children. My grandfather it is thought felt her loss very acutely, but he never spoke of her again, and no trace of her was found at his death, save the name 'Mary Collins' in some old books. A little over a year after her death he married again. His second wife was Mary Pearson Carnarvon, only daughter and heiress of Dr Thomas Carnarvon a physician of Greenwich. He had married one Jane Pearson, daughter of Dr John Pearson a physician of York, whose wife Elizabeth was heiress of Sir Hercules Buck, the last of a Yorkshire family with strange Christian names descended from Sir Bezaleel Buck *temp*. Charles I. The Buck property had descended through Mrs Pearson to her daughter Mrs Carnarvon, and through her daughter it eventually came to our family. The landed property appears to have been sold, but Miss Carnarvon brought to my grandfather a sum of £36,000 in East India Stock and a considerable amount of house property in Greenwich and elsewhere. There was a large portrait in oils of Dr Carnarvon in the breakfast-room at Bashley. It represents a small man with a round, fair, clean-shaven face with delicate thin features and blue eyes, the hair powdered and tied in a knot behind, a scarlet coat with large polished steel buttons and frill on the breast. My brother Harry and my second son Frederick closely resemble him, and I am looking out for the re-appearance of the type among my already numerous grandchildren.

Old Carnarvon's temper was nearly as bad as my grandfather's and they were constantly quarrelling, especially about money matters. So much did they disagree that they judged it advisable not to live in the same house any longer, though they had arranged to do so when the young couple were married. As my grandmother was very much attached to her mother, Mrs Carnarvon, the two ladies did not like the idea of being separated, so a compromise was arrived at. Dr Carnarvon lived in a big red-brick house on Croom's Hill. This house faces north. It is still standing (1896) and is called Croom's Hill House.[1] Opposite, but a little to the east, is another equally large red-brick house facing south which also belonged to him, and this he gave over to my grandfather who moved into it and lived there for some years. The two houses are on the brow of the steep hill leading down into Greenwich and are just outside the wall of the Park opposite the Ranger's Lodge.

In this house was born on 1 February 1815 my father, Thomas Beames. He was named after Dr Carnarvon, a departure from the old family custom of calling the eldest son John, which, if one were to be superstitious, one might say brought him ill-luck. In the same house on the 22nd February 1817 was born my Uncle John V. These were the only two children born of this marriage.

Soon after my uncle's birth old Carnarvon died, and his widow removed from Croom's Hill to a large white house in Park Lane, just opposite the eastern gate of Greenwich Hospital. It has been pulled down now. Here she lived for many years in company with a queer old Yorkshire woman, Miss Smith, who was my godmother and left me a legacy when she died thirty-odd years later. My father was very fond of his grandmother and often spent his holidays with her. The unfortunate dispersion of my grandfather's library and the destruction of all his private papers after my father's death during my absence in India deprives me of the power of assigning accurate dates in many cases to the events I am now relating. I can therefore merely record what I have been told by my father and grandfather, only in a few instances can I give the actual or approximate dates from the few papers which I have been able to secure.

About this time, that is, in or about 1818, my grandfather gave up the house at Greenwich and lived in his town house 24 Bedford Square, spending his vacations chiefly at Wrington. There was good shooting on the Cowslip Lodge estate, which he much enjoyed, and my grandmother had many friends in the neighbourhood, among whom was Mrs Hannah More, who lived close by at Barley Wood, and was in her time a cele-

[1] Editor's Note. This house was pulled down in the spring of 1938.

18

brated authoress, though probably now forgotten. My grandmother was a highly educated woman with strong literary and artistic tastes, and had much cultivated society round her in London. My grandfather too was an extremely well-read man and when in a good temper could be very charming. There was great fascination in his talk even as an old man, and my father has told me that as a younger man my grandfather was highly popular in society. Some of the verses he has written in his wife's album, which I have still, are very graceful and witty.

He visited his mother Mrs Powell regularly every time he passed through Bristol on his way to or from London, but he quarrelled so much with her about the management of the property that there was not much cordiality between them. Nor was he on much better terms with his sister Mrs Burroughs who was a very religious woman, but whom he always spoke of as 'that canting Jezebel'. He was also much disliked by his mother-in-law, old Mrs Carnarvon. He often used to take his wife down to Greenwich on Sundays much to the old lady's distress. On such occasions he would frequently send down fish, game or venison the day before so as to secure a good Sunday's dinner, and usually made a great fuss because it was not properly cooked. He was an enormous eater but drank very little, a rare thing in those days of hard drinking.

It was in these surroundings that my father's youth was spent. His father he saw very little of; he was at his chambers all day at No. 2 Old Square, Lincoln's Inn, and did not come home till late, when he ate a huge dinner, drank a little beer at dinner and a couple of glasses of port afterwards. Then he retreated to his study where he shut himself up with his papers till often long past midnight. His iron constitution enabled him to rise early the next morning fresh and hearty and as bad-tempered as ever. He was making, I am told, at this time about £5,000 a year and he had nearly £2,000 a year with his wife. So he must have been a rich man for those times. He was a man of middle height, very broad-shouldered and strongly built with a keen, sunburnt face, an aquiline nose, piercing brown eyes, a lofty and broad forehead, and the most snarling, ill-tempered expression I ever saw on any human countenance. But when pleased or interested in anything his face lighted up, the cruel lines vanished and he looked an extremely handsome, intellectual man. My grandmother, judging from her portrait, was not particularly handsome. She was a large, heavily-built woman with solid, square features and big bags under her eyes. When I saw her she was old and had had a paralytic stroke. She struck my childish imagination as a very big, fierce old woman with a loud, harsh voice. But my father always spoke of her as a mild, gentle, refined, delicate woman. He admitted, however, that she was extravagant, fond of display, and loving rich dress and furniture.

In 1822 my father was sent to a school on Richmond Green kept by one Delafosse. I observed lately that Sir Richard F. Burton, the famous traveller, was at the same school, but at a later period. The school was still standing in 1868, but now calls itself a 'Collegiate Institute', which is as Milton might have said, 'old school writ large'. My Uncle John went there also a year or two later. The boys do not seem to have learnt much at Delafosse's, and in 1825 they were removed and sent to Winchester, then under the Headmastership of Dr Williams, afterwards Warden of New College, of whom my father always spoke with the greatest affection and reverence. He spent eight happy years there in spite of fagging and other barbarities, and loved the glorious old school, and was always proud of being a Wykehamist.

The selection of Winchester was part of a general move into Hampshire which my grandfather conceived and carried out about this time. Old Mrs Carnarvon was fond of spending the summer at Southampton, then a quiet seaside town, and my grandfather occasionally took his wife there to stay with her mother. He had left her there one summer—I think it was 1825 or 1826 but cannot be certain—and had himself gone on to Cowslip Lodge for some shooting. Captain Powell, his stepfather, had a paralytic stroke a little while before this, and on partially recovering desired to make his will. For this purpose he consulted my grandfather. But the young Burroughses, William, John, Ben and Dick, youths of from fifteen to twenty, took it into their heads that my grandfather was trying to induce both his mother and stepfather to make wills leaving all their property to him. So they made a sudden irruption into the room and summarily ejected my grandfather—kicked him downstairs—as they themselves expressed it. Old Dr Burroughs, their father, had been dead some years—he died in 1823—and the youths considered themselves bound to protect their mother's interests. What the real truth of the story was I never could ascertain, whether my grandfather was merely giving honest advice, or whether he was really acting so basely as the youths supposed. At any rate it is certain that they turned him out of Hillfield House, and that he never saw it or them or his mother or sister again.[1] The whole lot of these people were so constantly quarrelling with my grandfather about money matters that one is not surprised at the most violent actions or extravagant stories about them.

[1] This is perhaps too sweeping. See note on p. 23 which seems to show that he did see some of them afterwards. He certainly, however, saw very little of them.

My grandfather retired to Cowslip Lodge, but a day or two later he received a letter from Bristol one morning which enraged him so much that he ordered his gig, left his breakfast untouched, and started off in his slippers. Drunken old James Parrett, his butler, rushed after him with his boots, but had a long run before he could persuade his master to stop and put them on. He purposed to go to meet his wife at Southampton and for this purpose drove through Warminster and Salisbury. At the latter place he heard of a small estate for sale in the New Forest, and though it was somewhat out of his road he drove round to look at it, and was so pleased with it that he eventually bought it, and lived and died there. It was called Bashley Lodge.

It is situated in the parish of Milton six miles west of the town of Lymington and about the same distance east from Christchurch. The house, or cottage, was a low two-storeyed building painted white with pointed Gothic windows, a veranda and two gables each with a wooden cross on it; the whole having a sham Cockney–Gothic look about it, only partly redeemed by a profusion of roses and myrtles growing all over the front. There were some 180 acres of baddish land, ornamental grounds, two long and beautiful avenues—each half a mile long, it was said, but I never measured them—leading up to it, and a magnificent view across the Solent, with the Isle of Wight and the Needles in the distance. Inside, the rooms were low, small and inconveniently arranged, but my grandmother furnished it in the most expensive style of those days—costly but tasteless. The books, however, and the collection of china were valuable and beautiful.

On the 15th August 1832 my grandfather was appointed 'King's Counsel' and a Bencher of Lincoln's Inn. In the same year he insisted, in spite of the remonstrances of the Headmaster, on removing my father from Winchester though he was only seventeen, and sending him to Oxford. He was entered at Lincoln College and proceeded at once to waste his time considerably. He went in for hunting and for boxing, which latter was one of the fashionable sports of the day. He appears also to have been very particular about his dress, and to have had a long bill at his tailor's. Enormous quantities of kid gloves and gorgeous satin neckties were also among the undergraduate vanities of those days, and though a temperate man himself, it was considered necessary for him to buy a tolerable quantity of port and sherry, the only two wines that were usually drunk then. In fact he led the life which the eldest son of a rich man and the heir to a good fortune might be expected to lead. If he ran up heavy bills, his mother, whose favourite he was, had no difficulty in supplying him with money to pay them with, and I never heard of his being troubled with Oxford debts in later life. I think I should have heard of them had there been any, for my dear father was very fond of talking to me about his own and his family's affairs and past history. Learning appears to have been at a very low ebb at Oxford in those days—in the smaller Colleges at any rate. Lincoln certainly was not Oriel nor were the tutors like Arnold, Newman and their company. My father appears to have taken no part in the intellectual life of the University though he was there at the time of the Tractarian Movement. In later life it was Arnold, not Keble or Newman, that he followed. He left Oxford in 1835 with a pass, declining to go up for honours. It is wonderful that he even passed with such tutors as he had. I used to meet one of them in after times, old Calcott, a greasy, wine-bibbing, unclerical old parson with a red face and a small flaxen wig usually awry, whose breath always smelt strongly of sherry. Though possessed of an amazing store of knowledge (so at least my father affirmed) he never could be persuaded to make any use of it. It was said that at his so-called divinity lectures, which consisted of hearing men construe the Greek Testament, he invariably asked three questions—and no more. These were the difference between 'genuine' and 'authentic', the three divisions of the Holy Land (Judea, Samaria and Galilee), and the names of the twelve Apostles.

On leaving Oxford my father wished to go into the Army. A Cavalry regiment was his earnest desire. He was a splendid rider to the last day of his life, and would probably have made a very good soldier. But England was now in the middle of the long peace that followed Waterloo and he would have seen no service till the Crimean War twenty years later. My grandfather, for some inexplicable reason, insisted on his going into the Church, a vocation for which he felt the strongest dislike. It was not without a severe struggle that he yielded. As, however, he was then only twenty, he was too young to be ordained. So he spent his time idling at Bashley; or at Greenwich with his grandmother, Mrs Carnarvon, where he had, as will presently be shown, stronger attractions than his venerable relative could afford.

Life at Bashley must undoubtedly have been somewhat dull for a young man of his tastes, for though he had not worked hard at Oxford he was gifted with a great love for learning, and read a great deal. He had also got into the habit of associating with cultivated men, and was passionately fond of long and profound arguments on difficult and abstruse subjects. My grandfather had retired from the Bar in 1835 disgusted at not being made a Judge. His contemporaries always said he would have had a Judgeship but for his temper. He was a Commissioner in Bankruptcy and held one or two other good appointments, but he could never attain to his desired Judgeship. His disappointment together with a very serious illness he had in that year led him to retire.[1] Then he set up for a country gentleman at Bashley. He was made a Justice of the Peace, Deputy Lieutenant of the County, Chairman of Sessions and several other things. He became the terror of all poachers and evil-doers for many miles round. He had a 'Justice-room' at Bashley where he tried cases and inflicted punishments. He domineered over his fellow justices, was the abiding terror of the town clerk and all the local attorneys, and soon became a notable character in that part of Hampshire. He also took greatly to the sport of coursing, kept a number of greyhounds of celebrated breeds and filled notebook on notebook with records of their performances, recipes for dog-medicines and hints on training. Also he took up the subject of scientific farming and believed that he was going to make money out of the stiff clay soil of Bashley. He spent large sums of money on this hobby but, as might have been expected, without reaping any profit from it. He read also a great deal—reading of the most varied kind; after his death there was hardly a book in his extensive library that had not its margins covered with pencil notes in his small, clear hand. He also wrote and published a novel in three volumes. It was called *Madness the Rage*. I read it once but have forgotten what it was like.

My grandmother read poetry, played the piano, talked aesthetic and sentimental talk with my father and such female friends as she could induce to stay with her, made preserves and pickles, and wrote, as was the fashion of those days, interminable letters to her friends, and kept them until she could find a Member of Parliament to frank them for her. My uncle John was a coarse, brutal youth, a regular Tony Lumpkin, who loved to sit boozing in alehouses, and go shooting or ferreting with all the idle boors in the countryside. His powers of eating and drinking were enormous, he used to be called 'the Bull and Mouth'. He was understood to be keeping his terms, and he did go and eat some dinners at Lincoln's Inn and was eventually called to the Bar.

My father gradually got sick of my grandfather with his greyhounds and guano, my grandmother's sentimental talk and my uncle's coarseness, and spent more and more of his time at Greenwich. This led to an important event.

Greenwich Hospital had not then been deserted by those for whose benefit it was built. In its immense rooms lived hundreds of old sailors

[1] I find that in this illness he was attended by his cousin John Burroughs, then practising as a doctor at Clifton. My father told me this.

disabled in the great war with Napoleon, each in his snug little wooden cabin built along the walls of the vast saloons. There was a large staff of Naval Officers, all more or less wounded in service, to whom these posts had been given as a sort of pension. Among these was a certain Lieutenant Joseph Dewsnap, a big, burly, fair-haired, red-faced, hearty old sailor who had seen much active service before his career was cut short by a bullet in the shoulder at the battle of Cape St Vincent. This bullet was never extracted, and continued to be a cause of pain and irritation in bad weather. The pain required to be allayed by copious draughts of rum and water and much trolling, or rather bellowing, of Dibdin's famous sea-songs. He was the son of a glover at Woodstock, who came of a Huguenot family that took refuge in England at the time of the revocation of the Edict of Nantes. The name is said to have been Du Chenappe or Senappe, corrupted into Dewsnap. When at St John's, Newfoundland, in the course of his service he had married[1] the daughter of a merchant named Little, whose wife was a French-Canadian named Le Jeais. On settling at Greenwich Hospital he began to beget children, and before long had burdened himself with six daughters and two sons. They all grew up half-wild, racing about the stately corridors and playing with the old pensioners. The eldest girl, Eliza, got some sort of education and was expected to teach the others. Most of the girls were very pretty, two indeed even beautiful, but the boys from an early age devoted themselves to blackguardly conduct of every description.

A fine band used to play in the square of the Hospital once or twice a week and all the *élite* of Greenwich society used to assemble there. On these occasions the Dewsnap girls were all dressed, and behaved themselves properly, and as they grew up attracted the attention of the young men of the place. The eldest married George Steuart, a retired sea-captain and partner in a leading firm in Colombo, Ceylon. Two others, Louisa the second and Virginia the fifth, also married fairly well. My father fell in love with the fourth, Susannah Amelia. She was nearly four years older than him, but the family spared no pains to catch him, and they were married on the 6th April 1836 at Camberwell Parish Church.

The marriage was severely disapproved of by both his parents. His mother, an intensely proud woman, in spite of, or perhaps because of her love for him, was bitterly mortified, and never spoke to or took any notice of her daughter-in-law as long as she lived. My grandfather told him with brutal frankness that as he had chosen to cut his own throat by this *mésalliance* he would do nothing more for him, and refused to

[1] About the year 1804 or 1805.

receive either him or his wife at Bashley. He made my father an allowance of £100 a year, which sum he never increased and not infrequently stopped for a time whenever more than usually displeased with him. My father, finding he had now no chance of having a commission in the Army purchased for him—the usual way of getting into the Army in those days—resigned himself to his fate, and after spending a rather long honeymoon in Jersey,[1] left his wife with her parents at Greenwich and went up to Oxford to take his M.A. degree preparatory to going into the Church. Then he had a severe illness which lasted some time. What he did with himself all the winter of 1836-7 and the following spring I do not know. Bashley was closed to him, Mrs Carnarvon disappointed and not very cordial, and the Dewsnap family not very pleased at the attitude of the Beames family, whom they to the last spoke of as 'haughty', 'stuck-up', 'giving themselves airs', and the like.

Under these untoward influences my father and mother felt naturally unhappy, and began a system of mutual reproaches and fault-finding which lasted for the rest of their lives. They began to find out that they were quite unsuited to each other and had not a single idea or feeling in common. With his marriage my father's happiness in this world came to an end, and a life-long struggle with poverty and disappointments began which closed only with his early death twenty-eight years later.

---

[1] On this occasion he nearly had a duel with a Jersey gentleman named de Carteret, who annoyed him by remarking that the Jersey people had once conquered England—alluding of course to the fact that Jersey was once a part of Normandy and as such belonged to Duke William—the Conqueror. My father, instead of laughing at this, called Carteret a 'crapaud Français'. Some sensible friends interfered and pacified the hot-headed youths.

CHAPTER II

CHILDHOOD, 1837–1844

I WAS born at one o'clock in the morning of the twenty-first of June 1837, at Lieutenant Dewsnap's quarters in the Royal Naval Hospital, Greenwich. A few hours before my birth, the window of my mother's bedroom being open by reason of the intense heat, she heard the sound of the tolling of the great bell of St Paul's Cathedral which announced the death of King William the Fourth. Her present Gracious Majesty Queen Victoria, whom may God long preserve, ascended the throne only a few hours before I came into the world. I am nearly sixty now and she is reigning still!

I was baptized in the chapel of the Hospital. My grandfather, who in spite of his displeasure still intervened whenever he thought fit in my father's affairs, expressed a wish that I should be christened Ayliffe Greene, after the old Bristol merchant from whom the Clifton property was derived. No one could understand why he should have fixed upon this name, and my father so strongly objected to it that it was given up, and it was then settled that I should receive the old family name of John. Towards the close of the year my grandfather made an arrangement with an old friend of his, the Revd David Williams, Rector of Bleadon and Kingston Seamoor in Somerset, for his giving my father a 'title to orders'. Accordingly early in 1838 we made a move into the old county. My mother and I were left with old Mrs Powell at Hillfield House while my father went on to arrange for lodgings. My father was not very fond of his grandmother nor of the Burroughs family but my mother seems to have got on very well with them all.

It was at this time and place that occurred the first incident that I can remember, or to be more accurate, that made a permanent impression on me though I did not know what it arose from till many years later. I was one day when I was perhaps fifteen or sixteen, telling my mother that I sometimes had a peculiar nightmare, in which I seemed to be lying on my back pressing hard with both hands at some solid substance a few inches above me which I was unable to move. It was as if I were shut up in a box, the lid of which I could not open. She was much struck with this, the more so when I told her I had frequently had this night-mare as far back as I could remember. She then told me that while

26

we were staying at Hillfield in 1838 she had put me to bed in a large old-fashioned four-post bedstead and had propped me securely up, as she thought, with pillows. She had then gone down to the drawing-room to pass the evening. Suddenly they heard loud shrieks from upstairs. My mother and the two Burroughs girls, Sarah and Mary, rushed up to the bedroom and found the bed empty, but guided by my roaring they felt under a large wardrobe close by the bed and to their amazement found me lying on my back and pushing frantically against the bottom of the huge wardrobe which was just a few inches above me. I must have wriggled myself out of bed—being always restless and given to tossing about in my sleep—and somehow rolled under this big piece of furniture. I continued to dream of this event for many years.

After a short absence my father returned and took us away to Clevedon, then a pretty little rural sea-side village. Kingston Seamoor was only two miles away. We had lodgings in a damp, dreary, dismal farmhouse, the only rooms my father could secure for the low rent he was able to afford. He got of course no salary while working for his title and had only £100 a year to live on. The parish was low-lying and marshy, the inhabitants scattered far and wide, an uncouth, brutal sort of people, immoral, drunken, and thievish. Their broad local patois would have been unintelligible to him, had he not spent so much of his youth at Wrington close by. There was next to no society. The Rector was a pluralist and absentee, and there were hardly any resident gentry. My father used to spend much of his time walking long distances about the parish, and reading the few books he could get. For books and genial talk, encouragement and advice he was indebted to another curate like himself, the Revd H. Thompson, a highly educated man who eked out a scanty income by taking pupils and translating German books. My mother, who was in delicate health, lay on the sofa in the damp little parlour terribly alarmed at the rats which coursed freely about the room. After a time, however, my father succeeded in getting more comfortable lodgings in the village of Yatton close by, and there, on the 21st December 1838, was born to them a second son. My grandfather again intervened to select a name for the child, and fixed upon Pearson Thomas. My father pleaded hard for Thomas Pearson but the old man insisted on having his own way this time, so the name was given and the child baptized by my father in Kingston Seamoor church. Bad food and the privations she had undergone had weakened my mother's health and my brother Pearson was a weak and sickly child for the first year or so.

In 1839 my father was ordained priest by Bishop Law of Bath and Wells, and the rector then somewhat unwillingly allowed him a salary of £75 a year, but it was not long before my father got made Curate of Clevedon with a salary of £120 a year. This, with the £100 a year from his father, relieved him from the extreme pressure of poverty. He took a small but pretty cottage on the sea-shore. The sea-bathing did my mother and the children good, and my father who was always a strong and skilful swimmer used to get his swim regularly every morning before going to nis work. There was more society here, and the great man of the place, Sir Abraham Elton of Clevedon Court, was kind to them and used to invite them to his house. The relations from Bristol used to go to Weston-super-Mare every summer and it gave my mother much pleasure to go and visit them, so that on the whole prospects brightened considerably in 1839.

My parents, however, by their own account, continued to quarrel and misunderstand each other. It has always been a wonder to me how two such diametrically opposite people could ever have got married. Mentally and bodily they were strongly contrasted. He was a big red man, nearly six feet high, broad-shouldered, large-limbed, very strong, and active. He had flaming red hair, rather wild-looking light blue eyes, a lofty white forehead and features that might have been handsome had he not been terribly disfigured by smallpox. He talked incessantly, and was disposed to be noisy and boisterous when in good spirits. He was fond of exercise, a good boxer, cricketer, rider, walker and swimmer. At the same time he was an omnivorous reader and had the most wonderful memory. He was certainly, like all his family, very hot-tempered, though easily pacified; very outspoken, straightforward and honourable. Though attaching very little importance to outward ceremonies he was a sincerely pious and earnest Christian. He always seemed to us to be the perfect type of that 'muscular Christianity' of which his friend Charles Kingsley used to talk so much. Although he did not want to go into the Church, yet when once he found himself there he devoted himself to his work as a clergyman with the utmost heartiness and fervour, so that one keen observer,[1] after saying of him that he was 'a good cut-throat spoiled', added that he was the best parish priest he had ever known.

My mother was a very tiny woman, very beautiful both in face and figure. Her hair was a deep, almost blue, black, her complexion rather pale and sallow, her features fine and regular. She was a thorough Frenchwoman in appearance, *petite et proprette*, as was only natural seeing that she came of French Huguenot race on her father's side and French-Canadian on her mother's. She was very strict and correct, prim and methodical, and in temper cold and hard, though very religious and

[1] My wife's father, Mr Geary.

28

even puritanical. She had no taste for learning of any sort, and spent her time in endless work with her needle. My mother in fact is always in my mind associated with needlework of some kind. How so excitable, noisy, passionate a man should have been attracted by so quiet, un-emotional a woman is one of those mysteries which are past all finding out. The first serious misunderstanding between them arose, like so many subsequent ones, from my mother's intense and perhaps injudi-ciously displayed attachment to her own family. When she went into Somersetshire, she kept up an active correspondence with her mother and sisters. This was only natural, and in the present day would have caused no trouble. But in 1839 there was no penny post; letters cost a great deal to the recipient, because it was not the sender who paid the postage as it is now, but the person addressed. It was no uncommon thing for poor people to have letters addressed to them lying at the post-office for weeks or even months because they could not afford to pay the postage. When my mother got once a fortnight or oftener a heavy letter from one of her sisters for which my father had to pay half-a-crown or more, he naturally objected, and the more so as he knew that these letters contained nothing but the idlest tittle-tattle and abuse of himself. 'Tom', as he was called, had grown to be a monster and bugbear to his wife's family. When my poor father, struggling as he was with extreme poverty, threatened to refuse to pay for these frequent letters, my mother and her family raised a great outcry and a very bitter quarrel ensued.

Fortunately for all parties my father determined early in 1840 to leave Somerset and go to London. He obtained, I know not how, a curacy at Stamford Hill Chapel near Clapton, a suburb in the north-east of London. It was then almost in the country. Young as I was—only three —I remember vaguely our journey to London. My mother and our nurse Emma Cameron, with myself and my brother Pearson, were put into the coach one evening in Bristol. Then followed a long hideous night in a rocking, jolting machine, during which I and my brother were constantly tumbling off the knees of the two women as they dozed and rolling in damp musty straw at the bottom of the coach among the feet of the passengers till our cries woke someone who picked us up again. In the morning we arrived at the Saracen's Head on Snow Hill in London where my father and my Uncle John met us, and took us in a hackney coach to Stamford Hill. We lived in a very small semi-detached house in a terrace with the usual small square of garden in front and longer strip behind. Here was born on the 18th June 1840 my third brother, William Carnarvon. He was called after William Burroughs, my father's cousin, the eldest of that family who was then in London studying for the medical profession, and who attended my mother in her confinement and refused payment, as my father was too poor to pay for a doctor. The name Carnarvon was added in memory of my great-grandmother, old Mrs Carnarvon, of whom my father was very fond, and who, I think, died about this time. We did not stay long at Stamford Hill. The vicar, a Mr Heathcote, was too High Church—too Puseyite as it was then called—for my father, who in 1841 got a curacy at Chelsea. The Rector, the Revd Charles Kingsley, was a genial old man and his sons, Charles the celebrated writer and Henry, were great friends of my father's. I can remember sitting on a small chair pushed back into a corner of the room while my father and Charles Kingsley put on the gloves and had a sparring bout, much to my terror. Then they sent out for a pewter pot of porter, and began a hot discussion (as I was told in later years) on socialism, the working man and similar topics. There was also William le Breton, afterwards Dean of Jersey, a strikingly handsome man, and one or two others in whose society my father took much delight. Le Breton fell in love with Annie Martin, the very lovely daughter of the lady in reduced circumstances in whose house on the King's Parade we lodged. There was no reason why he should not have asked her mother and brother's consent, and married her openly. But for some reason they thought it more exciting and romantic to elope. So one morning they got away quietly and were married at a church in the City. My father, among other friends, went in search of them and, I know not how, discovered them in a cottage in a village in Kent and induced them to return home.

But le Breton thought it advisable after this escapade to leave Chelsea and we saw no more of him for some years. We also moved to a house in Marlborough Square, a quiet little nook now pulled down and built over, in the fields and market-gardens which then lay between Chelsea and Brompton, where I and my brothers used to enjoy rambling.

My mother had a serious illness in 1842 and a child was born prematurely and never lived. Then she and my brothers went to Margate to recover and I was left with my father to undergo an operation.

Some time before this I had fallen downstairs and cut my left eyebrow badly against the lock of an open door. The wound healed at the time but there grew on the place a tumour which increased so that it hung down over the eye. The doctors at last decided that it must be cut off. I remember the whole affair well though I was only five years old. One fine summer's day my father came home to lunch accompanied by three grave and solemn gentlemen, and they all sat down and ate and drank. Then our family doctor arrived and took me upstairs into the big bedroom where I was strapped down on a high narrow, deal table, while Emma Cameron stood by me half-crying but telling me somewhat inconsistently that there was nothing to be afraid of. I was in mortal terror when the three solemn gentlemen came in and began to feel the tumour and whisper to each other. Suddenly I was aware of a sharp pain and our own doctor bathing my eye with a sponge and warm water. I was in bed after this for a long time with my eye bandaged up. The learned gentlemen carried my tumour away with them and, I believe, have it preserved in spirits somewhere still, for I was told it was an altogether remarkable and unusual tumour, and had excited much interest in the medical profession. Perhaps if I had been older I should have been proud of it.

When my mother returned I was well, but she seemed to repent having left me and was more loving and tender to me than I remember her to have been either before or since. I believe she had been sent away from home in ignorance of what was going to happen, as her health was too weak from her recent illness to stand the shock of the operation. I was much petted about this time and became a conceited little prig. Fortunately much—I hope, all—of this was thrashed out of me when I went to school. But I was made to learn all sorts of things, and soon learnt to read with ease, and used to spend hours lying on the floor poring over a book, half of which was not intelligible to me. My mother's assertion that I could read when I was three years old seems incredible, but she was a severely, not to say offensively, truthful person, and would not have said it if it had not been true. I remember beginning to learn Latin at Chelsea, and reading the Bible every day to my mother. We used to walk together in Cheyne Walk and on Battersea Bridge, a quaint, clumsy old structure on huge wooden piles, and discuss scripture. Chelsea was, however, a damp, unhealthy place and we were always ailing there, so my father at last, somewhat reluctantly, decided on leaving it. Among his numerous friends at Chelsea was Jasper Blunt, who held a high position in the Colonial Office. His brother, the Revd Henry Blunt, had been for many years incumbent of Trinity Church, Sloane Street; and a very popular preacher of the then prevalent Evangelical School, but was at this time Rector of Streatham. Jasper Blunt also removed from Chelsea to Streatham and hearing that my father wished for a change induced his brother to offer him a curacy.

So to Streatham we went about the beginning of 1843. Our stay at this place was always looked back to by us all as the happiest period of our boyhood, and by my father as a bright brief oasis in a life of care and disappointment. Young as I was I remember the place well, probably my memory has been assisted by my frequent visits and long stay there afterwards. When I saw it last year, 1895, it was so changed that I had difficulty in finding my way about. It was a quiet country village in 1842; now it is a busy suburban town. The high road to Brighton, after passing through the long rows of cockney villas called Brixton, came out at the fifth milestone from the Exchange, London, into open fields with luxuriant hedges interspersed with a few scattered parks and houses of rich city merchants. An occasional shop of a small and old-fashioned kind, an inn or two with swinging sign and horsetrough in front were dropped down at intervals. Passing these the road skirted a small three-cornered green with a few more, rather smarter, shops; an inn and a dear old-fashioned smithy, a lock-up with its door thickly studded with nails and the parish stocks and pump in front. On the western side stood the church in a large graveyard and beyond it the comfortable Rectory with its shady garden. Two roads branched off here, one leading to Tooting, the other to Mitcham. At the junction of these roads were three or four roomy old houses, one of which my father took.[1] The high road after leaving the Green passed on between fields again, with here and there a handsome house standing in extensive, well-kept grounds, till it reached Streatham Common, a large open space which then, as now, sloped up the hill to Norwood. On the south side was a row of large houses and at the top several very fine and stately ones. Beyond these were bowery lanes where the hedges were white with May in the spring, and where we found rich store of horse-chestnuts in autumn, and from the top of the Common a glorious view over a wide expanse of undulating country from London on the north to Wimbledon on the west, and Croydon on the south.

My father's salary here was higher than before, and being unable to find furnished lodgings suitable for permanent residence he determined to furnish a house for himself. I did not learn till many years later how he did it. It seems that old Carnarvon, disliking and distrusting my grandfather, had in his will left his property (£36,000 in East India Stock with house-property at Greenwich) to his daughter, so tied up that my grandfather should have no control over it. He left the interest of the money and the rents of the houses to my grandmother for life, and to my grandfather for his life if he should survive her. On the death of the survivor it was to be divided equally between the children, and as there were only two, my father and uncle, each of them had a reversionary interest in £18,000. My grandfather allowed each of his sons

[1] It has since been pulled down and there is now a Roman Catholic church and priest's house on the site of it (1896).

£100 a year, neither more nor less, however great their need might be; and whenever—as often happened—he was displeased with them he would stop their allowances, a step which often, occurring as it had a habit of doing at the most inopportune moments, threw my father into the most serious difficulties. It is not possible, and it would not be becoming if it were, for me to sit in judgement on my father and grandfather. All I can say is that there was perpetual strife and wrangling between them, and that I was brought up to regard my grandfather as an iniquitous, hard-hearted old tyrant who, though rolling in money himself, denied his sons the bare necessaries of existence. He was always associated in my mind with old Ralph Nickleby, and it is certainly singular that the pictures of Ralph in the original illustrations to Dickens's novel are strikingly like my grandfather. But there may perhaps have been faults on my father's side. It is not for me to judge. Anyhow, my father was driven as his family increased, and his expenses with it, to anticipate his reversionary property by raising money on the security of the £18,000 that would come to him at his father's death. The old man ere long found out what my father was doing and bitterly resented it. He took his revenge, as will be seen hereafter, by his will.

It was, I suspect, by thus raising money that my father was enabled to furnish our pretty home at Streatham, and very charming it was. The Rector, Mr Blunt, was dying of consumption and unable to do any work, so all the parochial work fell upon my father and his fellow-curate, and gloriously busy, noisy, active and happy he was over it. The society at Streatham consisted almost entirely of wealthy city merchants, who although disposed at times to be a little patronizing, were as a body genial, liberal and sociable. Many of these kind-hearted people remained our friends for the rest of their lives. The ladies liked to have us three boys to play with their children, and many a happy day we spent in their splendid houses—palaces rich with all delights they seemed to our childish minds. I loved the exquisitely kept gardens with their conservatories and greenhouses, their sweeps of velvet lawn and shady cypresses and limes, with the rocking-horses indoors and the swings hanging from a branch outside. The names of these kind people will convey no associations to anyone but myself, yet it is pleasant to recall them. There was sturdy old Coster, a silk-merchant—a genial, broad-built old Dutchman—and his two pretty daughters Julia and Emma. Julia was my second love though some fifteen years at least older than me. My first love—first in point of time and by far the first in strength of attachment—was Juliana Arroyave, daughter of a Spanish merchant married to an Englishwoman. I loved Juliana with the most ardent,

33

devoted affection. I was six and she was nine. Never was there such a heroine, so lovely, clever and brave. She rode a pony, a fiery steed of the most dangerous character; she could climb trees, and run along the top of the garden wall and do all sorts of Amazonian feats, and she always had apples or sweets in her pocket which she shared with me, and never would give any to Pearson or Willie, which was so sweet of her! Poor Juliana! She married very young a brute who ill-treated her, and she died before she was twenty. 'Whom the gods love die young.' Then there were the Cowies, whom I met afterwards in Calcutta; a great tribe of young Blunts, the sons of the rector and those of his brother Jasper; the Hutchinses of whom more anon; Dicky Drew, son of old Beriah Drew the great landowner of the parish, to whose refusal to allow any building on his land was due the fact that Streatham preserved its rural character so long. I cannot name them all, they were all kind, dear people and they lived in a lovely place. Streatham was a paradise, an earthly paradise, inhabited by rich city angels.

Beyond the Rectory was Tooting Common. It is there still, but alas! *quantum mutatus*—then it was a rough, wild, woodland place, and on one side of it amidst tall thick trees, a rookery of elms in front, a lake on the right, shady walks on the left, stood a long low white house with a columned portico in front—Streatham House where the Thrales once lived and where the great Dr Johnson so often visited. We knew the people there and often went to spend the day with the children. In the depth of the wood on a mound was a small round summer house where we were always solemnly told Dr Johnson wrote his dictionary; even then I used to wonder how he managed it in so small a place. But out on the Common beside the beck under the great elm trees we spent many a happy morning with our faithful old nurse Emma Cameron, weaving baskets of rushes, collecting acorns and chestnuts, hunting for blackberries and hips and haws, and torturing beetles and all such small deer as we could catch. In another direction was Mitcham with its perfumed fields of lavender and roses. In another was breezy Streatham Common down which we ran races and Juliana fearlessly galloped her pony, beautiful, reckless darling that she was. At the top of the Common was a delightful up-and-down lane leading to a house of the Duke of Portland's, where we had small children's picnics under the trees. Then and for many years afterwards I used to imagine the scene of all the poems, plays and novels that I read as being in and about our favourite haunts at Streatham. In Portland Lane lived Rosalind and Orlando, the duke with his following and Touchstone and Audrey. Melancholy Jacques sat by the side of a little brook that trickles down towards

Croydon. Schiller's Robbers lived there, and the Canterbury pilgrims and Coleridge's Christabel. I do not mean to say that I had read all those books at the age of six, but that when I did read them only a very few years later my fancy pictured them as living in these scenes. Oddly enough different sets of people *would* live each in their own place. Thus Falstaff and Prince Hal and their crew always lived on Tooting Common. I could not imagine them anywhere else; they did not go with Streatham Common at all.

Most of the scenes in English history occurred in the Temple Gardens probably because I did not read history till I went to live in the City. But Mary Queen of Scots was always beheaded just in front of the Pied Bull at the foot of Streatham Common.

I read all sorts of books even at that early age. No one took the trouble to select books for me. My father always boxed my ears if he caught me reading his books, and my mother always took them away for fear there should be something improper in them. Her own reading was as far as I could see confined to the Bible and a big volume of sermons. Emma Cameron had somehow become possessed of the *Mutiny on the Bounty*, a book which I used to delight in and pored over by the hour till one day my mother took it up and seeing the word 'd—d' in it scolded Emma for letting me read it. It then disappeared and I never saw it again. Being thus impeded in my reading, I naturally met force by fraud, and used to carry off books on the sly and hide them in a garret where I read them by stealth at odd moments. I shall never forget the awful blood-curdling paroxysm of fear I experienced on reading Hood's *Haunted House*. I was all alone in our house late one summer evening just as it was getting dark when I read it, and I was so frightened that I remained cowering against the wall behind the staircase till Emma and my brothers returned from a walk, when I was taken up and put to bed speechless.

About this time there arrived one day a ragged, dirty sea-faring man who turned out to be Joseph Dewsnap, the elder of my mother's two brothers. He had gone to sea in a merchant vessel some years before this and had been lost sight of. After a long absence he turned up with a long story, which no one quite believed, of having been shipwrecked somewhere in the Pacific and having lived a long time among savages. He was accommodated with a garret at the top of the house whither I used to accompany him of an evening and sit with him as he smoked his pipe and told me wonderful yarns about the sea and shipwrecks, pirates and savages which much delighted me. He left us suddenly and I subsequently learnt that he had been caught by my father misconducting himself with one of the maidservants. He was a singularly debased blackguard, as was also his brother Charles.

Then my father's fellow-curate, Cubitt, a 'muscular Christian' like himself, suddenly went mad. One Sunday morning, as my father was reading prayers in the church, Cubitt made his appearance in full canonicals, marched up the aisle and tried to force his way into the reading desk. My father had the presence of mind to go on reading calmly while the sexton vainly tried to remove the intruder. Aided by a strong young man from the congregation he succeeded in forcing the unhappy man a few paces towards the door, but could not get him further as he clung to the end of a pew. Thereupon old Coster left his seat and advancing to the spot turned round and, applying his broad back to the struggling Cubitt, slowly and steadily butted him all down the aisle and out at the door into the churchyard where several men seized him and carried him off. Then the ponderous old Dutchman stolidly returned to his pew, and went on with the responses as if nothing had happened. My father was warmly thanked and applauded for his calmness on this trying occasion. The incident added greatly to my father's already great popularity in the parish.

My grandmother had a paralytic stroke this year and though she lived some years longer one side of her body remained paralysed and she used to stump about on a stick. My grandfather invited my father to Bashley, where he had not been since his marriage, and began to display an amount of affection for him which was somewhat surprising. The old man also paid us a return visit at Streatham and was much pleased with the place and gratified at the evidences of my father's popularity there.

There used also to come on Sunday afternoons a tall stout man in a rough coat, accompanied by a number of dogs, who would sit and argue with my father by the hour together on religious subjects. He was a strong ultra-Calvinist and enjoyed the comforting conviction that he himself was 'elect' and sure of salvation no matter what he did, whilst most other people were equally sure of damnation. My father, though at that time somewhat Evangelical, was never extremely Calvinistic, inclining like his friend Charles Kingsley to that moderate party afterwards called 'Broad Church'. He and Mr Geary, as this big man was called, used to argue themselves into a white heat on 'Justification by Faith', 'Election' and similar topics without any definite result. Mr Geary had been an old acquaintance of my father's in the Greenwich days, and I shall have occasion to mention him again later on.

These happy Streatham days came to an end all too soon. Mr Blunt died in the autumn of 1843, and a deep gloom fell upon the parish, for he was sincerely loved by all who knew him. His earnest unassuming holiness, meekness and kindness were joined to a playful, genial spirit which never left him even in his worst sufferings. I saw him once or twice sitting before a blazing fire in the heat of summer, wasted and powerless, yet smiling and making little cheerful remarks, quoting scraps of his favourite authors as if the end were far off, though he well knew he had not many weeks to live. His manner made a profound impression on me young as I was.

The living of Streatham was worth, I believe, £1,200 a year, with a charming house, light work and agreeable society. The patron was the Duke of Bedford, by whom the presentation was put up for sale. Whether owing to his increased affection for my father, or moved thereto by my grandmother who wished to see her favourite son provided for before her death, my grandfather offered to buy the living for my father. It was a tempting offer—the place, the work, the position were exactly what he would have liked. But in the estimation of all honourable men the transaction would, it seems, have constituted the mysterious ecclesiastical crime of Simony, so my father felt it his duty to decline the offer. Great was his inward struggle and there were not wanting people, good and religious as well as indifferent and careless, who told him he was ridiculously sensitive. But he was undoubtedly right and true as ever to the noble principles of his life. He gave it up, and sadly but firmly set his face to the world again. The new Rector, Mr Nicholl,[1] was one of the then increasing school of 'Puseyites', and my father could not stay with him. The pretty house had to be given up, and the kind friends left. There was great grief at his going, the parishioners subscribed and presented him with a massive silver salver and a purse of £60 to buy books with. The sixty pounds were duly spent in books and the silver salver was sent to Bashley to be kept with my grandfather's rich collection of plate. My mother always declared that my father acquired from that date a taste for book-buying that led him into unjustifiable expense. For years afterwards he would refer to this gift of sixty pounds as an excuse for any extravagance in book-buying he might commit.

Several months went by before we left, and on the 23rd November 1843 was born my fourth brother, who was christened Henry Blunt after the lately deceased Rector, whose widow Mrs Blunt was his godmother. As soon as she was able to be moved, my mother went to the Isle of Wight to stay with some kind Streatham friends named Philips who had a villa

---

[1] Mr Nicholl is still Rector of Streatham as I write this in 1899, fifty-six years later! He is now described as a 'moderate High Churchman'; in 1843 he was thought very advanced.

at Shanklin; and from there she went on to Bashley. It was the first time
she had been invited there since her marriage. Meanwhile my father was
searching for a new curacy. He got one at St Bride's, Fleet Street, under
the Revd Thomas Dale, Canon of St Paul's, a short, fat, pompous,
irascible gentleman, a great contrast to his late Rector. Early in 1844 we
moved into London to a dull, smoke-begrimed house, No. 21 Bartlett's
Buildings, a bottle-shaped court entered by a passage on the south side
of Holborn near St Andrew's Church. It was a quiet, brown, ugly place;
an atmosphere of smoke, fog and stuffiness brooded over it. To us boys,
coming from the green lanes and breezy commons of our beloved
Streatham, it was like a strange prison in which we were confined for we
knew not what offence. We were all three very unhappy; moping, lonely
and neglected. Instead of the green fields we now had endless rows of
brick houses around us. Our walks were in Holborn, in Newgate and
Farringdon markets, and it was a bright day for us when a friend of my
father's gave us permission to walk in the Temple Gardens. We used to
go there every day, and the quiet garden with its formal walks and
bright flowers, the busy river full of boats and steamers, were a great
relief from the crowded streets and hurrying masses of human beings.
I began to people it with scenes from the books I read. It was chiefly
Henry VIII and Cardinal Wolsey, Sir Thomas More, Shakespeare and
Ben Jonson, Sir Walter Raleigh and good Queen Bess who lived there.

My father had a severe attack of cholera this year and on his recovery
he and my mother went to the Isle of Wight for a long visit. They took
the baby with them, but I, Pearson and Willie were left alone in the
attic of Bartlett's Buildings. Emma Cameron had married and gone
away, and the servant who had charge of us preferred to sit with her
fellow-servant in the kitchen and seldom came near us except to bring
us our food. It is a wonder we did not burn the house down or do some
other mischief. The window of our room was in the roof and we could
not get up to it to look out, while those of the back rooms looked out
upon grimy courtyards and the backs of the houses in Fetter Lane,
from which hung clothes to dry and where we could see the ragged
children of the pauper population of that slum, who made faces at us
and shouted oaths and other bad language. So we did not care to look
that way. In the evening they often forgot to bring us a light, and we sat
huddled together in a corner of the nursery which we pretended was a
castle or a palace full of all sorts of delights and mysteries, and told each
other long and wonderful stories about knights, magicians, fairies and
other strange things. Then we all somehow caught smallpox, and this
brought our parents back. I and Pearson had it very lightly and I have

only one or two pock-marks. As soon as I was well I was taken to Bashley by my father. We went by the new railway from the Nine Elms station at Vauxhall then the terminus of the South Western Railway. The line ended at Southampton, where Rowland, my grandfather's coachman, met us with 'Clarence' as it was called, a large, closed carriage with a pair of horses. We drove through the New Forest and I was delighted with the grand old trees and the flying herds of deer. We did not stay long and I do not remember much of the visit. An arrangement was now made by which my grandfather took my brother Pearson to live with him and we saw no more of him for many years. He had offered, I believe, to take me, but this was refused as I was to be sent to school.

My Uncle John came into our life again at this time. He had been called to the Bar at Lincoln's Inn, and with the still great prestige of my grandfather's name and his wide connexion among solicitors might have done well. But his dissipated and irregular habits prevented him from getting on. He left Lincoln's Inn and took chambers in a grimy little place called Staples Inn leading out of Holborn where, in the filthiest rooms I ever saw, he had gathered round him 'seven other devils worse than himself'. Through his cousin William Burroughs, a clever, idle, fast man about town, a doctor without any patients, he had managed to get some young medical students whom he was supposed to be coaching in Latin and Greek, which subjects were then required for the medical degree. But there was more drinking and gambling than anything else in my uncle's chambers. His principal associates were, besides William Burroughs, a dirty, villainous, low-looking medical student named Hurd, and a Mr Alfred Beeston, the husband of my mother's sister Virginia, or Virge as they called her. Beeston, or Uncle Alfred as I was taught to call him, was a curious character. His father, a man of respectable family, had, I believe, been an attaché in some Embassy, or something of the kind—vagueness as to their antecedents was a chief characteristic of all the Beestons—and when I knew him was living here and there, no one knew how, with two daughters Amelia and Anne. They were all highly accomplished, clever, witty, well-dressed people with charming manners, but absolutely devoid of honesty or principle. They were a sore trouble to my father because, wherever he might settle, as sure as fate the Beestons would turn up. They would give my father's name as a reference, and thus get credit, and furnish a house and run up bills with the local tradesmen. After a time when their creditors became troublesome they would suddenly disappear, paying no one. One never knew where they were for some time, and then they would be heard of in some very far-off part of England. I remember Alfred Beeston living at Exeter, then at Derby, and subsequently at Hastings. He also lived at one time near Primrose Hill. He was always well dressed and had many titled and highly placed friends.

He had served in his early manhood in the force of volunteers under Sir de Lacy Evans, which went to Portugal in support of the young Queen Maria against the pretender Don Miguel, and had been all through the campaign After that he had been engaged in some mysterious way on railways but it was, I believe, principally from gambling and betting on the turf that he derived what little income he had. As he never paid his tradesmen, he had always plenty of pocket money, and though his wife and children were often nearly starving, and went about with shabby clothes, *he* never suffered; he took good care of *himself*.

My father tried hard but in vain to separate his brother from this disreputable society. It however broke up before long owing to some disgraceful scandal arising from gambling transactions. My uncle left Staples Inn and went home to Bashley for a time. From there he went to stay with some friends at Salisbury, and there an event happened which, but for my grandfather, might have reformed him and secured for him a successful career. He fell in love with a charming girl, a Miss Burgess, daughter of a country gentleman near Salisbury. He proposed to her, and was accepted. Her father gave his consent, but in the fashion of the old school of fathers insisted on settlements being made. He engaged to give his daughter a certain sum—I forget how much—provided my grandfather would give as much. My grandfather, though the amount was not more than he could easily afford, absolutely refused to give it. He said that he allowed each of his sons £100 a year, which he considered was quite enough for them. He declined with much harsh language to give a penny more. The lovers were inconsolable. They used to meet secretly to consider what to do, and to make all sorts of wild plans, but old Burgess found them out, and at once sent his daughter abroad and refused to hold any further communications with my uncle or his family. My uncle was heart-broken. He went away no one knew where, and did not turn up again for some years. When he did reappear he was much altered for the worse, as I shall relate in the proper place. Alfred Beeston got an appointment in Ceylon, which, however, he only held till the gambling affair had blown over. Six months later he was in England again. William Burroughs went to Italy where he lived for a good many years. Hurd also vanished.

I was now promoted to male costume. Hitherto I had worn the usual child's costume of those days: a frock like a girl's and white calico drawers. But now I had a cloth jacket and waistcoat, very short trousers buttoning over the waistcoat, a stiff round cap of white horsehair with a long tassel and leather peak, and Blücher boots. In this costume I went to see the Queen and Prince Albert going in state to open the Royal Exchange. I could not see the Queen's face as it was hidden by a huge poke bonnet of white straw with a great plume of ostrich feathers. But the great gilt coach with the six cream-coloured horses made a great impression on me. After the procession had passed we went to see the Temple Church where I was much struck by the tombs of the Templars. That night I had a terrible dream in which I saw hosts of Templars marching along, trampling on lions and singing in a loud and awful voice: 'Thou shalt go upon the lion and the adder, the young lion and the dragon thou shalt tread under foot.' I awoke screaming and they had much ado to calm me. Truly in after life I have trampled on lions and adders many, and I have often thought of that dream.

CHAPTER III

MERCHANT TAYLORS', 1847–1855

IN January 1845 I was sent to school at dear old Streatham, and very pleased I was to get back there. Streatham Academy as it was called was kept by Mr Lewis Edwardes, a short, stout, kindly old Welshman. I was a great favourite with him and his wife, a fat, comfortable, motherly old soul. The school still flourishes. It is at the bottom of Streatham Common, a long, low white house, roomy and commodious. I visited it last year and found it almost unchanged. The boys were a strange mixture; the majority were sons of London tradesmen who were receiving 'a sound commercial education'. They stayed at the school till they were sixteen or seventeen, when they went, I suppose, behind their fathers' counters. A most offensive set of young cads they were. But there was a small number of gentlemen's sons who were being prepared for a public school. We gave ourselves airs—I did not know in those days that I was only four generations off from the victualler of St Mary Overy's Churchyard; nor I think did my father, though he knew all about the Norman Barons and Bishop de Belmeys. We gentlemen's sons learnt Latin which was a proud distinction, while the tradesmen's sons spent their time at arithmetic and book-keeping. I was encouraged in learning Latin, and my neglect of arithmetic was winked at. I have in consequence suffered all my life from want of knowledge of calculation and how to keep accounts.

Our life at Streatham was simple and healthy. A hideous clanging bell woke us at seven; after dressing and washing hands and faces we went into the large schoolroom, a gaunt, whitewashed room with rows of desks and benches where prayers were read, followed by lessons till nine. At nine servants came in with large trays of bread-and-butter and mugs of milk and water—'Skyblue and Scrape'—as it was called. After a copious meal we started for a walk, two abreast, up one side of the Common. At the top we broke ranks and played about for a while and were then formed into line again and marched down the other side of the Common. Morning school lasted from half past ten to one when we filed into the long dining-room and had a plentiful meal of meat, vegetables and pudding with one glass of small beer each. Food was always abundant at Edwardes'. We then played in a large gravelled playground till half past two, when afternoon school began and lasted till five—play again till six

—and at six the milk and bread-and-butter again appeared. After this we sat about till nine amusing ourselves, and in the summer we mostly spent the evenings playing cricket, rounders and other games on the Common, or walked down Greyhound Lane where we turned loose to play in the fields. At nine there were prayers and we were then counted and marched off to bed. I was at first a little home-sick and being the smallest boy in the school I was a good deal bullied. I was a fat, round, chubby boy and probably tempting to kick, but I soon learnt how to defend myself and got over my home-sickness. As to learning, I got on in Latin as far as Caesar and Ovid; I learned French grammar and a little history, and I devoured greedily all the books in a very well selected school library. The kind Streatham people, remembering my father, used to invite me to their houses on half-holidays. Juliana Arroyave was gone, but Julia Coster took her place, and became my goddess. She was, I suppose, at least sixteen or more, a tall, rather plump, rosy, smiling, benevolent divinity, who petted me and played and read with me. We had many a happy afternoon together and when I went back to school at night old Coster always gave me half-a-crown. Also there was a funny little shrivelled-up old dentist named Hutchins who lived in Hanover Square, but had a country house at Streatham where he and his numerous family spent the summer months. Two of his sons, Arthur and Philip, were at Edwardes' with me. Phil subsequently bloomed out into a great personage—Sir Philip Percival Hutchins, K.C.I.E., Member of the Viceroy's Council—and a stuck-up prig. Several of the young Blunts were at the same school; one is now a Bishop.[1] Altogether I was very happy at Edwardes'.

In 1846 my father, not being able to endure Canon Dale any longer, left St Bride's and got a curacy at St Pancras in the north of London. We moved to 34 Burton Street, Burton Crescent, a small, mean cul-de-sac of a place, but decent and respectable and far less gloomy and dirty than Bartlett's Buildings. At the beginning of 1847 I was taken away from Edwardes' and sent to Merchant Taylors'. My father would fain have sent me to his own beloved Winchester, but he could not afford it, and my grandfather would not help him. Edwardes' son, Stephen, had been at Merchant Taylors' and had got a postmastership thence at Merton College, Oxford, where he then was. Edwardes was so well satisfied with his son's success at Merchant Taylors' that he strongly advised my father to send me there. Arthur and Philip Hutchins, Frederick and Arthur Blunt, also were sent there, so I had some friends in the new school.

[1] Bishop of Hull and Archdeacon of Scarborough.

My grandmother died in the spring of 1846 aged 68, and my father was dreadfully distressed at her loss. In this year or the next my grandfather came to stay with us in London, being made Treasurer of Lincoln's Inn. In this capacity he was for that year Head of the Society, and it fell to his lot to receive Her Majesty the Queen at a great banquet given to celebrate the opening of the new Hall. It was officially notified that her Majesty would confer a Baronetcy on the Treasurer on that occasion, but much to my father's mortification my grandfather announced that he did not mean to be present. He had been told that the fees for being made a baronet amounted to over £300 and though he could afford it, he made up his mind not to incur the expense. So in spite of my father's entreaties he stayed away, and the next senior Bencher received Her Majesty and got the title.

Merchant Taylors' School, which I entered in the third form in January 1847, was situated in Suffolk Lane, a narrow street on a steep incline upwards from Thames Street. The school occupied nearly the whole of the eastern side of this steep lane; opposite it were two boarding-houses where many of the boys boarded. The Headmaster's house joined on the school at the lower end. The school was a long, double-storeyed building of red brick, dating from 1670, having been rebuilt after the great fire of London. It had eight tall, round-headed windows with pilasters between and was entered by an enormous massive door-way with the arms of the Merchant Taylors' Company over it. The lower storey contained a dark hall, or 'cloisters' as they were called, supported as to the roof by massive pillars, some classrooms, and a long narrow courtyard bounded by the school building on three sides, and on the fourth by a very lofty, perfectly plain wall, forming the back of the adjacent buildings. Only a narrow strip of murky sky could be seen from this dismal vault-like space. On the upper floor approached by a wide staircase was the principal schoolroom, a very long, lofty room lighted by eight tall windows on either side, with long rows of forms rising in three tiers on each side. A wainscote painted white ran all round the hall to a height of about eight feet, and above it the walls were bare and whitewashed, save on one side where on slabs between the windows were painted the names of all the monitors year by year from 1800. The upper end was occupied by a dais, in the middle of which placed lengthways of the hall was a massive ancient table, its surface cut all over with names of former boys, and at its head a desk and massive, handsomely-carved chair of Spanish chestnut, with the arms of the Company carved on the back. This was the Headmaster's throne, and at intervals down the hall were similar chairs for the under-masters. In

44

the south-east corner of the dais was a door leading into a classroom where the Head and Sixth forms retired for lessons apart from the vulgar gaze. Beyond this was the 'Chapel', so-called because of a tradition that on this spot had stood the Chapel of the Duke of Buckingham's house, which was bought by the Company as a house for their newly-established school. It was used as the Headmaster's private room, was lined with bookcases over which were full-length portraits of Sir John White, the Founder, and other eminent persons who had been taught at the school. This room communicated with the Headmaster's house.

The school generally contained about 250 to 300 boys distributed into ten forms. Every half-year there was an examination, and a great speech day at which the Master and Wardens of the Company attended in their robes, with a large company of visitors and former students. Speeches were made, scenes of plays acted, and the prizes distributed with much applause and ceremony. The 11th June, St Barnabas day, was *the* great day. The Headmaster, Dr James Augustus Hessey, of St John's College, Oxford, was a short, fat, fussy man, extremely kind, industrious and earnest. The other masters were not particularly remarkable except for the long canes with which they beat us unmercifully for the slightest fault. I have gone home at night with my shirt sticking to my back with blood which had congealed on it from 'benders'. The 'bender' was a form of caning peculiar, I believe, to this school. The master seized a boy by the forelock—boys wore their hair much longer then than they do now—and pulling him down lashed him hard on the back. Old Deane, the second master, a tall, wiry man who had been a cavalry officer, was particularly expert at the 'bender'. Our French master, M. Delille, a fat, genial, lively man, more like an Englishman than a Frenchman in face and figure, was our favourite master and taught us admirably, but French was held in small esteem in those days.

A day's routine of work at Merchant Taylors' was on this wise. Punctually at nine the Doctor made his appearance, struck his desk with his cane and said in a stentorian voice, 'Preces'. Immediately the lowest boy in the Sixth Form rushed to the great door at the lower end of the hall and shut it. It had no lock and was kept closed by the boy passing his arm through the large iron staples. His strength was severely tested by the boys who came late pulling at the door from the outside.[1] Then another Sixth Form boy rushed to the foot of the dais and there placed an open book face upwards. A good, soft old dictionary was kept for this

[1] Like Catherine Douglas when she held the door against the murderers of James I of Scotland. Only the Merchant Taylors' boy never got his arm actually broken, though it was often severely bruised.

purpose. Then one of the monitors whose turn it was took up a hand-somely illuminated book of prayers and, kneeling down on one knee on the dictionary, read the prayers in Latin as fast as he could gabble them, the whole school standing and shouting the responses. As the last words 'in Sœcula Sœculorum. Amen', were uttered the door was flung open and the late boys let in, each one's name being taken down for punish-ment which consisted in having to write out one hundred lines of Virgil. Lessons then began. Some of the forms went down into the classrooms on the lower floor and the others spread themselves over the space thus vacated.

In all the forms the first thing done was to repeat the 'Part'. This was a passage of some twenty lines from a Latin poet learnt by heart over-night. On Mondays it consisted of the Epistle and Gospel of the Sunday. In this way I learnt by heart nearly the whole of Virgil and Horace. Then came the 'exercise', a copy of Latin, and in the Sixth and Head Forms Greek, verses prepared overnight. In the Fifth and all the Forms below it books were used containing passages for translation in prose and verse. They were compiled by one T. Kerchever Arnold and had a great deal in them about one Balbus and his friend Caius. The famous remark of Balbus that it was all over with the Army (*actum est de exercitu*) passed into a standing joke. Indeed, all our work was embellished with jokes and several of us who were fond of drawing made pictures about everything that we read. My old school books are profusely illustrated on every vacant space and many a cut on the hand did I get from old Deane's ever-ready cane for my artistic efforts.[1] At one o'clock there were prayers again, very short ones this time gabbled by a Sixth Form boy who, to mark his inferiority to the monitors, was not allowed a dic-tionary, but had to kneel on the bare boards. Then we went home to dinner. Afternoon school was from two to four. The Doctor never attended this school, at which Euclid and Algebra were taught in the higher forms and arithmetic and writing in the lower. We broke up at four in the winter and at four-thirty in the summer. There was a half-

[1] Many years after I left school Dr Hessey told me he still preserved a Eu-clid interleaved, the blank pages of which I had covered with pen and ink sketches illustrating the speech of Pericles from Thucydides, the odes of Horace and other subjects. Pericles was a likeness of the Doctor himself in cap and gown with his fat cheeks and paunch. Once in Thucydides we came on a word τροπωτηρ which the Doctor told us was a kind of thong used to fasten the oars to the row-lock, and he added that the preceding holidays he had seen exactly the same kind of thongs in the boats on the lake of Zürich. So of course I had to draw the Doctor in cap and gown rowing a boat on the 'margin of fair Zürich's waters' with a huge τροπωτηρ, and puffing and blowing very hard over it! He recognized his own likeness and was immensely delighted at it!

holiday on Saturday, three weeks' holiday at Christmas, one week at Easter and six weeks in July and August.

The first two years I boarded at one of the boarding-houses opposite the school known as 'Townsend's'. It was kept by an old lady, Miss Townsend, alias 'Spitfire', and her niece, 'Miss Georgie'. Old Spitfire was a sharp-tongued, lynx-eyed, shrivelled little witch whom we all hated and feared; 'Miss Georgie', a large, meek, ox-eyed, patient drudge whom we all worshipped and who sheltered us from her aunt's wrath. We were of course very mischievous, noisy boys and the confinement in the large old-fashioned house which had once been the residence of a wealthy city merchant was naturally very irksome to us, and I daresay we gave poor old Spitfire enough to do, but dear Miss Georgie was our goddess and there was nothing we would not do for her. After a time, some doctor, I think, told my father that I required more exercise, and as I happened about that time to have had my hundred and fiftieth battle royal with Spitfire who refused to have me in her house any longer, I was taken to live at home and walked down to school every morning and back in the evening. Philip Hutchins, who lived in Hanover Square, used to meet me at the corner of the Quadrant (where Piccadilly Circus now is) and we walked, or rather raced, down to Suffolk Lane together.[1]

In 1846 or 1847 my father left St. Pancras, Canon Dale having unfortunately been transferred from St Bride's to that parish. He got the appointment of Preacher Assistant as it is called—virtually Senior Curate—at St James's, Piccadilly, under the Revd J. Jackson, a mild, holy but mediocre man, who was afterwards Bishop of Lincoln and eventually Bishop of London. We lived in the upper part of a house, No. 23 Great Pulteney Street, a quiet, shabby street near Golden Square.

On the 24th September 1847 my sister, Mary Pearson Beames, was born, after whom my parents had no other children. In this house all my youth was spent. It was a dull, dreary, monotonous kind of life and there are very few events to mark the flight of time. I learnt Latin, Greek and French (especially French, which I greatly delighted in), some Hebrew, a very little mathematics, some smattering of history and geography. But in the schools of those days 'Classics' were regarded as the chief

[1] Athletic sports which now (1896) form so important a part of a schoolboy's life, were absolutely non-existent in our life at Merchant Taylors'. One year indeed Dr Hessey hired a field at Hackney for us to play cricket in, but the distance was too great and so few boys went there that it was given up after one season. No other attempt at having any outdoor games was made all the while I was at the school (1847–56).

47

branch of learning; all other things were looked upon as subordinate and unimportant in comparison.

My father was stern, absorbed in his books and parish work, and harassed by poverty and the struggle to keep up the position of a gentleman on the wages of a servant. My mother was silent, cold and unsympathetic. I had scarlet fever in 1848 and my father, who had unfortunately for us been reading some books about diet and the preservation of health, took it into his head that we all ate too much, so from that time forward he steadily starved himself and his family, thereby, among other things, sowing the seeds of the disease from which he eventually died. One cup of weak tea, a small roll and two fingers' breadths of fried bacon constituted my breakfast, after which I had a long walk to school and worked till one, then had dinner at the Headmaster's house, and worked again till four when I walked home and worked again till seven. At seven a cup of weak tea again and two slices of very thin bread-and-butter completed my rations for the day. If it had not been for one copious meal of plain but wholesome food at Dr Hessey's in the middle of the day I should have fallen ill from insufficient food. Condiments, jams, sauces and even so harmless an indulgence as a lettuce or a little fruit in summer were rigidly forbidden. When a holiday occurred— most Saints' days were holidays—I was ordered off directly after breakfast for a long walk in the country with strict orders not to come back till evening. A shilling was given me with strict injunctions not to spend it save in case of illness or other dire necessity. If I did not bring back the coin intact I was subjected to a long and angry cross-examination, and was in disgrace for days afterwards.

With that longing for green fields and trees which grew upon me so strongly during the long months spent among the interminable bricks and mortar of London, I used on such occasions to walk for miles into the country, but sometimes hunger overcame me and not daring to spend my solitary coin I almost fainted from fatigue and emptiness of stomach and reached home scarcely able to drag one leg behind the other. If I arrived after tea-time I had to go to bed empty, for no eating was allowed except at meal times.

I have often wondered since that my mother did not provide me with at least a few biscuits or sandwiches in my pocket. But it was not her habit to think of such small attentions. Once, when I had walked as far as Barnet and back, I felt so faint and ill as I reached Regent's Park that I ventured to call on my Aunt Rose who was living in a house looking on to the Park. I found her and her husband Mr Mitchell at dinner, and on hearing my tale and seeing how ill I looked they administered a copious dinner, some hot wine and water and then made me lie down on a sofa and sleep for an hour, after which my aunt took me home in a cab. She scolded my father and mother severely for their inhumanity. The only result, however, was that I was in disgrace for a long time afterwards. Pearson came up from Bashley about this time, and was sent to King's College and Willie was taken on at Bashley in his place.

In 1851 came the building of the Great Exhibition Palace in Hyde Park. We watched every step in the progress of this novel and beautiful structure of glass designed by Sir Joseph Paxton, Head Gardener to the Duke of Devonshire at Chatsworth. It was, subsequent to the Exhibition, considerably enlarged and re-erected at Sydenham under the title of the Crystal Palace. When it was finished and opened we were frequently taken to see it, and I still remember the new and beautiful things collected there. London was crowded with people from the country, and foreigners. For the benefit of the latter, my father, with an old friend, the Revd T. Haverfield, got up a service in French at St James's Chapel, a small private chapel in York Street, of which Haverfield was the clergyman. Except my father and myself no one English or foreign went to these services.[1]

Old Haverfield was very proud of his French and was always making me talk to him and read French books to him. I daresay he taught me a good deal that was useful. Pearson was not much given to learning by nature and his long residence in the country had given him the country tastes. London was hateful to him and my father disliked him because he would not learn. They had a detestable habit at King's College (instead of honestly caning a boy and having done with it), of keeping him in for an hour after the school broke up and, in order that he should not hide this punishment from his parents, he had to take home a 'detention card' which his father had to sign and he took it back to school the next morning. Whenever Pearson came home, as he very often did, with a 'detention card', he got a severe thrashing from my father; and blows from him, accomplished boxer as he was, were no joke. Once my father thought he could coach Pearson in his lessons of an evening in order to help him, but this well-meant plan entirely broke down owing to my father's hasty and impatient temper, which Pearson loved to provoke by appearing more stupid than he really was. When he had purposely

[1] It is a curious coincidence that this chapel was originally built for Divine Service in French—at least for so much of Romish service as is conducted in a vernacular. It was built to serve as the private chapel for the French Ambassador in the reign of Charles II. He lived at No. 8 St. James's Square, close by. The chapel has now been pulled down (1896). It was half-way up York Street on the east side.

blundered for an hour over two lines of Caesar my father lost his temper and knocked him down, and then sent him to bed. 'Go to bed!' was my father's perpetual punishment for all of us. Two strong, healthy boys cooped up in a small, gloomy house naturally made a good deal of noise at times, and we frequently disturbed my father when reading or writing his sermon in the room below us and got sent to bed accordingly. My father's favourite was the youngest of his sons, little Harry, a bright, merry little fellow full of the oddest and quaintest imaginings, living in an imaginary world of his own peopled with strange beings whose sayings and doings he would solemnly repeat to us. The principal of these was a person called Jod C. Mazemaglastus, who possessed a liquor called Joby, which was liable to be attacked by crickets, and to run out in consequence. Harry had been very ill with water on the brain some time before this, and was very weak and sickly for some years. This small, pale, elfish creature would come down to breakfast and suddenly break its silence, in which all our scanty meals were eaten, by remarking, 'the Joby ran out last night, the crickets got at it,' whereat my father would roar with laughter while Harry looked at him sadly and wistfully.

Among the numerous visitors to the Great Exhibition came unexpectedly my Uncle John, looking very large, red-faced and coarse. It seems he had gone down to Yorkshire where Mrs Carnarvon's former companion old Miss Smith was living with her cousins the Seymours. She had been unable or unwilling to help him, and he had drifted somehow to a little town in the West Riding called Barnsley, near to which is the dirty little village of Chapelthorpe. Here he had established himself as a cattle-drover and had married a woman much below him in position and to my mind not in any way attractive, Ellen Barron, daughter of a land steward to Sir George Beaumont of Bretton. He took a great fancy to me and I used to accompany him on long walks in the course of which he used to astonish me, accustomed as I was to my father's extreme abstemiousness, by stopping at nearly every public house we passed, to have some beer. By my father's advice he went down to Bashley and was reconciled to my grandfather, who gave him rent-free a small cottage at Arnwood, a mile or so from Bashley, with a few acres of ground round it. On his return through London on his way to Yorkshire to fetch his wife and two boys, he took me with him, it being then our long holidays. I spent a fortnight in the north, the only time in my life I ever went to that part of England. I was not much pleased with the Yorkshire peasantry among whom my uncle lived. I could not understand their language very well, and I thought them very coarse and rough and brutal. But I enjoyed a visit to Manchester and Liverpool, and I went down a coal mine. The Christmas holidays of that year I spent with my uncle at his new home, Arnwood. Pearson was at Bashley with my grandfather and I used to be over there nearly every day. The old man took rather a fancy to me and I delighted in sitting at his feet and inciting him to talk. His manner seemed to me pleasanter than my father's. There was less sternness, more variety and grace. But then he was not engaged in a severe struggle with poverty as my poor father was. He was subject to violent fits of rage during which he would swear the most frightful oaths, grow purple in the face and make everyone tremble. He lived almost entirely alone, seeing no company, except when he went into Lymington to preside at the Bench of Magistrates. My uncle called on him occasionally, a formal call, when they began by talking to each other in a strain of very much overdone politeness and usually left off swearing at each other like bargees. Then my uncle would go into the kitchen to drink a glass of beer with old Eley the butler, and before he had been there long my grandfather would ring his bell and order Eley to turn that drunken scoundrel (epithets *ad libitum*) out of the house, and my uncle would go away imprecating the most awful curses on his own head if he ever set foot in that house again. But he went there again the next week, and the two met as if nothing had happened.

My uncle had very low tastes. He spent a great deal of his time walking about the country and dropping into the various public houses where he would sit for hours drinking and smoking in the company of the lowest and most disreputable scoundrels in the neighbourhood. He was supposed to be farming his half-dozen acres of land at Arnwood but he did not seem to pay much attention to that. He was walking about the country all day. Once he drove me through the loveliest part of the New Forest to Salisbury where we stayed two days, and I explored the old city and cathedral to my heart's content, while my uncle was buying cattle at Salisbury Market. It was on this occasion that he took me to the village near Salisbury where his first love, Miss Burgess, had lived and told me the sad story which I have already related. We sat on some rails by the roadside as he told it in front of the house where she had lived. It was a large, handsome house, but then shut up and deserted. The old man was dead and no one knew where the family had gone.

In 1852 my brother Willie was sent to Dr Burney's school at Gosport to be prepared for the Navy, and Harry was sent to Edwardes' at Streatham, my old school. Edwardes had retired, and had been succeeded by one Hodson, under whom the school had a good deal fallen off. I went again to stay with my uncle at Arnwood, and after being there some weeks was invited by my grandfather to spend the rest of my holidays at Bashley. The old man used to talk to me a great deal and once or twice tipped me handsomely. He was getting very infirm and used to be taken to bed every night at seven, when Pearson and I spent the rest of the evening in the kitchen, a large stone-paved room with an immense fireplace with settles inside it. In the warmest corner sat the housekeeper, Mrs Sleeman, a tall, handsome, bold-looking woman, dressed in black with large white collar and cuffs. It was the custom for her to go and sit with her master for an hour after dinner, sipping a glass of port wine, and amusing him with scandalous gossip about people in the neighbourhood. She had an illegitimate son, whom she passed off as her nephew and for whom, through my grandfather's influence, I believe, she secured a good berth as engineer on a steamer. He was a clever, pleasant young fellow who was much liked by Pearson. He used to come to Bashley for a visit now and then. Sleeman was a great drunkard. She and old Eley the butler used to drink together, and it was whispered that they had been privately married. At any rate Eley used to be seen coming out of Mrs Sleeman's bedroom early in the morning and it was not unjustly surmised that he had spent the night there. But of course these things were not told to Pearson and me, though our youthful curiosity was much excited by what went on. The evenings in the big kitchen were rather riotous, and my grandfather, who slept in a distant part of the house, seemed to be quite unaware of what happened. Eley would play his fiddle and sing songs while Mrs Sleeman drank brandy and water and nodded her head to the tune with a drunken leer. The songs it need hardly be said were not always of the most chaste or select kind. At nine the cook, Mrs Thomas, a poor, meek, crushed little creature, though a consummate artist, would put on the table a copious hot supper. I often used to reflect that there was as much eaten in one meal in the kitchen at Bashley as would have lasted us at my father's scanty table for a week. My grandfather's servants lived better than his sons did. Big jugs of strong, home-brewed ale, great joints of hot beef or mutton and quantities of hot pies, bread and cheese and vegetables were consumed, and we hungry and rather greedy boys were only too glad to join the feast. Then there was more drinking and fiddling till at last Mrs Sleeman was carried off to bed, either roaring drunk or maudlin drunk, by the housemaids. My grandfather was completely in the hands of three of his servants, Sleeman, Eley and Rowland. This last was his coachman, steward and factotum. He lived in a cottage near the stables. It was through him that my grandfather managed his farming operations, and lost so much money by his experiments with guano, phosphates and other chemical manures. Rowland was a little, wizened, wrinkled old man, a 'Particular Baptist' by religion and, we all thought, a consummate hypocrite. But he knew how to brew the most delicious beer, and his wife managed the dairy and produced delicious butter, and being a Devonshire woman, knew how to make such clotted cream as one could not get elsewhere. The lavish expenditure on eating and drinking at Bashley was a continual surprise to me after my father's system of starving us on so many ounces of meat and so many cups of very weak tea. But there was a great quarrel soon between Sleeman and Eley, I know not what about, and it led to Eley's resigning his post. He was succeeded as butler by a meek young man named Batts, who ministered to Mrs Sleeman's requirements with most devoted attention till the end. And the end was not far off. In the autumn of 1853, instead of inviting me and Pearson to Bashley, it pleased my grandfather to invite my father and mother. He was ill and in low spirits and perhaps wanted better company than us boys. One day my mother was reading the Hampshire newspaper to him, and when she came to some article on local politics in which he was much interested, something in the article displeased him. He started up and began to rave at the writer, and to curse and swear in his usual fashion. Suddenly he turned almost black in the face, his head dropped on his chest, and he began to choke. The servants were called and he was carried to bed, a man was sent on a horse for the doctor who, when he came, pronounced it to be an apoplectic stroke. For some days he lay unconscious while his stertorous breathing could be heard all through the house. On the 17th October 1853 he died, aged 72. He was buried in his family vault beside his wife in Milton Church and my father put up a marble slab to his memory.

In his will he left Bashley Lodge and land to my father, but entailed to me and my eldest son, failing issue to each of my brothers and their issue and to others and others as far as he could possibly entail it, and saddled with an annuity of £100 a year (nearly as much as the property was worth) to Mrs Sleeman, and another of £40 to Rowland. His estate at Aymestry in Herefordshire he left to my Uncle John similarly entailed, and burdened with annuities of £30 each to my mother and my uncle's wife. The original family property at Clifton and Wrington, with the houses at Greenwich and a large sum of money, were left to my brother Pearson also carefully entailed. Sums of £500 each were left to my brothers Willie and Harry and my sister Mary, to whom also he left all his wife's jewels. In his will he explained that he had tied up all his property in this way in order to prevent his sons from dealing with it as they had done with the Carnarvon inheritance of £36,000. There were also numerous conditions and legal technicalities inserted tending

53

to hamper all the legatees as much as possible in the enjoyment of their bequests. His books, pictures, china and plate were left as heirlooms to go with the Bashley Estate. He evidently expected my father to live there, forgetting that he had not left him any money to keep it up with. My father's share of the Carnarvon money, £18,000, had been almost, if not entirely, anticipated by the time he came into it. He tried the experiment of living at Bashley for some years, but was eventually obliged to give it up as he could not afford it. His (i.e. my grandfather's) death, however, came at a very opportune moment, and relieved my father of some part of his poverty though perhaps not of so much as he might reasonably have expected.

Our life now changed considerably. My father wished to retain Bashley in his own hands, though perhaps he ought to have let it, and he was not rich enough to do without his appointment at St James's. So my mother lived at Bashley and my father and I remained in grimy Pulteney Street, giving up most part of the house and retaining only two bedrooms and a sitting-room. We ate our frugal breakfast at home but I dined as usual at school and my father got his dinner at an eating-house. There were in those days none of the splendid restaurants in the West End, of which there are now so many. Simpson's in the Strand was the only place of the kind. We spent our holidays at Bashley. Here I had full access to my grandfather's large library. It was a strange medley. In addition to a huge mass of law books, there were old black-letter and other rare and curious volumes, a whole world of curious seventeenth- and eighteenth-century literature. I devoured all these greedily. I remember reading *Don Quixote*, Rabelais, *Gil Blas*, *The Rambler*, *Tatler*, *Spectator*, the edifying collection of British dramatists, Mrs Aphra Behn and Mrs Centlivre, Sheridan, Smollett, Goldsmith, and the like, also Fielding and some less known writers. There were also large volumes of the pictures of Hogarth, the caricatures of Gillray, Rowlandson, H. B. and others. Then there were shelves upon shelves of old Elzevir Classics and Aldine Editions, little dirty books an inch or two long, *Erasmi Colloquia*, More's *Utopia, Euphues*, Sidney's *Arcadia*, Barclay's *Argenis*; likewise all the poets from Ben Jonson to Byron, several editions of Shakespeare and more than I can now call to mind. I was never without a book in my hand; sometimes I would wander off into the lovely glades of the New Forest and lie the best part of a long summer's day under the great beeches poring over a book, at another perched high on the top of the steps in front of a bookcase deep in some ponderous folio. I began a catalogue, but as I had to stop to read every interesting book, it is needless to say I did not get far with it. We had a mail-phaeton and horse in which my mother went for long drives, mostly in to Lymington, shopping, for though it was six miles off there were no shops nearer. We had also a rough New Forest pony which I learnt to ride and on which I wandered for miles all over the Forest. Also the sea was not far off and Pearson and I used to go for a bathe and swim nearly every morning. I soon learnt to swim fairly well.

When the holidays were over I returned to London with regret, but much improved in health. My father used to talk to me of an evening, and his conversation was full of interest, as from his well-stored mind he would pour out floods of information of all sorts.[1] At this time I was getting impatient at the narrow limits of our school education. I had got into the Sixth Form, a form the numbers of which were limited to twenty, all of whom had the proud privilege of being allowed to wear 'stuck-up' collars and elaborate stiff neckties or cravats. The stuck-up collar, consisting of two stiffly starched triangular pieces of linen, cut the ears, pricked the cheeks, and was in every way inconvenient and uncomfortable but to us boys, as the badge of manhood, it was dear. But I was very lazy at school, being, as I have said, more interested in the wide range of things learnable out of school than in the limited one of things learnt at school. French I was still interested in, but Greek and Latin had no charm for me. I had bought, out of my rare tips, a German dictionary and Schiller's *Don Carlos* and *Wilhelm Tell*, and by the aid of a German grammar of Pearson's I was teaching myself to read them. Pearson learnt German at King's College and a good many things which we did not learn at Merchant Taylors'.

My father was as fond of walking as my uncle and on holidays would go for long—dreadfully long—walks with me. We would go to Hampton Court and back, Epping Forest and other distant places. He talked hard the whole way and if he had not taken me so far and given me so little to eat I should have enjoyed the walks much more than I did.

But I must not linger too long over this period of my life. The details would not be so interesting to others as they are to me. I will only

---

[1] I remember about this time going with my father to hear Faraday lecture at the Royal Institution in Albemarle Street. Faraday was as usual brilliant and instructive. At the close of the lecture the Duke of Northumberland who was among the audience advanced to the platform and complimented the lecturer. Faraday bowed almost to the ground. My father was indignant. 'There,' he said, 'is a specimen of British Toadyism. There is Faraday, the greatest chemist of his age, bowing humbly to that nobody because he is a Duke. It is disgusting.' But the Duke was not only a highly intellectual man but a munificent patron of art and science. I think such men are worthy of respect as much as the great savants whom they support. Moecenas has his uses as well as Virgil.

mention that I had regular lessons in riding at the Knightsbridge Riding School where we were taught by the riding-master of the Horse Guards, by whom I was taught the military seat with long stirrups which I have ever since retained; that I at one time had a few drawing lessons and took to water-colour sketching on my own account with great perseverance and energy; and that an attempt was made to teach me music, which utterly and absolutely broke down owing to my total want of ear and of any interest in the subject. The attempt was very soon given up as hopeless, much to my satisfaction.

CHAPTER IV

HAILEYBURY, 1856–1857

A WIDER existence opened to my view in 1854 when I was seventeen and thought myself a very grown-up person indeed. One day my father, walking down a street in the City, ran up against someone who turned out to be his old friend, Mr Frederick Augustus Geary, the same who used to come on Sunday afternoons to Streatham to argue about Election and Justification. They had not met for some years and were delighted to see each other again. Mr Geary invited my father to come and see him at Putney. Accordingly one lovely evening in July we went by steamer to Putney and found our way to Platt House, one of those fine old brick houses that used to be common in the suburbs of London in those days, but are now, alas! grown so rare. It had a fine large garden surrounded by a brick wall and in front a gateway of elaborately curled and twisted iron-work. There was a large company at table when we went in. They had finished dinner and were sitting over their wine. My father had, I need not say, arranged to arrive after dinner lest I should be betrayed into eating too much. He was so dreadfully afraid of eating! At Mr Geary's right hand sat a tallish girl in white, whose face I could not distinctly see in the gloom. But amidst the babble of voices I noticed her, and was much struck by the affectionate, caressing manner in which she waited upon her father, and the tender tone of his voice in speaking to her. There never having been any love in our own home or any outward display of affection between the members of our family, the affectionate hearty tone of this father and his sons and daughter struck me as quite a new and charming thing. My father as usual began lecturing the company about anything and everything. Mrs Geary shrieked and laughed and talked nonsense to Mr Ball and my father, while I watched Ellen Geary. We had a delightful evening. After dinner Ellen played the piano and her brothers Henry and Alfred sang. Their father sat by me and talked for a long time. It came into my mind, I know not how, that this was the woman that I would marry, and I went home that night fully resolved to do so as soon as the time should come. I had just come out of a precious, and, alas! unrequited attachment, having been for nearly two years deeply in love with Agnes Marryat, one of the daughters of Colonel Marryat of Chewton, near Bashley, and niece of Captain

57

Marryat, the once celebrated writer of the very popular sea-novels. We were very intimate with the Marryats, but the fair Agnes did not return my attentions. They left Hampshire about this time and we saw no more of them. My heart was thus unoccupied for the time, except for Lettie Beeston, my cousin, a tall handsome girl, but very stupid, whom I kept on hand as what actors call an 'understudy'—somebody to flirt with when there was no more serious affair on hand. Lettie of course did not count. The intercourse with the Gearys was unhappily interrupted for the time by the sudden death of Mr Geary in November 1854. He had for many years shared the house at Putney with a friend, Mr John Ball, a member of the firm of Quilter Ball & Co, Accountants, and on his deathbed he confided his wife and children to Mr Ball's care, a charge solemnly accepted and faithfully performed by him as long as he lived. But of course for some time they could receive no visitors, and a long time elapsed before I saw them again.

In September 1854 I went up to Oxford to try for a demyship at Magdalen. I did not get it but was marked 'proxime accessit', and the College offered to matriculate me, but my father was advised not to accept the offer and so the matter dropped. I returned to my work at Merchant Taylors' where I was now a Monitor, and had the proud privilege of wearing a tailcoat. Although these coats are now only worn for evening dress, in 1854 it was no uncommon sight to see men walking about in them in the daytime.

Pearson, having been left so well-off by my grandfather—his income under the will was estimated at about £700 a year—elected to go into the Army and was accordingly sent to Sandhurst. Willie entered the Navy in 1855 and went to sea as a midshipman on board H.M.S. *Arrogant*, commanded by Captain Yelverton, the husband of the Marchioness of Hastings, an eccentric old lady who lived at Efford, near Bashley, and had been a very great friend of my grandfather's. In consequence of this Captain Yelverton was very kind to Willie and looked after him. The *Arrogant* was sent to the Baltic as part of the flying squadron under Sir Charles Napier. The Crimean War was then going on, and Henry Geary the eldest son of the late Mr Geary had just passed out of Woolwich into the Artillery and was in the trenches before Sebastopol. The second brother, Alfred, a clerk in the War Office, had been sent, together with a brother-clerk, Robert Hamilton, to Balaklava to assist in the Commissariat Department which was in dreadful confusion. When therefore we resumed our visits to Putney, we and the Gearys were equally interested in news from the seat of war, and we followed with the closest attention and greatest anxiety every step of the campaign, especially during that cruel winter when our troops were well-nigh frozen and starved to death. This common interest took us much to Putney and my love for Ellen grew silently but deeply. In our many long walks together we found ourselves possessed of similar tastes and interests. She was nearly three years older than I was, but that did not matter. She was in those days rather disposed to be learned and literary, and this pleased my father very much. He used to lend her books and give her many of the interminable lectures he was so fond of delivering.

My father's absorbing interest at this time was the condition of the working classes. He and his friend Charles Kingsley, whom he used to meet often, were, or professed to be, Socialists and ultra-red Radicals, and I think it must have been somewhere about this time that Kingsley wrote his novel *Alton Locke*. Certainly many of the characters in that book strike me as closely resembling the working tailors and cobblers in my father's parish.

He used to visit many of these men in their close, fetid attics in Windmill Street, Archer Street, and that neighbourhood, and I went with him. They always seemed to be atheists as well as Radicals and my father succeeded in converting several of them, and they attended his Sunday evening extempore sermons in a dingy little room in Marshall Street. I always went with him and loved to hear him preach. His written sermons were very elaborate and profound, but when preaching extempore he was wonderfully eloquent and impressive. At last he wrote a book called the *Rookeries of London*—'rookeries' being the slang term for lodging-houses of the poorest kind, where human beings were herded together like cattle with no regard to health or decency. The book had considerable success and ran into a second edition. At this time a number of young officers in the Guards at Knightsbridge Barracks, Viscounts Ingestre and Lewisham, Sir W. Fraser and others whose names I forget, together with Lord Goderich, afterwards Marquis of Ripon, and some bishops and other big people got up a Society for the Improvement of the Dwellings of the Working Classes. They wrote a volume of essays called *Meliora or Better Things to Come* and my father edited it and contributed to it. He was then made Secretary to the Society, and with Lord Ingestre who was President did a great deal of visiting in the worst dens in London. I sometimes went with my father and saw something of this revolting side of life. The labours of the Society culminated in the erection of an enormous block of model lodging-houses in a very bad slum near Poland and Wardour Streets. The Duke of Cambridge laid the foundation stone and there was a big dinner at the London Tavern, and much flourish of trumpets and articles in the papers. Then the young lords got tired of it and turned to some new toy. My father had hoped that some good to himself might come from being associated with all these big people, but when the excitement was over they quite forgot him.

In November 1855 I went up to Oxford again to try for the Balliol scholarship. I did not want to go, feeling that I was not sufficiently prepared. But the Headmaster and my father decided that I was to go; so I went, and failed. The double life I was leading at that time quite unsettled me for school-work. The teaching I got from my father at home, and the knowledge I was picking up from my private reading, carried out under his supervision, introduced me into a larger and more real world than was ever dreamt of in the narrow routine of school-work. At night my father often gathered round him men of note and learning. I sat listening eagerly while they talked history, ancient and modern, politics, religion, art, manners and customs, society—everything one could possibly imagine. In the daytime I was tied down to Latin and Greek taught in the driest and barrenest way, and was expected to take a keen interest in subjunctives with ἀν or the exact phraseology suited for Ciceronian Latin. In the long holidays of this year my father invited Ellen Geary to Bashley, and she and I drove about the country together, or roamed in the Forest talking incessantly about every conceivable subject and building castles in the air for the future. These were happy days and insensibly drew us nearer together. Now, however, suddenly and unexpectedly came the turning point of my life. I was spending the Christmas holidays as usual at Bashley, when, on Saturday the 12th January 1856, the morning post brought me a letter from my father who was in London, enclosing one from Dr Hessey. It said that Mr J. P. Willoughby, a Director of the East India Company, had a nomination to bestow for the Indian Civil Service, and being an old Merchant Taylors' boy, had taken it to his old school and asked the Headmaster to recommend him a boy. The good old Doctor, knowing me to be a youth of 'erratic tendencies' as he put it, and one whose mind was not contented with Latin and Greek, had nominated me. I was then third Monitor, and the two senior Monitors were provided for by scholarships at St John's. I also should have got a scholarship at the same College had I stayed at school till June 1856, but the Doctor rightly judged that I should prefer to go to India. My father, in sending on the letter, did not urge me to accept the offer, rather the contrary. He had looked forward to a successful career at the Bar for me where he thought my grandfather's name would still have been of use. He said his life would be lonely without his boys, but he could not advise me to refuse so splendid a prospect if my health would stand the climate. His system of half starving us, and my mother's fondness for giving us strong purgatives on the slightest provocation, had resulted in making the health of all of us, and especially mine, far from strong, and my father had once or twice been anxious about me. But at eighteen one does not stop to think about one's health. There was no time to be lost, for the Entrance Examination was to be held on the following Monday. I did not hesitate for a second, but went up to London by the express that very day, and on the following Monday presented myself at the India House in Leadenhall Street where I and six other nominees were put through, what to me, was a very easy examination. The *Antigone* of Sophocles, Horace's *Epistles*, the Gospel of St Luke in Greek, Paley's *Evidences*, a paper of easy Mathematics (Euclid and Algebra) and another equally easy on History. We all passed without difficulty, were solemnly presented before the Directors assembled in a vast, stately Council Room, and after a speech from Colonel Sykes the Chairman, were admitted as students at Haileybury College. I have often wondered in after days that I was not more surprised at the time. So sudden a change in my prospects, and the unexpected opening of such a brilliant career ought to have filled me with amazement. But it did not; perhaps because such startling events do not strike us at the time. One has not time to think about them till afterwards. I remember that I took all the congratulations of my friends very calmly. What really pleased me most was the consideration that I should now be able to marry Ellen, for whom I had for some time been feeling a very deep attachment.

The next few days were spent in preparations. I visited the Gearys at Putney and Ellen and I agreed to write to each other, though as yet there was no word of love spoken between us and our correspondence was extremely polite and literary. Yet, I think, in some unspoken way, we understood each other already.

On the 21st January 1856 I commenced my new life. Arthur and Philip Hutchins, who had been at Merchant Taylors' with me all these years had also been sent there, having got nominations from Sir James Hogg, a friend of their father's, and as I knew no one else there, they became for a time my chief companions. Haileybury College is in Hertfordshire, twenty-one miles north of London. A commonplace ugly quadrangle of dingy yellow brick in the tasteless dull style of the beginning of the century. The front of the square consisted of a large library flanked by a chapel and a dining-hall, the outer side of which looked on to a small park and presented to the road a pompous façade of white stone with pillared porticos in the Cockney Grecian style. But it was

comfortable in spite of its ugliness. Our rooms occupied three sides of
the quadrangle. Each man had a small, snug room with an alcove containing a bed, and a closet which served as dressing-room. We furnished
our rooms ourselves and some men ran into great extravagance in this
respect. There was a good cricket field, racquet court and football
ground. We had boats on the River Lea at the Rye House a mile off,
and for indoor amusements a reading-room and gymnasium. Close by
were several rows of cottages in Hailey village and on Hertford Heath
wherein dwelt a colony of waiters, bedmakers and hangers-on. The
College was in the middle of a triangle formed by Hertford, busy
cheerful and pleasant; Ware, dingy, dirty and of evil repute; and Hoddesdon, airy, clean and dull. Our railway station was at Broxbourne on
the Eastern Counties Railway (now called the Great Eastern), a mile
south of Hoddesdon. The surrounding country was green and undulating; on one side the copses and woods of Hatfield, on the other the
pleasant meadows by the Lea and Stort. The professors lived in houses
at the corners of the Quadrangle and in an old house close by called
Hailey Hall or Bury. The Revd Henry Melvill, the Principal, was the
most eloquent and popular preacher of the day. Wherever he preached
in London crowds thronged to hear him. His eloquence had a fervour
which rapt and carried one away on the swift current of his thoughts,
so that it was intense exertion to listen to him. As he spoke there was a
dead silence in the largest congregations, and it was curious to note how,
when he paused, a storm of coughs broke forth showing that his audience
had been holding their breath so as not to lose a single word. He spoke
with a slight but pleasing Scotch accent, which, however, he seemed to
have the power of dropping or lessening as he pleased. He seemed to use
it to intensify stern or denunciatory utterances, when his voice became
harsh and rough, while when he wished to convey the opposite impression the voice grew soft and musical without a trace of Scotch
accent.

My father, who studied his preaching carefully, always said that he
was a finished orator, who understood how to make his voice an instru-
ment co-operating with his ideas. He was a tall, thin man with an ugly
round face and pug nose; short white hair stood stiffly up all over his
bullet head. But he had an eye that pierced through you, and a clear
cutting sarcastic tone in his voice when angry that made the dullest and
most licentious idler in Haileybury wince. To face 'the Prin' as he was
called was no light thing. Sir James Stephen, the Professor of Political
Economy, was also a man of note. A big, ponderous, pompous man with
a massive head covered with grey hair, he seemed to have an intense,

deep-seated admiration of himself, and always treated us as so much idle scum. Many of us fully deserved to be so treated. He delivered his lectures in a slow, measured tone with his eyes shut, as one who casts pearls before swine. Monier Williams, a little, swarthy, peppery Welsh-man but a renowned scholar, taught us Sanskrit. The Revd J. Buckley, Dean of the College, an elegant scholar and noted biblio-maniac, was kind enough to play at teaching classics, and the Revd J. W. Heaviside, a Cambridge Wrangler and afterwards Canon of Norwich, did the same by mathematics. E. B. Eastwich, a retired officer of the Bombay Army, taught Hindustani and some other Indian vernaculars; Colonel Jasper Ouseley (who was familiarly known as 'Old Jowzle') taught Persian, and J. F. Leith, Q.C., an old Indian barrister, made highly unsuccessful efforts to impart to us some knowledge of law.

Haileybury was a happy place, though rather a farce as far as learning was concerned. In fact you might learn as much or as little as you liked, but while the facilities for not learning were considerable, those for learning were, in practice, somewhat scanty. The Professors gave certain lectures and one or two of them would allow us to consult them at their houses, but for the most part we had to rely upon reading in our own rooms. The men, few in number, who really 'ground' or 'mugged' or 'sweated' (euphemisms by which the use of the word 'worked' or 'studied' was avoided) were looked upon by the majority as amiable but misguided enthusiasts and as fit objects for the more boisterous kinds of practical joking. There were about eighty or ninety students divided into four terms. The whole course of study lasted two years, and each year was divided into two terms: a long term from January to June, and a short term from September to December. But as the College was destined to be closed finally in December 1857, owing to the introduc-tion of the new system of appointing members of the Civil Service by Competitive examinations, the number continually decreased, no new men being appointed. When my first term (or half-year) ended and I passed into the second term, there ceased to be any first term, the fourth term men having completed their course went to India, and there remained only three terms and so on. A good many of the men (or boys as Monier Williams used contemptuously to call us whenever we were more than usually noisy at lecture) were sons of Members of the Indian Civil and Military services, had been born in India and sent home to be educated; many others were connected with Indian families. In spite of this, however, there was little or nothing in the tone of the place or in our habits indicative of our connexion with that country. India was not talked of or thought of except by the few who really worked, nor did we

as a rule care or know or seek to know anything about it. In accordance
with that singular English tendency to keep out of sight everything
relating to a man's profession which leads officers in the Army to wear
plain clothes whenever they can, and condemns all professional conversation as 'talking shop', it was considered 'bad form' to talk about
India or to allude to the fact that we were all going there soon. Even the
study of Oriental languages, which was the chief feature of the place,
and in fact the reason for its existence, was carried on as though we had
no personal interest in the countries in which those languages were
spoken, and no attempt was made to practise talking them or to acquire
any practical familiarity with them. If at any time one wanted to know
what sort of a place India was, or what one's future life or work there was
to be like, it was impossible to find anyone who could give the requisite
information, though three of the Professors, Eastwick, Ouseley and
Leith, had spent many years in that country. All we knew was that it
was 'beastly hot' and that there were 'niggers' there, and that it would
be time enough to bother about it when you got there. Once indeed,
just at the close of our stay there, Sir James Stephen, having been too
busy elsewhere to prepare a lecture, or having exhausted all he had to
say about the fortunes of a certain soap-boiler whose vicissitudes constituted what he was pleased to call Political Economy, pulled out of his
pocket a letter he had just received from a Civilian in the North-West
Provinces, and with his eyes half-shut in the pearls-before-swine manner,
read it to us. In his letter the writer described his daily life and the style
of work which we were shortly about to enter on. It interested me
deeply, but I found that by my fellows it was regarded simply as an
expedient of 'Old Jimmy's' for shirking a lecture and merely valuable
because it gave us one lecture less to take notes on.

Our manner of living was as follows. About 7 a.m. an aged 'bedmaker'
came in, lit the fire and disappeared. Then came the 'scout' or waiter,
who filled the bath with cold water, laid the table for breakfast, cleaned
the boots, and made as much noise as he could in order to awaken the
sleeping student. Gradually we got up, dressed, put on cap and gown
and hurried off to chapel at eight. The attendance at morning chapel was
scanty. A few of the studious men and the Professors were in time. Then,
just as the bell stopped, in rushed a tumultuous mob of the unpunctual
ones in every degree of undress, unshorn, unkempt. Many of them in
slippers and the long overcoat reaching to the heels which was fashionable then, and called a 'Noah's Ark', under which they had only a night-
shirt. Some fragments of a torn gown and a shapeless mass which had
once been a trencher-cap completed their costume. Other belated ones

kept dropping in at intervals till the second lesson began, after which the door was closed and all entrance denied. Attendance at chapel was compulsory for three days in the week, and those who did not attend the full number of chapels were liable to punishment. If a man arrived at the chapel door after the second lesson began, he was not admitted but was allowed to count half a chapel. Often, while the first lesson was being read, and only the voice of the reader broke the silence, one could hear from without the sound of windows being thrown open and voices shouting, 'Pope! Pope! Mark me half a chapel'—to which Pope, the chapel doorkeeper, would be heard replying, 'Very sorry, Mr . . . I can't do it unless you come to the door, sir.' Whereupon there would ensue a volley of oaths and the window would be slammed violently. After chapel the shady ones made a rush for their rooms so as not to be seen in deshabille by the dreaded 'Prin' or the Professors. When we regained our rooms we found our breakfast consisting of tea or coffee, excellent bread-and-butter, and on the tongs, artfully stuck in between the bars of the grate to keep it hot, a mutton-chop or a curried sole or something of the kind. Breakfast parties were a favourite thing, and at these there were all sorts of luxuries provided by the students, and generally tankards of beer or claret. Then those whose rooms did not look on to the Quad descended, pipe in mouth, and lounged about. At this hour a swarm of tradesmen from Hertford made its appearance. Two tailors, a hairdresser and some others walked round the Quad with pattern-books and bags, taking orders and bearing with an equanimity derived from long habit a torrent of chaff and coarse jokes; occasionally crushing some offensive joker with a clever retort.

At ten, the first bell rang for lectures, which lasted till twelve on some days and till one on others. Stephen Austin and Simpson, two booksellers from Hertford, had stalls in the anterooms to the class-rooms where they sold stationery and the textbooks in the various subjects. They also did a considerable business in cribs. These were translations of the textbooks in Greek, Sanskrit, Persian or any other language, printed in small type on thin paper so as to be slipped in between the pages of the textbook in the classroom. The lectures in Law, Political Economy and Mathematics were delivered by the Professors and we took down copious notes—at least, those who belonged to the small, studious minority did so; the majority only pretended to do so and begged, borrowed or stole (chiefly the last) the note-books of the studious a few days before the Examination. The Mathematical lecture was an utter farce. 'Old Heavy', as the Revd Mr Heaviside was irreverently called, would draw a big figure on the board, and begin, 'Now, gentlemen, we draw the line A—B, bub-bub-bub-be,' then he would see someone throwing an inkstand at another. 'Mr X . . . I mark you an L'—and going to his desk he would solemnly record 'Mr X—L', then resuming, 'The line A—bub-bub-be,' till he saw someone else making a disturbance when he would mark him an L and so on. What it was all about I never knew, but some of my most successful pen-and-ink sketches (which I was always making) were executed in 'Old Heavy's' lecture-room.

As soon as lectures were over there was a rush to our rooms where cap and gown were carefully hidden (for it was a law of the place that if you lost your own gown you might take anyone else's), and each man put on the costume appropriate to his special form of amusement. The cricketing, rowing and football men appeared in flannels of gorgeous hues, the fast men in rather too gaudy London costumes, and so on. A crowd then gathered at the 'trap', which is the same as the buttery at an Oxford College, and had bread and cheese and beer, served by two very pretty girls, nieces of the College purveyor. This, like all other cere-monies at Haileybury, was accompanied by a ceaseless flow of foul talk and coarse jesting, with occasional horse-play. Then everyone dis-appeared, the athletic men to their field, the rowing men to run a mile to the boats at the Rye House, the fast men on dog-carts to play billiards at Hertford or Ware, or perhaps to slip up to town by train for the after-noon, and the steady men to take a solemn constitutional along the roads.

The Quad was deserted till half past five when men began dropping in again. Dinner was served in Hall at six and evening chapel was at eight, after which everyone went to the 'trap' again to order the mor-row's breakfast, the orders being taken down by the two girls, Miss Clifton and Miss Coleman, amidst an indescribable hubbub and uproar of oaths, songs, indecent jokes and horse-play as before. I used to pity the two young women, who were modest, quiet, hard-working girls. They took absolutely no notice of anything that went on, but wrote down the orders peacefully through it all. One hopes they did not under-stand the meaning of half that was said.

After this the steady men retired to their rooms and read far into the night. The noisy ones assembled by tens and dozens in someone's rooms where they held what was elegantly termed a 'lush'; drinking, smoking and singing till two or three in the morning, when a 'beak', as the College watchmen were called, brought them a message from the Dean requesting them to retire to their own rooms. A bell was indeed rung at eleven and was, theoretically, the signal for everyone to go to bed, but I do not remember that any attention was ever paid to it.

Towards two o'clock in the morning, those who sat up late working, heard faint sounds of distant voices singing very much out of tune, 'we won't go home till morning . . .' and snatches of various ribald songs, accompanied by the sharp sound of horses' hoofs coming over Hertford Heath, and presently one dog-cart after another drew up to the back entrance and discharged with much noise its load of more or less intoxicated youths. Sometimes, one more drunk than the rest would have been brought home lying in the straw in the bottom of the cart and would fiercely resent being dragged out. After about half an hour's screaming and fighting, the inebriates would be somehow got to their rooms and silence would at last descend upon the Quad.

Though the Directors of the Honourable East India Company had promulgated very strict rules for the discipline of the College, no one seemed to take the pains to enforce them. If you wrote your name in a book which lay on a desk in the Dean's Entrance Hall you were said to have got 'gates', which meant that you could stay out till two o'clock in the morning. Many men, eluding the vigilance of the stern B. Jones, 'Marshal of the College', would slip up to town by the two o'clock train from Broxbourne and amuse themselves there, not returning till the last train at night from Shoreditch, somewhere about 11 p.m. B. Jones was a tall, very powerful man, whose duty was to preserve discipline, report all breaches of rules and to watch Broxbourne Station to see that no one went to town. But he could not be everywhere at once and very great ingenuity was displayed in foiling him. At a public house close by called the 'College Arms' a number of dog-carts with very fast horses were kept on hire, and the drivers, being well and constantly tipped, were on the side of the men and helped them to evade the College officials. The Professors too took a very lenient view of their duties. They said that we were all going out to India in the Civil Service and provided we scraped through College somehow we had a brilliant career before us. It was a pity to spoil such splendid prospects merely because of boyish freaks. The 'Prin' was extremely stern and punished heavily whenever a case was reported to him, but he made it a rule not to interfere unless the Dean or some other qualified person reported a man to him, and the easy-going Dean very seldom did so. The ordinary punishment for cutting chapel or being out too late was so many lines of Latin or Greek, and there were several young men living in the cottages on Hertford Heath who wrote lines at one shilling a hundred for Latin and half-a-crown for Greek, so the punishment of 'lines' practically resolved itself into a fine of the amount one had to pay for getting them written. As nine-tenths of the men had abundant pocket-money the fine was not felt.

MEMOIRS OF A BENGAL CIVILIAN

I was at first very shy and painfully conscious of my poverty and
shabby clothes among all these rich youths, for my father, whether from
necessity or on principle, stinted us as much in clothes and pocket-
money as he did in food. I was at length obliged to buy myself some
decent clothes and sent him in the bill which he paid with much
reluctance, and wrote very severely to me about it. But I felt myself
emancipated now, and was not so much afraid of him as I had always
been hitherto.

I began also slowly and shyly to make friends among my fellow-
students, chief among whom was my dear old life-long chum Frederick
Eden Elliot. The window of his room on the ground floor looked on
to the sunniest and most frequented corner of the Quad, while I had an
upstairs back room in a rather gloomy situation. I was passing his room
one morning as he was sitting at the open window talking to 'Jack
Hunter'. He dropped a pencil (as he afterwards told me, on purpose)
right in front of me, and asked me to pick it up for him. I did so, and as
the window was rather too high for me to reach, I went round into the
room to give it to him. The room was tastefully furnished, full of
pictures, cabinets, and knick-knacks, and he was very cordial and
friendly. The same evening I met him again in Philip Hutchins's room,
and the conversation turning upon painting and sketching, he invited
me into his room to see some pictures he had, and there for several
hours enchanted me with portfolios full of beautiful water-colour
sketches of West Indian scenery. From that night we became fast friends
and are so still as I write this forty years later.

Elliot was a short, slight man, but strong, wiry and active. He was of
a sallow complexion with black hair and wonderfully expressive deep
blue, almost violet, eyes. He had the sweetest and most charming
manners of any man I have ever met. He came of a good old Border
family—the Elliots of Minto—and had an indescribable air of *noblesse*,
an imperturbable temper, a ready flow of talk, a keen and subtle wit, and
an utterly calm and cheerful idleness, unpunctuality and fearless disre-
gard of consequences. He broke all the College rules whenever it suited
him, and took his punishment whenever it befell him sweetly and almost
condescendingly, never being in the slightest degree disconcerted or
abashed and never affecting any concealment. If summoned before the
dreaded 'Prin', he would smile courteously and with the tone of one man
of the world to another admit that he had 'unfortunately omitted' or
'unfortunately done' something that was entirely wrong. But he seldom
got into trouble. Men of that sort do not : there is a sort of spell or charm
that they carry with them, a tact and readiness that protects them. And

though no older in years than the rest of us, he had already lived half a life, and seen more than many men see in a whole lifetime. His father, Admiral Sir Charles Elliot, was a son of Hugh Elliot, the well-known ambassador at Berlin, and cousin of Lord Minto. On his mother's side he was related to Lord Auckland and to the great naval hero, Lord Dundonald. Born at Macao, in China, where his father was then in command of a British fleet, he was taken when very young to India to visit his uncle, Lord Auckland, then Governor-General. Shortly after this his father left the Navy and entered the diplomatic service, being attached in various capacities to several embassies. Thus Fred Elliot lived successively at Dresden, Naples and Brussels for some years. When he was, I think, barely ten years old, his father was appointed Governor of Bermuda and he went there with his parents. There he met his relative, old Lord Dundonald, who took him on his flagship to Halifax, where he was for some time at school, returning eventually to Bermuda through the United States. Then he was sent to England where he lived for a time with Sir Henry Taylor, diplomatist and poet of those days, and was subsequently sent to Rugby for two years. His father was next appointed Governor of Trinidad and took his son away from Rugby, provided him with a private tutor and brought him out to the island where he remained till he was nineteen. Then family interest was brought to bear and an appointment in the Indian Civil Service was secured for him.

It will readily be understood what a mine of delights the society of such a man as this was to me, but what he can have seen in me to like has always been a mystery to me. In Trinidad he had been well taught by an old Creole drawing-master, one Casabon, who had studied in Paris. Casabon's water-colour sketches, often only half-finished, taken as he and his pupil rambled through the exquisite scenery of that most lovely island were a source of endless delight to me. I had a strong though uncultivated taste for art, and under Elliot's guidance improved greatly both in drawing and colouring. We used to spend many a pleasant afternoon sketching in the woods or on the river. We used to take a boat at the Rye House, pull down the Lea to Ratty's Lock, then up the Stort to Roydon where Tennyson's 'Gardener's daughter' lived in my imagination, and his dying swan sang, and the Lady of Shalott sat in her tower (at Nether Hall, an old ruin close by) and 'waves of shadow went over the wheat'. We lived on Tennyson in those golden days.

Haileybury was much broken up into cliques. Elliot and I, with James Hunter and William Hathaway, formed a small set by ourselves and almost always spent the evening together. We were among the quieter and steadier, though not perhaps the very quietest, sets. The very quietest consisted of men who were rather 'goody-goody', read hard, kept regular hours, never missed a lecture or a chapel, drank tea with the professors' wives, and were generally at the head of the term and took most of the prizes. At the other end of the scale were the young gentlemen of the 'Supper Club' and other noisy associations, who kept no sort of hours, gambled, drank, frequented the *lupanaria* of Hertford and Ware and generally did whatever was forbidden. Between these two extremes we held a middle place. We were tolerably regular at lecture and chapel, never got into any very serious scrapes, did not gamble or drink more than was good for us and behaved on the whole very decently. We were sometimes out of College when we ought to have been in, but this was generally because we had roamed too far on a sketching expedition and had stopped to dine at some pleasant little roadside or riverside inn miles off in Essex or Hertfordshire.

On Sundays Elliot and I usually went to Roydon, a pretty village nestled among trees under a hill on the banks of the Stort. Mr Pyne, the Rector, took pupils and Elliot had been there for a little while before he went to Haileybury. We rowed there, tied up our boat at the foot of the Rectory garden, went to afternoon church, dined with the hospitable Pynes and rowed back to the Rye House where we had a parting glass of beer with two of Pyne's pupils, Byng and Johnson, who had accompanied us so far, and then walked back to College. Arrived there we went to Elliot's rooms where the other two joined us and Elliot would make us a little supper of delicacies which his mother used to send him from Trinidad, namely chocolate, cassava cakes, and a peculiarly delicious jam known as 'Governor's plum' jam. Then we would sit up till long past midnight discussing art and all sorts of other things.

Our special study in those days was Ruskin's *Modern Painters* which was just then coming out, over every page and every drawing of which we would argue for hours. During the later part of our stay at Haileybury we worked harder than at first and sat in our own rooms reading till three or four in the morning. My health also very greatly improved owing to the plentiful food and the open air life and exercise.

In the long vacation of 1856 Pearson and I went to Paris together, and spent a fortnight there. I was delighted with the trip, and found that owing to the excellent teaching of dear old Delille at Merchant Taylors' I could talk and understand French very well. I went everywhere and saw everything, but Pearson was bored and would not go anywhere with me. On our return we travelled via Havre and Southampton to Bashley

where Ellen Geary came and stayed with us. We went for long drives in
the forest taking with us my youngest brother Harry and her sister
Carry, a lovely child of about twelve. They, however, had the good taste
to keep as much to themselves as possible and did not interfere with us.
We were now beginning to understand that we were in love with each
other. Pearson did his best to annoy us by trying to flirt with Ellen, but
of course met with no encouragement. He soon left us, much to our
relief, having obtained a commission as Ensign in the 69th Regiment.
Under the purchase system then in force he had to pay £400 for his
commission. He joined his regiment at Dorchester. Harry was removed
from Streatham and sent to the newly started public school at Marlborough. The *Arrogant* had been through the naval campaign in the
Baltic and Willie had been under fire at Helsingfors and Bomarsund.
On his return he brought back a Russian helmet and some other small
trophies, and was quite a local hero for the time. His ship was under
orders to take the British ambassador to St Petersburg at the close of
the war, but at the last moment a change had been made and she was
sent off to the West Indies.

CHAPTER V

LEAVING FOR INDIA, 1858

ON the 25th September 1856 my brother Willie died of rheumatic fever in the hospital at Port Royal, Jamaica. My father had been spending a few days at Bashley and had returned to London by a late train. He reached Pulteney Street, let himself in by his latchkey, lit his candle at the gas burner in the hall and went up to his solitary chambers. There on his writing table he saw a letter with a foreign postmark. He said afterwards that a sudden fear seized him, he knew not why—a presentiment of bad news begotten perhaps of the fatigue of the journey, the loneliness of the large, gloomy room, the silence of the night and the depression caused by other troubles. For a few moments he was unable to open the letter. When he did so he read the news of the death of his favourite son! The shock was terrible. Coming as it did on the top of other troubles it completely broke him. He was never the same man again. It is to that shock that his friends always traced the origin of the terrible malady that fell upon him a few years later. Poor Willie! He was only sixteen, a tall, lithe, handsome boy, with bright brown eyes, full of spirits, clever, and adventurous. 'Whom the gods love die young.'

My father had experienced a very bitter disappointment shortly before this. The living of St James's, Piccadilly, had become vacant owing to the promotion of Mr Jackson to the see of Lincoln. My father had been many years in the parish, was very popular there and earnestly desired the living. Many influential parishioners favoured his claim, and for a time he was sanguine of obtaining it. But for some reason which we never could fathom it was offered to several people and refused, my father's claim being tacitly ignored. Ultimately it was accepted by the Revd J. E. Kempe, an unknown man who, it was said, did not very much care about having it. My father felt this disappointment very keenly. Then he began to find that the cost of keeping up Bashley was more than he could bear. He had clung to it in hopes that on getting St James's he would be able to keep it up, but now this hope vanished. The carriage was put down and severe retrenchments made, and on the night when he got the news of Willie's death he had returned to town in order to consult his lawyers about letting the place.

William Burroughs also had about this time returned from Italy, where he had been living ever since the gambling scandal.[1] He was a morose, cynical man, prematurely aged and worn out by excesses. He exercised an unwholesome, morbid influence over my father, with whom he constantly associated.

From this sad condition of affairs arose the first hitch in my relations with Ellen. My father, who had grown very strange and difficult to deal with—at one time profoundly melancholy, at another wildly hilarious—suddenly started the theory that it was not proper for a young man and woman to correspond and go about together unless they were engaged. I quite agreed with him, and proposed to get over the difficulty by getting engaged at once. But this did not suit him at all. William Burroughs I believe it was who put the notion into his head that I had a splendid career before me, and might aspire to the hand of some rich man's daughter, even the Governor-General's. My father discovered from the *Peerage* that Lord Dalhousie had a daughter, Lady Susan Ramsay, and in the maddest way he formed the idea that I had only to make up to her on my arrival in Calcutta to be at once accepted! It was marvellous what a lot of wild nonsense he would talk about this matter. Ellen and I had many a hearty laugh over it. Her mother, Mrs Geary, also objected to our engagement, not indeed from any consistent or intelligent policy, for she was a vain, selfish, frivolous woman, quite incapable of connected reasoning on any subject. She had been beautiful when young and had been surrounded by admirers, and could not understand that she was no longer young. She regarded all attentions paid to anyone but herself as so much deducted from her lawful rights. My father and Mr Ball paid her extravagant compliments, and she disliked me because I did not do the same. My father and I spent a great deal of our time at Putney. I in fact managed to stay there whenever I could get a day or two away from Haileybury. Henry Geary, the eldest son, was a dull, pompous youth, very proud of having been through the Crimean campaign, and affected to look on me as a schoolboy though he was only three months older than me. But Alfred Geary and his friend, Robert Hamilton, were great friends of mine and made up with Ellen a delightful little party which I was always happy to join.

In 1857 my father again tried to separate us, but this time I induced Mrs Geary to sanction my engagement to Ellen and my father reluctantly gave his consent. The year 1857 passed by happily enough. I was thoroughly happy at dear old Haileybury with Elliot and our other two chums. I liked the work and the life. I was extremely happy at the Platt House with Ellen, and happier still when I could get her down to

[1] See p. 40.

73

Bashley to wander about the New Forest with me. We had then no carriage, and the narrowness of our means was rather painfully obvious, but love made up for everything.

In the summer we heard the news of the outbreak of the mutiny in India, and as one of the victims of Delhi was the 'Prin's' daughter, and many others had relations in that country, the event produced a deeper impression than outside events usually did. There was a general day of Humiliation prescribed for the whole Kingdom, on which Melvill preached a sermon such as it is not often given to us to hear. The old grey head bowed in sorrow, the rough but beautifully modulated voice and the majestic eloquence of the preacher who at last in one awful burst of passionate oratory hid his face in his hands and wept aloud—all this made an impression not to be effaced from the memory.

So also in October the news of the taking of Delhi reached us and was celebrated by a general illumination, after which we made a big bonfire in the Quad and sat round it singing and drinking half through the night. One consequence of the Mutiny was that many Bengal civilians lost their lives, and to fill the vacant places men who had been previously destined for the Madras and Bombay Presidencies were transferred to Bengal. I had been a Bombay man and Elliot a Madras man; we were now both transferred to Bengal.

The first batch of men appointed to the Indian Civil Service by the new system of competition had gone out to India in 1856, thus getting two years start of us, so that the two systems were working side by side. The Directors of the East India Company were determined that their system of appointment by nomination should die brilliantly and had exercised an unusual care in selecting men of promise from the principal public schools for the last term. The competition for medals and prizes in this term was consequently very keen and some six or seven men were working hard against each other. Elliot, in his sweetly ingenuous insouciance, announced that he would be satisfied with a place not lower than half-way down the list, while I was led by my own ambition and by the often repeated exhortations of my father and Dr Hessey to try for a high place. There were seven subjects—Classics, Mathematics, Law, Political Economy, Sanskrit, Persian and Hindustani. The first man in each of these would get a gold medal, the second a prize. I certainly did work uncommonly hard during the last half of that year; and eventually came out fourth out of a term of thirty-two men, getting the gold medal for Persian, prizes in Sanskrit and Classics, and being third or fourth in all of the other subjects except, alas! Mathematics, which, ever since the Streatham days, had been a sore stumbling block to me. It was generally thought that if I had not got such low marks in mathematics I should have been Head of the Term. C. E. Bernard was first, Philip Hutchins second. Elliot was tenth or twelfth.

On the 7th December the prizes were distributed by the Chairman of the Directors before a distinguished company. It was our last day at the old place. After the prizes followed a sumptuous lunch. My father and many other parents and friends of the men were present. Then came a hasty packing up, a last run round the old familiar scenes, handshakings, tips to the servants and last farewells to dear old Hailey. How often both then and since have we quoted those lines from Thomson's 'Castle of Indolence':

> *The Castle hight of Indolence*
> *And its false luxurie;*
> *Where for a little time, alas!*
> *We lived right jollily.*

Although the discipline was shamefully lax, and the moral standard very low, the Haileybury men in most cases turned out well in India, and our having been two years together gave us a camaraderie which the Competition men had not.

The next two months were spent in preparing my outfit and saying good-bye to relations and friends. I had also to sign the 'Covenant' with the East India Company which made me a 'Covenanted Civil Servant', as we are called in India. Over this a difficulty arose. This remarkable document, a survival from the days when the Company was only a body of traders, begins with the words 'This indenture' between the Honourable East India Company of the one part and John Beames of the other. It goes on to stipulate that the said Company admits the said J.B. into its Civil Service in the Bengal establishment and covenants to grant him such pay promotions pension and so forth as the rules and practice of the Service provide, and the said J.B. agrees to a long string of conditions for the most part obsolete and impracticable. It has to be accompanied by a security bond executed by two sureties, one the said J.B.'s father in the sum of £1,000 and the other anyone else for the sum of £4,000. The whole thing was entirely a matter of form as the conditions of the covenant had been framed in days when circumstances existed which had long ceased to exist, so that it was next to impossible for anyone either to keep it or break it. But my father did not know this and he suddenly took a step which surprised us all. He refused to sign the bond unless I promised not to marry Ellen till I had been two years in India, hoping, as I soon learnt, that I should forget her when I got to

India and make a more advantageous match. Lady Susan Ramsay was, as we used to say half-jokingly, half-bitterly, evidently in his mind. So there arose great searchings of heart. Mr Ball and Mrs Geary advised me to resist, but Ellen and I felt that this was useless, so at last, sadly and reluctantly, I yielded and gave the required promise. The second surety was an old clergyman, a friend of my father's, the Revd J. F. Stainforth, Rector of a city parish, who had been in his youth in the Company's Bengal Cavalry, the famous old 'light blue and silver', now no more, though its gallant exploits live in history. The Covenant was signed on the 7th January 1858 and from that date began my long service under Company and Crown.

My passage was taken in the P & O steamer *Pera*, one of their newest vessels. She was a ship of 2,000 tons which was thought in those days very large. I naturally spent most of my time at Putney with Ellen and many were the discussions and arrangements between us as to our future. Mrs Geary was ill in bed, and we had thus much opportunity of being alone together, though with characteristic selfishness she tried to keep Ellen as much as possible in her sickroom attending on her. Good old Mrs Ball, however, a worthy but low-born, commonplace woman, who was severely snubbed and neglected both by Mrs Geary and Mr Ball, came to the rescue and took Ellen's place in the sickroom as much as Mrs Geary would let her.

At last the parting came. On the 6th February we met in my father's study in Pulteney Street and kneeling down prayed God to keep us faithful to each other and unite us again when the two years were over. The next morning, after saying good-bye to my mother, I left for Southampton accompanied by my father, and at two o'clock went on board the *Pera*, which soon after moved slowly out of dock. As he left me my father kissed me and wrung my hand. Our hearts were too full for words. As the great ship slowly made her way round the pierhead I saw his burly figure pushing his way through the crowds, caught a glimpse of his face, pale with extreme emotion, heard his stentorian voice shout, 'God bless you!' and shouted back a 'God bless you!' in return. In a few seconds he was lost to sight. It was the last time I ever saw him. With all his sternness and even at times (as I thought) injustice I loved him very dearly. He was my most truly cherished, honoured and regretted friend and companion. As he himself often said, he was the father not only of my body but of my mind. It is to his long-continued care and stern self-denial that I and my brothers owe the education which enabled us to take such excellent places in the battle of life, and I felt the parting from him deeply.

But most feelings were for the time swallowed up in the rapture of being free and going out into the world independent. As we passed down the Solent I saw all the places known to me during my youth: Beacon Bunny where we used to bathe, Chewton where I had sighed for Agnes Marryat, Highcliff Castle, and lastly the tower of Christchurch Minster. Then the sea began to be too much for me. I went below and knew no more.

The next five days passed like a horrid dream; we were caught in a violent storm in the Bay of Biscay and I lay sick unto death as it seemed, watching the light which came in through the porthole making a little round spot on the cabin wall which rose and fell as the vessel rolled, while occasionally a rush and a shiver with a gleam of green light showed that some larger wave than usual had washed over us. I believe we were in some danger but I was too ill to care for anything. At last we sighted Cape Finisterre, and the sea got calmer. I recovered, managed somehow to get into my clothes and crawled on deck. Next morning, before a stiff breeze, we steamed gaily into the Straits of Gibraltar. It was charming; the air was bright and fresh, men and houses, the giant rock with its guns peeping out of the lines of embrasures cut in the face of the cliff, the gardens, the shops, everything that met the eye was new and delightful. It was the beginning of a new life.

The voyage to India by a P & O steamer is now so familiar to everyone that there is no need to enter into details. I will merely mention a few of the incidents. At Gibraltar there came on board a party of Spaniards bound for Manila, and two of them had berths in my cabin, Don Manuel Reyes and Don Francis de Yriarte. With these noble and amiable hidalgos I foregathered immensely, and Don Manuel, aided by one of his friends, Don Antonio Morales, began to teach me Spanish. I took great interest in this, being always fond of languages, and by the time they left us at Ceylon I had picked up a considerable amount of knowledge of the language.

At Malta we witnessed the Carnaval and took part in the fun. At Alexandria we landed and went by rail to Cairo where we waited a short time for the passengers from Marseilles. Here I met dear old Elliot, to our mutual delight. There was also a delightful little Swedish artist named Lundgren[1] on board with whom Elliot and I consorted, watched

[1] Lundgren was going out to India to make sketches of the principal scenes in the Mutiny for Prince Albert. He made a capital sketch of me by the by, reading on deck. I have it still—it is a good likeness of me as I was then. Lundgren talked German, French, Spanish and English fluently. Only his pronunciation was sometimes queer. He said 'yolly' for 'jolly', and 'ahveefull' for 'awful'.

him sketch and got much valuable advice from him about our own sketches. We sketched of course everything we had time for all the way out.

We left Cairo early in the morning by train but, after an hour's journey, the railway suddenly left off in the middle of the desert. Our baggage was put on camels led by Abraham, Isaac and Jacob living in the flesh, and the passengers were closely packed into small green omnibuses on two wheels drawn by mules, six of us in each. There was a long procession of them, and they plunged and jolted most uncomfortably. We reached dirty Suez as the sun was setting and after a wretched fly-haunted meal in the bare caravanserai of an hotel went on board the *Bengal*, a large, roomy old tub of a vessel long since broken up. Elliot and I had the same cabin and Lundgren was next to us. It was a sleepy, languorous life we led on board this slow, old ship but we were very happy sketching and talking art and travel with Lundgren; talking Spanish with Morales, Yriarte and Reyes, and French with M. D'Harcourt and his family. He was going out as Governor of some French colony, I forget which. Thus we passed burnt-up Aden, green Ceylon, straggling Madras, and finally on the 16th March landed at Garden Reach, Calcutta, after a voyage of close on six weeks. The first view of Calcutta impressed us very much, the long rows of shipping, the lines of stately white houses of the 'City of Palaces', and the beautiful villas with their luxuriant gardens composed an attractive picture. Several old Haileybury comrades came to meet us, and thus full of life and spirits buoyant with hope and excitement, eager to begin my new career, I landed in India on that 16th of March 1858.

CHAPTER VI

CALCUTTA, 1858–1859

WHEN we landed in Calcutta the Mutiny was not yet crushed. Lord Canning, the Governor-General, was living at Allahabad and Mr John Peter Grant, President of the Council, was ruling in his place in Calcutta. Everyone was in terror of the sepoys, who, in contempt of all geographical arguments, were supposed to be on the point of making a raid upon Calcutta at every moment.

Elliot and I went, on landing, to D. Wilson's Hotel (now called the Great Eastern), a large, stuffy, vulgar, noisy place permeated with a mixed odour of cooking and stale tobacco. We could not stand it for long and were advised to take rooms in a boarding-house. Fortunately we obtained rooms at the best house of the kind in Calcutta—Miss Wright's, 3 Middleton Street—a large, comfortable house, where we obtained on the first floor a vast, airy, handsomely furnished sitting-room about the size of a church in England, with two spacious bedrooms. For this we paid the modest sum of rupees 300 (£30) a month including board. We had to keep our own servants besides. My salary I found was to be Rs 333 3a 3p, equal to £33 4s. od a month or £400 a year. Out of this I had to pay my half share of the rent of our rooms, Rs 150, about Rs 50 for three servants, a bearer or valet, a khidmatgar or footman, and a mehtar or sweeper, and I had of course to buy my own wine and beer and my clothes. The income, though not large for so expensive a place as Calcutta, would have been sufficient with economy. But we had neither of us the slightest idea of economy. We were both utterly inexperienced in the management of money, I from never having had any, and Elliot from always having had as much as he liked to ask for.

We took our meals at the public table where we made the acquaintance of a number of very pleasant people. Boarding-houses, which are very numerous in Calcutta, are like private hotels in England with the addition of the public table. People holding the highest positions in society who wish to avoid the trouble and expense of keeping up an establishment in one of the vast, palatial houses of Calcutta with the troops of servants and other expenses which it involves, often take a suite of rooms at a good boarding-house. Bachelors of all ages especially favour these

79

comfortable refuges for the homeless where they are well cared for and looked after. They are always kept by women of the middle class, such as would be found in the position of housekeepers or matrons of an institution at home. Of those whom I have known most were widows; one was the widow of a pilot, another of an indigo planter, a third of a captain in the merchant service. These good ladies are very kind to young bachelors, look after them when ill, get their clothes made and mended, help them to get servants, talk the language for them to natives when they cannot do so themselves, and generally do their best to give a home-like tone to their establishments. Miss Wright was a cheery, fat old maid, the daughter of a newspaper editor, deceased, who had left her this and some other houses in Calcutta. She was also part proprietor of the *Englishman*, the leading newspaper in Bengal.

The first thing we did was to report our arrival to Colonel Lees, Secretary to the Board of Examiners, who informed us that we were attached to the North-West Provinces and would have to pass an examination in Persian and Hindi, for which purpose a native tutor or munshi[1] would be assigned to each of us. An imaginary institution called the College of Fort William, consisting of Colonel Lees who conducted the examinations and a staff of native tutors, was supposed to exist and certain high officials constituted nominally a Board of Examiners, but their duties, as far as I have ever been able to ascertain, were non-existent. Each young Civilian on his arrival was supposed to have a munshi from the College assigned to him, and the Government paid the munshi thirty rupees a month. But the number of munshis was too small for the number of Civilians; each munshi therefore took several pupils—three was, I believe, the number to which he was limited. At any rate three was the highest number for whom he could draw the allowance in any one month. Moreover there were three or four of these men who were much better teachers than the others and were therefore much sought after. A man who wanted to pass quickly or to pass with honours had to secure one of these three or four, and as their sanctioned number of pupils was always full we had to pay them out of our own

[1] It will be as well to remark here once for all that in using Hindustani words, those that have become to a great degree naturalized in English will be spelt in the conventional form in current use. Such words as Raja (prince), Zemindar (landed proprietor), ryot (peasant), jungle (forest or bush), punkah (fan), loot (plunder), are now well known and it would be pedantic to spell them according to the scientific system of transliteration. Words however which have not been naturalized, many of which I shall have to use, will be spelt correctly and where necessary their meaning will be explained. Only occasionally will it be necessary to insert accents or other diacritical marks. The same rule will apply to names of places.

pockets. This is one of the muddles so common in British Admini-
strations everywhere.

A few days after my arrival a fat old Bengali gentleman called on me,
and gave his name as Hari Prosad Dutt. He said he was the best munshi
in the College and as he had heard that I had taken the Persian medal at
Haileybury he, and he only, claimed the honour of being my munshi.
As, however, his list was full I should have to pay him out of my own
pocket, but he promised to give me the first vacancy that occurred. On
asking some of the men who had been some time in Calcutta I was
strongly advised to agree to this, which I did. Hari Babu then put a
Persian book before me and asked me to translate at sight. This I did
quite correctly. I also translated correctly an English exercise into
Persian. On this he assured me that I should certainly pass the first time
I went up. An examination was held on the first of every month. I went
up and was plucked! Hari Babu was full of indignation. He said he had
seen my papers and there was only one very slight mistake—hardly in
fact a mistake at all, merely the use of a word in a sense which was somewhat antiquated. He then told me this was a favourite trick of Lees'.
He often refused to pass a man who was perfectly competent, because
he had only been a month in India, holding that no one was fit to be
passed who had not had longer training under his College munshis. This
disgusted me and for some months I idled considerably and did not
finally pass in Persian till my fourth month. Elliot also had a munshi but
as he was new to Persian, or nearly so, not having paid much attention to
it at Haileybury, he did not make much progress.

We usually got up between five and six in the morning and sat in our
sleeping jackets and pyjamas on the veranda having tea. Then we dressed
in riding breeches and went for a ride till seven. We usually rode on the
maidan, the broad plain round which Calcutta is built, but sometimes
went for long scrambling rides in the country. Elliot was an excellent
rider and could sit any horse. He rather liked a vicious or troublesome
horse. I used to accuse him of liking to show off his skill, which made
him very angry. At seven we came in and got into pyjamas again. Many
of our old Haileybury friends would drop in and our cool, shady veranda
was full of men drinking tea, smoking, reading the papers or letters,
talking, laughing and enjoying themselves. At nine the chota haziri
party broke up and we went to have our baths, put on clean clothes and
went down to breakfast. This was rather an elaborate meal consisting of
fish, mutton chops, cutlets or other dishes of meat, curry and rice, bread
and jam and lots of fruit—oranges, plantains, lichis, pineapples, papitas,
or pummelos—according to season. Some drank tea but most of us had

iced claret and water. After this we returned to our rooms and worked at languages till twelve. The munshis appeared and read with us one hour each, daily. About twelve we usually went out either in a buggy or a palki, custom having appointed this, the hottest time of the day, for making calls. Buggies are seldom now seen in Calcutta, the present generation preferring dog-carts. But a buggy has a hood which a dog-cart has not, and it is therefore more suited for going out in the middle of the day. It is a light gig on two wheels with a hood. I bought one second-hand but in good condition, with horse and harness, for Rs 750 (£75). Elliot also had one. We each had, besides, a saddle horse. We went out at twelve and made a round of calls on the principal ladies in the fashionable quarter of Calcutta—Chowringhee. We were often asked to stop to tiffin (lunch) at some one or other of these houses. If not we returned to 3 Middleton Street for that meal. This was also an elaborate meal of soup, hot meat, curry and rice, cheese and dessert, with claret or beer. After this we felt (naturally) lazy and drowsy and lay about idly dozing—a sort of siesta in fact—under the punkah. About five o'clock we got up and dressed, for during the heat of the afternoon a good deal of clothing had been dispensed with. Then we ordered our horses and rode on to the course. This is a road along the banks of the river; on one side of it were the Eden Gardens, not then so well cared for as now, where the band played. All the rank and fashion of the town collected here in carriages or on horseback. Round the Eden Gardens there was at that time a turf road for riders. The remains of it are there still but in 1858 it was longer, wider and more frequented than now. After meeting our numerous friends and acquaintances, and having a canter round once or twice we dismounted at the bandstand and went and talked to the ladies in their carriages which were drawn up in rows, or fetched them ices from a refreshment pavilion in the gardens. We got home to dinner at half past seven and were generally in bed by nine unless, which often happened, we were invited to dine out or to a ball.

This method of life was certainly expensive, and though we did not know it at the time we were both getting into debt. So were all our contemporaries, and so had been many generations of Haileybury men before us. It was the fault to a great extent of the absurd system which was then in force, by which all the young Civilians were kept for a time in Calcutta 'to learn the languages', as it was phrased. This was not only unnecessary but led to their wasting their time and getting into debt. In those days it was not the custom for all the high officials and rich non-officials to desert Calcutta for the hill-stations as they do now, from March to November every year. Simla and Darjeeling, Musooree and

CALCUTTA, 1858–1859

Ootacamund, had only recently been discovered and very few houses had been built there. There were very few railways, so it was not easy to get to them, and the P & O steamers did not run so often as they do now, so it was not so easy to get to England. Consequently the upper classes of society lived in Calcutta all the year round, and rich men inhabited, and dispensed a lavish hospitality in, the palatial houses of Chowringhee, which are now turned for the most part into boarding-houses and offices. The young Haileybury men were, in very many instances, related to the high officials, and even if they were not, their position as members of the Covenanted Civil Service secured for them a ready admission into the best society. The Civil Service was in those days an aristocracy in India, and we were the *jeunesse dorée* thereof. We were invited everywhere and dined out three or four times a week besides numerous lunch and garden parties. Mamas angled for us for their daughters for, as the phrase then went, we were 'worth three hundred a year dead or alive'.[1] Then of course we had all sorts of amusements among ourselves. Men met to play, and for high stakes too; they had dinner parties, billiard-playing parties at the Bengal & United Service Clubs, cricket, horse-racing, steeple chases and many other less reputable diversions. It was not surprising that they did not work very hard. And Colonel Lees made matters worse, for instead of doing his best to pass men and get them away from what my father called 'that unwholesome Capua', Calcutta, he plucked them one examination after another and so kept them there longer. When a man had been plucked twice or three times running as I was, on each occasion for one trifling mistake, he naturally lost all interest in his work and turned to the numerous attractions of society. Thus it came to pass that hardly any man left Calcutta without getting heavily into debt; a man was said to have 'turned the corner' whose debts exceeded one lakh of rupees (£10,000). And all this while they were not really learning the languages. They had mostly learned these languages as far as they could be learnt from books at Haileybury, and it would have been better to have sent them at once, on arrival in India, to some station in the interior where they could live among the natives and learn to speak the languages from hearing them speak. This is what they do now, and if they had done it in our time it would have saved many a man from life-long indebtedness and misery.

In the first writing of this narrative in 1875 I inserted here a long description of Calcutta as it was in 1858 when I landed there. But on

[1] This means that a Civilian's pay on first entering the Service was supposed to be £300 a year (in fact it was rather more) and his widow's pension is £300 a year, so that a woman who married him would be sure of £300 a year whether he died or lived.

83

reading it over again now in 1896 it occurs to me that the city has changed very little in all those years. It is rather bigger, new houses have been built in between the old ones; docks, railway stations and bonded warehouses have sprung up; the place is more crowded, infinitely cleaner, and perhaps more stately than it was. But the general features are not very much changed. It is still the somewhat sleepy, stately, palatial city with its wide, park-like maidan, broad streets, huge white houses and enervating atmosphere. Gay and busy for three months, from December to March, dull drowsy and empty for the rest of the year. Thanks to Messrs Cook & Co and the 'increased facilities of communication' India is now so well known that a description of Calcutta is unnecessary. I therefore omit what I wrote in 1875.

Elliot and I idled our time away in this pleasant place for some three months when Miss Wright gave up her boarding-house and we all had to turn out. We took rooms temporarily at Schoenerstedt's Hotel, a dark, stuffy place in a cul-de-sac leading out of Tank Square. The change from the airy rooms in Chowringhee to the close business part of the town disagreed with us and we both got our first attack of fever. The smells in this part of the town were exceeding awful and unimaginably disgusting. They are nearly as bad now though the sanitation of Calcutta as a whole has immensely improved. As we lay tossing in the heat the great adjutants looked down on us from the tops of adjacent houses which rose high around us shutting out the air. The adjutant is a gigantic crane with a beak some three feet long, a bald head, evil grey eyes, and a huge crop of red crinkled flesh hanging down in front—altogether a loathsome bird. They nest in the great forests called the Sundarbans between Calcutta and the sea, and used in those days to frequent Calcutta in large numbers, especially during the rainy season. They, the crows, and the jackals, were in those days the licensed scavengers of the city. Very few of them are seen in Calcutta now, a testimony to the greater cleanliness of the place. In our sickness we were attended by Mrs Howe, whose acquaintance we had made at 3 Middleton Street. Mrs Howe was a typical Calcutta character and as such merits description. She was a half-caste or, as she preferred to call herself, a Eurasian, old and ugly in face but had probably been good-looking when young and had still a tall, fine, well-shaped body. She was the wife of a gentleman who spoke of himself habitually as 'Captain Enery Ow'. He had been skipper of a merchant vessel, one of those once very numerous sailing ships that plied between Calcutta, Singapore and Hongkong—but are now superseded by steamers of the British India and other Companies. He was, when we knew him, Master Attendant of the Port of Calcutta.

CALCUTTA, 1858–1859

A very strikingly handsome, pleasant-mannered man, but very illiterate and rather coarse in his language. The Calcutta half-castes are for the most part a lazy, immoral, useless set; but there are exceptions to the rule and one does occasionally meet with an honest and industrious half-caste. Some among them too are wealthy and occupy high and respectable positions in society. Mrs Howe was one of the good specimens. She was very charitable and indefatigable in soliciting contributions for her many good works from the rich Europeans. She was the centre and leading spirit in all the benevolent schemes and institutions then existing in Calcutta and spent hours every day driving about in her large shabby old barouche with a pair of jobbed horses carrying help to the poor, begging for them or writing letters on their behalf. She had an immense crowd of women hangers-on, old and young, mostly of the Portuguese section, who are the idlest, loosest, and most improvident of the half-caste community. These 'high-born beggars' who bore the lofty names of Da Souza, D'Almeida, Da Silva, D'Rosario, Da Cruz and the like, sponged upon her unmercifully and for them she slaved cheerfully. The old lady was romantic and sentimental; 'dear Mr Elliot' and 'dear Mr Beames' were model young men in her eyes, and were constantly being introduced by her to slight, graceful, coffee-coloured young ladies with Portuguese names in want of an income and a position in society. She was much distressed when I told her I was already engaged, and though she did not even then give up all hope of entangling me she devoted her principal efforts to capturing 'dear Mr Elliot', who, as she poetically observed, had such 'Raffaelesque eyes'.

Calcutta was full of refugees from the upper provinces; English officers and their wives who had escaped with their lives, but with the loss of every scrap of their property, from the stations where the native troops had mutinied. One body of these excited deep sympathy. It consisted entirely of ladies and children who had escaped from stations in Oudh. The husbands of many of them had been killed, those of others were detained on service. These poor creatures, after spending several months in the fort of Allahabad, had been sent down to Calcutta by steamer. They had been in many cases obliged to flee for their lives only half-dressed, and reached Calcutta in a state of complete destitution. That noble, gentle-hearted woman, Lady Canning, provided a house for them, and called Mrs Howe to her aid. She went round to all the Englishwomen in Calcutta and collected not only money, but old clothes, and under-linen of all kinds. She might be seen in all corners of the town day after day with the old barouche piled high with clothing, which she then distributed to the poor refugees. Then she would carry them off to the shops, and make them happy by buying gowns and bonnets for them.

There was also at No. 1 Little Russell Street a hospital temporarily fitted up for the reception of wounded officers. We used to accompany Mrs Howe there to visit and cheer up these poor fellows. Some of them were horribly wounded. One man in the Rifles had lost his left arm, and four fingers of his right hand, besides having a sabre cut across his forehead. He, like many more, had been saved by the devotion of his native servant. By degrees, all the ladies and officers were shipped off to England and Mrs Howe had to seek other channels for her charity.

About this time Captain Howe induced me to become a Mason, and I was duly initiated in Lodge 'Star of the East', No. 80, of which he was Master. Elliot and I also became Volunteers. The volunteer movement was in full force in Calcutta and in all the large stations in India. It was of course strictly confined to Europeans. In Calcutta we had a fine force of Artillery, Cavalry and Infantry. Elliot and I were in the Artillery and learnt to handle a gun pretty well by dint of constant practice. Our uniform was a white helmet with a dark blue 'pagri' or roll of muslin round it, blue tunic with red facings, white corduroy breeches and dragoon boots up to the knee. Elliot and I were drivers and rode the two leaders of the four half-broken Cabulee horses which dragged our light six-pounder howitzer. In the Cavalry each gentleman trooper rode his own horse. It was a handsome little troop, commanded by Colonel Montague Turnbull. Dear old 'Monty' as he was called was a great racing man, a shining light of the Calcutta turf, and a general favourite, being a genial, kind-hearted old fellow. His wife was a daughter of Colonel Apperley, a writer on sporting matters well known under the *nom de plume* of 'Nimrod'. She was a splendid rider and a good artist. She used to paint large pictures of dogs and horses, and her compound at 'The Hermitage' in Alipore was an asylum for old and broken-down animals of every description.

We knew everybody in the higher circles of Calcutta society, and the summer wore away pleasantly enough. In those days, as I said before, it had not become the custom for everyone who could get away to rush off to the hills as soon as the weather became warm, leaving Calcutta almost empty. The members of the Government of India and the heads of society stayed in Calcutta all the year round and life was very pleasant there in consequence. I wrote to father and to Ellen occasionally and got tolerably frequent letters from them. I fear, however, I rather neglected them both. Not that I was indifferent but that I was a little carried away by the attractions of my new position, and I had no regrets for England. Both my father and Ellen were constantly urging me to leave Calcutta and go up-country to begin the real work of my profession. They both seemed to think I was wilfully idling away my time, and I could not make them see that it was not in my power to go till I was allowed by Colonel Lees to pass.

Most of our Haileybury contemporaries as well as the Competition-wallahs (as they were called, who had been appointed under the new system of open competition) completed their studies and were sent off to their stations in the mofussil[1] by about September. Only a few of us lingered on; Elliot and I moved back into our old quarters at 3 Middleton Street where the Howes and all the old lot had then returned. I passed at last in Persian with honours and got a gold medal, the second I had gained for that beautiful language. I then had to take up Hindi and this compelled me to stay some months longer in Calcutta. It was now October. Henry Geary, Ellen's eldest brother, came to India in command of a small detachment of Artillery and went up country to Goruckpore where fighting was still going on against the remaining bands of mutinous sepoys. We were very glad to see him and he seemed to enjoy our society.

Then we had an entirely new sensation. We made the acquaintance of Chaloner Alabaster, a clever little man in the Chinese Diplomatic Corps. He was living in a big half-furnished house—one of those huge palaces, half in ruins, situated in the remains of spacious grounds half overgrown with jungle that one so often sees in the neighbourhood of Calcutta. This was at Tollygunj, and in it was living the Chinese mandarin, Yeh, who had recently been made prisoner at Canton and sent in charge of Alabaster to Calcutta. Yeh himself, with whom we had one interview, was not interesting; a tall, fat, hideous Chinaman with scanty beard and moustache, rolled up in a sort of dressing-gown of light blue flowered silk, he grunted out a few words in answer to our remarks which Alabaster interpreted. He refused to see the sights of Calcutta or even to leave his house, alleging that there could be nothing in the land of the barbarians worthy of his notice. But his aide-de-camp, Lam, was a merry young fellow who gave us capital dinners after the Chinese fashion and made jokes, and drank neat brandy like water, and amused us in many ways.

---

[1] 'Mofussil', properly 'mufassal', is an Arabic word meaning 'scattered', 'separated' and in Anglo-Indian slang is used to denote the rural parts of India, the interior of the country in general as distinguished from Calcutta, Bombay and other capitals. It is the 'country' as distinguished from 'the town'.

With Alabaster I went one day to call on Lady Birch, wife of General Sir Richard Birch, Military Secretary to Lord Canning. The General was still at Allahabad with the Governor-General, but we saw Lady Birch, an aged half-caste of vast rotundity, and her two lovely daughters. Emily, the elder, was in ill-health, but Louisa, the other, was very active, bright and clever. 'Lulu', as she was called, became a great friend of mine; we used to ride together, and talk on all sorts of subjects. Both girls had been well educated in London and Paris, they spoke French, Italian and German, sang and played admirably. We used to go for excursions to the Botanical Gardens and elsewhere and return to delightful little suppers at their house. Lulu and I read German together and talked 'geist'. We sketched and discoursed on Ruskin and art. Men said in after times that this was flirting. I did not so regard it. I told her I was engaged to Ellen Geary and she told me she was also engaged to a Captain Baker who was at Haidarabad. We agreed that there was no reason why we should not be good friends all the same. She was very religious, and my own religious feelings were passing at that time through a stage of excitement and enthusiasm, so we talked a great deal about religion, and certainly no conversation about love, and for my part at least, no ideas of love-making ever obtruded themselves. There was a man named Thomas, an opium and indigo merchant, who was in some way connected with the Birches, who was always hanging about the house. He was a fat, flabby, overdressed, purse-proud snob; loud and vulgar, but good-natured and always ready to help poor old Lady Birch in her housekeeping difficulties during Sir Richard's absence. He was fond of dropping in on Lulu and me in our quiet *tête à tête* conferences. Whenever she got enthusiastic on some subject and would look into my eyes with that deep, flashing, yet tender look which the half-caste woman can so readily assume, blond, plump Thomas would suddenly stroll up and, looking blankly into space, utter the word 'Harris' and disappear. Lulu would look like an angry tigress for a second, bite her lips, and hiss out some violent words of contempt. One day I asked her what was meant by this word 'Harris' and she told me that Thomas used it to remind her of her absent lover. Even to unsuspecting me the explanation seemed hardly satisfactory, as the lover's name was not Harris, but Baker. Long afterwards I learnt that Lulu had been engaged to several men but had thrown them over one after the other. Thomas himself had been so jilted by her in favour of one 'Harris' who was also rejected in his turn. Thomas now thought, or affected to think, that she was trying to 'Harris' Captain Baker in favour of me.

CALCUTTA, 1858-1859

Lord Canning with all his secretaries and staff returned to Calcutta in the first week of November and on the 9th of that month took place the memorable ceremony by which Queen Victoria assumed the Government of India and the Honourable East India Company ceased to exist. Elliot and I attended the ceremony on duty as volunteer Artillery men and sat on our horses with our gun behind us in the compound of Government House while the proclamation was read. It was a gorgeous sight, and so were the illuminations and fireworks that followed for two nights, though the fireworks were somewhat spoiled by the sudden blowing up of thousands of rockets before they were intended to. For nine days and nights there was a ceaseless whirl of excitement; balls, parties, durbars and reviews. Everyone was more or less crazy and no one did any work. I fancy the outburst was due more to a sense of relief that the mutiny was at an end, than to any real preference for the Queen's Government over the Company's. Indeed, many old officers openly said that we should not be long in finding that we had lost a good master in old John Company, and not got so good a one in Her Majesty's Ministers. Undoubtedly the good old Company was a very considerate master, and looked well after its own servants whatever may be thought of its merits as a ruling power in India.

With old Sir Richard Birch, who returned to Calcutta with the Viceroy (as the Governor-General was now for the first time called), I soon became a favourite. He was a large, fair-haired man, very stout and unable, from an old wound, to ride or walk. I used to go and sit with him of an evening while his wife and daughters went for their drive, and I learnt a great deal about the upper provinces from his conversation.

Elliot had left Calcutta and gone up-country in November, and I now longed to go too. During December and January I worked hard and got a Degree of Honour in Hindi with a prize of Rs 800 (£80). My father, though sensible of the value of the medal and prize, and rather hoping that I should throw over Ellen for the daughter of a General and K.C.B., had constantly urged me to try and get away from Calcutta, and so had Ellen. Elliot's letters from his new district were full of the charm of mofussil life, and finally I resolved to stay no longer. I might have stayed and gone in for higher honours still, but I was getting rather tired of the aimless existence and determined to bring it to a close. So I reported that I did not wish to go in for any more honours and wished to join my district. In a few days I got orders to go to Benares and report myself there, but before I could start I received fresh orders countermanding the previous ones and directing me to proceed at once to

Lahore and report myself to the Chief Commissioner of the Punjab.

As the time for my departure drew nigh, Mrs Howe, who had wept over Elliot when he went away, wept over me also. She had formed the idea of marrying 'dear Mr Elliot' to one of her daughters, Sophie; and 'dear Mr Beames' to another, Nellie. But as both Elliot and I persisted in leaving Calcutta before those young ladies, who were then at school in England, could arrive, this plan broke down. She was none the less practically kind to both of us, and kept a small army of tailors at work in her veranda on my wardrobe. As we had clean clothes on every day—clean white duck trousers and coats or jackets, shirts, drawers, banians and socks—our stock of clothes in those days had to be very extensive. Mrs Howe also laid in abundant stores for my use on my journey. Calcutta people then, as now, had an idea that the whole of India except Calcutta was a vast, howling wilderness where none of the provisions required by Europeans were procurable. Acting under her advice I laid in so large a stock of provisions that I had been months at my station in the Punjab before I got through them. Bottled beer, brandy, sherry, tinned meats, jams, marmalade, biscuits, sauces, tea, sugar and numerous other things were bought and packed. I engaged a dâk gâri[1] from Raniganj to Lahore, bought a pistol and some cartridges and engaging an up-country bearer recommended by Sir Richard Birch, stood ready to start.

My last evening in Calcutta I spent at the Birches'. After dinner the old man kindly wrote me several letters of introduction to high officials up-country, some of which were afterwards very useful to me. As the moment for saying good-bye arrived Lulu got very restless, and Thomas, who was as usual present, watched her closely. At last I took my leave of the General and the ladies, and as I did so Lulu whispered, 'I will meet you in the veranda' and left the room. Thomas had already disappeared. In the carriage porch Lulu was waiting. She said, 'I could not bid you farewell before them all.' Taking both my hands in hers, she wrung them and sobbed out, 'Has it come to this—must we really part?' I was much moved at this, and I know not what I should have said or done, when suddenly Thomas emerged from the shadow of a pillar, uttered the word 'Harris' and vanished into the darkness again! Lulu flashed a glance of anger at him, wrung my hands once more and dashed away. I never saw her again. Many years afterwards a man who knew her well told my wife and me that she was a notorious flirt, and that it was obvious to all Calcutta society that she was trying hard to catch me—a rising young Civilian being preferable to a Captain

[1] Literally 'stage-carriage'.

90

in the Haidarabad contingent. People were, he said, very much amused at my evident unconsciousness of all Lulu's wiles. Poor Lulu! She was very beautiful, very clever and very accomplished. I cannot bear to think she was a hypocrite. I was never in the least in love with her; I liked her very much as a companion, and I used to write frankly to Ellen about her, and talk about Ellen to her. I suppose I was a very green, conceited young prig in those days. I heard afterwards that she married Captain Baker, had two children and died after a very brief married life.

The next morning 12 February 1859 I left Calcutta by train for Raniganj. I had spent eleven months there, an idle, happy time; not doing much good, nor much evil, beyond, as I discovered afterwards, over-drawing my account with my bankers by some Rs 5,000 (£500) and thus forming the nucleus of a debt which clung to me and harassed me throughout my career. As to the languages, which were the pretext for keeping us in Calcutta, I can honestly say that I knew very little more about them at the end of the eleven months than I did at the beginning.

CHAPTER VII

PANJAB–GUJRAT, 1859

THE train started from Howrah terminus about nine o'clock in the morning and crawled slowly along all day reaching Raniganj—120 miles —at six in the evening; a speed of about fourteen miles an hour. It now (1896) does the distance in about half the time, and an ordinary English express would do it in two hours. Raniganj seemed to be a rambling, chaotic place, a mere jumble of rusty rails and dusty trucks. Here the railway left off, and after a dinner of sundry tough and tasteless dishes at a nightmare of half-finished and half-furnished rooms, sarcastically called the Hotel, I found my dâk gâri waiting for me. This vehicle, which I now beheld for the first time, was an oblong four-wheeled carriage—like a box upon wheels—with a sliding panel door on each side, windows and canvas shades all round it and a board behind for the syce.[1] It had once been painted green, but that was long ago. When I saw it, it had a general air of dust, rust, and various kinds of dirt and looked as if it might tumble to pieces at any moment. Inside there were two seats and the space between them, where in an ordinary carriage the legs of the passengers would go, was boarded over with a movable plank, forming a sort of well in which were stowed all my provisions. From the roof hung a network of cord, fastened at the four corners of the vehicle, and in this were oranges, soda-water, and wraps. In front under the driver's seat was a shelf which held books, a surahi[2] of water, drinking-cup, purse and various odds and ends. The flat surface obtained by boarding over the well was, together with the seats, covered with a mattress on which my bearer spread a rug, a 'razai'[3] and a pile of pillows. On the roof were my boxes amongst which the bearer dozed, curled up in a heap. I got in and lay down comfortably at full length, the bearer clambered to his airy perch, and the coachman to his, while a ragged, wiry, ungroomed pony was coaxed between the shafts by the united efforts of two or three ragged syces. Then they all shrieked and howled and one smote the pony under the belly, whereupon, with a snorting cry, a kick, and a plunge which nearly burst the old rotten

[1] 'Groom'.
[2] Long-necked jug of porous earthenware used for keeping drinking water in.
[3] A quilt of bright red calico stuffed with wool.

harness, he started off at a breakneck speed. This was rather alarming as the carriage swayed and rocked from side to side and came at times perilously near the edge of the road, which, being raised some height above the country on either side, affords facilities for an upset. The pony soon, however, subsided into a loping canter which he kept up till the end of the stage where a fresh pony was put in with the same cere- monies. Sometimes when a more obdurate animal than usual refused to start on being slapped on his belly, they fastened a leathern twitch round his upper lip and dragged him till he moved of his own accord. Some- times they even resorted to the extreme measure of bringing a lighted wisp of straw and putting it under the pony's belly. If even this failed, as it sometimes did, they took the pony out and put in another. Every ten miles was a change of ponies, and each stage took about an hour.

Thus I went on all night, sleeping soundly, and thus I travelled for many days and nights, reading, dozing, looking at the scenery, stopping from time to time at the numerous staging bungalows for breakfast or dinner. The Grand Trunk Road was then a magnificent, broad, level, well-metalled road with staging bungalows every fifteen miles where travellers could get meals and sleep if they wished to do so. At Topichanchi in the Sonthal Hills just below the grand towering peak of Parasnath I met my old acquaintance Lundgren, the Swedish artist, who was returning from the upper Provinces with several huge port- folios full of sketches. I stopped a couple of days at Benares and saw the beautiful sacred city, also at Allahabad, then a chaotic, half-built place; the new station of Cannington having only recently been founded by Lord Canning. The Government of the North-Western Provinces was just then in process of being transferred to Allahabad from Agra, and all was confusion. Part of the vast mass of offices and records had arrived, and part was still on its way.

Here there was a bit more railway by which I travelled as far as Cawnpore where it left off again. The fading daylight lasted long enough to enable me to take a hurried glance at the ghastly place; a desolate, sandy waste it then was. The dreadful well was marked by a few boards, the walls of the roofless houses were riddled with shot and tottering; ruins, dust, flies, evil odours and general misery and distress were all one could see. A rough sort of hotel had been formed out of the ruins of an old mess-house where they gave us a very atrocious dinner, after which I got into my dâk gâri and fell asleep, glad to get away from the horrible place. I spent a pleasant day at Agra seeing the Tàj and Akbar's tomb at Sikandra, and went on to Bulandshahr, a pleasant leafy station, the headquarters of the district where Elliot had been appointed Assistant Magistrate and Collector. He was in camp some miles off and I had to go a long distance in a palki, and found him at last in tents with Charles Currie the Collector. I had a very pleasant time for five days with them, riding about the district, and learning a great deal about the work, and then travelled on again through Delhi and Ambala to Lahore, where I reported myself and was admitted to an interview with Sir Robert Montgomery, the Lieutenant-Governor. I also then saw for the first time Mr Richard Temple. Sir John Lawrence had just left for England. I was appointed to be Assistant Commissioner of the district of Gujrat, and ordered to go there at once.

The problem now was—where was Gujrat, and how could one get to it? By dint of much inquiry, I found that it was some seventy miles off on the way to Peshawar. No dâk gâries could run on that road as it was a mere unformed mass of mud and sand. So after engaging a khansaman or butler, and leaving my heavy luggage with him to bring after me, I went to the Post Office one evening at 6 p.m. and secured a seat on the mail cart. This turned out to be a small box painted red, on two wheels. The top of the box was divided into two seats, front and back, by an iron rod, so contrived that at every jolt it caught the passenger sharply in the small of the back, inflicting acute pain. One small pony was harnessed between the shafts, and a second outside the near shaft, after the manner of a Russian droshky. I was allowed to carry a small valise weighing ten pounds. The driver wore a postin or sheepskin jacket with the wool inwards, and kept on perpetually blowing a bugle to warn the wayfarers. He drove like Jehu the son of Nimshi: he never slackened speed, and very nearly drove over everyone and everything he met. Thus we went on all night long, on and on, jolting and bumping over the rough, half-finished road. The night was bitterly cold, and I, clad to suit the warm climate of Calcutta, was almost frozen through. Towards three in the morning we crossed the broad sandy bed of the Chenab and after seven more miles of the agonizing bumping and the piercing cold we suddenly stopped in the mist at a little lonely post-house on a broad plain. A sleepy policeman with a lantern came out and took the mail bags, and the coachman threw down my valise and bowing asked me for a tip. As I looked surprised he explained that this was Gujrat! I gave him his fee, got down, and stood stupidly staring while the driver gave a terrific blast on his bugle, lashed his horses, and vanished into the darkness, leaving me half-frozen, bewildered and aching in every limb by the roadside at Gujrat at four in the morning of the 7th March 1859. It had taken me twenty-four days from Calcutta, about sixteen of which were spent in actual travelling. Nowadays the journey takes three days only. The distance by road is about 1,250 miles or perhaps a little more.

It was now necessary, as the first thing, to find a roof to shelter myself under and as in an Indian station the dâk bungalow is the stranger's natural home, I turned to the sleepy policeman and asked where it was. He pointed vaguely into the darkness, said something in Panjabi which I did not understand and turned to retreat into his tower. This evidently would not do, and it then occurred to me that I was one of the officials of this district and entitled to some attention. The position was new to me, but I had noted the respect paid to Elliot at Bulandshahr and knew that I was entitled to the same here. So I announced myself in Hindu-stani as the new Assistant Sahib, and sternly demanded that someone should go with me to show me the way. This at once produced the effect desired. The sleepy policeman suddenly became wide awake and rushing inside woke up his chief, the jemadar[1] or sergeant, who came out buckling on his sword and with many bows and courteous words provided me with another policeman to show me the way. The night was so dark and the fog so thick that nothing could be seen, but we seemed to be standing on the edge of a broad, flat plain with no houses or trees near us; no signs in fact of any inhabited place. But my police-man putting my valise on his head stepped out across the plain, re-questing 'my Honour to do itself the grace to follow its slave.' He explained that we were on the encamping grounds for troops, which accounted for the bareness. After crossing this plain we got into a net-work of what seemed to be grassy lanes bordered by young trees; we passed several buildings looming dark and lofty till my guide stopped and announced that he had lost the way! I was about to administer corporal punishment with my umbrella. It would not have been a wise or proper thing to do, but I was young and hot-tempered, and after all the sufferings of the night this last contretemps was really too exasperat-ing. To be within a few yards of rest and shelter and not to be able to find it! Suddenly, a sepulchral voice from somewhere near my toes uttered the words 'Kyâ huâ' (what is the matter?). I jumped and looking down saw a lump of rags at the foot of a tree. My guide explained that the lump of rags was a very holy ascetic who lived under that tree, and proceeded to ask the holy man which was the way. He told us in a few words and relapsed into a lump of rags again. After going a short distance we came suddenly on a wall with a door or two in it. Here we

[1] In this case a sort of Head Equerry—but jemadar means all sorts of things. The general notion of the word is a Head man of sorts—head of a gang—ser-geant.

knocked and shouted for some time, till at length a greasy, half-dressed Musulman with a smoky native lamp opened the door. I saw a room within and a bed in it on which I incontinently flung myself dressed as I was, and fell asleep immediately.

When I awoke it was broad daylight and I was lying just where I had thrown myself a few hours before. By degrees I arrived at the consciousness that I was greasy, dust-begrimed, aching all over, with a parched mouth and a swimming head. So I fell to shouting 'qui hy'[1] till the greasy Musulman appeared and was induced to bring me a cup of tea. This done he prevailed upon one greasier even than himself to bring several earthen jars of cold water into the bathroom. I stripped, bathed and scrubbed and deluged myself with water till the aching left my limbs; then I put on clean clothes and felt myself a new man. The physical weariness was driven away by my anxiety to see my new home and begin my new work. I looked out and found myself in a tumbledown building of red-brick—not plastered as houses in India mostly are—the British administration in the Panjab was then still so newly established that there had been no time for refinements and luxuries such as plaster. Buildings were hastily run up to serve the emergencies of the moment, and if they tumbled down again as hastily, it did not matter—they were professedly only temporary. In front of me was a dusty unmetalled road bordered with young sissoo[2] trees just budding into leaf. Beyond I could see here and there the tops of brown brick houses half-hidden by scanty trees, broad fields, and above them the glorious snowy summits of the Kashmir Himalayas. The air was sharp and fresh, and felt light and invigorating—a good atmosphere for activity of mind and body.

On the other side of the bungalow was a well-kept aloe hedge and beyond it a sparkling garden, gay with flowers, in the middle of which rose a curious-looking house, half-native and half-European in style. This I was told was the Báradari or 'House of 12 doors', once a native palace, now the Deputy Commissioner's residence. It being by this time past nine I judged it advisable to go and report my arrival to this officer under whom I was to serve. Crossing a small grass plot I entered

[1] The cry by which we summon our servants in Bengal, there being no bells in the houses. It is a corruption of the Hindustani words 'Koi hai'—Is anyone (there)?

[2] Sissu pronounced in Panjabi 'shisham', the Dalbergia Sissoo, a large forest-tree with beautiful bright foliage. The wood is hard, of a dark, purplish-brown, and is much used for making furniture. Quantities of these trees were planted along roads in the earlier years of British rule in the Panjab. The country was very bare when we took it.

by a huge but unfinished gateway of brick, Saracenic in style, with two lofty towers, in the lower storey of which lounged the native guard of Afghan troopers. From this a broad walk shaded by trees led up to the house. A sentry with musket paced up and down in front, and four or five chaprassees armed with sword and shield stood or sat about on the steps. I handed my card to one of these, and was admitted into a large, bare room with whitewashed walls, lighted by small windows high up near the roof. The floor was bare save in one corner where there was a shabby carpet and on it a small table heaped high with papers. Presently a thick curtain at the other end of the room was lifted and the Deputy Commissioner came in. Major Robert Roy Adams of the Guides, one of the numerous military officers in Civil employ, was a man about my own height, five feet nine, thick-set and strong but light and active in his movements. A very handsome man about thirty, a bright eye, a look of command, and a long, thick moustache and beard. He shook hands cordially and said, 'Where have you come from and what powers have you got?' I did not understand what he meant by 'powers', so I simply said that I had just arrived from Calcutta and that this was my first district. He looked disappointed, and an angry scowl passed over his face, but quickly vanished as he said, 'It's a great shame —but of course it isn't your fault—have you had any breakfast?' I replied 'No,' then he said, 'Come in and have some, we are just sitting down.' Then he led me into the next room, a small but lofty square room lighted by windows high up, and beneath them three lovely Saracenic open-arched doorways on each side, making twelve in all, from which this class of building, common in India, takes its name of Bāradari. What little wall-space there was between and above the arches was gaily painted with flowers and figures of dancing girls in the native style. Through this we passed into an English drawing-room with numerous wide open french windows looking on to a deep-thatched veranda. Here I was introduced to Mrs Adams, the most lovely woman I have ever seen, and as kind and charming as she was lovely. She had been a Miss Bellew and had that inexpressibly fascinating beauty of face and manner which so many Irishwomen possess. We sat down to a good and substantial breakfast in the room with the twelve doors, and after kind Mrs Adams had condoled with me, not without some laughter, over my adventures of the past night, I asked my host why he had said it was a shame to send me there. He explained that he himself had been hitherto only an Assistant, and as this was the first district of which he had charge he had particularly asked for an experienced Assistant to help him, and lo! the Government had sent him a youth fresh from

college. To exonerate the Government, partly at least, I told him what
I have omitted to mention further back, that it had been their intention
to station me at Delhi and orders had been sent to the Commissioner of
that place to stop me there on my way up. But he had failed to do so
owing to my not stopping at the dâk bungalow where he had sent a
letter for me. When I turned up at Lahore the Secretary to the Government was much surprised to see me there and half disposed to send me
back but, finding that Gujrat was vacant, sent me there instead. I
apologized to Adams for my inopportune presence there and could only
hope I should soon learn enough of my duties to be useful to him.
'Powers' is a technical term, the meaning of which will appear later on.
Then he asked me to come and stay at his house and sent a man to
fetch my luggage from the dâk bungalow. Breakfast over, Adams,
ignoring in true Panjab style the possibility of anyone being tired, or
wishing to do anything but work, said, 'Now let us go to cutchery.'
Whereupon a chaprassee brought him his pistol in a belt which he
girded on, and bade me get mine, load it and put in on. He advised me
to wear it always except in my own house, and this caution was not
unnecessary for it was not unusual in those days for European officers
to be fired at by Musulman fanatics. Poor Adams himself met his death
in that way a few years later. Duly armed we walked down the avenue
followed by a crowd of chaprassees and policemen to the cutchery
close by. It was a large, long, and not very hideous building in the
middle of a plain dotted here and there with clumps of young trees in
whose somewhat scanty shade sat groups of suitors waiting for the courts
to open.

Adams led me first to his own court, a large-roughly-furnished room
full of native clerks sitting on carpets on the floor, who all rose and
saluted, bowing almost to the ground as we entered. Here I was sworn in
with the oaths which it was still the custom to adminster in those days,
and signed a certificate to the effect that I had that day in the forenoon
assumed charge of my office. Then he took me into another room
similar to, but smaller than, his own, pointed to a small group of clerks
who were all bowing elaborately and said in his sharp, jerky way, 'This is
your court, and these are your amlà,[1] now go to work,' and before I
could open my mouth to ask him a single question he had turned and
abruptly left the room! This was throwing one into one's work with a
vengeance! Here was I, as ignorant of the whole business as a child,
with a hundred questions to ask, and no one to ask them from. I had
heard from Elliot and from other men that it was customary to allow a

[1] Clerks.

man on joining his first district to sit on the bench beside one of the older Magistrates for a few days so that he might gradually pick up some ideas of how to do the work, and I had expected something of the kind myself. But Adams had told me as we walked along that the work was so heavy he could hardly get through it, so I suppose he had no time for teaching beginners. My stock of available knowledge consisted of Persian and Hindustani, the latter language I already spoke fluently and tolerably correctly. Of law and procedure I, of course, knew nothing.

However, no time was to be lost; the people were already staring at me rather wonderingly as I hesitated for a minute, so I took my seat at a plain and rather dirty table separated from the rest of the room by a plainer and dirtier railing. The amlà took their seats, some on a form beside the table, others on carpets on the floor, and the head man of them a young, slight Musulman named Mushtak Ali, who I afterwards learnt was my sarishta-dar, rose and pointing to a pile of papers covered with writing in the Persian character, said in beautiful Delhi Hindustani with many courteous periphrases, 'These are the cases on your Honour's file for trial—what is your order?' I said as by instinct, 'Call up the first case,' though what I was to do with it I knew as little as the man in the moon. Mushtak Ali smiled and looked round at his fellows as who should say, 'Guessed right the first time'. Then he mentioned some names to a six-foot-high Sikh with a turban as big as a bandbox, armed with sword and shield, who went out into the veranda and bawled loudly for some minutes. Then entered a dirty, greasy shopkeeper, the plaintiff, who was sworn by the tall Sikh, and had a wooden tablet given him with the words of the oath written on which he held tight all the while he was making his statement. I was furnished with a printed form and requested to fill in what the greasy man said in a certain column, other columns being intended for the statements of the defendant and witnesses. The defendant was next sworn and deposed. He was a big, powerful zemindar, i.e. peasant with a long black beard. Both these people spoke Panjabi, of which I could not understand one word, but the sarishtadar translated it into Hindustani as they spoke, so I got on wonderfully well. By four o'clock I had disposed of all my cases and went back to Adams's house where I spent the evening pleasantly with him and his wife, picking up a great deal of information about the place, the people and the work. I went to bed intensely tired but very much interested in, and pleased with, my day's experience.

Next morning I rose early, refreshed by a sound night's rest, and went forth to view the place. On the other side of the cutcherry was the jail, a large, ugly building of the universal dull-brown brick, and close to it was a small one-storeyed house of four rooms in a pretty garden surrounded by tall poplar trees. It was to let for Rs 40 a month, and as it was the bungalow always occupied by the Assistant, I took it. There was, in fact, no other to take, except a much larger house which was shortly after taken as a dâk bungalow instead of the ruin where I had passed my first night.

An officer in the neighbouring station of Jhelam was about to leave and, as is the custom, circulated a list of his furniture for sale, from which I bought such things as I wanted, and my servants arriving with my heavy luggage I was able, after about four days' stay in Adams's hospitable house, to set up house on my own account. I also bought a pretty white mare of the excellent native breed of the district, half-Arab. She had never been ridden before. I paid Rs 120 for her and had to break her myself.

Gujrat was one of the smallest districts in the Panjab having an area of about 1,200 square miles. It occupies the country between the rivers Chenab and Jhelam, the Kashmir territory, and the desert of the Southern Panjab. The town is situated on a high mound crowned by the old fort, from the top of which there is a splendid view. In the European station there were only five houses and a few public buildings. The society was correspondingly small, consisting of Major Adams, the Deputy Commissioner and his wife and child, Major Terence O'Brien, a jolly little fat, round Irishman with a strong Cork brogue (he called his native place 'Cyârk') and his wife, a sickly half-caste and child, and my humble self. There were also two half-caste clerks and their families. For doctor we had a Bengali who spoke English well.

I had four chaprassees and a sowâr to attend on me. The former, so-called from wearing a large brass badge (in Hindustani 'chaprâs') were very warlike-looking Sikhs with long beards, huge turbans, swords and shields. Their duties were to hang about in attendance two and two by turns all day, to carry letters and messages, and to make themselves generally useful. In court they had to keep order, call in the witnesses, and carry papers to and fro. The sowâr or trooper was an Afghan, a big-booted, truculent-looking scoundrel from the regiment, a troop of which was stationed at Gujrat. His duty was to accompany me on my rides, and to go on messages where greater speed was required than the chaprassees could achieve.

I next began to learn Panjabi, for which purpose I engaged an old Sikh priest, Bhai Mihr Singh (Bhai = brother, is the title borne by all Sikh priests). Like most Panjabis of those days the good Bhai was a kindly, simple-hearted old child. He had not the most rudimentary idea of teaching but he used to come and sit with me of an evening and read Panjabi books to me, translating into Hindustani as he went and elaborately explaining all the difficult words. He also composed for me a poem called 'The luminous history of the Panjab' which he used to bring in instalments as he composed it, and chant it to me to the great satisfaction of himself and the chaprassees, who would crowd into the open doorways to listen to him. The Bhai wore an immense triple turban, red next his head, over that green, and outside of all, white. He had large gold ear-rings, brass-bound spectacles, a tight white coat, and extremely tight white trousers, with a large, loose muslin scarf floating about his shoulders and a voluminous waistband of the same rolled several times round his middle. His beard hung down below his waist. It was by nature grey, but he dyed it black with henna and indigo, about once a month or so. For the first few days after the operation it was a lustrous, glossy black. Then by degrees it got rusty and the grey began to show near the roots of the hair. It went on getting greyer and greyer till the time for dyeing it came round, when it suddenly shone out lustrous and glossy again. By dint of constantly talking to this good old man and using the words I picked up from him I succeeded in learning to speak Panjabi pretty fluently. It was necessary for use with the peasantry and lower classes in towns only. All the upper classes and educated people spoke Hindustani. By degrees all the Sirdars or chiefs— the native nobility and gentry—of the district came to call on me and finding I liked their society, used to drop in of an evening and sit talking for hours. With their swords across their knees they would tell me long stories of their adventures in war and foray under Ranjit Singh, their beloved old Maharaja. Barring their love of brandy, which was excessive, these old lions with their long beards were very good company and I learnt a great deal about the people, their ideas and feelings from them. They are a fine, manly race and in those days at least were very friendly to their European conquerors. The majority of the population could still remember the tyranny and oppression of native rule and contrasted it with the justice and security of our rule.

My work consisted chiefly of trying petty cases of assault, theft and the like; and equally petty civil suits in which the village moneylenders sued peasants for small debts. I had also to visit the jail twice a week and see that everything was in order. There was no law in the Panjab in those days. Our instructions were to decide all cases by the light of common sense and our own sense of what was just and right. From time to time a high official, called the Judicial Commissioner, issued printed circulars with directions as to the procedure to be adopted in doubtful or difficult matters and another equally high official, the Financial Commissioner, issued circulars respecting the collection of revenue and taxes. But on the whole our procedure was simple and expeditious. The weak point was that almost every case was appealable, and as the people availed themselves very largely of the power of appeal, the higher courts were often flooded with futile and frivolous appeals. That they were frivolous and futile is shown by the fact that from eighty to ninety per cent of them were dismissed by the Appellate court. It was partly the frequency of appeals and partly the suitability of physical punishment for a simple race that led to the frequent use of the cane. Many offences were punished by a flogging, and the people themselves preferred this summary disposal to the tedium of imprisonment or the long indebtedness resulting from a fine.

My powers at first were limited. Until an officer has passed what is called the Departmental Examination in law and languages he is only invested by the Government with 'third-class powers'; that is, he can only give one month's imprisonment in some cases and generally very light punishments: consequently only petty cases can be given him to try. However, Adams made up for my want of powers by the immense number of petty cases he gave me to try, so my time was fully occupied. I was generally in office from ten to six every day.

At the end of April Adams was transferred to another district. It was a practice, and certainly a very annoying and injudicious practice in the Panjab in those days, to keep moving officers about from one district to another. This was originated by John Lawrence, the first ruler of the Panjab. The signal services rendered by this great man have caused him to be regarded as a sort of popular hero, and it will seem almost blasphemy to say a word against him. But it is undeniably true that by those who served under him, he was intensely disliked. And this was not unnatural. He was a rough, coarse man; in appearance more like a 'navvy' than a gentleman. His ideal of a district officer was a hard, active man in boots and breeches, who almost lived in the saddle, worked all day and nearly all night, ate and drank when and where he could, had no family ties, no wife or children to hamper him, and whose whole establishment consisted of a camp bed, an odd table and chair or so and a small box of clothes such as could be slung on a camel. Such a man must be ready to go anywhere at a moment's notice. Personal government was the only form of rule which the rude and simple Panjabis could understand, therefore the ideal Magistrate must show himself to all his people continually, must decide cases either sitting on horseback in the village gateway, or under a tree outside the village walls, write his decision on his knee, while munching a native chapatty or a fowl cooked in a hole in the ground; and then mount his horse and be off to repeat the process in the next village. Heat, sun, rain, climatic changes of all sorts were to be matters of indifference to him. But, of course, he could not always induce his subordinates to lend themselves to this wild, unresting life. Especially the Civilians, who had been accustomed to the more civilized conditions of the older and more settled provinces, objected strongly to being turned into homeless, vagrant governing-machines. To wean them apparently from their weak, effeminate liking for clean shirts, a decent house, and a settled life, he adopted the practice of keeping them constantly on the move. Thereby he effectually prevented any one from being 'comfortable'—a word he had a horror of—and at the same time, as many men pointed out, also effectually prevented them from acquiring that local know-ledge of their districts, and that influence over their people which had proved such inestimably valuable factors of good government in the older provinces, and to the possession of which he himself owed his promotion and success. He had left before I came to the Panjab, but much of his system was still in force, though his successor, Sir Robert Montgomery, was a much milder, more refined and civilized man, and gradually mitigated the extreme rigour of the system. Still, much remained; Elmslie, one of my Haileybury comrades, imprudently brought a piano to the Panjab with him. Such refinement was un-pardonable, and poor Elmslie was moved five times from one end of the Panjab to the other in the course of two years. 'I'll smash his piano for him,' John Lawrence was reported to have said, when he first heard of such a degradation as a Panjab officer having a piano. I had brought from Calcutta a handsome dinner-service, and I was strongly advised not to let the fact be known lest I, too, should be kicked about from one place to another till it was all smashed. So Adams was sent away after three months' stay at Gujrat, and Bradford Hardinge came in his place. Hardinge was a man of my own service and only a few years senior to me. We took to each other from the first and became very great friends. Before long it became a regular custom for me to dine at his house every night. We built a big swimming-bath and every even-ing after cutcherry we and O'Brien had a bathe, with feats of diving, fighting on masaks, and lots of fun. Then we adjourned to Hardinge's house—the Bāradari—and dined. He had an old tin-kettle piano, which he bought, as he told us, directly he heard that John Lawrence was gone—he had not dared to do so before. He used to play and sing to us all the evening, in the intervals of talking about our work—talking 'shop' was universal in those days. He kept six horses, and I, by this time, had two (horses were very cheap), so we were in the saddle by five in the morning and worked on horseback for two or three hours, riding about inspecting police-stations, roads and bridges and public buildings under construction, tree-planting, ferry-boats, settling disputes about land and property between villagers, and such-like business. Or we would walk with our horses led behind us through the narrow lanes of the ancient town, accompanied by a crowd of police officers, overseers and others giving orders for sanitary improvements, repairing roadways and drains, opening out new streets, deciding disputes and a variety of similar matters. Of an evening we would often ride seven miles to the Chenab, have a swim in the river, and then repair to the flat roof of the Serai where our servants had brought our dinner. After dining, we would sit in our loose calico pyjamas and coats, looking down on the motley throng of travellers with their carts, mules and camels, in the courtyard below. After sleeping on charpoys on the roof in the open air we returned to Gujrat the next morning. Hard work as usual filled up the day from ten to six with unvarying regularity. This kind of happy, busy existence lasted all through the hot weather, broken only by one or two incidents.

Sometimes we rode over to the neighbouring stations of Jhelam, Sialkot or Gujranwala and spent Sunday with the men there. Or some of them would ride over to see us. We all lent our horses to each other. It was an established theory that no horse could go more than ten miles, so there had to be a fresh horse at every tenth mile. If you were going fifty miles, you had to provide five horses, and eked out your own number by borrowing from friends. The horses we used to ride were country-bred. The Government kept several magnificent Arab stallions at various stations and the breed between them and country mares yielded a very useful animal. We also rode Cabuli horses, but they were rather heavy and given to stumbling. A few rich men indulged in Arabs or Walers.

I had been a regular attendant at Lodge while in Calcutta, and it became known in the Panjab that I was a Mason, so I received an invitation to attend a great Masonic function in Lahore and, for a wonder, got leave to go. It was not easy in those hard-working days to get leave even for a day. One of my horses broke down on the road and I had to finish my journey in a dooli, whereby I was kept out in the sun all a burning June day without any food. I made the bearers stop at every well they came to and pour pots of water on the dooli and over my head and neck, and thus escaped a sunstroke, but when I arrived a little before sunset at the ancient tomb of the Emperor Jahangir at Shahdara on the Ravi, opposite Lahore, I was in an almost insensible condition. Knowles, an Assistant Engineer, who lived in a vaulted chamber in the tomb lifted me up the narrow stairs, helped me to strip and, summoning two water carriers, made them pour the contents of their masaks over me. Then I had some food and a stiff tumbler of brandy and water, after which I fell asleep and woke up the next morning none the worse for the exposure. Sandeman, the Accountant General, who was a very high Masonic dignitary, received us all hospitably and there was a grand function. I stayed with the 79th Highlanders, a very nice set of fellows, and after two days pleasantly spent at Lahore, Knowles and I rode back to Gujrat with some officers of the regiment who were going for a tour in Kashmir. We had managed relays of horses all along the road, and rode back a very joyous company, in two days, sleeping at bungalows on the road. On my return to Gujrat I had a sharp attack of fever which laid me up for nearly a month.

In July I got a letter from Mr Ball reminding me that the period of two years, which was to expire, according to my agreement with my father before I married Ellen, was drawing to a close, and as it would take some time to make the necessary arrangements he thought it was high time I should begin to think about it. Ellen had had a bad attack of measles in the spring of 1859 and I had been duly informed of it, but had not realized that it was serious, and being in a state of great excitement over my journey up-country and settling in my new district, had not shown as much sympathy for her in my letters as I ought. She told me afterwards that my letters at this time were short and cold, and she had persuaded herself that I was getting tired of our engagement. This letter from Mr Ball was a sort of feeler, to see what my intentions were. I immediately wrote to Ellen a very, very long letter—a dozen sheets or more—in which I gave her the fullest information about the voyage, and all the arrangements I had made for her reception. It was, as was natural, a lover's letter; and lovers' letters are not meant to be seen by the public, so although that memorable letter is still in my wife's possession, I will say no more about it. It ran a risk, however, of never being posted. It happened on this wise. I had been looking round for a married lady to chaperone Ellen out to India, and had found that the wife of Brigadier-General McCausland, commanding at Sialkot, would be coming out at the same time. The Brigadier, a kindly old man, invited me over to Sialkot to discuss the subject. In those days it took six weeks for a letter to go from India to England and there was a mail only once a fortnight, so it was necessary to make one's arrangements a long time beforehand. As soon as I was well enough to ride, viz. on the 18th July, I sent out my horses and wrote to the brigadier that I would be with him by dinner-time that evening. I put my precious letter in my pocket intending to post it as I passed the Post Office. But I found that the wretched postmaster had no postage-stamps, so I rode on intending to post the letter at Sialkot. It was securely deposited in a leather courier's bag which I wore slung over my shoulder by a strap. When I got within ten miles of Sialkot I was told by a policeman who passed me that the River Chenab had risen in flood and the waters were out all over the country. He said, however, that I could not lose my way as the road was well raised and ran between two continuous lines of trees. He forgot to mention that a small stream—probably an arm of the big river—crossed the road. The sun was setting but the road seemed plain enough and I rode on, my horse splashing through the water which was only a few inches deep. Suddenly, without any warning, he went down into deep water almost over his head. I slipped off and holding by his mane with one hand struck out with the other. We were carried down some distance but at last gained the opposite bank and with difficulty managed to scramble up. Some villagers, attracted by my shouts, ran up and showed me the way into Sialkot which I reached at eleven o'clock at night, wet through. On undressing I found my letter also wet through, and had to spend some time spreading it out to dry on a mantelpiece. It was dry the next morning, and I posted it with a brief postscript explaining how it came to be in such a state.

In August Hardinge fell ill and had to go away for a month. I was put in to act for him. This was an amazing piece of promotion for one so new to the work, but dear old Hardinge in his generous way had praised my work and had said I was quite fit to have charge of a district. During my brief incumbency of one month the following incident occurred. One of the constantly recurring petty outbreaks among the wild Afghan tribes on the frontier caused the Government to send the 7th Dragoon Guards to Peshawar in a great hurry. The big Panjab rivers were usually crossed by bridges of boats, which, however, had to be removed during the rains, when only ferry boats could be used owing to the strength of the current and the liability to floods. The rains were just over and I was ordered to see that the bridge of boats over the Chenab was put up at once so that the Regiment might not be delayed. Generally this took some time as boats had to be hunted for and hired. I had, however, only three days in which to collect, anchor, and put in position seventy-five boats, and fasten down the planked roadway over them. The Darogha, or officer in charge, had collected sixty-two boats and had all the planking ready, but he reported that he could not get any more at short notice. Taking a slice or two of bread, a few eggs and a brandy-flask, I got into a small rowing-boat with half a dozen police-men and rowed up the river all day long. Wherever we found a boat we seized it and sent it down to the bridge in charge of a policeman. By about ten o'clock that night I had collected and sent down a number of boats and then rode home to snatch a little sleep. Next day I was on the spot again by daybreak and went down the river. By five o'clock I had collected seventy-four boats. One only was wanting. A large boat laden with corn was lying at Vazirabad, a few yards from the bridge, and the owners were imploring me with tears not to take it as they said the loss to them would be serious. While I hesitated there was a sound of horses galloping and up dashed Mr Richard Temple, Commissioner of Lahore. He had half a dozen mounted orderlies behind him. He wore a helmet with gorgeous scarlet and gold turban; his huge and hideous moustaches stuck out in stiff points, in imitation of the Emperor Napoleon III whom he fancied he resembled. He was, in fact, an ugly likeness of Punch's caricatures of that sovereign. He examined what I had done, approved, and then to my surprise told me to go back to my station and he would do the rest. After I was gone he seized the grain-boat, put it in its place, got the bridge ready, and was found standing in a picturesque attitude giving the last touches to the work as the Colonel, followed by his Regiment, arrived on the bank. He was asked to dine at the Mess that night, where they drank his health, and the Colonel reported the important service he had rendered by bridging this large and difficult river. He received the thanks of the Lieutenant-Governor. My name was not even mentioned. He thus, a man already well known and secure of his advancement, stooped to filch even this small amount of credit from a young officer who had his name yet to make, to whom the praise would have been valuable.

Hardinge returned soon after this; and in October I received a letter from Ellen Geary telling me she was about to start at once. I inter-preted the two years which my father had imposed upon me in the strictest and most literal way. I had left Haileybury on the 7th December 1857, and I had so arranged that Ellen would reach India in time for our wedding to take place on, or as near as possible to, the 7th December 1859. Mrs McCausland having changed her plans, another lady was found for chaperone, Mrs Becher, wife of Colonel Septimus Becher. Now Hardinge, who flattered himself that he was quite a lady's man and one who knew what ladies required, undertook to fit up my simple bachelor bungalow in the proper style. I bought a buggy in Calcutta and took to training my white mare to carry a lady. Hardinge improvised curtains, looking-glasses, a sofa and various other decorations, and specially prided himself on constructing a dressing table with a red valance round it, covered with white muslin which we all agreed was most successful and correct. I applied for a month's leave to go to Delhi where I was to meet Ellen. Delhi was one of the few places where a clergyman could be found in those days. But when I got there, the clergyman was a hundred and fifty miles off visiting an outstation! I thought at once of Elliot and travelled across the thirty miles further to Bulandshahr where he welcomed me and introduced me to the Joint Magistrate, a man named Colledge. Mrs Colledge entered into the subject with all a woman's interest in such things and insisted on the marriage taking place at their house. Next day Elliot and I went off to Meerut where we were the guests of the Bengal Artillery whose head-quarters it was. Elliot had a cousin in the Regiment. We secured a padre, the Revd J. W. Rotton, also two bridesmaids, and by favour of the Mess Sergeant of the R.A., a magnificent wedding-cake. I also got a suit of clothes at a Meerut tailor's, and at another shop bought some presents for the bridesmaids. The Artillery subalterns who took a warm interest in the proceedings insisted also on my buying two 'goes' (as they put it) of orange flowers without which they affirmed no marriage could take place. After a jolly time at the R.A. Mess we returned to Bulandshahr.

CHAPTER VIII

MARRIAGE, 1860

A LETTER from Ellen, written in Calcutta, had reached me at Delhi. She had been taken care of by good Mrs Howe. Her brother, Henry Geary, had taken leave and joined her at Calcutta, and she was about to start for Delhi in company of him and Captain Keyworth of the 51st. Mrs Keyworth, a charming, lively little Irishwoman, was to chaperone her. They might be expected at Delhi by about the 2nd or 3rd of December. My plans having been now changed, mounted policemen were stationed at Khurja, the point on the Grand Trunk Road where the road to Bulandshahr branches off, with letters from me telling them to come on to that place. This was on the 24th or 25th of November, so we had a week to wait. Now, however, occurred a hitch. Lord Canning with all his staff and an immense escort of troops—I forget how many regiments—was making a semi-royal progress through India, holding durbars, receiving assurances of loyalty from all classes, rewarding those who had done good service, and satisfying himself that the last embers of the mutiny were extinguished. All the district officers were busily engaged in collecting supplies for feeding this great army, enlarging and laying out encamping grounds for them and seeing that everything was in proper order. The process of disarming the native population was also being vigorously carried out. Elliot could not be spared for a week to do nothing in the station, but had to go into camp, and as I was his guest and he had to take all his scanty establishment with him, I was perforce compelled to go too. Colledge, however, promised to send out a mounted policeman to call me in as soon as Ellen and her party should arrive. So we went and pitched our camp at Nabinagar, twenty miles from Bulandshahr, where his work chiefly lay. The people, knowing that their arms were to be taken from them, had hidden them beneath the floors of their houses or buried them in their fields, and pretended that they had none. But as this was known to be false, force was resorted to and many a stalwart old Rajpoot was stripped and publicly flogged before he would give up his old sword or match-lock. The measure was a stupid political mistake, brutally carried out, and Elliot, like most of the officers employed in this duty, was disgusted at having to do it. After some days of this sort of life we were sitting one

night about nine in the tent after dinner when a sowàr arrived with
a note from Ellen—a little pencil scrap—saying that she had arrived
and asking me to come over. The note was worded as if she thought I
was living just across the road, and this was, as I afterwards found, what
she really had thought. In her ignorance of India it had never occurred
to her that when Mrs Colledge had said I was not far off, she had meant
only the trifling distance of twenty miles. It seems the party had arrived
at 6 p.m. Ellen and Mrs Keyworth were shown into a bedroom, Harry
and Keyworth into tents. When they asked where I was, Ellen was told
to write a note to me which would be sent at once. They were much
surprised when dinner was announced and I did not appear, and it was
not till then that they learnt how far off I was. Then arose a discussion,
some maintaining that I could not get in that night, while others
asserted that if I had any go in me I should certainly get in. Meanwhile,
the sowàr, not being in love, did not hurry himself but took three hours
to do the distance. As soon as I got the letter I took Elliot's fastest
horse—luckily he had not been ridden far that day—and started. It was
a bright moonlight night and I did not spare the horse, but dashed
rapidly along fearing they would all have gone to bed before I arrived.
And so they had; as I galloped up the avenue to the house all was dark
and silent. It was just eleven and I had done twenty miles in an hour
and a half. I shouted loudly for the syce, and made as much noise as I
could to let them know that I had arrived; on which out came Colledge
in his pyjamas and dressing-gown and begged me to be quiet. He said
(which was not true) that they had not expected me and, being very
tired, had gone to bed. He then took me into a spare room and sat by me
till I was undressed, so as to make sure I should not try to obtain an
interview that night. However, no sooner was his back turned than I
rapidly dressed again, let myself out and wandered round to the side of
the house where I knew Ellen's room was, where I rattled at the
shutters and called her by her name. As no answer came I concluded
she was asleep and retired to bed. In fact, she and Mrs Keyworth had
quite made up their minds that I should return that night, and though
much to their disgust Mrs Colledge made them go to bed, they sat up
till midnight waiting for me and at last went to sleep disappointed and
with a very low opinion of me as a lover. How it was they did not hear
me rattling at the shutters of their room and calling her, I do not
know; nor why on earth Colledge did not allow me to wake them.
However, the romantic ride by moonlight, the ardent lover in his
picturesque dress-boots and breeches, huge blue and gold scarf round
waist, the panting steed, the warm embrace—were all *une affaire*

manquée. Our actual meeting next morning was very tame and prosaic. I met Henry Geary first, who disliked my spectacles—I did not wear them when in England—and thought they would make a bad impression on his sister, so he took them off. The consequence was that when I went into the room where Ellen was I could not see her distinctly, and the figure, seeming strange to me, I thought it was Mrs Keyworth, and merely bowed and said politely, 'good morning!' Then a well-known voice cried, 'Oh, John, is *that* all?' and I recognized my mistake and rushed to her and greeted her as I ought. But the sense of coldness remained for a time, and it was not till we had had a long talk together after breakfast and I had told her how far off I had been, and how I had ridden directly I got her letter, and how stupid old Colledge had prevented our meeting, that the cloud passed away. The incident only shows how much mischief stupid people can do in this world.

There was a large party staying in the house and we had a merry time for some days. At last we were married on the 10 December 1859 in the drawing-room of Colledge's house, there being no church in the station. Henry gave his sister away and Elliot was my best man. There was a sumptuous wedding-breakfast, after which we departed in the carriage of a native Raja under a shower of rice and old shoes to the dâk bungalow a mile off, where the usual dâk gâri awaited us. There we changed our festal clothes for plain ones, and my wife was persuaded, not without some difficulty, to take off her crinoline, a huge balloon-like petticoat with steel ribs which would have left very little room for me in the gâri. We went on to Ambala where we spent our short honeymoon of two days, and then started again for Gujrat. When we reached Vazirabad, at the point where the road crosses the Chenab, my handsome new buggy was waiting for us, and from thence to Gujrat we had a triumphal progress; all the principal natives of Gujrat came out to meet us on horseback and escorted us home. My wife was delighted at this reception, the light and colour, the strange, picturesque figures were new to her and the heartiness of this unexpected welcome touched her very much. She had so long felt herself a homeless wanderer that to come among people who regarded her as something more than a mere traveller made her feel at home again once more. And there was some pride mixed with wonder at finding him whom she knew as yet only as the insignificant boy who had left England two years ago, a person of importance and influence, looked up to and respected by all these crowds of people. At last we reached our own little house, looking bright and gay amongst its poplars and rose bushes. Then we dismissed our friends and were 'at home' at last. After dinner, when the curtains

were drawn and we sat together before a blazing fire of logs, we felt
very happy in thus beginning life together and I was much pleased to
see how cheerfully my dear wife took to all the new ways and new
people, and how much she admired my humble little house and all the
things around her, and seemed thoroughly satisfied with her surroundings. I could write much about the perfect happiness of my married
life and of my dear wife's many excellencies, but such things are too
sacred to be written about.

In the words of Tennyson:

> ". . . not easily forgiven
> Are those who setting wide the doors that bar
> The secret bridal chambers of the heart,
> Let in the day."

For some days after our return all the chief natives of the district
kept coming to see us. Our chaprassees placed two chairs in the centre
of the drawing-room and we were invited to take our seats while a
procession entered at one door and left by another. Each man as he
approached bowed, uttered a speech of congratulation and good wishes
and deposited some rupees at our feet. The number of rupees must,
according to native custom, be uneven. Some gave one, others eleven,
others even twenty-one. They refused to have this money returned to
them. It was, and perhaps still is, customary in the Panjab for every
native when visiting a superior to hold out a 'nazar' or offering. The
poorer bring one rupee on the palm of the hand, the richer two or three
gold coins on a folded handkerchief; soldiers tender the hilt of their
sword. We used merely to touch the money or the swordhilt and then
put the hand to the forehead as a salute. I thought these rupees were
meant to be touched and returned in the usual way, and was much
embarrassed when I found that I should be wounding their feelings by
so doing. In my embarrassment I consulted Mr Charles Saunders, the
Commissioner of the Rawal Pindi Division, of which the Gujrat district
formed a part. He happened to be encamped at Gujrat at the time, and
knowing that it would be an insult to return a 'neundrà', or wedding
present, while on the other hand it was quite out of the question that I
should take the money from natives, he suggested that I should spend
the money in giving a great dinner to them all. I acted on this suggestion.
For the Hindus and Sikhs, whose religion would not allow them to eat
with men of other creeds, I caused to be prepared by a Hindu trays of
food, one of which was sent to each giver of the 'neundrà'. Each tray
contained a pile of fine wheaten flour, rice, ghee, sugar and spices. A

goat or sheep was sent with each tray. For the Musulmans, the most numerous of my wellwishers, I had a large tent pitched and carpets spread, and invited them to a feast. Huge cauldrons were prepared in which sheep were boiled whole, with rice, saffron, pistachios and flour. Piles of native sweetmeats, curried fowls, vegetables and other native delicacies were also prepared and a large number of my native friends sat down and gorged to their hearts' content. Meanwhile, I gave a lunch to the Europeans. When the natives could eat no more they sent a message asking to see us. So we all went out, and as we approached the tent were greeted by a thunder of eructations from the assembly. We were rather shocked at this, but it was explained to be a compliment, and was meant to show us that they had thoroughly enjoyed their banquet! Then followed speeches in Hindustani, after which they all dispersed very happy. The cost of the whole thing was Rs 400, the total amount of the offerings we had received.

Early in 1860 Lord and Lady Canning arrived. All through the provinces from Calcutta to Lahore the new Viceroy had been making a semi-royal progress. His camp covered many acres with its town of tents, not the flimsy marquees used in England, but substantial canvas structures with fireplaces, doors, windows and double walls. He had an escort of his own splendid bodyguard, regiments of English cavalry and infantry, native horse and foot also. But a fire broke out in his camp at Delhi wherein many tents and much property were destroyed, and when he arrived at Lahore it was represented to him that the wild country between that place and Peshawar was too poor to support so large a company, nor could tents be quickly found to replace those lost in the fire. The English officers governing the various districts through which he must pass invited him to trust himself to their hospitality and guardianship and to come among them with only a small cortège. His excellent sense at once showed him how great would be the moral impression made by the fact that scarcely a year after the suppression of the mutiny the Viceroy of India could safely travel with only a small retinue through the most warlike province in the country. So he came, travelling in a carriage drawn by four camels with only half a dozen native troopers following him. He was accompanied by the Commander-in-Chief, Lord Clyde, and a few secretaries and aides-de-camp. Lady Canning, with a similar retinue, followed him one day later. Hardinge's house was prepared for their reception, and he was delighted to be able to borrow from us plate, glass and ornaments such as were rarely seen in those rough districts, but which my wife had brought out with her as wedding presents. My wife with rare disinterestedness

lent her looking-glass, the only one in that part of the Panjab fit for a
lady, for Lady Canning's use. It was sent on from camp to camp, on a
special camel to itself, and did not return to us for many weeks.
Saunders, Hardinge and I rode down with an escort of a dozen sowàrs
to meet the Viceroy at Vazirabad, where our district began. He arrived
about 8 p.m. and got out of his carriage while the camels were being
changed. We were all introduced to him, and he shook hands and conversed courteously with us for a few moments. Then he said good-bye
to the Gujranwala officials who had accompanied him thus far, and
proceeded on his journey, Hardinge and I riding one on each side of
his carriage and answering as best we might the innumerable questions
which he kept asking us about the people and the district. His thirst for
information seemed insatiable. We had provided relays of torch-
bearers at short distances, wild, long-haired men who ran in front and
beside the carriages. At last we reached the Baradari. The long avenue
was bright with torches and lined by troopers of the 14th Panjab
Cavalry. It was a weird and picturesque sight, the fitful red light flashing on lances and drawn swords and the many-coloured equipments of
cavalry, police and native noblemen, the tall, awkward camels advancing at a rapid trot, the horses cantering, the torches flaring, trumpets
sounding and the crowd shouting cries of welcome. We soon sat down
to supper in the large front room where I had first met Adams. It was
now transformed with flags, carpets, wreaths of flowers and a long, well-
decorated, and laden dinner table.

Lord Canning was a tall man, stately in bearing with a cold, pale,
handsome face, rather spoilt by a long, straight upper lip. Old Lord
Clyde was an odd little crumpled being with a bright eye and a face
like a winter apple. He was the life of the party; the young aides-de-
camp played off practical jokes on him, filling his glass with different
wines, all of which he drank without distinction while he told amusing
stories which kept us at the lower end of the table in a state of subdued
laughter. At the upper end, stately, silent Lord Canning took nothing
but pickled salmon and tea. This struck us as rather an unsatisfactory
meal, but he explained that he had been so often stopped during the
day to have refreshments on the journey that he had no appetite left.

Next morning they all started off again and that evening we went
down to the Chenab again to meet and escort Lady Canning. My wife
was in attendance at the Baradari to receive her. She was worn and
old-looking but very graceful and pleasant in manner. She made my
wife give her some tea in her private apartments and was very much
amused when the khansamah sent in Hardinge's battered old Britannia

metal teapot, reserving my wife's handsome new silver one for the gentlemen, it being unnatural from a native point of view to provide for women in preference to men. She kept my wife a long time talking, being, as she said, much surprised to find a newly-married English girl in so wild a place. Her sweetness and gentleness of manner impressed us all.

When they had all gone we went out into camp, and thoroughly enjoyed this our first camping tour together. We rode all the marches escorted by troopers, one of whom solemnly carried the precious silver teapot, and the other my wife's morocco dressing-bag. The kindly old, long-bearded Sikh sirdars in their handsome cloaks of green or scarlet embroidered with gold would come to meet us, and got up hawking parties for our amusement. They were very picturesque figures as they rode, hawk on fist, over the bare sandy plains among the low scrub jungle where the partridges lay hidden. They were very curious about my wife; thought it wonderful that she should ride a horse—and very well she rode too—and were still more amazed when my servants told them that she could read and write and keep accounts. They were all very anxious to know how much I had paid for her (wives being always purchased in the Panjab), and utterly rejected as incredible the assertion of our people that I had not paid anything at all for her. One fine young Sirdar with whom I was riding alone one morning told me that he knew the English worshipped a woman, whose head they put on their coins, and they had images of her in their churches. This impression, a confusion of ideas between Romish images of the Virgin and the Queen's head on our coins, was very general in those days in the Panjab where very few Englishwomen had been seen, except in the military cantonments. Only one English lady before Mrs Adams had lived in Gujrat, and Mrs Adams had only been there a few months. So my wife was a startling novelty and the women in the remoter villages would crowd round the camp peeping shyly at her, and there were, I was told, hot discussions as to whether she was a man or a woman. The absence of a beard was advanced in favour of the latter view, while the fact of her riding on horseback seemed a strong argument for the former.

The Viceroy and his party returned while we were in camp, and I rode by the side of Lady Canning's carriage pointing out to her whatever was noticeable. She saw our tiny camp of two tents pitched on an open plain near the road and being told that my wife was in it, insisted on my going back to her, as she could not bear to think of the young bride being left alone among native servants in that wild place. Lady Canning was always kind and thoughtful for others.

A large meeting was held at Sialkot, where a durbar of some importance took place, at which the Maharaja of Kashmir attended to pay his respects to the Viceroy of his Suzerain the Queen of England. His tents were constructed of the richest Cashmere shawls and his throne was of the same embroidered in gold. Those who saw it said it was the most gorgeous thing of the kind they had ever seen. Hardinge was ordered to be present, and he summoned me into Gujrat to carry on the district work in his absence, so my wife and I had to ride in about twenty miles. This over-exertion knocked her up, and brought on a miscarriage. The ignorance of matters relating to their health when married, in which many young Englishwomen are brought up, often leads in India, where they have no older women to advise them, to disastrous consequences. My wife did not know that in her condition she ought not to ride, and a long and tedious illness was the consequence. We had only the Bengali doctor at our station and she shrank from consulting him, so I wrote to Dr Aitchison, the Civil Surgeon of Jhelam, and he very kindly came over to see her. Jhelam was thirty miles away, and his duties there prevented him from leaving the station oftener than once a week. But regularly every Sunday he came over by the mail cart, and this comforted her. She was very brave and patient, but it was great grief to me that I could not get more constant attendance for her. She did not thoroughly recover till May.

Meanwhile, in April, I went to Rawal Pindi to pass my examination in law, the rules of practice, and languages. When first appointed, a young Civilian had only what were then called 'ordinary powers'; he could only pass very light sentences, and consequently could only try petty cases. After six months he was expected to pass a first examination, and if successful he was invested with 'second-class powers' enabling him to try more important cases. Six months later he again had to pass a second, and more difficult examination, when he obtained the 'full powers' of a Magistrate and could try cases of all kinds, and perform revenue work of every description. On this occasion both examinations, called the 'lower' and 'higher' standards, were held at once, the examination which ought to have been held in the previous November having been for some reason postponed. We were allowed, as a special case, to go up for both standards at once. This was very difficult, but I was successful, and so was my contemporary Charles Edward Bernard. We two, I think, were almost the only men who ever passed both standards at once, and the first time of going up. It is only fair to say that the examinations were far less difficult then than they are now, not only because the examiners were more lenient, but because the

Panjab system of government was far simpler than the present. We had no Acts and Regulations, no complicated rules of civil and criminal procedure, no fearfully intricate systems of accounts to study. We had to show that we possessed sound judgment, and knew the few and simple circulars issued for our guidance. The linguistic test was much harder as we had to show that we could converse fluently, understand and make ourselves understood by rude peasants speaking various kinds of rustic patois. As the result of my success I was invested with 'full powers' and my salary was raised from Rs 400 to Rs 500 a month.

In June a change of air was recommended for my wife, and as I could not get leave to go to the hills, Hardinge kindly made over to me the management of the western part of the district. In this region is a low range of hills called the Pabli, running parallel to the Jhelam River, on the top of which a former Deputy Commissioner had built a delightful little bungalow at a place called Bani. It had a garden round it, with buildings for the amla and servants, and commanded lovely views of the Kashmir hills. Here we lived very happily for some time, and the change did my wife much good. Dear old Aitchison rode over from Jhelam—it was only six miles—constantly to see her, and we often went to Jhelam to spend a day or two there. This was a very happy time.

Here a curious incident occurred. The Indian chaplains of those days were not a very clerical class of men—at least those we fell in with, for it is perhaps hardly fair to include the whole body under one sweeping condemnation. Some that we met were certainly rather lax in their conduct. One morning, as I went out to inspect the adjacent police-station, I was met by a doleful procession: the Thanadar, Moharrir and Jamadar with their heads artistically bound up in bloody rags, blood dried in clots on their faces, and their clothes torn and dusty. In answer to my questions they stated that in the night a Padre had arrived from Jhelam in a dooly. He was intoxicated and as his relay of bearers could not immediately be found, he had got angry, called up the police officers and, after swearing at them, had beaten them all with a thick stick, after which he had flung himself, exhausted by his violence, into his dooly and, the fresh bearers having arrived, had been carried on his way. Of course the police officers had, after their custom, made the most of the incident, and had taken care to exhibit as much blood and wounds as they could. But I was bound to take notice of the matter, and Aitchison coming up at the time, I asked him if he knew who the Padre was. He laughed and said he had been dining the night before at the Mess of a Regiment, then stationed at Jhelam, that the Padre (whose name he told me) had been there and the officers had amused themselves by making him drunk and had then put him into his dooly and started him on his journey. Not wishing to have the scandal of summoning the Padre and punishing him in open court, I wrote him a studiously moderate letter telling him of the accusation and advising him to make it up with the police officers by giving them a little present to induce them to withdraw the charge. I also told him, without however mentioning Aitchison's name, that I had been informed of what took place at the Mess. In a few days' time I received a letter in about forty pages from the Padre accusing me of spying upon his actions, instigating anonymous accusers to bring slanderous charges against him, and winding up by calling me 'Pontius Pilate', 'Judas Iscariot', 'an assassin thrusting in the dark' and similar other violent clerical abuse. He did not, however, deny the charge. On this I wrote to the Bishop, whom I had met once or twice, and asked him for his advice. That good and kindly man, Bishop Cotton, replied that he thanked me very much for not bringing the Chaplain into the police court, regretted the quite unjustifiable violence of the Padre's language and the utterly unnecessary and irrelevant tirade of forty pages which he had written, and said that he had written to the Padre requesting him at once to follow my very friendly advice, to compensate the police for the assault, and to apologize to me for his insulting letter. In due course there arrived a letter from the Padre—a very short one this time—in which he tendered a sort of half-apology, winding up with the singular remark that 'we have both much to forget and to forgive'! This was hardly satisfactory, but as he compensated the police, at Hardinge's request, I allowed the matter to drop.

Hardinge now announced his intention of taking furlough, much to our distress, for he was very much liked by both of us. He left in September and was succeeded by a Lieutenant Paske, another of the military men in Civil employ, of whom there were so many in the Panjab then. He was a great friend of Mr Donald McLeod, then Financial Commissioner, and had been in the Educational Department, whence his patron pitchforked him into this favourite station. His wife was a very ill-bred, offensive little woman, puffed up in a most ridiculous way with the supposed grandeur of her husband's position, and expecting my wife and myself to toady her and wait upon her. She repeatedly annoyed us by telling us that we were 'only Assistants', and other offensive remarks, which affected us all the more because of their contrast to the uniform courtesy and kindness of dear old Hardinge. Added to this, Paske made many changes in the district arrangements, most of which, owing to his ignorance of district work, were distinctly changes for the worse. The old Sirdars and Choudhries used to come to me complaining of the new régime, and though I was as irritated as they were, I had no power to do anything. The cold weather passed unpleasantly enough under these circumstances, and early in the New Year I unfortunately allowed myself to be so goaded by this man, that I lost my temper and had a savage quarrel with him, the result of which was that I was transferred to another district, and we left our dear Gujrat for our new district, Ambala, in February 1861.

CHAPTER IX

AMBALA AND LUDIANA, 1861

THERE was great sorrow at our departure, and a calvacade of the principal natives accompanied us some miles on our way where they took an affectionate farewell of us. I had perhaps no great cause for complaint, for I had been two years in what was considered one of the best districts in the Panjab, a very unusual thing in those days when, as I have mentioned before, men were generally moved once in six months or even less. Still, it was a grief to us to leave our pretty little house, and the numerous friends we had made in those parts, and the more so as we were now moved quite to the other end of the province where we knew no one, and all the conditions of existence were very different. My wife, too, was not in a condition to travel. We reached Ambala on the 21st February 1861, after a fatiguing journey of seven days, and were hospitably received by Colonel Busk, the Deputy Commissioner, a shy, silent and somewhat unsociable widower. He took a liking to us, however, and was less reserved to us than to others. My poor wife was so much knocked up by the long journey that we feared a miscarriage. She, however, recovered after a few days' rest, and we found an empty house where we settled down with a tolerable amount of comfort.

I felt strange and rather at sea at Ambala, for although all the districts in the Panjab were supposed to be governed on precisely the same system, yet an absolute uniformity is not attainable in this world, and the circumstances of the country were so different from those of Gujrat that there was much in the work that was entirely new to me. It was a much larger and more civilized district than Gujrat and the work was in consequence not only heavier, but more intricate. Instead of the simple cattle-thefts and adulteries which constituted the staple crimes of the Jats and Gujars of my old district, I now had complicated cases of forgery, perjury and embezzlement, and occasionally had to try a European soldier out of the cantonment in virtue of the powers of a Justice of the Peace which had recently been conferred on me. There was a very large military force at Ambala, some six miles away from the Civil Station in a spacious and well laid-out cantonment with several miles of broad, tree-shaded roads crossing each other at right-angles, numerous houses in big compounds, shops, bazaars and barracks. There was also a large, populous native town enclosed in high walls and protected by a strong fort, and all round a barren, hungry, waterless plain of sand and rocks, with the snowy peaks of the Himalayas on the northern horizon. Shortly after my arrival the wheat crop, which is the chief harvest of the year in those parts, failed; and famine reigned not only in Ambala, but for miles and miles around. I was sent out to take charge of the parganas[1] of Ropar, Kharar and Morinda, lying along the left bank of the Sutlej River just below the hills. I was in tents, and every morning rose before dawn and rode through village after village accompanied by the Tahsildar, carefully examining the state of the crops and making notes as to the amount of the relief which it would be necessary to give to the people who were already on the verge of starvation. At each village the people flocked round us in crowds showing us their parched-up fields and the granaries nearly, if not quite, empty. Reaching my tent about eleven, I spent the day in trying cases, and writing reports. At four we were all in the saddle again riding round another circle of villages. We did not get back to our tents till long after dark. All along the barren rocky spurs of the mountains, and far down to the Rajputana desert in the south the crops had failed. The scanty stalks of the wheat stood barely three inches high and the ears already formed were dry and empty. The wells were nearly dry, many of the cattle dead, and the people waiting in silent and hopeless misery till death should overtake them too. This part of India, the immemorial battlefield of all the invading races, is thickly sprinkled with castles. Strangely resembling the medieval castles of Europe, they consist of a central lofty keep, a courtyard or two, an enceinte of high and strong battlemented walls, surrounded by a moat, crossed by a single draw-bridge. In each of these castles dwelt an old feudal chief. They all came out to meet me in their finery, and complained bitterly of their sufferings from the scarcity. I remained under canvas till the middle of April when the heat became insupportable and I was recalled to the Station. My wife did not go with me on this tour as her health was not strong enough to stand the fatigue and exposure. Even I, strong though I was, was a good deal knocked up. But there was no rest for me. Relief centres—i.e. places where food and shelter were given—were opened in the station and at various places in the district and crowds of

---

[1] A pargana is an ancient division of the country for revenue purposes. There are parganas in all parts of India but they differ very much in size, some being as large as the largest English county while some are only the size of a parish. On average a pargana may be considered equal to a middling-sized county.

famished wretches poured in from all the country round. They received twice a day a dole of food, under the eye of the Deputy Commissioner and his Assistants, for not even in such a bitter emergency as this could native officials be trusted not to embezzle. So each one of us had to preside daily at the distribution of food, while the ordinary work of trying cases went on all the same. The immense jail was crowded with people who had committed petty thefts on purpose to get put into prison where they would get food. It was a strange and dreary time.

On the 14th May 1861 my wife was delivered of a son, a beautiful and large baby with blue eyes. Our joy was great, but of short duration, for our beautiful child died quite suddenly on the 22nd. We afterwards found that the doctor, a drunken, careless old fellow, had injured its head in bringing it into the world and had concealed the fact from us. On the night of the 22nd I was, as usual in the Panjab, sleeping on a charpoy in the garden when I was called in to see my wife. She had the child in her arms, and said it was in great pain, crying and moaning, and squinting very strangely. She begged me to go and fetch the doctor, so I dressed, called for my horse, and galloped off into the cantonments where the doctor lived; for they gave us no Civil Surgeon for the Civil Station. I found him asleep in his garden. He paid very little attention to me, and when I had described the symptoms he laughed and said, 'Only a little wind in the stomach. Give it some rhubarb. I will call in the morning,' and turned over and went to sleep again. Much relieved I galloped back, went into my wife's bedroom and told her what the doctor had said. She heard me out, and then said quietly, 'The baby is dead.' This was a terrible shock to us both, and especially to my poor dear wife. She was a long time recovering and might have been longer, but for the kindness of Dr Ince, a brilliant young surgeon, just fresh from home, well-up in the latest medical knowledge, and having as much in his little finger as stupid, careless, drunken old B——l had in his whole carcase. Ince was prevented by professional etiquette from attending my wife. Such was the official tyranny of those days that we were bound to employ the doctor appointed by Government and as the charge of a Civil Station was very lucrative, the senior medical officers claimed and obtained it. Many of these old fogies had not been home for years, they never read medical books or kept themselves abreast of the progress of medical science, they did their work in a perfunctory, careless manner, and spent most of their time in playing cards and drinking. My wife was a young, strong, healthy woman, and the child was healthy and well formed. There were no complications about the confinement.

Old B——l was probably only half sober; no monthly nurse could be procured; had one been present she might have prevented the doctor from doing mischief. As it was the child's skull got injured in some way and it died. Ince was very indignant and as he could not openly attend my wife, we used to invite him to dinner and after dinner he would have a little talk to her, and prescribe for her. Old B——l avoided her, and well he might. Thanks to Ince she recovered by degrees. The child was buried in the cemetery at Ambala, but as it died so suddenly that we had no time to have it baptized, the chaplain refused to read the burial service over it, and was only with difficulty persuaded to allow the grave to be dug in consecrated ground. I wrote to my father about this, and he replied in a long and affectionate letter giving me the whole history of the Church's teaching on the subject, and winding up by saying that he had too firm a belief in God's mercy and justice to suppose that the soul of an innocent child could possibly be lost for lack of baptism. So we were comforted. But the weather was very dreadful and retarded my wife's recovery. The heat day and night was intense; a sort of simoom, a 'dust-storm' as it is called, frequently blew for days together. A storm of this kind blows up clouds of fine sand from the Rajputana deserts, and this sand penetrates everywhere, even into apparently closely shut houses, and covers tables, beds, floors with a fine layer of gritty dust. The storm usually lasts four days, during which the sky is obscured by the flying sand, the sun cannot be seen and a low moaning in the air continues. My drive of two miles and a half to my cutcherry every day in the teeth of the storm was a very unpleasant experience. At last we felt we could not stand Ambala any longer and I applied for a transfer. Sir Robert Montgomery wrote me a very kind letter and transferred me to the adjacent Station of Ludiana.

We left Ambala on the 15th June 1861, having been there less than four months. Our move, as it turned out, was from the frying-pan into the fire. If we were uncomfortable at Ambala we were more so at Ludiana. The Deputy Commissioner of this place was Colonel McNeill, well known as a despotic, determined man, a perfect Tartar; and to his subordinates a brutal bully. He was, it is true, the right man for the district, for the large city of Ludiana was full of Kashmiris who are known all over India as the most desperate ruffians. There was also a numerous population of Afghans attracted by the sort of court held by some Afghan princes who were detained there as political prisoners. There is a well-known verse current in Upper India which stigmatizes Afghans and Kashmiris as the worst of men. To keep the turbulent population of this large and flourishing place in order a stern, strong-handed

man like this McNeill was wanted. But though we gave him all praise
for the vigour of his administration, we European officers serving under
him felt that he had no right to treat us in the same harsh way as he
treated the thieving, brawling cut-throats of Afghans and Kashmiris.
He was peculiarly severe upon us, because I was a Civilian, and he
disliked all Civilians, and because a particular friend of his had been
moved to make room for me. So I and my wife were subjected to a
variety of petty annoyances. In most Indian Stations there were clubs
for the supply of such articles of food and other comforts as could not
otherwise be procured. There was a mutton club for instance. Every
European in the station paid a certain sum every month, and the
Civil Surgeon managed it. He bought the sheep, paid the shepherd, saw
that the sheep were properly fed, and once or twice a week had a sheep
killed and joints sent to all subscribers. Mutton of an eatable description could only be obtained in this way. McNeill ordered that we were
not to be allowed to subscribe to this club, and though he had no right
or power to give such an order, so great was the fear of him, that no one
dared to disobey him. So we had to live on coarse goat's flesh, such as
we could buy in the bazaar, till the doctor kindly shared his joint with
us. After a time one of the subscribers to the club was transferred to
another station for a time, and during his absence retained his share in
the club, and we bought the mutton from him. Many other petty
persecutions of this sort we had to suffer from this man. But his
brutality defeated itself for the other people, being English men and
women, were indignant at his conduct, and tried to make up to us for
it by extreme kindness.

The only pleasant event in our stay at Ludiana was a visit from dear
old Elliot. He took it into his head to marry about this time, and much
to his wife's disgust came to spend his honeymoon with us. I am not
writing his life, and I have no right to divulge his secrets. I will, therefore, be silent on the subject of his marriage. They stayed with us three
weeks, and after their departure I fell ill and was sent to Simla by the
doctor for change of air. We spent a pleasant month there, in a house,
part of which was rented by my Haileybury friend, C. E. Bernard,
who lent it to us, as he had to go to Calcutta as Under-Secretary to the
Government of India. The other half was inhabited by another old
Haileybury man, R. T. Burney, with whom he chummed, and a very
merry party we were. We did lots of sketching in the glorious scenery
of the Himalayas.[1]

[1] I had a narrow escape while at Simla. Instead of riding the small surefooted
hill ponies as they did at other hill stations, people at Simla used to ride their

Shortly after our return to Ludiana I received, without any previous notice, orders informing that I was transferred to Bengal—the Lower Provinces. In great distress I started for Lahore, saw Sir R. Montgomery and begged to be allowed to stay in the Panjab. He received me very coldly and assured me that there would be a much better career awaiting me in Bengal; that I was far too independent and insubordinate for the Panjab, and that having been asked to supply three officers for Bengal, which was then short of hands, he had specially selected me—because I suppose he wanted to get rid of me—and as he had already reported my name to the Government of India it was too late to make any change. I was somewhat comforted by this and after hurriedly disposing of my furniture, left Ludiana on the 22nd November 1861 and the Panjab two days later—for good.

Thus closed a chapter in my career and a totally new existence opened for me in a different part of the country. Looking back now at this period after many years, I see that I had much cause for thankfulness to that loving Providence which guides our steps.

Strong in body and in mind, enthusiastically interested in my work and in the people and the country, I was at the same time hot-tempered, independent, and horribly careless as to what I said or did. If I had stayed longer in the Panjab I should almost certainly have got into serious trouble with the military men in Civil employ—the 'Cutcherry Captains' as we used to call them. We junior Civilians resented the presence of these men, because they stopped our promotion, were harsh and stuck-up and overbearing, and introduced military ideas of subordination instead of the genial, brotherly relations which subsisted between members of our own service. Under a Civilian Deputy Commissioner and with a Civilian Commissioner over us all, we lived and worked together in the most perfect harmony; the respect due to an official superior being tempered by the *esprit de corps* which made us all support each other, and by the feeling that official rank was a mere temporary accident and that we were all really English gentlemen

big horses from the plains. I rode my Biluch mare, a beautiful animal and very fast. One day I rode alone to see a waterfall and by mistake took a wrong path, which rose and rose along a lofty hillside narrowing as it went. At last it grew so narrow that riding was no longer safe. I therefore slipped off and taking the reins over my arm led the horse. I had not dismounted two minutes when her foot slipped and she went over the edge. I tugged at her with the reins but I could not hold her. The poor beast struggled hard but the soft earth gave way and she rolled down, bumping from one rock to another till she landed in a pool at the foot of the waterfall. Slowly and painfully I climbed down and found her dead. I managed to get the saddle and bridle off and carrying them over my shoulder trudged sadly and wearily several miles back to Simla.

socially equal. Under a military Deputy Commissioner on the other hand
we were treated as if we were something by nature inferior, and they
assumed an offensive air of superiority. They were, moreover, inter-
lopers, put into Civil posts at a time when the Government chose to
assume that it had not sufficient officers in the Civil Service to administer the newly-conquered territory of the Panjab. But when the
number of Civilians was increased Government had got so enamoured
of a system which so largely increased their patronage, and enabled
them to provide for sons and relatives of influential persons, that they
broke the pledge which they had given to the Civil Service, that this
intrusion of military men into their domain should be temporary only,
and refused to send back these Colonels and Captains to their regiments.
They did indeed promise, in order to pacify the Civilians, that their
promotion should keep pace with that of their fellows in the regulation
provinces, but whenever a Civilian was promoted in fulfilment of this
promise, all the Cutcherry Captains raised a howl. Then we Civilians
reminded them that they had been sent out to India to fight, and drill
troops, not to govern districts and try lawsuits; that all the Civil appointments were ours by right, and finally, if they did not like it, it was
always open to them to go back to their regiments, which was their
proper place, and where they would get about half the pay they now
did. Perhaps no one felt this matter so strongly as I did, for I had
experienced the difference between the *camaraderie* of dear old Bradford Hardinge and the snobbish pride of the Paskes, followed at a little
interval by the cruel persecution of McNeill. One day I electrified
that terrible Tartar McNeill by telling him (alluding to the notorious
fact that soldiers got into civil employ by backstairs influence, nepotism
and jobbery) that our respective positions reminded me of St Paul and
the Centurion. The Centurion said, 'with a great sum obtained I this
freedom' but Paul said, 'but I was freeborn.' It was probably remarks of
this kind combined with my quarrel with Paske that led to my being
transferred to Bengal. Paske belonged to a small but very influential
clique which surrounded the Lieutenant-Governor and shared among
themselves all the best appointments. They were commonly called 'the
Royal Family' and to quarrel with one of them was fatal to one's
prospects. It was therefore fortunate for me that I got out of this part
of the country when I did. Besides, I got very much more rapid
promotion that I could have got in the Panjab. So everything was for
the best in this best of all possible worlds.

We travelled down-country in the usual leisurely way, in a dâk gâri,
the only mode of conveyance for long journeys. Our progress was slow,

for the wretched ponies kept by the dâk gâri company had been more than half-starved during the recent famine. We stopped a week with the Elliots at Bulandshahr, two days at Agra, seeing once more the beautiful Taj and the lonely grandeur of Akbar's tomb at Sikandra. Then we had to drive some ten miles to the railway at Shikohabad which was open only up to that point from Allahabad. At this latter place we had some trouble in finding a resting-place for the night, and were finally accommodated very roughly at a hotel in course of construction. Canningtown, the new European quarter of Allahabad, was a wilderness of half-finished bungalows. Thence to Benares we had to travel by dâk gâri again, the railway not being yet opened. At Benares we were received by my wife's brother, Captain Henry Geary, whose battery of Artillery was quartered there, and by his friend, Major Priestley, Executive Engineer. We spent a happy week, with parties, picnics and amusements of many kinds in this charming station, and visited the quaint and beautiful ancient city and the ruins of Sarnàth, a celebrated Buddhist monastery, and tope. A letter awaited me here from the Government of Bengal containing the good news that I was to be Joint Magistrate of Shahabad on Rs 700 a month, a rise in salary of Rs 200. This is the frontier district of the Lower Provinces and only a short distance from Benares. But though not far off, it was not very accessible and we had some difficulty in getting to Arrah, the capital of the district. We went by dâk gâri to Ghazipur, a large city and Civil Station on the Ganges, and thence in a large native boat down the Ganges to Buxar, the first town in the Shahabad district. There we struck the railway again, but though the line was finished, no trains were as yet running, so we had to go on a trolly. It took us all day to get to Arrah, a distance of only thirty miles. Finally at 6 p.m. on Thursday the 19th December 1861 we arrived, and stayed with Steuart Colvin Bayley, the Magistrate and Collector of Shahabad. I took the oaths and assumed charge of my new duties the next morning.

CHAPTER X

SHAHABAD AND PURNEA, 1861–1862

THE change from the rough, wild Panjab to sleepy, civilized Bengal was very marked and we both felt the difference acutely. Socially the tone was more formal and less genial. People were friendly, but a little stiff, and punctilious about calling and invitations. At Gujrat Hardinge would say, 'Come and dine tonight and bring your dinner with you,' whereupon we would send our servants over with our dinner and join it to his and all eat of the combined meal in happiness. Here they sent us written invitations in which they 'requested the pleasure of our company', etc. We did not at first slide easily into our new grooves and I fear we were looked upon as rather wild and uncivilized for a time. But the station was a nice one, the houses of the Europeans were stately, roomy mansions, standing in large compounds, and were handsomely furnished. All the Europeans had horses and carriages in plenty; they entertained handsomely and lived, as it seemed to us fresh from the rude fare of the Panjab, luxuriously. They also dressed fashionably and the *toilettes* of the ladies were not much behind the latest Paris fashions. I soon found that my increased pay was not more than sufficient to meet the cost of living in this much more expensive place. Some things it is true were cheaper; such articles as were imported from England through Calcutta cost less at Arrah than in the distant Panjab, owing to the distance and consequent cost of carriage being less. At Gujrat for instance we depended for our bottled beer, our universal and almost only beverage, on a shop kept by an enterprising Parsee named Jamasjee at Jhelam. He charged us thirteen or fourteen rupees a dozen and often ran out, and we had to wait till his fresh stock came slowly up the Indus to Jhelam in boats. Here abundant supplies could be got from Calcutta through Dinapore for five rupees a dozen. Good and cheap claret was also always obtainable. But grain for our horses was three or four times as dear and we had to dress better and spend more money on clothes. We secured a pretty house and furnished it nicely, and as our horses and buggy arrived before long from the Panjab the New Year found us comfortably settled.

As regards public work the contrast to the Panjab was great. The so-called 'Lower Provinces' of Bengal consisted of five provinces: 1. The ancient Kingdom of Bengal, or Bengal Proper as it was called; 2. Orissa; 3. Behar; 4. Assam; 5. Chota Nagpur. Arrah was the capital of the district of Shahabad which was in Behar. In the three provinces of Bengal, Behar, and Orissa, the first acquisitions of the East India Company, the Permanent Settlement prevailed. Under this system the country had been from of old divided into immense estates, each held by a zemindar who was held responsible for paying the revenue assessed on the estate to the Government. These zemindars had been in 1793 confirmed in the permanent and hereditary possession of their estates on the condition of paying the revenue, the amount of which was fixed in perpetuity. If they failed to pay, the estate was put up to public auction and knocked down to the highest bidder, who entered on possession, subject to the same conditions as his predecessor. It was held in 1862, and for long after, that the Collector and other public officers had no right and no business to inquire how the zemindar managed his estate, or how he dealt with his immense body of tenants. If any difference arose between them they could go to law about it, and a celebrated statute (Act X of 1859) provided for the decision of all such matters. This was quite the opposite of the Panjab system, where there were no large landholders, and the officers of Government settled the rent to be paid by every cultivator, and were always actively intervening in all matters connected with the land, and expected to see that rents were punctually paid. It was the 'ryotwarry' system in fact. When I spoke to my new Collector, Bayley,[1] about the welfare of the peasant class and suggested intervention in cases where they were oppressively treated by the zemindar, he laughed at me and told me it was no business of ours; the zemindar had a right to do what he liked with his ryots. My Panjabi zeal was in fact laughed down by all the Bengal men. No one took any trouble about anything. I do not mean that they were lazy, on the contrary, they did their work regularly and conscientiously. But this was a Regulation Province, an old possession, which had been under British rule nearly a century, and where laws and rules had had time to take root and harden into a settled system of procedure in which there was no room for the exercise of individual character on the part of officials. Here, when a case arose, they consulted their law-books, found the law that applied, passed orders in accordance therewith, and troubled themselves no further. In the Panjab, on the contrary, when a case arose, as there were no laws to go by, each officer had to think the matter over, and make up his mind as to what was the best thing to do. He had to do it promptly too, for there was no time for prolonged

[1] Afterwards Sir Steuart Bayley, Lieutenant-Governor of Bengal.

reflexion or hesitation; and having issued his order he had personally to see it carried out, and to take care that it worked satisfactorily. He had often to get on his horse, ride to the place concerned and in person see to the execution of his orders. In Bengal such a thing was unheard of. An order once passed was made over to the proper native officer to be carried out, and any further instructions that might be required were applied for and given in writing. In Bengal before you could issue an order you had to find a section of an Act or Regulation empowering you to do so. In the Panjab you did so, because you thought it was the proper thing to do. It is not surprising that it was a long time before I got accustomed to this very new state of things, and that I was liable frequently to be reprimanded for acting without authority. 'Taking the law into my own hands' was here my principal offence, while in the Panjab the promptness and decision with which I acted on my own judgment had won me much praise, and on one occasion I had even been written of as an officer who displayed 'great administrative ability'. I got to have the same words applied to me in Bengal twenty years later, but at first I was often found fault with.

My first great success was in criminal work. Bayley, the Collector, though also Magistrate, disliked criminal work, and like many Collectors in those days left it entirely to the Joint Magistrate. The Indian Penal Code and the Criminal Procedure Code had been compiled many years previously by a Commission of able men, chief among whom was the great historian Macaulay. They were not received favourably by the Bengal Civilians, and their introduction had been postponed for many years. The Bengal officers had been so long accustomed to administer justice by the light (or darkness) of a string of old regulations that they could not regard the prospect of being tied down to the precision of the new law without some apprehension. There was a muddled, jumbled book—a ponderous quarto—called *Beaufort's Digest*, in which, under the head of each crime arranged alphabetically, were given abstracts of decisions of the old chief Criminal Court of Bengal, the 'Sadr Nizàmat Adàlat', and Magistrates were supposed to gather from these some idea of the punishment that might be imposed. The evidence of witnesses was taken down in writing by clerks who sat round the court-room and read over to the Magistrate, often many days later. Altogether the whole system was an inefficient, intricate chaos out of which, as a natural consequence, it resulted that offenders were very inadequately dealt with and crime was rampant. I had the misfortune of sitting as Magistrate for some days at the close of 1861 and felt acutely the uselessness and inefficiency of the old system. The new

Codes were to be introduced on the 1st January 1862, but Bayley told me that I need not bother myself about them. He said, 'We shall all go on the old system as long as we can. Government will perhaps find out that we are doing so, and will issue circulars insisting on our introducing the new Code, but it will take six months or a year, or perhaps more before they make us do it, and in the meantime we may go on in the old way.' I surprised him by saying that I was impatiently longing for the day on which the new Code would come in. It had been introduced in part in the Panjab six months before I left, and we had all liked the new system very much. Somewhat reluctantly he consented to my doing so, and confined himself to chaffing me before other men for actually liking the new Codes which had so long been a bugbear and a stock subject for chaff among the Bengal men. When the day arrived and I took my seat in court and called up the first case on the board there was great excitement among the amla and pleaders, and my court was thronged with people looking on to see how I did it. I went through all the new procedure with ease owing to my six months' familiarity with it, and instructed the amla and the audience, pointing out the various sections of the Act under which I was acting. It got soon to be a custom for European officers to come into my court to sit on the bench and watch my proceedings, and I gained considerable *kudos* thereby.

At this time also the new police were introduced, and here also the Panjab had been in advance of Bengal, so that I was better acquainted with the new system than the other men. In this matter of the organization of the new system I was useful.

We were not destined however to remain long at Arrah. In May I was appointed, much to my surprise, Officiating Magistrate and Collector of Purneah on a salary of Rs 1,250. This was a great stroke of promotion, and quite unexpected, for in those days we had no 'Quarterly Civil List' to tell us how we stood for promotion. My wife was expecting to be confined, but we thought we should have time to get to our new station before the event occurred, so again we sold our furniture, and prepared to set out on our travels. My brother Pearson, who was with his Regiment the 69th Foot in Burmah, took leave and joined us and was very helpful to us. We left Arrah on the 3rd June 1862 in palkis and reached Patna next morning. There my wife, probably from the jolting of the palki, felt ill and was afraid to continue her journey. We did not know anyone at Dinapore except the doctor, who told us of a strange old man named Good, who kept a large and comfortable hotel at Deega between Dinapore and Patna. This eccentric person was always very much offended if a traveller drove up to his door and treated the place as if it was an hotel. So the doctor went to him and represented that some of his friends were passing through Patna, and one of them, a lady, was ill, and as they had no place to go to, he would be much obliged if Mr Good would kindly take them in. He consented to do so, and after spending some hours on a steamer, by which we had intended to go on, if my wife's illness had not intervened, we found ourselves at Mr Good's hotel. We stayed there four days, during which time the worthy man and his wife kept up the farce of our being their guests. They took their meals with us, and Mr Good always offered his arm to my wife, and I had to take in Mrs Good. They were very vulgar people but kindhearted. He was a coach-builder by trade and did a large business in repairing the carriages in Patna and the surrounding stations. The eccentric way in which he kept his hotel was typical of the tone assumed by the middle and lower classes of Europeans in India, every one of whom considered himself a 'Sahib' or gentleman. After a few days' rest my wife felt well enough to continue the journey, so we started again. Mr Good did not forget to send in his bill when we left—it amounted to Rs 80, as much as the best hotels in Calcutta would charge.

We were so fortunate as to find a Government steamer going down the Ganges, on which, as an officer joining his station, I was entitled to a free passage. These steamers have a 'flat' or large barge lashed to each side, so that the whole concern consists of three boats abreast. The cargo is placed on the flats and the steamer is reserved for passengers. Though it was June, the hottest month of the year, the swift movement of the vessel produced a cool breeze and we sat at the forecastle in long cane chairs and enjoyed the journey very much. On the 12th June after four days in the steamer we landed at Caragola, the entrance to the Purneah district, and reached the station the next morning, Friday the 13th June 1862.

The first appearance of the district was decidedly uninviting. On passing the rocky promontory of Colgong the Ganges gradually widens, the hills on the right bank recede, and on the left a river nearly as wide as the Ganges itself, the Kusi, pours in with a turbid mass of thick yellow water. The united stream is nearly nine miles wide. The left or northern shore is low and flat, save where a high raised bank came down to it at right-angles. This was the Ganges and Darjeeling road. On either side of it were clusters of squalid mat huts, with a few small white-washed brick buildings amongst them. The ruins of a fine old Mahommedan tomb and garden were gradually tumbling into the river which was cutting away the soft, sandy soil. Inland stretched in all directions a

SHAHABAD AND PURNEA, 1861-1862

flat plain covered with tall, waving grass, higher than a man, topped with white plumes. Caragola was not a regular settled village, but a sort of emporium which had risen into a squalid, mushroom sort of existence owing to its being the entrance to the district, and the way to the rising sanitarium of Darjeeling. It is now no more, having been entirely washed away by the river in 1864. We were hospitably received at Purneah, and after a short time found ourselves a house, and bought some furniture. We had hardly got settled when the long-expected confinement took place. On the 25th July 1862, at a quarter past eight in the morning, was born our eldest living son, David. He was not baptized till the 3rd September when Henry Geary came to stay with us. He and my brother Pearson were the godfathers. My wife recovered rapidly and was soon able to enjoy her morning rides with me again.

The new work and new surroundings of my position in Purneah caused me at first some embarrassment. To be appointed to officiate as Magistrate and Collector of a district after only four years' service was unprecedentedly rapid promotion. Even if I had spent those four years in Bengal, becoming familiar with the Bengal system, the charge of so large a district would have been a difficult task for so young an officer. But having passed nearly all the time in the Panjab, where the system was entirely different, it was still more difficult for me to do the work. Purneah was a district of more than 5,000 square miles, and was officially described about this time as 'the most lawless district in Bengal'. Owing to its notorious unhealthiness it was shunned by all officers whose ability or personal influence were sufficient to secure them favourite districts. Thus it was generally entrusted to men of inferior calibre, or to men who were in disgrace, for the Government has the habit of reserving some of the most unhealthy districts as 'penal settlements' to which they send any man whom they wish to punish. I was sent there because I was a stranger whom no one knew or cared about. Peacock, the son of Sir Barnes Peacock, Chief Justice of Bengal, who was of the same standing as myself and was appointed Collector at the same time, got the healthy and favourite district of Monghyr. But malarious Purneah was good enough for a friendless man like me.[1]

[1] During the whole of my career in India I corresponded with my dear friend Elliot. I wrote a long letter to him on an average twice a week, and sent him short scraps in between. He wrote me also; his letters were not so frequent as mine but generally longer. All his letters I have destroyed, but all mine he kept. Before leaving India in 1893 I succeeded with some difficulty in inducing him to give me my letters. There was a large box full of them, and as they contain a fairly complete history of my life in India written day by day, extracts

133

The officer designated 'Magistrate and Collector' is the actual ruler of a district, usually a tract of country between two and five thousand square miles in extent and containing in most cases about a million and a half or two millions of inhabitants. He is the pivot on which the whole administration turns; all those below him are under his orders and engaged in assisting him, all those above him depend upon him for information, and are engaged in giving him orders and instructions. But like Joseph in the Egyptian prison 'whatsoever is done there he is the doer of it'. From this date then begins the really active and important part of my life. All before this was merely training and preparation. Now began action.

At first I began too hot and strong. The very qualities which were most required to bring this lawless district into order—activity, sternness, and a somewhat high-handed self-will were precisely those which I was always being told by Alonzo Money were my chief faults, and I was often warned by friends and well-wishers not to be so hot-headed, or as they expressed it, 'so Panjabi'.

To take things quietly; never to act on one's own responsibility if it could be helped; to sit calmly in court hearing reports read and dictating orders for a certain number of hours every day; to write long, decorously-worded reports to the Commissioner; to see that all periodical returns were punctually submitted; to listen patiently to long-winded pleaders arguing for their clients;—all this was proper and becoming and in the eyes of my new acquaintances constituted the whole duty of man. Whatsoever was more than this savoured of evil.

The first difficult and important business that fell to my lot to manage was the Darbhanga Estate. Money had urged me to give my most careful attention to this matter, when I called on him at Bhagalpur. So the first thing I did on taking charge was to tell my Head Clerk to bring the papers of the Darbhanga affair. He looked a little surprised, but only said one word, 'All?' 'Yes, all,' I said, wondering why he should ask such a question. I understood the next morning when a string of coolies arrived laden with large bundles which they simply said were 'Darbhanga papers'. When deposited on the floor they made a heap about three feet high reaching all along one side of a large room.

One of the largest estates in the Lower Provinces is Darbhanga, the proprietor of which is the greatest noble in Behar and bears the title of Maharaja. The estate consists of a large number of parganas and

from them will give a more vivid impression of what the life really was than a dry record compiled years after the events occurred. I shall therefore quote from them largely in these pages.

stretches in an unbroken expanse along the country between the Ganges and Himalayas for about 200 miles. Its total area is 2,460 square miles, larger than many European kingdoms. A portion of it called Dharmpur lies in the district of Purneah. It is about forty miles long with an average width of twenty miles, the area being over 600 square miles. The great River Kusi runs through it from north to south dividing it into two nearly equal parts. The proprietor of this vast estate was just dead, leaving his estate heavily in debt. His son and successor was an infant of three years of age. Under such circumstances the estate, as is customary, was taken charge of by Government and placed under what is called the Court of Wards. This so-called court is really no court at all. The estate is managed, and the minor's maintenance and education provided for, by the Collector of the District acting partly on his own authority and partly under orders of the Commissioner of the Division, who in his turn is subject to the general supervision of the Board of Revenue in Calcutta. When, as was the case with Darbhanga, the estate is scattered over several districts the Collector of each district manages that portion which lies in his jurisdiction, and a General Manager is appointed who has charge of the person of the Ward and a vaguely defined power with regard to the administration of the estate. This arrangement provides that jumble of conflicting authorities, and absence of power definitely concentrated in the hands of one capable officer, which is so dear to the British mind and accounts for so many of our administrative failures both at home and abroad.

The General Manager, who lived in one of the Maharaja's palaces at Muzaffarpur, the capital of the district of Tirhut in which most part of the Darbhanga estate lay, was one Forlong, who had been an indigo planter. He was a big, pompous man, but clear-headed and active. He wore a long cloak theatrically flung around his shoulders, and drove about in a barouche and four, followed by mounted attendants in dark green uniforms, armed with swords and carbines. The sub-manager for the Purneah portion of the estate was one Richard De Courcy, also an indigo planter, an old resident of the district well acquainted with the people, their manners and customs.

All this organization was quite new. Forlong, De Courcy and the others had only just been appointed. The first thing that had to be done was for the Collector to write an elaborate report—nothing can be done in India without the 'report'—giving minute details of the number of farms on the estate, their extent and condition, and the rent paid by each, with numerous other particulars. The piles of papers I had obtained from my office were rent rolls, reports from native subordinates, and a mass of correspondence between the Board, the Commissioner and the Collector relating to the first steps which had just been taken to bring the estate under the Court of Wards. These preliminaries having been completed my report was awaited in order to begin the actual management. The task of compiling such a report would have been difficult for anyone, but it was peculiarly so for one who was unacquainted with the intricate details of land revenue management in Bengal—a subject which, writing as I do now after thirty years' experience of it, I still consider the most difficult, confused, and complicated I have ever known. Fortunately for me, I had in De Courcy an honest, laborious, and deeply experienced helper, and with his assistance I was able, after about a month's hard work, to produce a report of formidable magnitude setting forth the present condition of the estate and making proposals for its future management. My proposals were approved and I was directed to put them into operation at once.

The Dharmpur portion of the estate, constituting my charge, lay mostly to the east of the Kusi River, and had never been visited by the Maharaja. The Brahmins, in whom, though himself a Brahmin, he implicitly believed, had set afloat an ingenious tradition that if ever the Lord of Darbhanga should cross the Kusi, his estate would pass into other hands and his ancient family come to an end. Having thus secured this portion of the estate from inconvenient surveillance, they set to work to profit by the superstition. It is an ancient custom for wealthy Hindu land-holders to make gifts of land free of rent to Brahmins, ostensibly for their support and to defray the expenses of the worship of some idol. They are taught that by so doing they store up for themselves rewards in a future state, and that to take away these lands is a sin of the deepest dye. Thus all the idle vagabond Brahmins in the countryside had obtained rent-free grants of land in Dharmpur, and where they got a grant of ten acres, they contrived by fraud, and by pushing to the uttermost limit the traditional awe and respect for their caste, to get possession of fifty or a hundred. So that extensive tracts of rich arable land which ought to have yielded revenue to the landlord were held free by these impudent beggars. The fraud was not detected by the Maharaja, and it is doubtful whether he would have dared to remedy it even had he been able to detect it. The whole system of management was faulty. It was followed by our Government at that time and for some years later. Eventually, however, its faults were recognized, and it is now universally condemned. Anyone who in 1862 had ventured to attack it would have been snubbed as a visionary and an innovator. My own timid remonstrances, at what appeared to me, owing to my Panjab training to be a monstrous system, were ruthlessly silenced.

The system may be thus described. Every peasant who cultivated land in the estate had, of course, to pay rent for it, but as the task of collecting rents from so large a body of men would have been almost impracticable without a very large and expensive staff, the custom was to break up the estate into groups of from one to a dozen villages, and to leave each group to a contractor or 'mustàjir' who engaged to pay a certain lump sum yearly, reimbursing himself, and making a handsome profit into the bargain by collecting the rents from the cultivators, and leasing unoccupied lands to new-comers. These leases, which ran for a term of three, seven, or ten years, were put up to public auction and knocked down to the highest bidders. No attempt was made to ascertain, record, or fix the rents to be paid by the cultivators, and where competition was keen, a system of rack-renting arose in the highest degree oppressive to the ryots, and detrimental to the estate. It had only one merit, if it be a merit; that it saved the zemindar a great deal of trouble and expense, and if it led to the grinding of the wretched peasantry—well, who cared for them? There were the law courts, and a peasant who thought himself overcharged could bring a suit to have his proper rent determined. But the poverty and ignorance of the peasantry, and their fear of offending the all-powerful mustàjir, not to mention the formidable and well-organized system of false witnesses, false accounts, bribery and corruption at the disposal of the latter, combined to deter the mass of the peasantry from having recourse to law. They suffered, hungered, and died in silence. It is true, as I shall presently mention, that a very strong agitation was at this time going on about the Rent Law—the then celebrated Act X of 1859—but though the effects of this movement were strongly felt in other parts of the district, the Dharmpur estate was hardly as yet touched by it.

Thus, in assuming the management of Dharmpur, I was not expected, nor even permitted, to alter the existing system. All that was expected of me was that I should collect the arrears due from the mustàjirs in possession, and lease out the unleased villages to the highest bidders; that I should extricate the accounts from the confusion in which they then were, and defend the estate in a large number of impending law-suits—and introduce an orderly, punctual and methodical system of management in place of the existing chaos.

The last named duty had to be done first. The mustàjirs did not pay their rents into the Maharaja's treasury at Darbhanga but to a native manager resident in Purneah, who had a large staff of clerks, a Treasury, and an army of peons (guards and office messengers). This man was by caste a Kàyasth and, like most of his caste, a wily, money-grubbing intriguer. He had leased to himself and his friends and clerks, under feigned names, all the best villages in the estate at absurdly low rents, which they never paid; the manager contriving, by clever jugglery with the accounts, and by sending to Darbhanga circumstantial reports of imaginary destruction of crops by flood or drought, to conceal the knowledge of these defaults. He had also numerous friends at the court of the Maharaja who were induced by bribes and presents to assist in the fraud, and to prevent complaints from reaching the ears of the timid and indolent Maharaja.

Thus, while Jhabbu Lal the manager was accumulating wealth and building himself a great house in his native village, the revenues of the estate were daily diminishing and it no longer paid its way. Rs 60,000 had to be sent every year from Darbhanga to pay the land revenue due to the Government. When the old Maharaja died and the Government assumed charge of the estate this condition of affairs caused much anxiety and one of the first tasks Alonso Money laid down for me was to devise a remedy. This is the way with the Bengal Government. They put an inexperienced young man into a difficult post, and expect him to be equal to all the duties it entails. It is like throwing a boy into the water to teach him to swim. Somehow most of us swam.

In putting down abuses it has always been my plan to go straight at the throat of the biggest game. It is waste of time to attack and demolish the small fry. If they are crushed the big man can always find fresh tools to take their place. In digging up a white ants' nest it is but lost labour to kill the working ants, for the queen ant soon produces a fresh swarm; but if you catch the queen and destroy her, the whole nest perishes. Like Virgil's bees—'*rege in columi mens omnibus una, Amisso rupere favos,*' etc. So, much to the dismay of De Courcy, I determined to go for Jhabbu Lal. He had paid no rent for many years, though he held some of the fattest farms on the estate. This fact came out clearly as soon as the accounts were properly made out by De Courcy and his clerks. Being thus confronted, Jhabbu Lal produced a long bill of sums which he said the estate owed to him, and dangled this bill before De Courcy's eyes whenever called on to pay his arrears of rent. At last I procured a complete list of all defaulters and summoned them to appear on a certain date at De Courcy's office. On arriving there on the date fixed, we found a large concourse of people, mostly Jhabbu Lal's friends and adherents, defaulters like himself. There were also many who had come there out of curiosity to see how dexterously the great and clever Jhabbu Lal would handle the inexperienced boy-collector. Jhabbu Lal's name was called out first. He approached smiling and bowing—a tall, handsome man with a keen, intellectual face, clothed in flowing white robes. I explained that I was ordered to call for an immediate settlement of outstandings, and observed that there was a sum of so-many thousand rupees due from him which I requested him to pay at once. He smiled sweetly with half-closed eyes, and professed his readiness to obey my orders; at the same time he produced a long roll of paper covered with figures, and respectfully begged that I would order De Courcy to pay to him the amount due as shown therein, being sums which he had disbursed in the interests of the Maharaja from his own pocket. I glanced at the total and found that it was twice as much as what he owed us. For a moment I was staggered, but as I looked over the items an idea flashed into my mind. I said, 'As I am an officer of the Government I cannot do or sanction anything illegal. This account shall now be read out item by item and I will allow you for every item payment of which you could enforce against us by a law-suit—*and no more.*' It was as if a thunderbolt had fallen; a sort of sympathetic shudder ran round the dense crowd. Jhabbu Lal shook for a moment all over, then recovering he began to plead that as manager he had been obliged to pay money for purposes the law would not recognize, and if I took that course he would be ruined. De Courcy whispered to me not to go too far. But I was inflexible and the items were read aloud. They consisted, as I had seen already, mostly of alleged bribery of court officials. Rs 500 to the Judge's Serishtadar for 'favour' in a certain case, Rs 200 to the Nazir for early issue of summonses, Rs 800 to four witnesses for swearing 'in our favour' and so on. 'Tell me,' I said, 'if you sued the estate for repayment of those sums, do you think the Court would give a degree in your favour?' He was obliged to confess that he dared not sue on such a cause of action. After an hour's wrangling we got to the end of his bill, and then found that the items which he could legally claim were about one-tenth of the whole. Deducting this amount from our claim against him there remained a heavy balance due. Quite crestfallen and humble he prayed for fifteen days' grace in which to pay up. This I granted him. I was then about to go on to the next man on the list, when the whole crowd cried out with one voice that they would pay whatever was due without any further objection. They did so, and in the course of a month nearly fifty thousand rupees were paid in. I then ejected the whole lot of them from their farms, and leased the farms to really substantial men. Thus was the clique broken up, ruined and dispersed, and though many minor matters remained to be settled, further measures were effected with ease. There was, of course, no doubt in the mind of anyone who understood the subject that Jhabbu Lal's bill for bribes paid to court officials was most grossly exaggerated, he having written down 500 where he had paid fifty; also that there was not the slightest necessity for his having paid even that fifty, and that nearly all his bill in fact was a shamelessly impudent fraud. Darbhanga gave no trouble when once he and his clique were turned out. Before I left Purneah it was yielding a very handsome profit to the Maharaja. The credit of this, I need hardly say, was due far more to De Courcy than to me. My only merit, if it be a merit, was that I supported him faithfully and strongly in all he did and he nobly repaid my confidence in him.

Darbhanga affairs, however, did not occupy the whole of my time. There was all the work of the district to be attended to at the same time. One extremely important matter was the new police, the introduction and organization of which gave me much trouble. The district was divided into thirteen circles or Thànas. At some centrally situated town or village in each was a police station, also called a Thàna. In fact, the Hindustani word 'Thànà' means a station, but the use of the word was extended to the area under the jurisdiction of a station. At each Thàna was located a small force of police consisting of a head officer, called a Darogha (or sometimes Thanadar), a Muharrir or clerk, a Jamadar or sergeant, and some twelve to fifteen constables or barkandazes. The appointment, promotion, punishment and dismissal of all these men was vested in the Magistrate of the District.

The old Daroghas were a remarkable class of men, of a type now quite extinct. They ruled as little kings in their own jurisdiction, and reaped a rich harvest of bribes from all classes. The Darogha of the Purneah Thàna was a good specimen of the class. He was a tall, portly Mahommedan, grey-bearded with a smooth, sleek look, crafty as a fox, extremely polished in manner, deferential to his superiors, but haughty and tyrannical to his inferiors. With his huge scarlet turban laced with gold, his sword hung from a gold embroidered baldric, spotless white clothes and long riding boots, he bestrode a gaunt roan horse with grey eyes, a pink nose, and a long, flowing tail. The beast's legs, up to the knees, and the lower half of his tail were dyed red with henna, which was explained to imply that his rider had waded in the blood of his enemies! Thus he rode in state about his jurisdiction, followed by a crowd of barkandazes and village watchmen carrying his luggage on their heads. Everyone trembled before him, for if you offended him he could report to the Magistrate that you had committed some offence, that he suspected you of harbouring bad characters, or that you had refused him assistance in arresting criminals, and then, woe betide you! The Darogha Sahib could command as many witnesses as he wanted, all of whom would swear to anything he chose to tell them, and unless the Magistrate were uncommonly keen at detecting false evidence, your doom was sealed. In a lesser degree the Muharrir and the Jamadar imitated their chief and the barkandazes followed suit. These latter were a ragged crew getting five rupees (10/-) a month wages and eking it out by bribes. Under them again were the chaukidars or village watchmen, one or two to each village. These nominally got three rupees a month, raised by levying a few annas from each householder, but they were mostly left unpaid for months, or even years, and did not dare to incur the odium of the villagers by applying to the Magistrate to compel them to pay. In some cases instead of money they had a small plot of land given them and supported themselves by tilling it. They wore a little brass badge on a belt of coarse scarlet cloth, and were armed with an old-fashioned spear, or a rusty sword, or with an iron-bound bamboo staff. It was their duty to patrol their village by night, and if any crime was committed they were bound to go off to the Thàna at once and report it. Thus they wielded, poor and despised as they were, considerable influence. If it suited an influential zemindar or a leading villager to conceal a crime the chaukidar must be bribed or bullied to hold his tongue. Everybody was interested in keeping the matter quiet, for a visit from the Darogha was a thing to be dreaded. It cost, of course, far more to induce the Darogha to hush up a case, not to mention the cost of feeding the great man and his followers and the loss of time to villagers who were pressed into the service to carry his luggage and that of his ragged regiment. Moreover, the police seldom visited a village without practising a little torture on persons whom they pretended to suspect in order to get money out of them. Undoubtedly a great amount of crime was concealed, innocent men were tried and sentenced on false evidence dexterously got up by the police, while guilty ones got off by paying the same potent body to screen them. On the other hand the Daroghas were often splendid detectives, and they certainly knew all the criminals and suspicious characters, and could lay their hands on them whenever it suited them to do so. Under a strong-willed, active Magistrate whom they feared they did excellent work. If honest, or passably honest—and there were, here and there, some who were so—they kept their Thànas in capital order, and from the powerful personal influence which they wielded, and their profound acquaintance with the people, they were able to do much that their over-drilled and over-regulated successors cannot do, and apparently never will be able to do.

However, the old system was undoubtedly unsatisfactory and an Act was passed sweeping it away and introducing a new one. There was an Inspector-General of Police in Calcutta who was to rule over all the police in Bengal. In each Division there was to be a Deputy Inspector-General, and in each District a District Superintendent with Assistants under him who was to supervise the police of the District. He was to be subordinate to the Magistrate in all matters relating to the detection and suppression of crime, but independent of him in regard to the drill, discipline, and internal organization of the force. In fact, there was to be a regularly organized Police Department. The higher officers down to the Assistant Superintendents were all English and mostly gentlemen. They had not the faintest or most rudimentary idea of their duties, but they held and loudly proclaimed the opinion that the power of the Magistrates was at an end, and that they were going to rule in their stead. Many of them were old military men, like the 'Cutcherry Colonels' of the Panjab; for the Indian Government in those days acted on the assumption that military men were fit for any duties; and were apparently not required with their regiments.

The introduction of the new police into Purneah took place in June 1862 a few days before I joined and all the measures for organizing it fell on me, aided (or rather hindered) by the new District Superintendent, Major Francis Crossman. He was about the most absolutely unfitted man for such a post that one could imagine. A tall, handsome, soldierly man, a perfect *beau sabreur*, extravagant, witty and wild, he had begun his career in a cavalry regiment and was always getting into scrapes and being with difficulty saved by influential friends, of whom he had a large stock. Though he has long been dead, yet there are sons and daughters of his still alive, for whose sake I hold my pen, and refrain from relating his numerous reckless and amusing escapades. Peace to his memory! He cost me many an anxious moment while I was painfully labouring to collect suitable men for enlisting in the new police, and when I had assembled a batch for him to select from, I would find him playing cards with some friends, drinking brandy and soda and singing *grivois* French songs to his guitar. If I did succeed in getting him to ride down to the parade ground, he would glance scornfully at my recruits, make one or two very witty and very indecent jokes in excellent Hindustani which set them all laughing, and ride away without either approving or rejecting any of them. At last, in despair, I enlisted the requisite number myself, and sent the enlistment rolls to Crossman who signed them without looking at them. Having thus collected some 800 men and distributed them to the various police stations, the next job was to get the old Daroghas whom we had been obliged to retain to teach them their duties. These old gentlemen were metamorphosed as regards their outward appearance, but *cucullus non facit monachum*, and the dark blue military coat with sword and belt and cartouche box did not make them into soldiers. But they all had to wear it, and learn drill into the bargain. Old Army drill-sergeants were sent out to teach the new force and long and weary were their labours. It took years before the new police looked or moved like soldiers. The great point however was to prove that this new and heterogeneous force officered by an equally heterogeneous mass of military men, clerks, protégés of bigwigs, and broken-down planters, none of whom had ever had the slightest practise in detecting crime, would indeed work the wonderful reforms that were expected from them. So it was first pointed out to me that Purneah had long borne a bad name for 'dacoities', and that now I had that excellent mechanism the new police to work with there would be no excuse for me if I did not at once suppress all crime and disorder. This was in 1862. When I last visited Purneah in 1889, more than a quarter of a century later, dacoity was as rampant as ever. You cannot make an ignorant peasant into a clever detective merely by dressing him in a blue coat and red turban, nor even by teaching him the manual of platoon drill.

Dacoity (correctly 'dakàiti') is robbery by a gang organized in a peculiar way. Living ostensibly as mere ordinary peasants, there are in every district in Bengal, numbers of men generally of low caste who really earn their living by this crime. They are all known to one or two experienced old hands who act as organizers and leaders. The leaders are constantly on the watch and find out some house where there is property to be plundered. When the house is fixed on, two or three of them meet and plan the job; then they go round separately and privately to the various rascals whom they select to help them, choosing purposely men living as far apart as possible, and by preference unknown to each other. These they bid to be present at a certain time and place. At the appointed hour, generally a little before midnight on a dark and rainy night, fifteen or twenty men assemble in a lonely spot. All are armed with sticks with perhaps a sword and a gun or two. They carry torches and usually have their faces muffled in black cloth. When all are assembled they march to the spot and on reaching it surround the house to be attacked, light their torches and rush into the house shouting aloud, whence the name of the offence (*dâk* means 'shout', and *dakait* 'shouter'). All the villagers roused from their sleep, often also the village watchman (who ought to be patrolling the village but who is frequently an accomplice) barricade themselves in their houses from fear, and the dacoits break into the house, bind the inmates, striking and wounding all who oppose them and plunder everything they can lay their hands on. They then carry off their booty, and hearing them depart the villagers come out and follow them at a respectful distance in hopes of being able to recognize one or two of them. But a shot or two, or even some threatening shouts from the dacoits, usually suffice to prevent them from coming too close, and the band runs off with its plunder to some lonely place where the booty is divided. Each man takes his share, and they disperse in different directions, usually burying the plunder in some quiet place where they can find it later on. Some are careless enough to take their share home.

Such a crime is obviously very difficult of detection. The Daroghas of the old school, unscrupulous as they were, knew the people well and were often very successful in detecting crime. Many of them knew the leaders of the dacoit gangs and tolerated them in return for such share of the proceeds of their robberies as might be agreed upon. But if it happened, as it occasionally did, that the Magistrate insisted on any particular dacoity being detected, the Darogha would send for the leader and tell him that he must positively arrest someone this time. The leaders would then meet and selecting three or four of the younger members of the gang would tell them that it was their duty to suffer for the rest. A few of the least costly articles plundered, such as brass lotahs (drinking pots), platters, and a bracelet or two of coarse silver, would be placed in the houses of the selected victims and duly found by the Darogha who had been previously informed of the arrangement. Then the culprits would be arrested, tried and sentenced to various terms of imprisonment. After their release they were received back into the gang with honour as men who had given their proofs and passed their apprenticeship to the trade. Thus the gang flourished unmolested, the Darogha acquired a reputation for ability, the Magistrate and Judge were satisfied, and everyone was happy.

In the new police the mistake was made of supposing that crime could be detected by rules and laws. The new police Inspectors were tied hand and foot by elaborate formalities, they were obliged to report daily every step they took, and were severely punished—ridiculously so considering how new they were to the work—if they did anything not laid down in the law and rules. Consequently they were utterly and hopelessly unsuccessful. The old Daroghas shrugged their old shoulders and said that if this was the way we were going to work we should never succeed. They held, and not without reason, that you must to a great extent fight the criminal classes with their own weapons, fraud, bribes, spies and torture—'set a thief to catch a thief' in fact—and that if you were tied down to a law invented by foreigners who did not half understand the ways of the natives, you must fail. And fail we did, ignominiously for some years, until the new police learnt how to use the 'extra-legal' methods of the old police without being found out. Even after they had got into the way of their work this new police was not after all very much better than the old, in spite of the flourish of trumpets with which it was introduced.

CHAPTER XI

PURNEA, 1862–1864

TIME went rapidly by for me, engaged as I was from early morning till late evening in a never-ceasing variety of occupations, revenue, police, magisterial, roads, jails, education, crops and condition of the people, and a dozen other things. In the middle of September we had a mighty flood. The low, marshy, alluvial plain of Purneah is intersected by many rivers flowing from the Himalayas to the Ganges. These rivers are constantly changing their course, and none so badly as the great Ganges itself. In this flat country the rivers run on beds of silt brought down by their waters from the mountains. Thus they are higher than the surrounding plains, and when they are swollen by the rains of August they often break through their soft, sandy banks and pour a devastating flood all over the fields and, scooping out fresh channels, leave their old bed in the condition of a half-empty, almost stagnant, marsh.

One of these deserted river-beds called the Saurà ran through the town of Purneah, and though fordable in many places was never quite dry. In some places, especially just under the town, it was for some distance very deep, and a large, rickety bridge spanned it. The Saurà was an offshoot of the Little Kusi, which itself was an offshoot of the Great Kusi. The Little Kusi ran to the south-west of the station, some two miles off. Between it and the Saurà, in the heart of the station, lay a large stagnant marsh or swamp closely connected with both rivers by numerous half-choked channels. On the 19th of September, after several days and nights of incessant rain, the rivers overflowed into the swamp and the waters rose and spread all over the country, submerging large numbers of native huts, carrying off men and cattle, breaking down bridges and embankments, tearing up large trees, and entirely cutting off all communication between the town and the European station.

When I woke in the morning police Inspectors were already waiting at the door for orders. A native official when in any difficulty has only one idea—to obtain instructions from his official superior—the old joke is hardly an exaggeration which represents the Bengali stationmaster of a small railway station in the jungle as telegraphing to the manager in Calcutta: 'Furious tiger on station platform. Please wire instructions.'

So I got up and found my house an island in a far-stretching waste of water. It did not take long to dress and mount, and in pouring rain to start for the edge of the submerged tract, not without difficulty wading through the water. There we found Barnfarther, the Executive Engineer, and Windle, his Assistant. Far across the waters we could see people in trees and clinging to the roofs of their huts, and could hear their cries for help. With characteristic selfishness the merchants who shipped cotton from the town had carried off all their boats, and feeling that help, if it came at all, would come from the Europeans in the Civil station, had carefully hidden them away among the bamboo thickets on the opposite shore far down below the town. Their object was to prevent our seizing their boats and using them in the work of rescue, by which they feared their business of shipping off the cotton might be delayed. After long search we at length found two boats which the owners had not had time to remove, and in spite of their opposition, though I offered a very large sum for their hire, we seized them and set off. It was awkward and dangerous work poling these heavy boats across the strong current and we constantly were nearly upset by striking against the roof of a hut under water or the trunk of a tree. We, however, were eventually successful in rescuing all the people in danger, though many of them, especially the old women, were very unwilling to quit their insecure perches on the roofs lest someone in their absence should steal their poor shreds of possessions. We found the Roman Catholic priest in the upper storey of his little house. His chapel was full of water, and he was in great fear for his life. But he was reluctant to leave. He could only speak Italian, and in those days I could not speak that language well. By degrees we discovered that he was loath to leave his sacred vessels and robes in the sacristy, and it was not till I promised, half in broken Italian and half in Latin, to place a guard of police over the chapel that he consented to jump out of his window, with his beloved violin in one hand and his breviary in the other, into our boat. We broke down from fatigue and the ceaseless drenching rain several times and had to go home and change our dripping clothes and snatch a mouthful of food. Five times we explored the submerged country and brought boatloads of natives to land. The last time, late in the evening as we were returning in a small dug-out canoe, my bamboo pole snapped off short and we drifted towards the broken bridge on the high road over which the water was rushing in a cataract. Our lives seemed lost, but Barnfather, who was in the stern of the canoe, flung me his pole which I caught and with one despairing effort sent the light boat hard and fast into the branches of a tree which overhung the water.

Then my head began to go round and I hardly knew how we managed to wade ashore or what became of the boat. But everyone had been rescued, and provision made for food and lodging for them. Next day Barnfather, Windle and I were prostrate with fatigue and rheumatism, and aching in every limb. The floods soon subsided but fearful damage was done to life and property. And yet, to such an extent does familiarity with danger dull the fear of it, the people soon rebuilt their huts on the same sites and in a few months nothing but the huge trees lying where they had been swept by the current remained to tell of the great flood. Even these were soon cut up and sold for firewood. We got the thanks of the Government for what we had done.

We began now to know the indigo planters. The planters of Purneah were almost a class apart, being on a different footing from the Bengal planters on the one hand and those of Behar on the other. They were nearly all Eurasians and had been settled on their estates for two or three generations. India was their home. Most of them had never been to England and did not want to go. They were nearly all Roman Catholics. The girls were educated—often brilliantly—by the nuns of the Loreto Convent at Darjeeling which was little more than a first-class boarding-school. There they were taught English, French, Italian, music and singing with some less showy but more useful accomplishments. The boys went to the Martinière, St Paul's School, or St Xavier's College, Calcutta. The planters were in some cases owners of the land on which their indigo was grown, in others they held it on long leases. This feature in their position gave them great influence over the ryots in all the villages composing their large estates or farms of several thousand acres, and as they were on the whole mild and liberal they were generally popular. If autocratic, this was no more than what the ryot was accustomed to. In all departments the Indian native prefers a benevolent despot to a red-tape administrator. There were, of course, among the planters despots who were not benevolent, but these were the exception, and there are exceptions to every rule. There was, however, hardly a single exception to the rule of open-hearted, lordly hospitality. The factory was open to all, and all were welcome to a good dinner, lots of drink and a bed for the night or a dozen nights. Elephants for tiger-hunting, horses for journeys, boats, buggies, guns, spears—all were readily lent to any European official or non-official who asked for them civilly. Nothing delighted them more than to invite some sixty or seventy guests to a party lasting three or four days, with hunting and shooting for the men all day, dancing for the ladies all night and perpetual feasting, billiards and cards all day and night for those who liked it. There were in Purneah in 1862 some thirty of these factories, chiefly in the south and west of the district. Old Joe S—— was the acknowledged doyen of the planter class. At his factory, some sixteen miles from the station, he kept open house. His family was of patriarchal dimensions—there were over twenty children. They all lived together in the great old house in perfect harmony, with a numerous horde of servants who lived in a range of huts in the grounds as big as an ordinary village, and brought their own children into the house to serve as soon as they were old enough. Then there were the factory servants, clerks and overseers—a large crowd; also outdoor servants such as gardeners, grooms, boatmen and the like. Joe's elephants, horses, bullocks, cows, goats and sheep and his big pleasure barges or 'budgerows', and cargo-boats required quite an army of attendants. There was room for all of them in house, huts, outhouses, cabins and warehouses about the premises, and old Joe never seemed to know how many there were of them. In fact he hardly knew how many children he had. I have seen him take up a little coffee-coloured imp that was crawling about the veranda and look at it for some time before he was certain whether it was one of his own offspring or not. He was a short, stout, oldish man, very dark in complexion with a full, round face, rather puffy features, slightly bald; and with good nature beaming in every line of his face, and every curve of his jolly, broad back and fat paunch. But with all his geniality he was sharp as a needle, and an excellent man of business, making every year large profits from his indigo. He subscribed handsomely to the support of the Roman Catholic chapel at Purneah, which his father or grandfather had built, and the poor, half-starved priest would have been wholly starved had it not been for the liberal gifts of food and money he received from Joe and his family.

The Purneah system of indigo-growing was that of lease and advance. On a 'dihàt', or group of villages held by a factory, of some sixty or eighty thousand acres all the ryots were compelled to grow indigo on some portion of their lands, and when the crop was ripe in June, to cut it and bring it to the factory where it was manufactured. They all received advances of seed, and cash, and the value of the indigo plants which they delivered at the factory was credited against the advance. The indigo, which is a small bush or shrub, was bound in bundles and measured by passing a chain of a certain length round the bundle; a rupee was paid for so many bundles. Then the ryot, after his accounts were adjusted, had to accept a fresh advance for the next year. They were thus always in debt to the factory, and were purposely kept so, to ensure their subserviency.

It was my duty to see that the ryots were not oppressed, while at the same time I was expected to keep on good terms with the planters. The task was easy with good, liberal, just-minded planters, but I once or twice had a little difficulty with those who were not so. On the whole, however, I got on very well with the Purneah planters. My difficulties occurred later on with a very different lot.

About this time we had bad news from home. My poor father, who had never recovered from the double shock of my brother Willie's death, and the disappointment of not getting the living of St James's, fell very ill and was ordered by the doctor to go to a German bath. He chose Langen Schwalbach, a place which he had read about in a charming book, Sir Francis Head's *Bubbles from the Brunnen of Nassau*. My brother Pearson, who had exchanged from the 69th to the 1/11th Regiment at Dublin, got leave and accompanied him. It was supposed (erroneously, as it turned out) that having learnt German at King's College, he was able to speak it, and my father's knowledge of languages was confined to a little French. But Pearson found himself unable to talk a word of German and as his leave soon expired he left my father alone in Germany and went home. My poor father tried to get home alone; he got down the Rhine, and managed somehow to reach Antwerp where he appears to have quite lost his head. He was put on board the steamer for London, and reached home safely, no one seems to know how. But he left all his luggage behind him, as also a handsome gold watch and chain, and arrived at Hereford Square, Brompton, where he was then living, absolutely penniless and unable to give any clear account of how he had got home. With much difficulty some of his friends traced his movements, and recovered his luggage and watch from the hotel at Antwerp. The hotel-keeper had kept them till his bill was paid, and the captain of the steamer had kindly taken my father home, seeing that he was a man of good position and trusting to find his friends and so get paid. My father's friends, James Knowles and Stainforth settled with both. But it was found necessary to put my father into a private asylum where he remained for about six months. In March 1863 he was sent home sane, but in very feeble health. The parishioners of St James's subscribed a handsome sum which was handed to my mother by Mr Kempe the Rector. My father had, of course, to resign his appointment, and I had to send home as much money as I could spare for the support of my parents. After his recovery he wrote me several long letters, very affectionate in tone but rather incoherent in style.

In June 1863 my youngest brother Harry, having inherited a sum of

£500 under my grandfather's will, emigrated to Natal intending to be a farmer there. Of his subsequent history I shall tell more at a later date.

In the beginning of 1863 I lost my appointment for a short time, as a senior man came out from home and had to be provided for. He was Sir William Herschel, son of the celebrated astronomer and though a man of very eccentric habits was an extremely charming companion, full of reading of all kinds, a fascinating talker and a most enthusiastic worker. We enjoyed his society very much and he taught me a great deal during the short time he was at Purneah. He did not stay very long and by the end of March he got another berth, and I recovered my appointment.

All this year passed in the monotonous but ever interesting round of business. Governing men is grand work, the noblest of all occupations though perhaps the most difficult, and as I acquired by degrees more experience and greater familiarity with those petty but indispensable matters of routine which hang about all work, I began to feel my strength and enjoy my duties more and more. Sir Cecil Beadon, the Lieutenant-Governor of Bengal, and his Secretary, the Hon. Ashley Eden, passed through Purneah twice on their way to and from the hill station of Darjeeling, and approved of my work, though they laughed a little at my "Panjabi" ways, which were too hot-headed and impetuous for them. But I made a favourable impression by my sanitary measures and by two *causes célèbres* which I carried through with success.

The first case was that of Jaynaràyan Singh, one of the most influential zemindars in the district. His brother, Uday Narayan, had taken a large farm in the Darbhanga estate in collusion with the manager under the old régime. He had never paid any rent and never meant to, and the amount due from him had run up in the course of years to a considerable figure. We had obtained a decree against him in the Judge's court, but this is only one step, and the easiest, in the process. The real difficulty is in realizing, or as it is technically called 'taking out execution' of, the decree. For this purpose the creditor has to indicate some property of the debtor's, and to apply to the court to attach and sell it. But Uday, being a younger son, had no property of his own, merely a joint share in the family estates. If he had any money or other effects which were his sole property, he had so concealed them that our agents could not discover them. At length De Courcy got news that our debtor was staying with his brother Jaynaràyan, and advised that we should apply to the Judge for a warrant for his arrest, seizure of the person being the last resource allowed by the law when no property is found. The warrant

was granted, and as opposition was anticipated, the Judge ordered
that the Magistrate should send police to assist his peons (or bailiffs).
The police were sent, but the sergeant or head constable in command,
holding that 'discretion is the better part of valour', discreetly posted
them in hiding some little distance from Jaynaràyan's house, a large
and strongly-built place surrounded by trees and bamboos. The peons
approached the large entrance tower, the gate of which was apparently
closed and barred. Someone from an upper window hailed them and
asked what they wanted. They produced their warrant, flourished it in
the air, and demanded the body of Uday Narayan. The voice replied
that he was not there, and added that if they did not go away they
would be fired on. Simultaneously the barrel of a musket was thrust
out through the window. The peons fled and sheltered themselves
behind the trees, whence they shouted to the police for help. Those
gallant warriors, some six or eight in number, advanced in all the
bravery of their new uniforms but without their rifles, which they had
humanely left behind. Thus reinforced the heroic band dodged about
from one tree to another till they reached a point whence they could
safely make a rush to the great gate, which turned out not to be barred
or locked, but only put to. Penetrating into the courtyard, they found
it empty, as were also all the rooms around it and those in the tower.
While uncertain what to do next they heard a great noise of shouting
from some inner court, whereupon they rushed out and hid behind the
trees again. Then from the gardens at the side of the house, which like
all native gardens were a dense mass of foliage entangled with luxuriant
creepers into an impenetrable screen, there emerged a procession of
elephants, surrounded by a crowd of Jaynaràyan's retainers armed with
swords and spears and an old, rusty matchlock or two. The police said
there were two hundred men in all, a conventional way of saying about
twenty or thirty. On the first elephant rode Jaynaràyan armed with a
good, modern rifle, and on the next the debtor Uday, also armed. Some
of the rabble caught one of our peons, snatched the warrant from him,
stuck it on the top of a spear and carried it off in triumph. All the while
the guns were kept pointed at the peons and at the valiant police who
did their best to keep out of harm's way. The procession then moved off,
Jaynaràyan shouting to the peons to give his salàm (compliments) to
the Collector and tell him he was taking Uday away out of the Collector's jurisdiction. Thereupon they all marched off across a small stream
into the neighbouring district of Bhagulpore. The effect of this step
was that we must now move the Judge to send the warrant for execution
to the Judge of Bhagulpore, some hundred miles off. This would take

time, and meanwhile our debtor would disappear into space. As soon as the procession was out of sight the police arose in their might, entered the house, and in a backyard found and most heroically arrested, two old men; one a washer of pots, the other a gardener; bore them off to the police station, and sent in a long report together with these two hardened ruffians for trial on the charge of resisting the officers of the Government in the execution of their duty. Of course, the facts as stated in the police report were very different from those given above, which only came out by degrees in the course of a strict investigation. I was in camp close by at the time and had I anticipated that there would be such cowardice on the part of the police I should have gone myself with the warrant. As it was I held a searching inquiry, and succeeded in arresting two of the men of Jaynarayan's escort who had pointed their guns at the peons. The next morning, about nine, I had just got back from a long ride on some other business and was standing in front of the tents talking to my wife and playing with my boy David, when a palki arrived and a tall, handsome, old native gentleman, dressed in cloth of gold with richly embroidered turban and Cashmere shawl, got out and approached, bowing respectfully. I noticed that, as if by accident, the Head Constable of my guard with two constables came up and stood behind me at this moment. The old gentleman said that he had only just heard that two of his servants had been arrested and as he was in a position to prove that they were both perfectly innocent he begged that they might be released on bail. I asked him who he was. He replied, 'Your slave is Jaynarayan Singh.' 'Oh,' said I, 'you are just the man I am in search of—arrest him!' The old gentleman leapt back a pace or two and made as though he would run away, but the Head Constable, who had evidently anticipated this, sprang forward and seized him. So he was led off into the prisoner's tent and had to remain there about a month, during which time he marched handcuffed along with other prisoners day by day as my camp moved through the district. By the time we got back to Purneah the witnesses had arrived and he was duly tried and sentenced to two years' rigorous imprisonment (i.e. imprisonment with hard labour). He appealed to the Judge who upheld my sentence, and he then appealed to the High Court. It took that august but not expeditious tribunal six months to dispose of the appeal, and during that time, day by day as I went to inspect the jail, I saw Jaynarayan, no longer in cloth of gold and Cashmere shawl, but with a single loin-cloth hoeing cabbages in the jail garden. He put a bold face on it and would look up with a laugh and ask me, 'Has the order for my release come yet?' When I said, 'No,' he would reply, 'All right, it will come soon.' Sure enough it did come. The High Court fastened on a minor point in the evidence, misunderstood the rest; was led by a clever barrister who ingeniously distorted the whole case, and finally, with some hesitation, gave the prisoner the benefit of the doubt and directed his release. It cost Jaynaràyan Rs 6,000, and after his release he admitted to De Courcy that the charge was true and chuckled over the way his counsel had misled the High Court. Though he put such a brave face on the matter, it broke his heart and he died a few months after his release. Sad as this was, the case did incalculable good. It taught the proud, lawless, oppressive land-holders of Purneah that they could no longer defy the law and tyrannize over their poorer neighbours as they pleased. From this case dates the commencement of a new state of things in that district, which was described by the Inspector-General of Police, as 'the most lawless district in Bengal'. In the task of bringing about a better state of things I received the most valuable help from Henry Michael Weatherall, who succeeded Crossman as District Superintendent. Mike, as he was called, was a man born in India of European parents; so at least he said, but that there was 'black blood' in him from some ancestor or ancestors was undeniable. His native place was Rishra near Serampore. He spoke English with a slight accent, but Bengali and Urdu absolutely like a native. With his dusky complexion, when dressed in native clothes, he passed as a Musulman among Musulmans themselves. He was as wily as a fox, and a born detective. Having lived among natives all his life he was intimately acquainted with all their ways and tricks and superstitions and, being absolutely unscrupulous, he was a match for the craftiest criminal. He was of much use to me in the following case.

Isri Prosad was the head steward and confidential agent of Raja Lilanand Singh, a zemindar who owned large but scattered estates. The Raja was sickly, indolent, and very extravagant, but he had occasional fits of activity. In one of these fits he examined into the state of his accounts and discovered that Isri Prosad had been guilty of various acts of peculation and mismanagement, whereupon he flew into a rage and dismissed him from his service. Isri had, as usual, bestowed upon himself and his relatives long term leases of the best farms on the estate, and, of course, had paid no rent for many years. The Raja sued him for arrears of rent amounting to Rs 40,000, a part only of what was due from him. The case was tried by Ricketts, an old, experienced half-caste Deputy Collector. In his defence Isri astonished the plaintiff and the Court by producing a document, apparently in perfect form and bearing the Raja's seal, which purported to be a receipt

for the whole amount! Ricketts's experienced eye, however, detected
this as a forgery and he ordered Isri to be tried by the Criminal Court on
that charge. Mike Weatherall went to work in some mysterious way of
his own and soon produced proof that the Raja's seal had been abstracted from the box where it was usually kept and an imitation made of it
in wax, the original seal being then put back again before its absence
was noticed. He also found out and caught the men who had assisted
Isri in the business and brought the crime home to them in a con-
vincing manner. Isri and his accomplices were therefore committed
to the Sessions to take their trial for forgery and uttering a forged document. They got down a barrister from Calcutta, a man new to India,
one Coryton, who, finding his client had not got the ghost of a defence,
took to abusing the other side. The Raja, who had a disease in the hip
and could not walk, was carried into court, and as a mark of courtesy
usually accorded to natives of his rank, was allowed by the Judge a seat
on the bench. He could not have stood in the witness-box. Coryton
objected to this, but Muspratt, the Judge, a quiet, experienced old
hand, silenced him, saying, 'Mr Coryton, I will thank you to confine
yourself to your brief, it is for me to decide where the witness shall sit.'
Coryton's Old Bailey manner and brow-beating tone were quite lost
upon the Raja who did not understand a word of English and did not
even realize that he was being addressed. Such adjurations as 'Remember that you are on your oath, sir,' fell quite flat.

Asked how many servants he kept, the Raja, on the question being
translated to him, smiled and said he had not the faintest idea. Coryton
waxed furious at this and began to bully, with, 'Do you mean to tell the
court, sir, that you do not really know,' etc. But Muspratt again stopped
him by remarking that it was highly probable that the Raja did not
know how many he had. In fact, if the lawyer had ever seen a Raja's
palace with its numerous courtyards and straggling village of outhouses
all swarming with hangers-on, he would not have asked such a question.
When all the evidence was taken Coryton made a long speech, forgetting,
as barristers so often do in India, that he was not speaking to a simple-
minded, impressionable jury, but a hard-headed old judge on whom his
eloquence made no impression at all. Muspratt used on such occasions
to say that he supposed the barrister was bound to talk for so many
hours in return for his heavy fee, and he used to occupy himself during
the inevitable infliction in looking over his notes and weighing the evidence. On this occasion Coryton, having nothing to urge on behalf of
his client, fell to abusing Weatherall and Ricketts and lastly me. He
said so much about '*this* Mr John Beames—this Magistrate,' and so

on, that at last Muspratt looked up and observed, 'We are not trying Mr John Beames but Isri Prosad and I beg that you will confine your remarks to him.'

Eventually Isri Prosad got fourteen years' imprisonment and was sent to the Andaman Islands to do it. Mr Coryton was a good deal laughed at, and I was calmed in the midst of my indignation by the general sympathy I received. This is perhaps an extreme case, but there is a perpetual and perhaps natural antagonism between the Civil Service and barristers in India.

But legal matters were not by any means the sole, or even the chief, interests of the Distict Magistrate. Sanitation was even then beginning to attract attention and to present almost insoluble problems. The extreme filthiness of native habits, the apparently unconscious and unintentional, but for that very reason all the more unconquerable obstructiveness of the whole population, combined with the difficulty of draining and scavenging such towns as we had in Bengal began to thwart all our efforts. Purneah, though called a town, was in reality a collection of small, scattered hamlets dropped down promiscuously in a swamp and buried in a luxurious overgrowth of trees and bamboo jungle. Everywhere one came upon pools of black, stagnant water covered with weeds and fetid from receiving the sewage of the adjacent houses. Dark, slimy patches of mud haunted by myriads of vermin bordered the narrow, winding roads; the walls of houses and huts were green with mould, every hedge and thicket was used as a latrine, and the smells were indescribable. Nine-tenths of the population were in the lowest depth of poverty and ignorance, and even the richer and more educated classes were as indifferent to cleanliness as the rest. Like all large towns, Purneah was created a Municipality and had a body of Municipal Commissioners who had power to levy certain taxes to be applied to road-making, conservancy, scavenging and other public purposes. But the funds were always inadequate, and the half-dozen pleaders and merchants who were appointed Municipal Commissioners neither understood nor cared about any of the objects for which they had been incorporated. In fact the houses and gardens of the wealthier citizens were the most insanitary spots in the whole town, and they deeply resented any attempt at interference. The doctor and I were the only ones who really did anything. We did what we could by setting up a staff of sweepers to remove refuse and filth, cutting down the jungle, and fining people for not keeping their premises clean. Drains were made and kept clean, roads and bridges mended and a few other improvements were introduced. It got to be a regular habit with me to ride round the town every morning, attended by the Overseer, giving orders and seeing that they were carried out. But it was a hopeless task, and I was not very successful. Malarious fever was permanently endemic, with its sequela of enlarged spleen; cholera was seldom entirely absent, and the whole population was anaemic, stunted and cachectic.

Fire was my best helper. From March to June a dry wind blew from the west and the air by day was like the blast of a furnace. The huts in which the majority of the people lived were built of bamboo mats for walls and grass thatching for roofs; a woman would be cooking food on an earthen stove in one of these inflammable dwellings, a spark from the fire would alight on the dry straw, and in a moment the hut would be in flames. As soon as the fire reached the thatch, small wisps of flaming material would be blown into the air and alight on neighbouring roofs. In less than an hour the whole bazaar would be in flames, and before long a mile or more of street would be burnt to the ground. No loss of life and very little of property would occur, and the scavengers had a grand opportunity of cleaning away masses of refuse, while the fire consumed still more. The people soon rebuilt their slight huts, and the place where a fire had occurred was unusually healthy for some years afterwards.

Once, when returning from a long tour in the interior of my district after a fatiguing ride and drive of seventy miles, I saw as I approached home dense columns of smoke rising. I pushed on anxiously, for our house had a thatched roof and I knew how quickly such houses burnt. On the way I passed my boys and their ayah in a palki. My wife had sent them to a neighbour's for safety and had got much of the furniture and all our few valuables out into the garden. It was only the grass in the compound that was on fire, but the flames were creeping on, fanned by the strong wind, and were not far from the house. Servants were running aimlessly about, throwing water from earthen pots without any system, sometimes on the flames, sometimes not. I tore off my long riding-boots, had them filled with water and dribbled the water from them carefully along the advancing flames; made the servants bring branches of trees, throwing abundant wanter on the leaves, and beat out the flames with them. In an hour's time we had put it out. Like most people in that part of the country we had grown a crop of oats that year in our compound, and they had been reaped and were being threshed when some burning straw from a neighbouring hut alighted on the threshing floor and set the whole place in a blaze.

To avoid such dangers in future, not only to myself but also to the Government offices, I resolved to remove the native village lying to the west of the station and issued an order to this effect to Raja Lilanund Singh the owner. He removed the village and rebuilt it two miles off. I then established a large bazaar further to the south on some Government land. This grew and prospered, for the native town was four miles off and the residents had long been inconvenienced by having to send their servants so far to buy provisions, a business which kept them away half the day. In my new bazaar they could get their supplies close at hand. At the request of the natives I allowed it to be called 'Beames gunj'.

I visited it in 1889—twenty-five years later—and found it a flourishing mart.

CHAPTER XII

PURNEA, 1865–1866

NOW comes an important period in my service. In September 1864 it was resolved by Government to make war on Bhutan. A little before this the Hon Ashley Eden, Secretary to the Government of Bengal, had been sent on a mission to that wild, mountainous country, and had been grossly insulted when he appeared at the Court of the Raja. One of the bystanders had taken out of his mouth a quid of betelnut and thrown it in Eden's face. So the stain must be wiped out, and the 'dogs of false Tarentum' made to expiate the insult. A very large force of troops, in two columns, was to march on Bhutan, and the whole of the left column was to come through my district.

The Magistrate-Collector of an Indian district is supposed to be very much what Joseph was in the Egyptian prison, 'whatsoever was done therein, he was the doer thereof'. From vaccination to education; from warding off a famine to counting the blankets of convicts in his jail; from taking a census to feeding an army on the march, all falls on him. If he protests in the least, or fails to do everything satisfactorily, he is punished by stoppage of promotion, public censure and removal to a less important post; if he does everything well, he may, perhaps, if he has interest, get some reward. If he has no friends in power he is left to meditate on the scripture text: 'Say, we are unprofitable servants, we have done that which it was our duty to do'. Eden wrote me a hasty scrawl, not uncomplimentary, though peremptory, 'The whole of the left wing of the Bhutan field force will pass through your district, you must feed them and find carriage for their baggage and ammunition. Any expense you may incur will be sanctioned, but you will not be forgiven if a single soldier or a single bag of grain is delayed for a day on the route. If any man in Bengal can do the work, it is you. Go ahead.' This was plain speaking and I went ahead accordingly.

Heavy absorbing work was welcome to me at this time, for I had been severely shocked by the news of my poor father's death. This occurred in August 1864 and the news reached me just before Eden's letter. He died very suddenly and, to all appearances, painlessly. Sitting on a sofa he fell back and when my mother ran to lift him up, he was dead. The post-mortem examination revealed that he had been suffering from ossification of the heart and water on the brain. He was buried in Kensal Green cemetery. He was only forty-nine when he died. Ever since his marriage he had led a sad life of poverty and struggling which he bore bravely as long as his strength lasted. A highly intellectual man, with an amazing memory; a brilliant but rather overbearing talker, rather noisy and loud in his manner; a fine preacher and a most earnest, devoted parish priest, extremely popular with the radical, atheistic cobblers in Windmill Street and the adjacent slums, several of whom he converted to a true faith; physically powerful and athletic, a typical 'muscular Christian' like his friend Charles Kingsley. He belonged to the 'Broad Church' party and was equally opposed to the sacerdotalism and ritualistic excesses of the High Church and the ultra-Calvinism of the Low. A sincerely pious and earnest believer, though in his later years he had studied German books on theology to such an extent that, as he used to say, he had reduced his religion to the smallest dimensions. His loss was a great blow to me. I inherited Bashley, but the receipts from it seldom came to £200 a year, and out of this had to be paid £100 to Mrs Sleenan, and £40 to Rowland yearly, besides taxes, repairs of cottages, succession duty and lawyers' bills. Whatever was over I gave to my mother, to whom I also made a regular monthly remittance down to the day of her death twenty-three years later.

The business of the Bhutan war came thus as a relief to my mind from melancholy thoughts. The road by which the troops were to march ran for 120 miles through my district, and there were twelve encamping grounds ten miles apart, at each of which they would stop for a day and would require food for man and beast. It is one of the conditions of the permanent Settlement under which the zemindars hold their estates that they shall provide provisions for troops passing through their lands. Three of the stages through which the road passed were in the Court of Wards Estate of Darbhanga, the rest were in the estates of other zemindars. Purneah itself produces nothing but rice and the troops indented on me for wheaten flour, pulses, spice, gram and grass for the horses and cattle, firewood, straw and many other things. The date of their arrival was not known. The Government supplied me, at my earnest request, with a number of junior Civilians, one of whom I stationed at each encamping place. He had to clean and prepare the ground, see that the wells were in good order, build sheds for the supplies, arrange for the said supplies being got in, stored and served out to the regiments as they arrived, as well as to provide them with carts and other carriage. I myself from Purneah supervised the whole line. Orders were issued to the zemindars to provide the necessary supplies, and they were put to great expense in sending to Calcutta for such things as the district did not produce. With great difficulty I collected 8,500 bullock carts, nearly every cart in the district, in fact. A system was also organized for paying the carters regularly. The people of the district were shy and timid and could only be induced to work for the troops by high pay and scrupulously mild treatment. The carts had to be changed at various stages and sent back to be ready for the next regiment. Fortunately Weatherall, the District Superintendent of police, had served in the Commissariat Department during the mutiny of 1857 and his experience and knowledge of natives were of very great use to me. I placed him at Kishanganj, forty miles north of Purneah where he organized the relief of carts. There were also got together 4,500 pack bullocks and eighty elephants for use in the jungles where there were no roads for carts.

Almost before the arrangements were well finished there began a shower of telegrams from the Adjutant-General, the Quartermaster-General, the Commissary-General and various other fussy military authorities. These telegrams would often arrive in the middle of the night. After having been up since five in the morning, paying and dispatching carters, writing instructions to the various assistants about a dozen different things, riding sometimes twenty or thirty miles to settle difficulties and inspect arrangements, snatching a mouthful of food when I could, I would try to get some sleep late at night, having sent out my horses for a long ride to some important post next morning. Before I had been in bed half an hour would come a telegram, and three or four times during the night others would come. In despair I took at last to sending a stereotyped reply, 'all right, everything ready'. The ignorance, indecision and nervous fussiness of these old military blokes was indescribable. At last, after fixing several dates for its arrival and not arriving on any of them, the first regiment landed at Caragola, and for the space of about six weeks a fresh regiment arrived every two or three days. Sometimes they would come one day behind another, so that there would be seven or eight regiments on the road at once. I had to keep up a running fight with the Colonel of each regiment, every one of whom insisted on doing or having something which was, from the nature of the country, impossible or unprocurable. Then the soldiers beat the carters, who ran away and had to be pursued and brought back again, or the harassed zemindar was behind time with his supplies and severe pressure had to be put on him to bring him up to time. One or other of the youthful assistants would lose his head in the confusion, and I had to ride out thirty miles to put him straight; or the Colonel of a regiment would refuse to pay for the provisions supplied and had to have a dose of very strong language to bring him to reason. Several of them, as it was, got through without paying, and I had terrible trouble in realizing the money afterwards.

All this while the Commissariat officers sat idly by and quietly declined to help, saying that their duties did not begin till the troops reached the front. At the same time they complicated matters by pouring tons and tons of flour and other stores into the district, and calling upon me to send them forward. Thus it was my daily task for some six or seven weeks to organize, provide, supply and pay for everything, to get back from the Colonels the money I had advanced, to drive my team of assistants at the encamping grounds, to keep the zemindars up to the mark and to answer all sorts of troublesome, meddling letters from superior officers.

At last all the regiments got through to the front—there were nineteen regiments and some artillery besides a very large quantity of stores and ammunition. Just as the last regiment passed through at the beginning of November, a difficulty arose about carriage at Ilwabari, a desolate spot on the road sixty miles from Purneah, and my presence was as usual required. There was only a small, unfurnished inspection bungalow on the encamping ground but I had placed one of my Assistants there in charge and, as customary in India, relied on him for food and a bed. I picked up Weatherall at Kishangunj as I rode through and we visited several places and settled various matters on our way. When we arrived very tired at Ilwabari late at night we found that the Assistant, a careless inefficient youth, had left his post without orders and ridden on to the next encamping-ground with a regiment which had just passed through, in which several of the officers were his friends. So there was no food and no bed for he had taken his tent with him. All we could get was a tin bowl full of cold potatoes which the Musulman Head Constable kindly brought us, and some trusses of straw to lie on. After settling all the difficulties I rode back the weary sixty miles to Purneah the next morning, and, of course, found twenty different people waiting for orders and instructions, others wanting money, supplies, carriage and all sorts of things. I worked through them all as well as I could till late at night. The next morning I woke up with as bad an attack of fever as I ever had in my life. For some time I was delirious and my wife had to keep guard over the house to prevent me from being worried by military officers who would come riding up and imperiously demand to see me. She fought bravely to keep them out. When I recovered I was sent off to Darjeeling for a fortnight where I was hospitably taken in by Hereward Wake, C.B., the Deputy Commissioner.

I soon recovered in the cool, pure mountain air, and when I returned all the troops had passed through and there was a lull for a time. The cold weather was devoted as usual to camping about the district.

The war was a short and not particularly glorious one. It was over in a few months and early in 1865 the troops began their return march. First, sick and wounded officers began to straggle back, and we had to nurse them. Our house became like a hospital. General Duncombe who had commanded the left wing was brought back in a palki unable to move hand or foot from rheumatism, others had dysentery or fever; very few had wounds. Then came the troops, and all the old trouble of getting them through the district had to be gone through all over again. By March we had done it all and I then sat down to examine my accounts, and found that I had spent four lakhs and a half of rupees (say £45,000) without any sanction! A Collector is not as a rule allowed to spend any money out of the large sums that lie in his District Treasury without sanction first obtained from some higher authority, and he has to render periodically long and intricate accounts to the Accountant-General in Calcutta. That worthy's equilibrium was grievously disturbed by the spectacle of so much money spent without sanction, and in accordance with the routine of his office wrote to ask if I had any reason to assign why this unauthorized expenditure should not be debited to my personal account and recovered from my salary. Colonel Haughton at Julpiguri, who had done the same as I had and received a similar letter, replied that the Accountant-General would not recover the amount if he confiscated the income of the Colonel and his descendants to the fifth generation. This reply was deemed flippant and the Colonel was rebuked. My dear, careful wife had fortunately preserved Ashley Eden's letter above quoted and by sending a copy of it to Government, with an indignant protest, I got the whole sum passed, but it was not until far into 1866 that I recovered from the military authorities the sums I had advanced to them.

When all was over I received a curt, formal letter of thanks from the Government of India—John Lawrence, who was then Viceroy, never praised his subordinates if he could help it though he punished severely for the slightest fault. The praises of the Government of Bengal were, however, warm, and I had to be satisfied with that. My health was much injured by my exertions and I was not for some years to come as robust or active as I had been before this terrible strain on body and mind.

On the 7th March 1865 was born my third son Rupert. He came into the world very precipitately—before my wife could reach her bed,—and was caught by the nurse in her apron! My wife soon recovered but David and Freddie had begun to feel the effects of the deadly climate of Purneah. David especially suffered from enlarged spleen, the normal sequela of malarial fever. Eventually I was obliged to send them all to Darjeeling, where I took a house for them. They stayed there from April to November, and thoroughly recovered their health. I took in some of my assistants to chum with me, and for the first time learned the newly introduced game of hockey on horseback, or polo as it is now called. We used to play every evening, riding small ponies from Manipur, the original home of the game; or hill ponies from Darjeeling or Bhutan.

I did not, however, succeed in shaking off the effects of the overwork caused by the Bhutan campaign, and in July I was obliged to take three months' leave and join my family at Darjeeling. This place is now so well known that no description of it is necessary. It was very much smaller then than it is now and there was no railway to it. I soon recovered my health in the sweet, cool air and getting tired of doing nothing I planned an excursion into the interior of the mountains. A young ensign of the 80th Regiment, named Howard, accompanied me. We took about a dozen coolies, each bearing on his back a large basket or 'kilta' in which were our bedding, clothes, cooking utensils, food and wine. We had also an interpreter and guide, a merry old Lepcha named Kin-lé. Howard did not like his first day's experience and returned to the station leaving me to continue the journey alone. I found climbing up the steep mountain paths very trying at first, but after a day or two I got more used to it. Our road lay over high, steep ridges one after another. To avoid the malaria of the deep narrow valleys we slept every night in a native hut on the summit of a mountain. Early in the morning we rose, and while Kin-lé cooked coffee and eggs I went out with towel and soap to some pool among the rocks where a clear, fresh spring of cold water gushed out. Then I performed the strange and, to the Lepchas inexplicable, ceremony of washing. This amused them very much. After a light breakfast our luggage was packed in the kiltas and we started off in Indian file down the steep slopes by scarcely discernible footpaths. Roads beyond British territory there were, of course, none.

Six hours' walking, always lower and lower, brought us at noon to the bottom of the hill where there was usually a cane bridge over a small river. The vegetation was dense and tropical—wild plantains, tree ferns, orchids, creepers in tangled masses—and the heat intense. Here we rested and lunched on biscuits, cold hard-boiled eggs and *murova*, a slightly acid fermented drink made from millet. Then began the long and toilsome ascent. All the afternoon we laboured up and up with frequent stoppages till nightfall found us at the top, some seven or eight thousand feet above the plains. The villages are all built at this elevation. They seldom consist of more than five or six huts with an occasional Buddhist temple. We always entered the best house in the place and were always heartily welcomed by the smiling housewife. She swept a corner near the fireplace for me, on which my bedding was spread, brought me a pot of murova with which, and a pipe, I solaced myself after my walk. Sometimes my stockings would be glued to my legs with congealed blood from countless leech bites. The leeches hang to the bushes and stick to the legs of people brushing their way by. At first they are as thin as threads but they suck and suck till they swell big enough to be seen, when they can be picked off. The good woman would bring warm water and bathe my legs and put on a plaster of some leaves known to the hill people. After the first day or so I found it best to walk with bare legs. Kin-lé, who marched close behind me, kept a sharp look-out and as soon as he saw a leech on my calf he squirted a jet of tobacco on to it from the quid which he chewed. This made it drop off, and stopped the bleeding at the same time. A dash of ice-cold water from any one of the little springs we were constantly passing prevented the bite from getting inflamed. The Lepcha huts were spacious wooden structures containing one room often forty or fifty feet long by twenty broad. They are built on sloping ground so that while one side rests on the earth, the other is propped on strong wooden posts. The floor, walls and roof are made of massive slabs of wood. In the space under the house are kept the cattle and fowls. On the side of the hut which rests on the hill a space is left in the flooring where the earth is bare and three sharp stones are set up. Between these a fire burns night and day and a huge iron kettle or pan full of water is always boiling. Round the fire is a row of vessels made by cutting a stem of the giant bamboo into sections. As soon as a visitor arrives—and people seemed to be dropping in all day long—the housewife fills one of these pots with murova grain, pours hot water on it, and places it before the guest, who sits sucking up the liquor through a reed of a very small kind of bamboo hardly bigger than a straw. It tastes rather like weak hock and water.

Kin-lé would buy a fowl and cook it for me, and this, with a tin of sausages, some biscuits and a little brandy and water, made a decent dinner. Being Buddhists these simple people have no restrictions of caste, and greedily ate up my leavings. Their own meal of rice being over we sat smoking and drinking murova. The Lepchas are a very merry, cheerful folk, and I managed to keep up a pleasant conversation with them through the interpreter.

On the sixth day as we toiled up the southern face of a huge mountain, threading our way among the dense foliage, perspiring and leech-bitten, we suddenly came upon a bare shoulder on which ran, from north to south for 650 yards, the 'Gya-zhing-men-dong' or Prayer Wall of Sikkim. It is a straight wall of rough stones some four feet thick and six high, loosely put together without mortar. On both sides is an un-broken row of large slabs on each of which is rudely carved a lotus, on each leaf of which is one of the letters of the sacred Buddhist formula. 'Om mani padme hum'. At each end and in the middle is a square tower about twelve feet high bearing similar slabs and crowned with a mass of boughs from which hang rags of various colours, votive offer-ings from pilgrims. Beyond this was an almost interminable flight of stone steps, rugged and uneven which led up through brushwood to the high plateau of Reb-din-chi, the former capital of Sikkim. Here amidst ruined walls stood the ancient palace of the Rajas, a solid building of dark grey stone, three storeys high with a steep stone staircase on the outside. More steps led higher still to the crest of the mountain where stands the monastery of Pem-yong-chi, the richest in Sikkim. This also is a solid building of stone, three storeys high with huge gateway of wood richly carved. On our way up we passed numbers of Lepchas and Bhutias carrying presents of food to the Bhikkhus or monks—the Lamas as they call them. We found the monks just going in to service. Sturdy, good-natured fellows they looked, clad in red cloth gowns with capacious sleeves and cowls. The Abbot or Do-rje-la-ben (literally 'thunderbolt—wielder') wore a mitre of red with yellow flaps. He had a fat, sly Chinese face with narrow, oblique eyes and a scanty white beard.

The church, which occupied the ground floor, had a nave and two aisles. Every inch of wall, roof and pillars was covered with paintings done by artists from China in red, yellow and other glaring colours. They represented scenes in the past births of Gautama Buddha and the sacred Beings of the Mahàyàna School, such as Avalokita. An unlimited supply of dragons and other grotesque monsters filled the vacant spaces. Seen through the dim light from the open door and a few oil lamps, these paintings had a rich and pleasing effect. On the high altar was an image of Buddha some twelve feet high painted a dark blue, in the attitude of contemplation. Down both sides of the nave were low seats for the monks, the abbot taking the first seat on the right hand looking up the nave. Before him on a low stool was his do-rje, a small staff of brass fashioned in the conventional shape of a thunderbolt. They gave me a seat in a side aisle. When all were seated each monk plunged his hand

into the bosom of his capacious frock and pulled out a small wooden
bowl, into which a young attendant poured tea from a wooden pot
neatly laced with a woven covering of cane. Holding the bowls poised on
their finger tips they waved them slowly round over their heads while
they chanted a long, solemn litany in Tibetan, after which they drank
their tea, and with many bows to the altar departed one by one. I also
had a cup of tea. It was brick tea, made of broken tea-leaves, stalks and
refuse cemented into a cake with bullock's blood. It is made into a thick,
soupy liquid, with hot water, salt, and rancid butter and, strange to
say, is not nasty. When we emerged the monks had all disappeared and
the great stone platform in front of the temple lay bare and white in the
sunshine. All round was a view unparalleled in the whole world. Far
below us the steep mountain slopes sank away through many grada-
tions of colour, from rich, mellow green to deep greys and violets in the
dark, sunless gorges. Across these narrow winding valleys rose other
hills, and beyond them others, and yet others till, far off on the southern
horizon, the eye dimly perceived Darjeeling on its wooded crescent with
cloud-capped Senchal towering behind it. To the west the high shoulder
of the hill shut out the view, but all along the northern sky stood in
awful majesty the loftiest mountains in the world—a long white chain
of snowy masses rifted into peaks and domes and ridges, none less than
25,000 feet in height. The shadowy clefts down their white flanks were
deep purple and here and there a great glacier, like a waterfall suddenly
frozen, hung arrested in the midst of its leap from a grey scarred peak.
From the cloudy top of Kahsuperi, itself some 7,000 feet high, the eye
wandered down and up over peak after peak till stopped by the mighty
wall of iron-grey rock streaked and lined with snow which reared up
and up till it culminated in the triple top of Kanchangjinga. It was a
sight such as one only sees once in a lifetime. One feels as if hung in
mid-air between heaven and earth. The unfathomable depths of the
great purple gorges, the constantly varying play of light and shadow on
the soaring pinnacles of everlasting snow, the plumy, waving woods of
every hue made up a picture rare and never to be forgotten.

I turned reluctantly away to visit the Abbot who sent me a polite
invitation to murova and sweetmeats in his cell. It was built on the edge
of a deep precipice just under the crest of a plateau among some graceful trees. We sat on a couch of furs looking out over the unique landscape from a delicately carved wooden balcony. He had been over the
snows to Lhassa to receive consecration from the Dalai Lama, but he
was not disposed to be communicative to a European about the
mysterious sacred city. He was, however, very voluble about the late

Bhutan war and the iniquities of Tongsu Pinlo, the Prime Minister of Sikkim.

We returned to Darjeeling by another and less difficult route than that by which I had come. It was, however, less frequented and less populous. Here the Lepcha coolies had many opportunities of showing their dexterity with the 'ban', a long, straight knife which they carry. They would cut down bamboo and build a shed in less than ten minutes, or throw a bridge over a stream, lashing the bamboo poles together with tough creepers. We ran short of provisions and one night had nothing to eat but bamboo tops. They are the young, tender shoots of the plant and are cooked in butter. In appearance and taste they are not unlike asparagus. The last night, after eighteen miles of heavy walking over hill and dale we reached Gok, a small police station just inside British territory. I was hungry and weary, and the porters had lagged behind. The police had nothing to offer but coarse rice, and very little of that. As I sat waiting outside the little hut in the moonlight, up the steep hill path among the dark mossy trunks of the tall trees came, with a light springy step, a tall, active youth in Bhutia dress. To my great surprise he addressed me in good English, and told me that people in Darjeeling were wondering what had become of me. Then diving into the bosom of his capacious robe, the place where Bhutias carry all their luggage, he produced a bottle of brandy, a cold turkey cut into bits and wrapped in a newspaper, hard-boiled eggs, and a loaf of bread. These he generously shared with me and we made a hearty meal. Then he lent me his big upper garment and in a tight-fitting suit which he wore under it, he started off again to be out all night shooting bears. This was one Tommy Masson, a young Englishman born and bred in India, who had adopted native dress and customs side by side with English ones. His father, a Captain in the Army, had retired and lived at Darjeeling with a large family of sons and daughters whom he allowed to grow up wild and untrained.

Next morning, descending the hill of Gok, we crossed the cane bridge over the Rangit to commence the ascent to Darjeeling. To this spot my dear, thoughtful wife had sent my pony, also a bottle of claret, a cold pie and other delicacies with a white cloth to spread them on which made the meal look even better than it tasted after my long roughing in wild places. After doing ample justice to the good things I mounted my pony and scrambled up the long, interminable zigzags into Darjeeling. Of course it rained all the way, but at length, wet through and very, very dirty I reached home in safety about three o'clock.

The exposure and fatigue of the journey brought on a bad attack of fever and I was delirious for some time. The doctor pronounced that I must not stay in Purneah as the malarious climate had gained too firm a hold on me and, in fact, on us all. Eden kindly promised to transfer me on the first opportunity to a healthier district. As soon as I was well we returned to Purneah, and all the winter I was engaged in winding up the accounts of the Bhutan campaign so as to be ready to leave the district as soon as my transfer came. It did not come till April when we had almost given up hope. I was transferred to the district of Champàran and we left Purneah on the 16th April 1866 after a stay there of very few days short of four years.

CHAPTER XIII

CHAMPARAN, 1866–1867

WE went by train from Sahibganj to Patna where we stayed for a few days, guests of Dalrymple the Commissioner. Then by palkis to Muzaffarpur, the headquarters of the large district of Tirhut. The next night we started again in palkis for Motihari, a distance of fifty-two miles. At dawn the next morning we woke to find our palkis on the ground and the bearers standing round. Asked why they stopped they said we had come to Barah Factory, and must get out and have tea. In vain I protested that I did not want to stop here, that I did not know the planter, and that I very much wanted to get to Motihari. They replied that all English gentlemen stopped there and that the planter would be very angry with them if they let us go on. So we gave in and were carried through a large, park-like compound to an immense house. A respectable old bearer came and helped us out, and led us into dressing-rooms where we washed and changed our clothes. On coming out into the veranda we found a copious breakfast of tea, coffee, eggs, ham, cold meat, herrings, jam, fruit and other things. After we had well eaten and drunk we were thinking of going on when one of the owners of the factory, Dr Hills, appeared, greeted us politely and hoped we had been properly waited on. He did not ask our names or seem to care who we were. It was the pride of the owners of his factory to entertain all comers. They had even prevailed upon the Magistrate to have the public road diverted so as to run through their property in order that no one might escape them. This open-handed hospitality was the rule at all factories. When we reached Motihari the bearers took us to another factory, where Baldwin, the manager, received us quite as a matter of course. It took us about a fortnight to get settled down in our house, a beautiful, large bungalow on the bank of a pretty lake. Champaràn is the north-westernmost district in the Lower Provinces. It is a small district only about a quarter the size of Purneah and the work was extraordinarily light. It was in fact given me by Eden because it was so light. He thought I required rest after the heavy work of Purneah. It was not, however, a bed of roses to me. I felt from the first that there was going to be a fight though I did not foresee the shape it would take.

While staying with Dalrymple at Patna I had naturally had long talks with him about my new district. Dal, as everyone called him, was a clear-headed man though his extreme indolence prevented him being a good officer. His account of Champàran was, as I afterwards found, very accurate. He said that the indigo planters were very numerous and powerful; that owing to their being genial and hospitable the Magistrates who had ruled the district hitherto had preferred to let them have their own way rather than have any social estrangement or quarrelling. While he himself, in his pleasant, sybarite fashion said he did not blame them for doing so, still the practical side of his mind rebelled against a practice which produced the worst possible results, for which he as Commissioner got blamed by Government. It was obviously undesirable to have so much power in the hands of men who, not being Government officials, were responsible to no one, and who from the very nature of their position could not easily be impartial. The district, in short wanted a strong man to pull it together and to assert and maintain the authority of Government. Dal hinted with a quiet smile that he should not be surprised if I turned out to be just the man for the work. My prudent wife warned him to be careful how he started me on the warpath, but he only said he hoped I should assert myself.

On the morning of my arrival Baldwin took me for a drive in his buggy all round the small town and station. This was, of course, done to show the natives that he was on good terms with the new Magistrate. As we went along he kept pointing to this or that place and saying with a boastful air, 'That belongs to me—the Magistrate has no power there.' I said nothing, but Dal's remarks came to my mind. I learned later on that Dr Hills's indifference to who we might be, the morning we stopped at Barah factory, was assumed. He knew who I was well enough, but he wanted me to see that to him the Magistrate of the district was a person of no consequence at all, and his arrival a matter of no importance. It *was*, however, a matter of very great importance and the planters were in reality preparing for a struggle.

A man whose name I will not here mention, whom I had detected and exposed in several dirty jobs in Purneah, had been transferred to Tirhut, and out of revenge had been spreading injurious reports about me and inducing others to do the same, so that the planters as a body had conceived a bad opinion of me beforehand. Thus the elements of discord were ready prepared.

When I reached Motihari famine had just begun. In Purneah there had been some failure of crops, but in Champàran the failure was universal and severe distress had set in. A few days after my arrival a meeting of all the principal inhabitants was held in accordance with a notice issued by my predecessor, to consider what steps should be taken for the relief of the distress. As Collector it was my duty to preside. When I entered the room I found some twenty planters present who had coolly begun business without waiting for me! The conclusion they had come to, as one of them was good enough to inform me, was that each planter was to relieve the distressed villagers in his own 'dihât', and that 'they would not stand any Government interference'. To this I merely observed that I as Collector had been ordered by Government to organize a system of relief all over the district, and that as a sum of money had been placed at my disposal for that purpose, it would only lead to waste of funds and energy if the Government officers under my orders and the planters were all to work at cross purposes. Ultimately, but not until much time had been wasted in argument, they agreed to subscribe to a common fund to supplement the aid given by the Government. A Committee was formed, consisting of a certain number of officials and a certain number of planters, to devise and put into execution a properly organized scheme of relief for the whole district. Relief centres were to be opened at suitable places, and the dignity of the planters was saved and their self-importance flattered by selecting factories as relief centres and making each planter relief manager of his own centre. They refused absolutely at first to send in any returns of the number of persons relieved or the sums of money spent, but it was pointed out to them that newspaper reporters were about and that much honour and glory would accrue to those whose relief work was brought most prominently to notice both of the Government and the public. This touched them, and they consented to act in accordance with the rules and submit the required returns. When the meeting was over one or two of the older planters and officials congratulated me on the success I had obtained, which surprised them all the more because most of the planters had come to the meeting determined beforehand not to agree to anything I might propose. The two principal planters, Baldwin and Gibbon ('Tom' Gibbon was well known all over Bengal), however, stood by me and materially helped me to carry my point. The planters of Tirhut, a vast tract of country which included Champàran, were as a class different from those of Purneah, and their system of working was different. The original founders of the Champàran 'concerns', as they were called, had made their fortunes and retired to England, leaving their concerns in the hands of managers, many of whom were rough, uneducated men, hard drinkers, loose livers and destitute of sympathy for the natives. The concern had been built up on this wise. The Maharaja of Bettiah, a very wealthy zemindar, owned the land of the whole district, with very few and petty exceptions. His practice was to let out the villages in his estate for long terms of years to farmers called 'mustàjirs', who agreed to pay him a fixed yearly rent, recouping themselves by levying the rents from the villagers. An Englishman would obtain from the Maharaja a long lease of a group of contiguous villages—fifteen or twenty perhaps. In this area, which he called his 'dihàt' (a Persian word meaning 'villages') he built one principal and several subordinate factories. Then he sent for the headmen of each village and compelled or coaxed them into signing a document by which they agreed for themselves and all the cultivators to grow indigo on a certain proportion of their lands, generally four cottas in every bigha, that is to say, one-fourth of the whole area. When the season for sowing came round each ryot received a quantity of seed sufficient to sow his land, also a small advance of money for expenses of ploughing, sowing, weeding, etc. At the harvest time the ryot had to cut the indigo and carry it to the factory where it was duly measured and paid for at a certain rate, after deducting the amount previously advanced. If the amount of indigo plant delivered by the ryot fell short of the quantity which, according to the planter's estimate, ought to be the out-turn of the seed sown, a proportionate sum of money was deducted from the payment. In this way the ryot was always in debt to the factory, and it was the planter's interest to keep him so. I shall return to this subject later on. It is mentioned here merely to explain the difficulties of my position. The planters' policy was to get rid as much as possible of the authority of the Magistrate, because it interfered with the despotic control which they considered it essential to exercise over the ryots. This control often degenerated into cruel oppression.

It was not, as some of my detractors alleged, from mere lust of power that I insisted on being master of my district and having my own way in all things, but because the district was a sacred trust delivered to me by the Government, and I was bound to be faithful to that charge. I should have been very base had I, from love of ease or wish for popularity, sat idly by and let others usurp my place and my duties. Ruling men is not a task that can be performed by *le premier venu* and though I was comparatively young at it, still I had had five years' training and experience prefaced by a liberal education, while these ex-mates of merchant ships and *ci-devant* clerks in counting houses had had neither.

I had not been many weeks in Champàran before Baldwin, who considered himself lord and master of Motihari town, wished to oust a man from house and home because he refused to grow indigo, alleging that other crops would pay him better, and that he was not bound by the agreement to grow indigo signed under coercion on behalf of the whole of the villagers by the headman. The headman, he said very justly, had no power to bind anyone but himself, and as he had never been consulted he was not legally liable. Now in the eyes of a Champàran planter, a man who refused to grow indigo was a rebel and a dangerous character and all measures were lawful against him. So Baldwin sent men with ploughs, who ploughed up every inch of ground round the ryot's cottage, sowed it with some coarse, cheap kind of pulse, put a fence of thorns round it, and so made the man and his family prisoners in their own house. He further gave the man to understand that if he set foot on the sown land he would be prosecuted for trespass and sent to jail. The wretched man and his family trembled and endured for two days, but when their food supplies were exhausted and they could not go so far as their well to draw water for household purposes, despair gave them courage. Although there were men put to watch them, the ryot managed to slip out at night and hide till the morning when he came into my court and told his tale. The action of Baldwin amounted to the offence known as 'illegal restraint' in the Indian Penal Code, so I issued a summons against Baldwin and his men. Seeing this unwonted action on my part, Baldwin, who was as great a coward as he was a bully, got frightened and paid the man a large sum to compromise the case. He also removed the fence and ceased to molest the man.

Edwards, one of Baldwin's assistants at an out-factory, was short of men to work at the press in which the indigo-pulp is compressed into cakes. The work is hard and unceasing, as the pulp has all to be pressed before it gets dry. It is also much disliked on account of the loathsome smell of the wet indigo. The men at first employed struck for a higher rate of wages, and when this was refused, bolted. Edwards in great distress sent a message in hot haste to Baldwin for aid, who incontinently sent out and dragged out of their houses at night three ryots ('his subjects' as he called them) and sent them off to the out-factory where they were kept as prisoners until the pressing was finished. Then they escaped and came to complain. This was also an offence under the Penal Code and I tried Mr Baldwin and fined him Rs 500, promising him six months in jail if he did such a thing again.

These two cases made a considerable stir in the district, and both planters and ryots recognized that there was 'a King in Israel'. The former took to flattering and courting me, inviting me to their factories and showing me and my wife many civilities. After a time also they took to asking me to settle their disputes with their ryots. The ryots also began to see that I was not a partisan of the planters, and having confidence in my impartiality began to come to me for justice when oppressed. In writing all this I mean to make no reflection on my predecessor. He was a good-tempered, easy-going fellow, extremely popular with the planters and, I have no doubt did his duty according to his lights. That was no affair of mine; I had to do my duty according to my lights.

All this while I was fighting the famine. Many thousands of starving people were daily fed at relief centres, which were opened all over the district at distances of about fifteen miles apart. The elaborate rules and procedure now in force were not then invented. We organized as good a system as we could and were fairly successful. There were very few deaths from starvation, and by strict economy the small supply of money granted by the Board of Revenue (about Rs 20,000), eked out by fairly liberal subscriptions from private persons, sufficed to stem the distress.

In August I narrowly escaped being drowned while trying to ford a river at night on my way back from a visit of inspection to a relief centre on the Nepal frontier. I and Cornish, the District Superintendent of police, had crossed the ford with only a foot of water in the morning; on our return late at night we found a rapid, swirling mass of water. Not knowing how deep it was we rode into it, and soon found our horses swimming. We slipped off our saddles and held on by the horses' manes. Eventually we reached the opposite bank wet through. It was a close shave.

Then my poor wife had a long illness. An Irish nurse whom we got from my brother Pearson's regiment at Fyzabad got drunk, wanted to fight me, knocked over half a dozen natives who tried to seize her, and frightened my wife dreadfully. She had a miscarriage and was in bed for several months.

But work had to be done all the same. The district bordered on Nepal, which was ruled at that time by a remarkable man, Jung Bahadoor. He was Prime Minister in name but *maharaja* or ruler in reality, the real Maharaja being a puppet, who was not allowed to go beyond the walls of his palace. Jung had won his way to power by shooting no less than seventeen of his uncles at a Durbar. He was a vigorous and intelligent ruler and careful to keep always on terms with the British Government. He rendered us good service in the Mutiny with his Gurkha troops. There was between him and us a 'reciprocity treaty' as it was called, by virtue of which any subjects of the one country caught committing crimes in the territory of the other were to be arrested by the authorities of that territory, and sent to their native country for punishment. Jung complained that the British officers did not carry out their part of the contract. Sir John Lawrence, who was then Governor-General, deputed an officer to hold an inquiry. This officer (J. D. Gordon of the Civil Service) reported that the complaint was unfounded, but Jung was not satisfied and continued to grumble all through 1866. Causes of complaint were constantly arising. There were gangs of dacoits composed of British and Nepalese subjects who plundered impartially on both sides of the border, and were protected by powerful zemindars with whom they shared the plunder.

According to the treaty, British subjects caught plundering in Nepalese territory were arrested by the Nepalese authorities and sent to me to be punished, and similarly Nepalese subjects caught on our side of the border were sent by me to the Nepalese 'Suba' (or Magistrate) for punishment. Jung complained that while his Subas always loyally punished everyone I sent to them, I constantly let off those whom they sent to me. This was true, but it was also inevitable. If my police caught a gang of Nepalese dacoits in my district they, in accordance with our law, collected all the evidence necessary to convict them. The prisoners, together with the evidence, were then sent to the Suba for trial. That worthy never troubled his head about the evidence—it was not the custom in Nepal. He merely said to the prisoners, 'You ——!' (in terms of abuse untranslateable), 'the illustrious English Sahib has sent you to me to be punished. Confess at once!' If they did not do so they were flogged and tortured till they did. The confession was then written down and they were sentenced to imprisonment, fine or other penalty. This was simple, if not satisfactory. When, however, the Nepalese caught British subjects they took them to the Suba who had them tortured till they confessed. He then sent them to me with the written confession. I could not sentence a man on that. The High Court would have been down on me very severely if I had done so. I was obliged to write to the Suba to send me the witnesses and other evidence. Of course, he had none to send. Probably he did not know what evidence meant. He used to send me the stereotyped reply: 'My respected friend,' (*mihrbàn i man*—they always wrote in Persian to show how civilized they were!), 'I have sent you the written confession (kàil-nàma). What more is necessary?' So after waiting in vain for a long time and failing to secure evidence of any kind I was forced to release the prisoners. This, of course, gave great offence to the imperious Jung—but what could I do? The bother about this question went on all through the cold weather till it culminated in a big row the following year, as I shall relate later on.

The Christmas of 1866 we spent at Gorakhpur, a district of the

North-West Provinces adjacent to Champàran. My dear old chum, Fred Elliot, was there as Joint Magistrate. We marched across in camp— the distance was 120 miles—at the rate of ten or twelve miles a day, having a double set of tents, one of which was sent on overnight. It was quite a patriarchal caravan. A Gorakhpur police officer who was camped in a magnificent grove of mango-trees, the Lákh-hazári Bágh or 'Garden of 101,000 trees' at Padraunà, described us to his friends. One morning he said there arrived a number of bullock-carts loaded with tents, with a dozen or so of chaprassees, tent-pitchers and police-men. They sent for the Tahsildar of Padraunà, and while waiting for him cooked and ate their dinner. After a time that lordly official ambled up on his horse followed by a string of peons. He and the chaprassees then had a long conversation, after which they walked about the tope (grove) to select a proper site for the camp. It was amusing to hear the chaprassees explaining that their Sahib liked this or disliked that in the way of sites. At last they found a place which suited them, and after having it carefully swept they proceeded with much noise and shouting to erect a 'Swiss cottage' tent as a sitting-room, two large, square sleep-ing tents, a smaller cutcherry tent, and several *pàls* for the servants. Then there was much wrangling as to the amount of food supplies required, the Tahsildar having been ordered by his own Collector to give the necessary supplies. The Tahsildar, after paying this short visit, ambled off again and the chaprassees and others curled themselves up and went to sleep. At dusk arrived coolies carrying hay, straw, cooking-pots, fire-wood, rice and other eatables for the camp.

Very early the next morning arrived more carts carrying the Sahib's kitchen, also tables and chairs, boxes and other things. With these came two milch cows, two or three goats, coops full of fowls and a fat sheep. The tents were then furnished and arranged, the kitchen set in order under a tree and the business of cooking the breakfast begun. His Highness the Khansamah on a pony, with several subordinate servants now arrived and took charge of the proceedings. An hour later there was a stir in the camp, the servants all put on their clothes and began to look very active and attentive. Two syces leading horses, and two more leading ponies now straggled in and announced that the Sahib was close behind. Presently there was a sound of hoofs in the distance, everyone stood up and the Collector and his wife, mounted on two hand-some Arabs, cantered into the tope and dismounted. Tea was brought to them at once and shortly afterwards a *champony* drawn by two bullocks trotted up, out of which emerged three little boys, an ayah, a bearer and a mass of rugs, clothes, toys and other things.

This is a fair description of the way in which a Collector camped in those days. I suppose it is still pretty much the same, but things change so much even in India, that perhaps camping is becoming a thing of the past. It was a very comfortable way of travelling.

After ten days spent in feasting, dancing and various other amusements we returned to Motihari and arrived about the 10th of January 1867. We were greeted on our return by my brother Harry. He had had an adventurous life for some years. Inheriting £500 under my grandfather's will on coming of age, he emigrated to Natal where he fell into the hands of unscrupulous persons who cheated him out of his money. Then he wandered up-country, lived in Kaffir kraals herding cattle, worked as a stonemason, kept a grog-shop and ferry over the Umvoti River in partnership with a sailor, for whom also he broke in horses on the veldt, and finally got together enough money to pay his passage as far as St Helena. There he was left stranded, and shipped as a common sailor before the mast in the capacity of cook and butcher's mate. He landed in London with £5 in his pocket, being his wages for the voyage. Through the kindess of Mr Ball he obtained enough money to come out to me, and I exerted myself to get him an appointment. Meanwhile he lived with us and set himself to learn Hindustani, an indispensable preliminary to getting an appointment in India. He was a tall, broad-shouldered young fellow, light-haired and blue-eyed, strong and active, a good rider, full of fun and high spirits.

The disputes with Nepal which had been going on all the cold weather broke out more virulently in January 1867. Certain native Christians of Bettiah made a livelihood by felling timber in the forests in the north of the district for Hershel, Dean & Co., a firm at Monghyr who contracted for the supply of sleepers to the Railway. One day a large and well-armed band of Nepalese forest-guards came upon them and ordered them to leave off work, with the significant threat that if they cut down any trees, the Nepalese would cut them down. Then the Christians, a timid folk, fled and reported the matter to their employer. He, of course, applied to me for protection, and having satisfied myself that the forest was in British Territory I sent a force of armed police to protect the woodcutters. Jung Bahadur appealed to the Viceroy, and after some correspondence I was ordered to go to Tribeni Ghat, the point where the Gandak River emerges from the hills, there to meet the Suba and settle the boundary with him. I took with me Harry and Ruddock, my Assistant. A very large fair was being held there at the time, and thousands of Hindus were bathing in the river, which at this point is held sacred. The Suba, a squat, sturdy, clever-looking Nepalese, who held as he told us the rank of 'Major-Captain' in Jung Bahadur's army, came attended by two 'Leftants' (Lieutenants). He presented me with a very fine kukri (curved Nepalese knife), a piece of richly embroidered Chinese silk and a yak's tail. We were not long in settling the boundary question, as my elaborate Government survey maps quite convinced him, and after a few complimentary visits to each other's camps we parted very good friends and I returned to Motihari.

But it was difficult to keep the peace with Jung Bahadur. He ruled Nepal with a rod of iron, and wished to be as peremptory with British officers as he was with his own subordinates. Sir John Lawrence treated him with extreme deference and we could expect no support from Government even when protecting the interests of our own subjects against him. Shortly after my return from the frontier a fresh case occurred. An elephant belonging to a wealthy merchant of my district got loose and strayed into the Nepal jungles, where Jung's elephant-hunters caught it and in spite of the evident marks of captivity on its limbs, took possession of it as a wild elephant and enrolled it on the Maharaja's stud. Shortly after the animal got loose again and returned to my district, where it was caught by the police and sent in to me. In accordance with the usual custom I issued notices inviting the owner to come forward and prove his ownership. The merchant came and proved his case convincingly. The animal was made over to him. Soon after this I received an insolent and imperious letter from Jung demanding that I should give the elephant up to him. This, of course, I could not do, so he appealed to the Viceroy, who called upon me for explanation. I gave it and it satisfied him, but he was much annoyed at my making some remarks on the unsatisfactory nature of our treaty with Nepal and the behaviour of Jung Bahadur towards British officials. I was told in reply that 'the Government of India did not look to officers in Mr Beames's position for advice as to its frontier policy.' On which the *Englishman*, the leading newspaper in Calcutta, remarked that it was just 'because Government did not look to experienced frontier officers for advice, that its frontier policy was so uniformly a failure.' In the Government letter, however, there was yet another sting. It was remarked that dacoity was not yet stamped out on the border (as if it ever could be!) and until I could do that, the less I said about the shortcomings of Nepalese administration the better.

This goaded me, for I had already done a great deal to put a stop to dacoity, and had I been properly supported by the Subas and my own police I might have done much more. In those days there were still many military men in the police. My District Superintendent, Major M., was one of them. I believe the poor old man was very honest in his narrow-minded way, and I daresay a very valiant old walking-stick in battle; but as head of the district police he was very nearly useless. For detective work he relied chiefly on a stalwart Sikh Inspector, one Tali-wand Singh, and another Inspector, Harak Chand, an Oudh Bania by caste, a wily fox. For some time past he had been worrying in an impotent way over the alleged misdoings of one Sheoprakàsh Singh, a zemindar who owned a small estate of two villages on the very edge of the district bordering on Nepal. This man, so M. was assured, maintained and protected a large gang of Magahya Doms, a low-caste, wandering gipsy race, who live by fortune-telling and thieving. He was said to organize dacoities which were carried out by his Doms from whom he received a fourth of the spoil. He roved about in various disguises on both sides of the border, moving backwards and forwards according as he made one side or the other for the time too hot to hold him. At the time the Viceroy thought fit to taunt me with failure, M. held in his hands the papers of no less than fifteen cases in all of which there was strong reason to suspect that Sheoprakàsh was the originator, yet so poor was his detective skill that he could not work up one of these cases to the point at which an arrest would be justified. Dacoities had been worse than usual during the past year on account of the famine, by which many of the lower castes had been driven to thieving by want of food, but this class of case was, to anyone but M., easily distinguishable from professional dacoity. I now felt the time had come for some earnest action, so I fell on him and his favourite adviser, Taliwand Singh, and insisted on these cases being worked up and proved. After much pressure I succeeded, and being in possession of satisfactory proof I issued a warrant for the arrest—not of the Doms, as M. expected—but of Sheoprakàsh himself, on the principle of flying at the highest game. My predecessor had several times tried and sentenced various members of the gang, but it was, of course, useless merely to put into jail a few Magahya Doms, so long as the head and leader of the band was at large and at liberty to hire fresh ruffians to fill their place. Sheoprakàsh made a desperate resistance and was only captured after shooting at and wounding one of the constables. His offence was bailable, but I fixed the bail very high and though it was reduced by order of the Judge, he was unable to give it, and therefore remained in the Motihari jail till the witnesses who had been summoned appeared. Some time necessarily elapsed before the case could come on for trial but my time was fully occupied in other matters. The sequel of the story will be told later on.

Although the ordinary routine work of this small district was light yet there were several very important matters on my hands which gave me enough to do. Indeed, but for the constant comfort and support of my dear, true wife I should have fared badly. I was in a low state of health both mentally and bodily and needed all her love and care and wise counsels. Among all the blessings for which I have to thank God, none can compare with the blessing He gave me in this good wife. I can never be sufficiently thankful for this inestimable treasure. God bless her!

From M. and his dacoities I now had to turn to a worry of quite a different kind. Nearly the whole of the land in the district was owned by the Maharaja of Bettiah. He lived at the town of that name, a busy mercantile place of some 15,000 inhabitants, thirty miles north-west of Motihari. The main street of the town led up to the palace gate, a lofty and beautiful structure, high enough for an elephant to pass under. This gave access to numerous large, untidy courtyards full of horses, elephants and retainers. In the centre was a stately pile of buildings three storeys high in which the Maharaja himself lived. He had also several handsome garden palaces a mile or two outside the town. He was a man of about forty, but looked much older from the effects of dissipation, for he was an inveterate drunkard and had a large harem. His great estates, some fifty miles in length by thirty broad, were very badly managed and he was heavily in debt. To save him if possible from ruin, the Government had at his request given him a European Manager, one Captain Cole, a retired military man, who had also served for some years as a Deputy Magistrate. My instructions were to afford the Manager all the support that was necessary without interfering in the management of the estate. I was in fact called upon to act and not to act at the same time, a false position in which Government is fond of placing officers by way of shuffling off its own responsibility, a regular Secretariat trick. Cole, an able, energetic, and good-tempered man, lived in a handsome house outside the town, with a salary of Rs 1,500 a month, carriages and servants supplied by the Maharaja. But he had a hard time of it. It is difficult to manage a large native estate when the owner is a minor and under control, but when the owner is of full age and his own master the task becomes much more difficult. With a live Raja who was constantly drunk, and in that state easily led to make presents and sign grants of land and money to his hangers-on, toadies, and other ministers to his base pleasures, always interfering under backstairs influences and upsetting the Manager's most carefully-studied arrangements; or refusing consent to his plans because they displeased the host of harpies who made court to him, and preyed on him

—with the Maharaja's mother and her nest of intriguers—with his wife the Maharani and her court of greedy parasites—with the large army of Brahmins working on the Maharaja's superstitions for their own profit —with the harem and its unscrupulous occupants—and last but not least a crowd of indigo planters clamouring for support to 'British Enterprise'—poor Cole's life was made a burden to him. Still, he struggled on manfully for a time. Through my help, he succeeded in getting the Maharaja to consent to a scheme by which his personal expenses and those of his wife, mother, son and household in general were limited to Rs 360,000 (£36,000) a year—sufficient income even for an Indian prince. The rest of the profits of the estate exceeding eleven lakhs a year (about £110,000—the rupee was worth two shillings then) was to be spent on paying the debts and discharging the Government revenue. But the night after he signed the agreement to this scheme, he signed while drunk a deed granting a long lease of an enormous area for a nominal sum to one of his parasites who was also the paramour of his mother, the dowager Maharani; and when Cole, on its being presented to him the next morning refused to act on it, there was furious uproar in the palace and so much abusive language and generally insulting behaviour that Cole, worn out by fruitless efforts to save a man who would not be saved, resigned his post and retired. He fortunately had a moderate private fortune of his own on which he lived in comfort in England.

This was an unfortunate termination to a struggle in which I had, for upwards of a year, taken a very great interest. I had been constantly consulted by Cole, had written reams of letters to him and spent hours in personal consultation with him and the Maharaja's officials. But my hands were too much tied by the orders of the Government for me to be of any real help. In Cole's place the Maharaja appointed Thomas Mitchell Gibbon, a leading indigo planter, an experienced, long-headed Scot from Aberdeen who managed the Raja by a mixture of flattering and bullying which outwardly at any rate succeeded fairly well. Gibbon was of tougher stuff than Cole; he was not the man to be worn out by intrigues, and was not above fighting the intriguers with their own weapons.

I was not much pleased at his getting the appointment, but the matter was arranged behind my back and I was not informed of it till it had been settled. This was done evidently to prevent me from opposing it. The relations between the planters and the ryots were becoming critical, and it was not desirable that a man like Tom Gibbon, himself a leading planter, should be able to wield the power which his position as Manager gave him, of granting leases to his fellow-planters throughout the extensive estates of the Maharaja. It was, in fact, principally in order to gain this power that he had undertaken the otherwise unenviable position of Manager. The planters were at this time—the summer of 1867—becoming frightened at the spirit of quiet, determined opposition which was growing among the ryots, and though they believed me to be the author of it, they came to me for help. I had not stirred up the ryots in any way, but they had been long dissatisfied, and finding that they had at last a Magistrate who would do justice impartially between them and the planters, they judged the time opportune for rising and resisting their oppressors. The real instigators of the movement were some pleaders and law agents from Tirhut who, as we found out afterwards, had been going about among the villages preaching to the ryots about their rights. When the time came for sowing their fields with indigo, many hundreds of ryots sowed them with other crops, saying (what was quite true) that it did not pay them to sow indigo. I have described a few pages back the system in force of taking a bond from a village headman on behalf of the whole village, by which they agreed to sow four cottas in the bigha, four-twelfths, of all their land with indigo, and to receive eight rupees for the produce of every bigha. They complained that these terms were no longer remunerative and clamoured for a reduction to three cottas in the bigha and ten rupees per bigha for the produce. They also complained that the planters picked out the best land for the indigo, and were always taking them away from their other crops to weed and hoe the indigo fields. In fact men with whips used to be sent into the villages to drive the ryots out to work. My own servants even, some of whom owned small patches of land in neighbouring villages, used to be driven away to weed indigo whenever it pleased Baldwin to do so. Of course, I soon put a stop to this as regards myself, and I felt it my duty to stop it throughout the district.

As both parties were anxious that I should decide their differences I took the matter up and went round the district from factory to factory, assembling the ryots and planters and examining the bonds on which their engagements rested. The agreements were generally for a term of twenty years, of which in 1867 some had expired, others had two or three years to run. The ryots were illiterate, and the planters ignorant and careless about law. The bonds had been drawn up by the factory clerks and were loosely and vaguely worded, and in many cases not properly signed or executed. After much wrangling I brought them at last to agree to a compromise. Those ryots whose bonds had yet a year or two to expire were to continue to work on the terms of the bond till the period for which the bond ran had expired. Those whose terms had expired were free to do as they liked and were not compelled to sign new bonds to grow indigo. I endeavoured to induce the planters to concede the terms of three cottas in the bigha and ten rupees per bigha for the produce, pointing out that since the old bonds were written—twenty years and more ago—the price of rice and other common crops had increased so much that it paid the ryots better to grow them than indigo, and that if they did not agree to some more reasonable terms every ryot, as his bond expired, would refuse to grow any more indigo, and their business would in a few years become extinct. They refused to listen to me then, but years afterwards they told me that they had ever since bitterly regretted not listening to my advice, as in the long run they had to concede even worse terms. Open violence was avoided, however, by my measures as long as I remained in the district. It broke out soon after I left. The ryots said when I went away that now the 'chashmawàlà' (the man with the spectacles), as they called me, had gone they would not trust any other Magistrate. The rioting was so serious in 1868 that Metcalfe, the then Magistrate, was obliged to call out the military to protect the station of Motihari. Five years later when Sir G. Campbell, the Lieutenant-Governor, visited the district, the people petitioned him to send back the 'chashmawàlà'.

Busy and anxious as I was all this hot weather and rains, I found time to begin my studies for the *Comparative Grammar of the Modern Aryan Languages of India* which I afterwards published. I generally managed to screw out an hour or two every day for a plunge into Sanskrit and Prakrit, which refreshed my weary soul in the midst of all the official trouble and worry.

My brother Harry used to want amusement—this was natural at his age—and he sought it amongst the rather wild young planters and the equally wild young officers of the Sixth Bengal Cavalry who were quartered at Segauli, a small station twelve miles from Motihari. One day as he was driving a frisky horse with a mad Irish doctor they were both thrown out. Harry broke his leg and was laid up for several months.

Thus passed the rains and the cold weather was upon us and we were planning to go into camp, when one morning, opening my letters calmly as usual, I read one from the Government telling me I was suspended! This came upon me like a bolt out of the blue—utterly unexpected. Sir William Grey, the Lieutenant-Governor, a man whose career had been spent entirely in the Secretariat, and who consequently had no knowledge of or power of sympathizing with a District Officer's troubles and difficulties, had read in the *Indian Daily News*, a very anti-official Cal-

cutta newspaper, several highly-coloured articles and letters reflecting
on my treatment of Sheoprakàsh, the old dacoit leader—'this aged
nobleman, torn from the comforts of his rank and station, rotting in a
felon's jail'—as the penny-a-liners put it. Having, as I learnt afterwards,
other reasons for wishing to remove me from Champàran, he made use
of the incident and commenced by suspending me. Then he called for
an explanation of my conduct, thus putting the cart before the horse.
I explained my conduct by reference to past events, and pointed to the
significant fact that since Sheoprakàsh had been locked up there had
been no dacoities at all, whereas there had been no less than sixty-five in
the six months preceding his arrest. The reason why he had been kept
so long before being brought to trial was that the police would not, or
could not, bring forward the witnesses on whose statements as recorded
in the police inquiries I had relied in arresting him. I subsequently discovered that the witnesses had all been spirited away across the border,
and Harak Chand had received a heavy bribe to connive at their dis-
appearance. M. had been transferred to another district and his successor knew nothing about the matter.

I sent in this defence and awaited orders, but there was a new
Magistrate in charge and I could not sit idle—my brother, my wife,
and my friends all urged me to take leave. I was worn out with work and
frequent attacks of fever and this last blow had utterly prostrated me.
The doctor gave me a medical certificate, and I sent in my papers for
sick leave to England.

Leaving the scene of so many difficult but interesting labours with
some regret, we went by boat down the Gandak and Ganges to Monghyr,
where I was obliged to stop for a time as my wife was about to be confined. On the 2nd January 1868 she gave birth to my eldest daughter,
Margaret, in a large, palatial house known as the Karan Chaurà situated
on a lofty bastion of the ancient fort of Monghyr.

CHAPTER XIV

HOME LEAVE, 1868

As soon as I could get away I went to Calcutta and saw Dampier, the Secretary to the Government, who told me that my explanation had been considered quite satisfactory, that my general administration of the district had been commended, that I had been reinstated and the full pay for the time I had been under suspension was to be allowed me. I was appointed to Balasore, a district in Orissa. He informed me that the reason I was suspended was not Sheoprakàsh's case, which, he said, though perhaps a little severe, was not a matter to suspend a man for, but because Sir John Lawrence, offended at my attitude in Jung Bahadur's case, had written privately requesting that I might be removed to some district away from the frontier. As it was not desirable to let Jung think that a Magistrate was removed to please him, the Lieutenant-Governor took the first opportunity of my making a slight slip to remove me. I said I wondered they did not shrink from treating an English official of good reputation in this way. Did they not fear it would make me lose all my interest in my work hereafter? They had reinstated me it was true, but what could compensate me for the unmerited disgrace, the suspense, the check to a successful career? He shrugged his shoulders and said, 'It does not matter how we treat an English gentleman, he is sure to be always loyal and to work well from a sense of honour and duty.' Perhaps this is why they treat native officials so differently.

My arrangements for going home took some little time to make but I finally got through them all and left Calcutta for England in the P & O steamer *Multan* on the 3rd March 1868—a few days short of ten years since I had first landed there. My brother Harry went to stay with Pearson, and soon afterwards got the appointment of tutor to the son of the Maharaja of Burdwan, a wealthy Bengal zemindar. The steamer was dreadfully overcrowded, as is usual in March when people go home in shoals, anxious to get away before the hot weather begins. There were about 200 passengers, and eighty-five children—a very large number for the comparatively small vessels of those days. My two eldest boys, David and Fred, had both suffered from attacks of dysentery at Motihari, and the crowded state of the steamer, the heat and bad smells and the unsuitable food brought on a return of the malady. Fred, who was weaker than David, was very ill for some days, so that when we stopped at Madras we had almost given up all hope of saving his life. The doctor, being, as these ship's doctors so often are, young and inexperienced, could do nothing for him, but one of the stewards had a couple of *bel* fruits. This fruit is an infallible cure for dysentery, and after taking three or four tumblers of the pulp mixed with water the poor little fellow recovered, and thanks to the sea air picked up so fast that by the time we arrived at Ceylon he was quite well. When we reached Suez there was the usual miserable struggle. The steamers lay-to a mile or more from shore owing to the shallowness of the water, and all the passengers with their luggage were bundled into a very small and dirty steam tug. Here an invention of mine came in useful. I had bought three stout leather straps with brass rings at one end. These were buckled round each of the children's waists and the rings went on to my finger, so I had them all three on a leash so to speak and thus escaped being separated from them in the crush. My wife and our native ayah, holding the baby Margaret in her arms, clung to my skirts and thus we got safe to the hotel. Here there were no bedrooms or dressing-rooms available for the ladies and children, so we had all to pass the day miserably in a big noisy room with no furniture but divans round the walls. The food was almost uneatable and the flies swarmed all over everything. At last, about 6 p.m., a big bell rang and we all moved off to a big open shed called the railway station where stood a train of a few carriages—not nearly enough for us all. I and one or two other men found our way with difficulty to the 'Bureau', a small room up a narrow staircase where sat four or five Levantines in fez and blue coats, smoking cigarettes. As I was the only one who could speak French I had to explain that we must have more carriages. They did not seem to be aware that a whole shipload of passengers had arrived that morning, and it took some time to get the fact into their heads. Some very energetic English from a colonel of our party finally stirred them up, and some more carriages were supplied. The train started about two hours late, which we were told was rather punctual for Egypt. We got a compartment to ourselves and reached Alexandria at daybreak next morning, where we were at once taken in a tug to the S.S. *Tanjore*, a clean and comfortable vessel. Most of the passengers, especially the children, went by the Southampton steamer, so we had lots of room and good food and enjoyed the four days' voyage through the Straits of Messina over the deep blue Mediterranean in delicious weather to Marseilles. There we had to stop three days as my wife was ill, but at length we started and after twenty-four hours in the train reached Paris, sick and faint and dizzy. A good night's rest in the hotel revived us, and we were able to spend the next day wandering about Paris. At every corner we met drums beating, bands playing and regiments of little red-legged French soldiers marching to the tune of *Partant pour la Syrie*, the rather mawkish air which did duty for a National Anthem under the Second Empire. I also called upon Garcin de Tassy, a celebrated Oriental scholar with whom I had had some correspondence. The next night we travelled to England, and astonished my wife's sister Carry and her husband Robert Hamilton by driving up to their door at 9 a.m. on Good Friday, the 12th April. We stayed with them one day, and the next day went to live with my mother, who had a small house at Richmond. As this was too small for us all, I took a larger house at Twickenham where we lived for the greater part of our sojourn in England. I found my mother very little changed in appearance. Her hair was still as jet-black as ever, but she suffered from hysterical attacks and was nervous and fretful. She did not recognize me at first. When I left England in 1858 I was quite beardless; when I returned ten years later I wore a beard and moustache and was still further disguised by gold-rimmed spectacles. In the days of my boyhood it was not the custom for any but military men to wear the moustache or beard. Men wore their whiskers long, and 'dandies', as they were called, took much pride in having them oiled and curled. They also wore their hair long and curly. But when our soldiers returned from the war in the Crimea in 1855 with splendid big beards and moustaches, their appearance excited general admiration and civilians began to let their beards grow. The fashion began with postmen, railway-guards and porters and though at first laughed at soon spread to the upper classes. The long, sweeping whiskers popularly known as 'Piccadilly weepers' began to die out, and boys at College began to try and grow a moustache, in spite of much mockery and chaff. When I returned to England in 1868 the moustache was pretty general. I found shaving a nuisance and gave it up for good in 1862, since when I have allowed my hair to grow as it would. The present almost universal fashion of shaving cheeks and chin and wearing only a moustache with close-cropped hair did not come in until many years later.

I spent the summer chiefly in rowing on the Thames, but I also enjoyed a good deal of London life in a quiet way. I joined a club and frequented the Royal Asiatic Society where I met many Oriental scholars, especially dear old Dr Rost, the Secretary, with whom we became very intimate. We also spent some very pleasant days at Oxford as the guests of Monier Williams, Professor of Sanskrit, who

had been our Sanskrit Professor at Haileybury. I also went to see
Bashley which looked very small and mean. Places one has known in
one's youth and thought of in after days as grand and lordly often
surprise one by their smallness when visited later in life. It was let to a
Captain Hughes and was poorly furnished and generally forlorn.

There is not much to be said about our stay in England. It was a
quiet, restful time on the whole, but uneventful and uninteresting. Our
relations were cold and disposed to be quarrelsome. Our ways and theirs
did not agree very well, and I found it too expensive to last. So in
January 1869 we determined to go back to India. We left our three boys
with a retired physician, a Dr Watson, at Prince's Risborough in
Buckinghamshire. It was a sad wrench to part from them. Rupert, the
youngest was only four years old. I have never seen him since. He is
now thirty-four, and I should not know him if I passed him in the
street! We took our youngest child Maggie back to India with us and
engaged an English nurse, Eliza Caffery, to go with us. Finally we left
England on the 24th February, spent two days in Paris, joined the
steamer at Marseilles and, after a voyage of the usual dull kind, landed
at Calcutta on the 4th of April. The only noticeable thing on our
voyage was the number of foreigners on board, with whom I consorted
considerably with a view to improving my French, Italian, Spanish and
German. We had a delightful series of polyglot conversations by which
I benefited much.

CHAPTER XV

BALASORE, 1869–1870

ON arriving at Calcutta I found that I was appointed Magistrate and Collector 1st grade of Balasore. The salary of the 1st grade was in those days Rs 1,916 a month and the rupee was still worth two shillings, though it began to fall very soon after that date.

I now entered upon my career of nine years in Orissa. This singular little province which has long dwelt apart has preserved a peculiar type of its own. It lies along the western coast of the Bay of Bengal at the northern or upper end, and consists of a narrowish strip of flat, fertile land backed by an extensive region of tangled hills extending far back into Central India. It is about two hundred miles long from north-east to south-west and about two hundred and fifty broad from the sea to the furthest inland frontier. The flat strip near the coast, which is under direct British rule, is divided into three districts, Balasore in the north, Cuttack in the centre and Pooree in the south.

Balasore I found was a small district, a long, narrow strip of flat land between the sea and the hills. In one part it was only nine miles broad, though in another it was nearly fifty. The picturesque little town of Balasore lies huddled up on a high bank overhanging the River Burhàbalang, about eight miles from the sea as the crow flies. It is a seaport, and strange grimy native craft ply thence to ports on the Madras coast laden with rice, the staple commodity of the district. West of the neat, clean town with its tall white houses lies the civil station on an undulating plain. Here are the houses of the European officials, the cutcherries and other public buildings, and a settlement of Baptist Missionaries from America who have a chapel with a high tower, and good houses.

My house was a fine, large, airy building surrounded by a good garden and close to it was the cutcherry. It was a very quiet little place and our life there was on the whole a very uneventful one. The first thing that happened was the birth of our second daughter, Edith, on the 31st May 1869 at 4.30 a.m.

Our small society consisted of a Joint Magistrate, a doctor, a Superintendent of police, an Engineer, a Harbour-master, and an Inspector of Telegraphs. There were also two police Assistants and a Deputy Magistrate. All the above were English, and several of them were married. The Missionaries hailed from Dover, New Hampshire, U.S.A. and belonged to a sect called Free Will Baptists. There was, moreover, a Belgian Jesuit, Father Sapart, and three Carmelite nuns—a Scotch woman, a German and a Belgian. The Baptists and the Catholics had each charge of a small number of native children who had been left orphans in the terrible famine of 1866 and taken care of by the Government, which paid the Missionaries three rupees a head *per mensem* for them.

Some of these people were interesting as specimens of the curious beings one meets in India. There are large classes of people of all nations in that country of whose existence the good folk at home have no idea. Worthy Father Sapart, for instance, the Jesuit priest, was a very curious character. By race a Walloon from Louvain (or Loewen as he called it), son of a journeyman carpenter or bricklayer, he was a tall, lean, cadaverous creature with a long, sharp-pointed nose, deep-seated eyes, a long, flowing beard and brown, sun-tanned face. Honest, simple-minded and very imperfectly educated at some Jesuit seminary, he had but one idea, the spread of his religion, and if he went the wrong way to work he certainly was not wanting in earnestness or sincerity.

He arrived at Balasore about a year before us, on foot, with a mat, a tin pot and a breviary as his sole luggage. He sat down under a tree and soon contrived to have a small bamboo and grass shed erected in which he lived, eating rice like a native. Then he began to beg from the Europeans and Eurasians (most of the latter class were Roman Catholics) until he got together money enough to build a cottage with mud walls and a thatched roof. He then secured a long lease of a patch of ground, and as the orphan children were made over to him he housed them in the cottage and in company with them dug clay, moulded, and finally burnt bricks. Then he set to work and drew on large sheets of paper a design for church, parsonage and school—all in one. Still begging persistently he scraped together money enough to pay for bricklayers, dug his foundations and began to build. In this slow way, begging till he got a little money together, carrying on the work till he had spent it, and then going begging again—all the while living on rice and inhabiting any corner of the building that was habitable—he toiled on till at the end of about six years he had constructed a singularly graceful little Gothic church with a fine airy crypt beneath, in which he held his school, and two large dormitories and rooms for the priest. The officers of the Public Works Department who inspected the building said it was an admirable piece of work. Then Sapart set to work and built a nunnery and chapel for the nuns. Whenever he had exhausted the liberality of the Europeans and Eurasians of Balasore he would start off, accompanied by a boy to carry his mat and cooking pot, and trudge four or five hundred miles to Cuttack, Sambalpur and other stations to beg for his church. I think he was altogether some seven or eight years at Balasore, building all the while. And as soon as he had finished his buildings and they were ready for use and had been consecrated by the Romish Archbishop of Calcutta, he was removed to a far distant station and never set eyes on his beloved church again! This is the Jesuit system. Poor, honest, simple-minded old Sapart was very fond of me and very much concerned at my being a heretic. He used to try to convert me, but as he only knew what he had been taught at his Belgian seminary he was not at all successful. He talked very fair English, but preferred, of course, to use French, and we always corresponded in that language.

Another curious character in this out-of-the-way nook was Captain Alfred Bond of the Indian Marine, whom we always spoke of as 'the Ancient Mariner'. He had been in India for upwards of sixty years and had never been to England once in all that time. His only tie to his native country was that he was related to the inventor of 'Bond's marking ink', which article he used always to recommend strongly to everybody he met. He was Harbourmaster, Superintendent of the Salt Warehouses and Commander of the brig *Orissa*. (She was a schooner in reality.) This vessel, a smart little craft, was a relic of a former state of things. In the early days of British rule when there were few roads, and those very bad, and when the British possessions extended only a little distance inland, the East India Company maintained a fleet of small vessels, generally armed, to keep up the communication between the settlements along the coast from Calcutta in the north to Madras in the south. These vessels carried officers joining their appointments, also opium and stores of all sorts. They were occasionally also employed in attacking the mud fort of some refractory zemindar, and even, in company with English men-of-war, in fighting the French. Those days had long passed away, but the brigs and schooners were still kept up. They still occasionally brought opium, stamps and stationery, and other Government stores from Calcutta, or cruised about in pursuit of salt smugglers. For the most part, however, the little brig *Orissa* lay placidly in harbour being constantly painted, scrubbed and polished and (as we afterwards discovered) being quietly devoured internally by white ants. Occasionally she took a trip to air her sails, and on some of these occasions, having too rashly put to sea in bad weather, was unable to get back again, and had to beat about in the bay till all her provisions were consumed and the Ancient Mariner and his crew suffered the pangs of hunger. Though he had been so long in India the Ancient Mariner's knowledge of the Indian languages was confined to a very small stock of horribly mispronounced words in nautical Hindustani, a curious jargon composed of Arabic, Persian, Malay, Tamil, Portuguese and Urdu. It is very generally spoken on board all the vessels of very various nationalities which navigate the Bay of Bengal from Singapore to Calcutta and from Calcutta to Colombo. This nautical life in the Bay of Bengal is very curious. It is a little world of its own. The ships are commanded and officered by Europeans, and the crews consist of 'lascars', i.e. men from Chittagong, the Madras coast, and Eastern Bengal. But a description of this kind of life would take a book to itself. In my capacity of Collector of Customs—one of the multifarious functions attached to my new post—I was brought into contact with it very constantly as I shall frequently have occasion to mention hereafter.

Mrs Bridget Bond, wife and ruler of the Ancient Mariner, was a small, shrivelled old lady who went about in a Bath chair and actively superintended the land affairs as her husband did the sea. She owned several houses and some land. Her special eminence, however, consisted in her being what her husband used to describe as 'a Plymouth Brethren'. In this capacity she was wont to hold prayer meetings in her house to which the Ancient Mariner used to invite us, saying, 'You should come and hear Biddy pray; Biddy prays beautiful.' I am sorry to say none of us ever went. Biddy was certainly a very clever old woman, and had evidently at some time or other been very well educated. She used to come and sit with us of an evening in our garden, and her conversation showed an amount of reading and acquaintance with various subjects which often surprised us. Who she was by birth, and how she had drifted into the arms of the Ancient Mariner and with him to the remote and obscure district of Balasore, was a mystery. They had a large family of sons and daughters all of whom, but one, were married and settled in various parts of Bengal in well-paid appointments. One unmarried daughter, Alice, a shrewish, leathery virgin of forty or more, lived with them and essayed her mature charms in vain on every young man that came to Balasore.

In this quiet place, among this strange society, we lived for four years. I quickly learnt Oriya, the language of Orissa, and assisted E. B. Hallam, one of the American Baptist Missionaries, in writing an Oriya Grammar. I also now began my *Comparative Grammar of the Modern Aryan Languages of India*, and completed it in about eighteen months, working at it for two hours every morning before breakfast, from eight to ten. This was the only time I could spare from my official duties, which though not heavy were incessant. People came about this or that at all hours of the day, and sometimes even late at night. At this time I bought my dear old horse, 'Balaclava', who was my faithful servant for nine years and carried me over many hundreds of miles. He was not beautiful, being a large, big-boned chestnut waler[1] with four white stockings and a vicious eye. I had been reading Kinglake's *Crimea*, and had just come upon the description of Lord Cardigan's charger at the celebrated Charge of the Light Brigade at Balaclava when my new horse arrived. He resembled the charger I had been reading about so exactly that I named him accordingly. My wife had a handsome bay mare, and we had many a grand scamper across country together. Balaclava was a vicious animal and bucked dreadfully. He used to bite his syces and I always had a struggle with him at starting of a morning. But he knew me and we were great friends.

The Christmas of this year we spent at Cuttack, guests of Robert Alexander, the Judge, a large, genial old man, a great friend of ours, and the most extensive consumer of bottled beer I ever met. We marched down the Trunk Road, living in tents and bungalows. All over Orissa—as in most parts of India—there are small bungalows by the roadside at distances of ten or fifteen miles apart. These are built and maintained by the Government principally for use of the officers of the Public Works Department when on duty inspecting roads and other works. They are, however, also available on payment of a small fee to other officers. They are simply furnished, with a few necessaries only, and every officer brings with him his bedding and food.

At Neulpur, a place about twenty-four miles from Cuttack, we found one of the small steamers of the Irrigation Department waiting for us on the canal, which had recently been completed up to this point. We were a merry company on board, twelve men and three or four ladies, with some children. We started early in the morning, and spent the day principally in eating, drinking, smoking, playing cards and singing, reaching Cuttack eventually, very tired, at eleven o'clock at night. The delay was caused by our sticking on the numerous sandbanks in the Mahanadi River. I will not here describe beautiful Cuttack, because we got to know it much better in after days. The charm of it struck us on our first visit, the broad, shady roads, and green parade ground, the picturesque buildings, the two broad rivers with their background of lovely blue hills, make it one of the most picturesque stations in India.

[1] A cavalry horse imported into India from New South Wales.

On a large plain a mile or so from the town was the race-course and a grandstand. In the early morning there were races to which the Maharaja of Vizianagram sent some good horses, in charge of a diminutive English jockey, who beat all the amateur gentlemen riders by his skill in handling his horses. Then there were great dinners to which twenty or thirty persons sat down, and after the ladies had retired there was hot whisky and water, with singing till past midnight. A Madras Regiment is, or was in those days, stationed at Cuttack and there was a grand dinner at their Mess. On St John's night (27th December) the Masons had a great function followed by a banquet at the Lodge, at which some fifty brethren were present, and there was deep drinking and a good deal of noise, ending towards morning in much horseplay and practical jokes.

It was a very lively place in those days, being a very large station and a centre of meeting for several smaller stations in the neighbourhood. It was one of the cheerfullest, healthiest, prettiest and most generally agreeable stations I have ever known—at least it was so in those days, i.e. from 1869 to 1878 when we knew it.

We returned to Balasore in the first week of the new year 1870. It seemed very small, quiet and dull after big, noisy Cuttack. The stream of pilgrims down the road was the busiest thing in it. The Orissa Trunk Road, a section of the great Imperial road between Calcutta and Madras, runs like a backbone down the whole length of the Balasore district for 120 miles. It is a work of almost Roman solidity, being raised fifteen or twenty feet above the level of the country across which it runs, visible from afar like a great dyke with its solid masonry bridges, long rows of shady trees and lines of telegraph posts and wires. The surface is metalled with laterite,[1] or iron-sandstone, a dark red stone found all over Orissa which makes admirable roads, bridges and other buildings. Along this noble road passes all the year round, but chiefly at the seasons of the great festivals—the Dol Jàtrà or Spring festival in January, and the Rath Jàtrà or Car festival in June—an endless string of pilgrims from all parts of India; the poor limping wearily on foot, the rich in bullock carts or palkis, to the great temple of Jagannath at Puri. To protect these pilgrims from being robbed or maltreated there are

[1] Laterite is a ferruginous clay of a dark red colour (so called from Latin *later* 'a brick' from its colour). It is porous and full of large round holes, like a sponge or like Gruyère cheese. When cut from the quarry it is soft, but hardens on exposure to the air. All the ancient temples, forts, palaces and bridges in Orissa are built of it. Broken into gravel it is used for metalling roads. It is the all-pervading laterite that gives the sombre dark reddish, grey colour to towns and scenery generally in Orissa.

regular patrols of police all along the road. There are also hospitals at several places where they receive medical assistance gratuitously if they fall ill from fatigue or disease on their way. Of course, large numbers of them fall ill and die, and they almost always bring fever and cholera with them on their return. The women, as usual, suffer most.

There is a class of Brahmans attached to the temple of Jagannath (*vulgo* Juggernaut) called Pandàs, whose business it is to travel long distances all over India, extolling the virtues of pilgrimage to Jagannath, and inducing people to undertake it. The decaying zeal of the modern Hindu for pilgrimage is kept alive by these touters, who are naturally most successful with the women. It used to be a common sight to see a strong, stalwart Panda marching along the road, followed by a little troop of small, cowering Bengali women, each clad in her one scanty, clinging robe, her small wardrobe in a palm-leaf box on her head, with the lordly Panda's luggage on her shoulders. At night they put up at one of the chatties or lodging-houses which are found all along the road. Here his lordship reposes while his female flock buy his food and cook it, spread his couch, serve his dinner, light his pipe, shampoo his limbs, and even, if he so desire, minister to his lust.

When at length they reach Jagannath the Panda leads his flock round to all the places of worship, sees them through all the ceremonies and, in collusion with the Parihàris, or temple priests, screws out of them all their money down to the last cowry, in fees and offerings. The ceremonies ended, he has done with them, and remorselessly turns them adrift to find their way home, a distance perhaps of many hundred miles, as best they may. So far from their homes from which they have in many cases started surreptitiously, purloining their husbands' hoard of money, these wretched women have to tramp wearily back through the rain, for it is mostly for the Rath Jàtrà, in the rainy season, that they come. What with exposure, fatigue and hunger they die in great numbers by the roadside. Those whose youth and strength enable them to survive the journey are often too much afraid of their husbands' anger to return home, and end by swelling the number of prostitutes in Calcutta. *Tantum religio potuit suadere malorum !*

Often journeying about the district and riding late along the road, we passed scores of white figures of Bengali women lying asleep on the damp ground muffled in their thin cotton sàris, their only garment. We never knew how many of them were alive and how many were dead. Only every morning a band of 'sweepers of the dead' (murdah-farràsh), as they were called, marched along with a cart to carry off and bury as many of the white-robed figures as had finished their mortal journey during the night. A large staff of these official *croque-morts* had to be maintained all along the road.

About this time we received a visit from that vivacious but not very accurate writer, Dr W. W. Hunter, who during a stay of seven days subjected me to such an unceasing fire of questions that on his departure I solemnly forbade anyone to ask me any more questions for a month. He was then a small, lean, hatchet-faced man with a newspaper-correspondent's gift of facile, flashy writing, and a passion for collecting facts and figures of which he made fearful and wonderful use afterwards. The light-hearted subalterns of the regiment at Cuttack had amused themselves by inventing for his benefit wonderful yarns, all of which he duly entered in his note-book and reproduced in his book on Orissa. He was rather a troublesome guest as he was not contented with our simple food. We lived as well as most people in our station of life in the rural districts of India. Our 'chotà hàziri', or little breakfast, was at five-thirty to six, and consisted of tea, eggs boiled or poached, toast and fruit. After this came our ride. Breakfast at eleven consisted of fried or broiled fish, a dish or two of meat—generally fowl cutlets, hashes and stews, or cold meat and salad followed by curry and rice and dessert. We drank either bottled beer—the universal Bass—or claret which we got good and cheap from Bordeaux through Pondicherry. Then followed a long day's work in office. Between four and five there was tea and cakes, after which we went for a drive or had a croquet party in our compound. Dinner at half past seven or eight consisted of soup, and entrée, roast fowls or ducks, occasionally mutton, and in cold weather once or twice beef, an entremet of game or a savoury, and sweets. We drank either beer or claret. This seemed to us a fairly good diet, but it did not suit our guest who wanted champagne every night, *pâté de foie gras* and other 'tinned' delicacies. We did not indulge much in 'tinned' things, believing them to be unwholesome and thinking them often very nasty. But by many people in India they are considered very great luxuries. We used often to be amused at our Eurasian friends saying, 'Oh you! you are so rich, you dine off tinned things every day of course!' They would not believe us when they were told that we lived on plain roast fowl and mutton like themselves.

Hunter's *Orissa* in two volumes was the result of his visit. It is a clever, brilliantly written work, though containing many inaccuracies. I supplied him with a mass of facts, and so did the Collectors of Cuttack and Puri, but he put all our contributions into an Appendix in small type and made very little use of them in the text of his work.

In this year the English doctor attached to Balasore fell sick and had to go away. The Government, never having a sufficient staff of doctors, was obliged to send us in his place a Eurasian apothecary. This man, of humble origin and not much education, had entered the public service as a Hospital Assistant, in which capacity it was his duty to wait upon the surgeons at operations, to clean the instruments, prepare bandages and perform other menial offices. In course of time he rose to be an apothecary and then had charge of the drugs, was entrusted with the task of making up prescriptions, and became at last a skilful compounder. After passing some sort of examination, he set to work to read books on medicine and surgery, and by living in hospitals and hearing the doctors talk picked up a smattering of medical knowledge. He was then lucky enough to be attached, in a subordinate capacity, to the office of the Viceroy's private surgeon and had the honour of compounding Lord Mayo's pills. He was also allowed to prescribe for the humbler members of the Viceregal household, the nurses, footmen and the like. This experience was eventually held to qualify him for the post of Civil Medical Officer of a district; the dearth of properly qualified surgeons compelled the Government to employ anyone with even the slightest pretence to medical knowledge. So he was sent to us.

He was a harmless if ignorant sort of creature at first, for if his medicines did no good, they at least did no harm. But as time went on, waxing bold with practice, he took to what he used to call 'exhibiting the pharmacopoeia'. This process consisted in administering one drug after another out of the work in question till he either killed or cured. He proceeded in alphabetical order. If the drugs under the letter A produced no result, he went on to B, and then to C, and so on. That he did not kill more than he cured was due to the sharpness of his patients, who, on hearing this peculiar phrase, understood that he did not know how to treat them and refrained from taking his medicines.

My wife felt that she could not trust herself to this man for her approaching confinement, and I was therefore obliged to take the long journey of 106 miles into Cuttack. There on the 16th December 1870 was born our third daughter and sixth child, Katharine. As soon as the event was over I started for my own district where I spent a lonely Christmas in camp at Noanand, a large Government estate in the desolate plains by the sea-shore. These are the plains where salt is made. I find the following descriptions of them in my letters to Elliot written in 1870.

'The salt-lands are like a picture in the *Illustrated London News* I remember many years ago of "Bulgarian fishermen on the lower Danube", which I have not seen for perhaps twenty years, but which now comes back to me vividly. Huge, sluggish stream,—"boom of the bittern" generally—dark evening—streak of light on the horizon, and that sort of thing. The salt-lands are wild, grassy plains; sandhills by the sea-shore; foul creeks half salt, half fresh; alligators—black, shiny mud—melancholy great sea, roaring and tumbling far off across wet sands—somehow it seems always to be low water. In the opposite direction is the one redeeming feature, a beautiful little range—far off— of the bluest of blue hills behind which the sun is just setting.'

——'Got back from these dreary salt wastes, red with samphire, white with salt, brown with withered grass, with its boundary of stunted screw pines and the muddy, roaring sea beyond; no houses, no people, no nothing!

> *A land where no one comes*
> *Or hath come since the making of the world.*'

There was a good deal of hard work to do in this desolate place and I remained there till the end of the year 1870.

At the mouth of the Balasore River stood an old ruined bungalow called Balramgarhi. It had been one of the East India Company's factories in the old days, and it was to this place that the few English who survived the 'Black Hole' fled for refuge. It belonged in my time to a rich native merchant, who, at my request, repaired it and let it to me for the summer months. We used to go there during the hot weather to enjoy the cool sea-breezes which blew all day and all night and rendered punkahs unnecessary.

In February 1871 Sir William Grey retired and Sir George Campbell became Lieutenant-Governor of Bengal, and a time of spasmodic activity began for Bengal. Grey was a mild, rather slow sort of man whose whole career had been passed in the Secretariat and whose knowledge of the rural parts—ninety-nine hundredths—of the province was in consequence purely theoretical. He was fond of writing interminable minutes, but he made no very great mark and no excitement was felt when he retired. Campbell was a very different sort of man. A restless spirit and an insatiable desire for change, joined to a profound belief in himself, led him to upset everything. In justice to him, however, it must be admitted that sleepy, muddy, stagnant old Bengal wanted a great deal of stirring up, and his measures were beneficial in most cases, though his successors did not carry them out in the spirit in which he conceived them. He did not reflect how short is the term of office of a Lieutenant-Governor—only five years and in his case even less—and it did not occur to him that he was likely to do more harm than good by commencing great reforms which would require more years of careful watching and guiding to bring them to a successful issue than he was likely to be able to give them. Much of what he did was good and has borne excellent fruit, but much, unfortunately, that went well so long as he was there to manage it, was subsequently spoilt by bad management on the part of his successors; and some of his projected reforms have even been entirely laid aside, much to the detriment of the country and the people.

Like most enthusiastic reformers he was quite indifferent to the feelings of those affected by his reforms. In his zeal for improvement, he rode rough-shod over the most cherished prejudices of the Bengalis, while at the same time he himself was extremely sensitive to public opinion. No amount of opposition or hostile criticism had power to turn him from a pet project, but he felt very much aggrieved at the attacks made upon him in both the English and Native newspapers, and showed his annoyance by issuing somewhat undignified circular orders in which he expressed himself with a freedom and homeliness of phrase very strikingly in contrast with the lofty decorum and stilted official circumlocution of his predecessors. Where another Lieutenant-Governor would have written, 'His Honour is constrained to express his dissatisfaction at . . .', Campbell would write, 'The Lieutenant-Governor abhors this kind of muddle and will punish severely anyone who behaves in this absurd way in future.' He afforded great fun to the comic papers by issuing a circular in which he solemnly informed all his liege subjects that he had been very much shocked at one station which he visited by meeting an Assistant Collector early one morning out for a walk engaged in training some 'puppy-dogs'. This he thought was a disgraceful waste of time. When the poor boy pleaded that he, thought he might amuse himself in his own way 'out of office hours', Campbell's indignation was unbounded. 'There are no such things as office hours,' he replied, 'an officer's services are at the disposal of the Government at all hours of the day and night.' Poor, witty, erratic Frank Bignold, my predecessor as Collector of Balasore, a brilliantly clever man but so unpunctual and unmethodical as to be the ruin of any district that might be in his charge, wrote some clever lines on this pronouncement of the new Lieutenant-Governor. It was a longish poem and I only remember parts of it. The lines I refer to ran thus:

> *The model Magistrate, our rulers say,*
> *Decides all night, investigates all day;*
> *The crack Collector, man of equal might*
> *Reports all day, and corresponds all night.*

Campbell had never served in the Lower Provinces. He had, it is true, been for a time a Judge of the High Court at Calcutta, in which capacity his eccentric ideas about law had made him rather notorious, but this was no introduction to the administrative work of Bengal. His service had been spent almost entirely in the North-West Provinces, and just before his appointment to Bengal he had been Chief Commissioner of the Central Provinces. He chose to assume that there was not, among the Civilians of Bengal, a single man fit to be his Secretary, and he therefore imported from the Central Provinces his favourite, C. E. Bernard.

Bernard, who had been my contemporary and rival at Haileybury, was a nephew of Sir John Lawrence and owed his rapid promotion partly to that circumstance. He was, however, a man of very great ability; had he not been so, he could not have risen as he did, even with his powerful interest.

Solid, judicious, indefatigably laborious, clear-headed, quick to perceive the bearings of a matter, but without much originality or initiative power—Bernard was just the man for Secretary to so masterful and original a chief as Campbell. If a lucid exposition of a long and intricate subject were wanted, Bernard would wade through piles of papers, missing no important point, never led astray by digressions, nor bewildered by conflicting opinions, and would produce a masterly minute which brought order out of chaos, and shed light on dark places. His services to Sir George were invaluable, and though there might have been found in Bengal eight or ten men as good as he, still it was not unnatural that Campbell, having already such a man to his hand, and being totally unacquainted with most of the Bengal men, should prefer to have him as his Secretary and should refuse to consider how much injustice he was doing to the Bengal men by giving one of the prize appointments to an outsider.

Sir George's activity was prodigious. He was never contented with the assurance often made to him by experienced officers, that this or that system had been in force for many years, had always been found to work well, and was well suited to the local peculiarities of the Province. He was full of theories which he had propounded years before in a book written when he was a very junior officer in Oudh. He attacked every department of the administration at once—police, criminal courts, judicial courts, jails, land revenue, collection of taxes, trial of rent suits, registration of assurances, public works, roads and ferries, education, vaccination, sanitation—('and everything else that ends in—"ation",' as Bignold remarked in one of his poems), municipalities, the excise on spirits and drugs, customs, salt—all felt his probing hand in turn. His plan was to issue a minute in which he stated that he was not satisfied with the working of this or that department, and therefore appointed a Committee consisting of Mr Bernard and some other officers to inquire and report on it. In due course there would appear an exhaustive report by Bernard, on which His Honour would base a series of rules often involving very sweeping changes. It is only fair to say that in many cases he effected marked improvements, though in some others he made very injudicious innovations. His general policy, it is scarcely necessary to add, was intensely distasteful to the natives on whose most cherished prejudices he tramped ruthlessly. Consequently he was very much disliked by them.

My official work at quiet, sleepy Balasore was not very heavy though varied. It had this advantage that owing to the smallness of the district I was able personally to supervise everything down to the minutest details. I was thus fortunately able to give satisfaction to Campbell by carrying out successfully many of his reforms. I might not approve of them all myself—and when I did not, I frankly said so—but as it was my duty to carry out orders I did so loyally, and Campbell was pleased at this. He also received very graciously a copy of the first volume of my *Comparative Grammar* which appeared about this time, and was good enough to say he did not at all object to officers occupying some part of their time in so useful a way. My *Grammar* was well received in England and on the Continent, was very favourably reviewed, and gained me some little reputation as a philologist.

It was difficult to find time for linguistic work, not so much because official work was heavy, as because of the constant interruptions to which one in my position is subjected. Still, I managed to devote some time nearly every day to my *Grammar*, and to extend my slight knowledge of European languages. I used to take up one language at a time and stick to it for a month or two, after which I went on to another. One cold weather I read *Don Quixote* through in the original Spanish and a great part of Ercilla's long and rather tedious poem, *La Arancana*, with which, after the glowing description of it in Humboldt's *Cosmos*, I was rather disappointed. Another time I had a spell of Goethe, or Tasso, or Balzac, a strange farrago! I was, however, more in need of German, because in writing my *Comparative Grammar* it was necessary to consult so many German authorities. Much painful wading through Bopp, and Grimm and Pott had to be done. It was a relief to turn from them to the grand old Spanish ballads of Rey Don Sancho, or el Cid Campeador, though both had often to be laid aside to settle some knotty point about the collection of revenue or detection of crime. It was a curiously mixed life as regards the mind and its workings that I led in those days.

About this time I became a contributor to a weekly paper called the *Indian Observer*, got up by a small number of brilliant young men in the Civil and Military Services, aided by some educational men and barristers. Most of the writing was clever and sparkling and, of course, very sarcastic. The paper was extremely popular and successful for about a couple of years. It, however, incurred the grave displeasure of several high officials, on account of the biting satire with which it attacked the measures of Lord Mayo's Government, and especially his two most prominent advisers, Sir John Strachey and Sir Richard Temple. Although I did not write any of the political articles, yet my connexion with the paper did me much harm when Temple, some years later, came to be Lieutenant-Governor of Bengal. Free and temperate criticism of the measures of Government by officials was not permitted in 1872. The article on Finance and Foreign Policy in the *Observer* did not exceed the limits usually considered permissible in England, but in India our rulers are thin-skinned, and by degrees made the writers in the *Observer* understand that it was not safe to write in it any longer. So they dropped off one by one. Poor Wilfred Heeley of our Service, then Inspector-General of Jails, was so persecuted that he died of a broken heart. I was cruelly persecuted also, and so were several others. I wrote a series of articles on the condition of the peasantry in Orissa, on the new Road Cess law, on the work and training of men in my own service and on various social questions. By degrees, however, the political element in the paper grew feebler and the purely literary element stronger. I then wrote them a long series of articles on the vernacular literature of India, giving a brief history of each of the principal medieval writers, with short versified extracts from their poems. I also wrote reviews of Morris's poem, 'Love is enough', and other work. The paper gradually declined and came to an end in 1873.

I have mentioned that some of my articles were about the Road Cess. This was a hotly debated question at the time, and much more trouble was anticipated from it than actually occurred. In fact, when the principle was once conceded, there was nothing more to fight about and the law having once taken its place on the Statute Book, was submitted to by the people with not more grumbling than the editors of native papers could manage to excite.

The point was this: the landholders of Bengal, having by the Permanent Settlement been secured in the possession of their estates (and so much of the estates of other persons as in the scramble of 1793 they could manage to get hold of) at a rent fixed for ever, imagined, or were said by their advocates to imagine, that the State had thereby pledged itself not to demand from them any further contributions to the expenses of the administration. They thought that they were exempt for ever from all taxes, imposts and cesses of all kinds. Money being wanted for the improvement of the roads in Bengal, and the finances not admitting, and not being likely to admit, of large sums being devoted to this purpose, further taxation was necessary. A bill was therefore introduced into the Council of the Lieutenant-Governor to provide for the levy of a cess. This cess was to be a rate upon the annual profits of estates, tenures, and holdings and was to be paid by landholders, by those who held tenures under them, and by the actual cultivators of the soil. Immediately a cry was raised that the Government was infringing upon the compact made at the time of the Permanent Settlement, and the war of words rose high. I took no part in this as I was from the first clearly of the opinion that the cry was not only baseless, but opposed to the most obvious historical facts. The fact that a former Government had bound itself and its successors for all time not to increase the demand from the zemindars on one account, namely the land, was no bar to additional demands being made upon them on other accounts. But it was the method adopted for fixing the exact amount of cess payable by each person that gave colour to the objection. An attempt was to be made to ascertain the profit on each estate and the tax was to be levied on this profit. Zemindars were to be called upon to submit statements showing their profits, and it was hoped that the threat of a criminal prosecution for submitting false returns would suffice to secure their truthfulness. The zemindar was moreover to be permitted to collect the sums due from his tenants and ryots and pay them to the Collector, after deducting a small commission for his trouble.

The weak points in this scheme were numerous. No one who really knew the zemindars could expect them to send in correct returns. Many of them were careless and indolent, mere puppets in the hands of unscrupulous followers. Many more were crafty, dissembling moneygrubbers. No reliance could be placed on their statements. The threat of criminal prosecution was mere *brutum fulmen*, because in order to secure a conviction it was necessary to prove first that the returns were false, and secondly that they were intentionally and wilfully misleading. We had no data whatsoever for proving the first point, for there had never been any official check or control over the management by zemindars of their estates, and as to the second it was easy for the zemindar to bring half the countryside to bear witness that he was easy-going and careless and had never kept any accounts in his life, and had not the slightest idea as to what were his profits, so that the return submitted was mere guesswork and not intended to mislead. Then again, so great is the dependence of the ryots on the zemindar that to give the latter the right of collecting the cess would open a wide door to all sorts of exactions.

I set forth all these considerations in my articles in the *Indian Observer* in the form of an imaginary history of what took place on the estate of a typical zemindar whom I created for the occasion. I also in several articles entered fully into the actual condition of the ryot and the relations between him and the zemindar. Sir George Campbell, as it afterwards turned out, knew that I was the writer of the articles, which made some stir at the time.

Nevertheless, though in my own mind I disapproved of the policy of the Government, it was my duty to carry out orders, and my small district of Balasore having been selected as the first into which the Road Cess should be introduced, I set to work actively and soon finished the assessment and reported my district as ready to pay the cess sooner than Government had anticipated. For this I was warmly thanked by the Lieutenant-Governor. I was frequently consulted by him and the Board of Revenue on points of detail and practical difficulties which arose in the course of the work, and my proceedings were handed round as a pattern for all other districts. This was one of the small triumphs which come now and then to encourage a lonely worker in a remote Indian district.

CHAPTER XVI

BALASORE, 1871–1873

SOME facts about our home life may now be chronicled. At the mouth of the Balasore River, sixteen miles from the town stood an old ruined house called Balramgarhi, famed as the site of the English factory to which the survivors of the 'Black Hole' had fled for refuge.

Although Balasore itself was so near the sea, yet there was a sensible difference between the climate of the station, and that of the sea-shore. For a long time the European residents had been in the habit of going for a few weeks in the hot weather to live in two small bungalows on the sandhills on the coast, at a place called Chandipore. But in my predecessor's time the bungalows had fallen into the hands of a doctor in Calcutta, who conceived the idea that he could make a popular sea-side resort out of it. So he published flaming descriptions of the poor little place, with fancy illustrations and scientific opinions as to its amazing healthiness and so on. But as there was no particular way of getting there from Calcutta, and no shops or supplies or drinkable water to be had when you did get there, the Calcutta public preferred to go to the hills, and the project fell through. Meanwhile, however, the doctor, by way of popularizing the place, took to lending the two bungalows to such of his Calcutta friends as he could induce to go there, and they were consequently lost to the Europeans of Balasore. It occurred to me that the old factory at the mouth of the river might be utilized as a hot weather residence, and the owner, a wealthy zemindar, agreeing to this, put it into thorough repair and let it to me. As soon as the hot weather began we all migrated there.

The old house was raised on a plinth about three feet high; it had, as usual in Indian houses, only one storey and contained three large and five smaller rooms. All round the front ran a deep veranda with a broad platform in front facing the sea, from which a broad flight of steps led down to a small garden. Beyond was a wide stretch of waste covered with tall jungle grass and a few clumps of mango and palm trees, beside which the river ran out to sea. Half a mile in front stretched the grassy plain away to a solitary palmyra tree on a point where sea and river met. Across the river to the south was Chandipore, a mile off on a low line of grassy hills, and behind us to the west the picturesque line of the Nilgiri Hills. Our boat manned by eight rowers lay close by, and every morning we were rowed down to the mouth of the river and went for a long walk on the sands. In the evening as we sat on the veranda a fleet of native sloops and brigs would appear on the horizon in a cloud of white sail, round the point and drop anchor in the river. The fishermen rowed out with the ebb and back with the flood, laden with delicious fish of which we thus had a very abundant supply.

We found the life here very pleasant. My wife and children lived there permanently and I rode into Balasore every morning to my work and back again in the evening. Provisions and drinking water had to be brought by boat from Balasore. Unfortunately the season that year—1871—was very unfavourable. Usually in March the south-west winds set in up the coast and round the headlands, turning to south up the rivers, so that as our house at Balramgarhi faced south we ordinarily had a sweet, cool breeze blowing right into it all day and all night. This wind blows over the flats into Balasore but of course loses much of its coolness and freshness by the time it reaches the station. The difference in the temperature between Balasore and the coast only eight miles off is very great. In the season we spent at Balramgarhi the course of nature was changed. The fresh sea-breeze was less regular. An abnormal land wind took its place, which, coming over the swamps to landward of us, brought with it malarious exhalations. Our native servants began to get fever and had to be sent into the station. At last we were also attacked and had to go back to Balasore and were ill for a long time afterwards. My poor wife suffered from malarial fever for a long time.

It was not merely the unusual season that made us ill. The circumstances had a good deal to do with it. When we first saw Balramgarhi, the old house was scarcely to be seen from the river owing to the dense jungle that had grown up all round it. All this was cleared away before the house could be got at to be repaired, but newly cleared land is always unhealthy in India, as elsewhere, and it is probable that even had not the weather been so unpropitious we should have suffered all the same. The salt-makers, however, lived there for many months of the year without getting fever, but they were a peculiar race and were acclimatized.

Salt-making is, or was then (for great changes have taken place since those days) a very flourishing industry along the eastern coast of India. There were two ways of making it. One way employed all along the Madras coast and in southern Orissa is known as Karkach. In this method large, shallow pans are dug in the sand on the foreshore and sea-water is let into them by channels at high tide. The heat of the sun evaporates the water, leaving the pans thickly encrusted with crystals of salt. It is then scraped off and stored in warehouses. It is a dirty, coarse stuff and not very strongly flavoured. The strict Hindus prefer it because, not having been touched by human hands, it is free from all suspicion of ceremonial impurity.

The other method, which is more complicated, is in use in northern Orissa and Bengal and is known as Panga. Channels are dug from the sea to small reservoirs dug—not in the sand, but in the muddy soil beyond. Then a mound about two feet high is made of earth and grass mixed. On the top is placed a large earthen vessel pierced with holes. A layer of grass and twigs is placed in the vessel, and on this again a thick layer of mud from the surrounding soil, which is largely saturated with saline matter from being constantly submerged by the sea. Water from the reservoir is then poured in till the vessel is full. This sea-water filtering through the saline earth becomes more salt than it was before, and the strong brine thus made is drawn off through a bamboo pipe into a second vessel. Close by is a rude, dome-shaped furnace consisting of a hole in the ground surmounted by a cupola, formed by fixing together with mud a large number of egg-shaped jars with their mouths outwards. These are all filled to the brim with the brine. Then a fire is lighted inside and fed with the tall, dry grass which grows around, till all the water in the jars has been boiled away. The crystals of salt are then scraped out and piled on mats for transport to the gola.

The making of salt is a Government monopoly. In the early years of British rule the salt was made by men hired by the Government, and a large staff of highly-paid officials was maintained to supervise the work. The 'Salt Agent', who lived in a huge palace at Contai on the Midnapore coast, was a senior member of the Covenanted Civil Service and drew a very large salary—Rs 4,000 or thereabouts a month. This system was, however, found to be expensive and inefficient. Fraud and peculation was rife, and smuggling on a large scale was winked at by the numerous and badly-watched native subordinates. Salt Daroghas, on a salary of forty or fifty rupees a month, bought large estates and built handsome houses and died worth large sums of money. The old system was swept away and a new one introduced. The Salt Agent and his army of Daroghas were abolished, and the long-suffering and over burdened Collector had the Salt department added to the already long list of his duties. Government gave up making salt on its own account, and private persons were invited to engage in the manufacture.

Enterprising merchants, contractors and others possessing a little capital readily embarked in this promising venture. Securing from the landowner the lease of a tract of land ten or fifteen miles square on the 'saliferous' region—a narrow strip of low land running along all the coast—the contractor applied for permission to make salt there. He had to fence his ground strongly, to build huts for the workmen and to hire them. He had also to deposit a sum of money with the Collector to meet the pay of a small guard of police and a 'Pass Officer' and weighmen.

As in every occupation in India, so in this, the men who do the work belong to a special caste, called in Orissa—Mallangis, in Bengal—Nûnias. Some of them engage in agriculture, but the most part live entirely by making (and smuggling) salt.

Work at the Arangs, as the salt enclosures are called, begins about December when the land has dried after the rains. The Mallangis clear the ground, build reed-huts, mounds and furnaces, dig canals to carry the salt water. They also cut great quantities of the tall, coarse grass that grows all about, which, with its thick stems and knotty roots, makes excellent and cheap fuel. At daybreak the fires are lit and the work goes on until an hour before sunset, when the salt, still wet and warm, is put into baskets and carried to the enclosure, where it is weighed and the day's out-turn recorded by the Pass Officer. The salt is thrown into heaps which are carefully thatched with palm leaves. Later on it is conveyed either by land in bags carried by pack-bullocks, or by boat up the numerous muddy creeks to the Gola or warehouse near one of the large inland towns or markets.

Every step in the manufacture and sale of salt is surrounded with the most minute precautions on the part of Government, and there is a distinct and separate kind of fraud practised at each stage. As each fresh precaution is evolved by the Board of Revenue, the Board of Smugglers invents a means of circumventing it.

The area of the Arang is extensive; except where actually cleared it is covered with tall, coarse grass and scrub. In many places there are swamps and quicksands. The narrow, winding footpaths on which only one man can go are known only to the Mallangis. The staff of police put to guard the Arang consists usually of only four men and a Head Constable. The work is unpopular because of the unhealthiness of the place and the difficulty of procuring provisions. Consequently only the worst men in the force can be got to go there and the salt Arangs are used as a penal settlement. A policeman who does anything wrong is sent to a Salt Arang as a punishment. Add to this that the smugglers are liberal with their bribes, and that they are backed up by wealthy and influential men who have no scruple in getting up a false charge against an inconveniently honest policeman and supporting it by any number of paid false witnesses, it is not surprising under these circumstances that malpractices should flourish and the revenue should be considerably defrauded.

In carrying the salt from the furnaces to the weighing ground, the Mallangis deposit parcels of it in spots known only to themselves in the jungle, to be removed later on and sold privately to the adjacent villages. When the fires are (apparently) put out at sunset, they will leave the furnaces with the loads of salt, but will sneak back again in the course of the night, blow up the embers and make salt all night, hiding it before daylight in the jungle. The police are supposed to patrol all night, and as the whole tract is as flat as a pancake it is only by mounting on the ruins of some deserted furnace of former years that they can see over the jungle and mark far off the light and smoke from some clandestine working. Then they have to steal upon the men silently and cautiously through the narrow, tortuous paths, taking their chance of meeting a leopard, or wild boar, or even an occasional wild buffalo. When they reach the spot, they often have a fierce hand-to-hand fight in which the smugglers, being numerically stronger, usually get the better of the police and escape into the darkness, where it would be useless to pursue them. Of course such courage and activity are not often displayed by the police. It is only when the Magistrate, angered by the increase of smuggling fulminates threats, that they are stirred up to such temporary efforts. But as soon as they have made an arrest or two they relapse into their former apathy and the smuggling goes on as merrily as before.

The salt itself by its nature plays into the hands of the smugglers. It is wet when first made, but dries by degrees and of course loses weight as it dries. It is weighed at the Arang before despatch and again at the Gola on arrival, and if the two weights do not agree the contractor is liable to a heavy fine. A certain allowance is made for dryage *en route*. A common trick is to prick holes in the bags when they are taken off the bullocks at night, for the journey takes two or three days. A good deal of salt is abstracted in this way. Then the bullocks are driven through some muddy pool or ditch—as if by accident—so that the salt gets wet and increases in weight and the loss by abstraction is covered.

If the salt is sent by boat it is not put into bags, but thrown loose—'in bulk' as the technical phrase is—into the hold of a large, undecked barge. The surface is then stamped all over with an 'àdal' or large wooden seal bearing the name of the contractor, and on arrival at the Gola it is carefully inspected before being unloaded to make sure that the àdal marks are intact.

Even from boats, however, smuggling takes place. One night a large, salt-laden barge was moored under a high, overhanging bank in a creek far from any inhabited place. The boatmen and police guard went up on to the bank, made themselves a snug retreat with piles of scrub and grass covered with a tarpaulin, cooked and ate their rice and went to sleep. Then from the jungle there emerged in Indian file sixteen or eighteen men, all stark naked and oiled. They had a long rope and baskets. They let themselves down into the boat and while some filled the baskets with salt others drew up the baskets by the rope. The salt was carried basket by basket to a boat hidden in a smaller creek close by and when it was full they got in and shoved off. They were afraid to row lest the noise should attract attention. So they softly and silently poled out of the creek. By this time it was just daybreak and as they turned out of the creek into the river they came full into the police patrol boat which happened to be coming that way. The constables at once smelt a rat and, boarding the boat, saw that it was full of salt and tried to seize the offenders. They, however, slipped through their hands owing to their bodies being oiled, and flinging themselves into the water swam ashore and disappeared into the jungle where it was useless to pursue them.

The reason for all this smuggling is that there is a heavy tax of Rs 3–4 a maund (in English weights, approximately £8 a ton). This has to be paid by the contractor before he can get delivery of his salt from the Gola. The salt is then issued to him under a pass in which all sorts of particulars are entered, name, father's name, caste and residence of everyone concerned, name of Arang at which the salt was made, where it is now to be sent to and so on and so on. The contractor sells it to wholesale vendors, who (also under a pass) sell it again to retail dealers, and they (also under a pass) to their customers the public. From the moment that the salt crystallizes in the pan to the time when it passes into the possession of the consumer it is guarded and protected by passes, espionage, supervision, official interference and legal penalties. The Collector's life is made a burden to him by the ceaseless vigilance necessary to protect the Government revenue. The price of salt is unduly raised thereby and the villagers living on the edge of the saliferous tract are harassed by incessant police visits. Close to them lies the broad, flat salt plain; they have only to dig up a little of the briny earth, boil it in salt water out of the nearest creek, and they can obtain a plentiful supply of this necessary of life. But if they do this they are liable to fine and imprisonment. The police, who are practically powerless against professional smugglers, used to display great keenness and energy in arresting some poor helpless widow whom they caught boiling a little brine in an earthen pot to make salt to eat with her rice. They dragged the wretched, frightened creature fifty or sixty miles into Balasore, and brought her before the Magistrate who was reluctantly compelled to fine her. The Board made matters worse by giving rewards to any policeman who discovered and arrested anyone having in his possession or making 'illicit salt'. But the way the thing was worked seemed to me and all the other Magistrates so absurd and oppressive that I first refused to inflict any fines in such cases and next refused to give the police any reward for 'detecting' them. Of course there was a great outcry, and I was angrily called on by the Board to say what I meant by such conduct. This gave me the opportunity I had been longing for. A lengthy correspondence ensued, and the matter ended by the Government conceding to the inhabitants of the saliferous tract and its neighbourhood permission to make small quantities of salt for their own use, but not for sale. This put a stop to the petty acts of oppression which fell so heavily, petty though they might seem to us, on the poorer classes of the rural population.

Very heavily oppressed they were, and it is wonderful how they contrived to exist at all under the numerous exactions to which they were subjected at the hands of their own countrymen. We did our best to protect them, but a mere handful of foreigners in so large a country cannot even hear of many of the things that are done behind their backs. The people are afraid to complain, knowing that if compelled by the English Magistrate to compensate their victims, the powerful oppressors will be able to find many opportunities for revenging themselves. It is only by accident that we find out many abuses, and it is necessary to practise the greatest caution in remedying them lest we should do more harm than good by our well-meant interference. Such a case occurred about this time, and caused much excitement. It was known as the 'Illegal Cess Agitation'.

One day my Assistant, Fiddian, in charge of the Bhadrakh sub-division which comprised the whole southern side of the district, was out in camp on one of his usual tours of inspection. In a very remote corner of the district, where the people understood little or nothing about the principles of British administration, a ryot came up to him as he was riding alone through the fields and asked him, 'Is it ordered that we are to pay *tikkus*?'

'What do you mean by *tikkus*?' asked Fiddian.

'Many things,' replied the ryot. 'Our zemindar makes us pay what he calls *tikkus*, he says he has to pay it to the Sirkàr, and we are to pay it to him, one rupee each house; then there is "tàr", one rupee, also "màngan", one or two or even three rupees each whenever he has a son or a daughter married, or wants to give a feast to Brahmans on some religious festival day, or wants to go on pilgrimage to Jagannath, or to repair his house, or many other things.'

'No,' said Fiddian, 'you have to pay your rent and nothing else.' The man went away, apparently well pleased.

But this set him thinking, and he made elaborate inquiries from which he found out that the zemindars were in the habit of levying contributions from all their ryots on all sorts of pretexts. 'Tikkus' was their pronunciation of the English word 'tax'. The zemindars had to pay the newly introduced and extremely unpopular income tax, and recouped themselves and more than recouped themselves by levying a rupee per house from all their tenants.

When the telegraph line was set up all along the Trunk Road, although the zemindars had not to pay anything towards its construction, they pretended that they had, and made a levy from all their tenants. This was the 'tàr', the telegraph being known as 'tàr bijli' or 'lightning wire'. Many other things were made occasions for raising contributions, so that the wretched ryots were ground down to the dust and lived in the direst poverty. I took the matter up earnestly and made inquiries from which it appeared that the practice of levying these illegal cesses was common all over the District. I reported the matter to Ravenshaw, the Commissioner, and he caused inquiries to be made in Cuttack and Puri, from which it came to light that the same practices were in vogue there also. He then reported it to Government. Meanwhile the news that the Hàkims had declared the 'tikkus' to be illegal spread all over the country and up into Bengal where it caused great commotion. In some districts it gave rise to rioting.

Various schemes were proposed for putting a stop to this, none of which were very effective. The Lieutenant-Governor then proposed legislation, and prepared a draft of a law declaring the practices illegal and laying down punishments for such offences. This was, however, stopped by the Government of India on the advice of Sir Richard Temple, then a member of Council, who knew absolutely nothing whatever about the matter or about Bengal, but who, as he afterwards told me, chose to consider it as a mere petty local agitation which it was not wise to encourage.

This was a great disappointment to us, but we did not give up the game. Seeing that the Government would not help us, we determined to help ourselves. We knew that the Government of Bengal was on our side though the far-off, ignorant 'India Government', as it is called, would not help us. So Fiddian and I commenced a series of tours into all parts of the District, in the course of which we assembled the ryots of each estate together with the zemindar himself, or if he were an absentee, his agent, found out by questioning the people and examining the zemindar's books what exactions he was in the habit of making, and explained to the people which of them was illegal. In this way we succeeded in opening their eyes, and stirring them up to resist illegal demands. For a time there was much confusion, underhand attempts at extortion by the zemindars, forcibly resisted by the peasants, in a few cases rioting and broken heads. But by degrees the strife ceased; most of the zemindars gave up their exactions finding they could not enforce them, and though with so timid a peasantry, so masterful a proprietary body, and so wily a crowd of agents, we could never be sure that extortions were not practised, we soon had abundant proof that they had everywhere very much diminished, and in most places entirely ceased. The result was, on the whole, considerable increase of material prosperity and comfort for the peasantry and a knowledge of their rights which would render a return to the old state of grinding extortion impracticable in the future. Had we been properly supported, the movement would have grown into a great revolution which would have been fruitful of unspeakable good for the down-trodden agricultural population. However, we did what we could and for the results we were thankful.

It was a great surprise to us all in the cold weather of 1871-2 to be informed that the Viceroy, Lord Mayo, was going to visit our neglected and benighted province. No Viceroy had ever visited Orissa since the establishment of British rule in India. Great were the preparations for his reception, and great were the stirrings of heart among the 'Kings of the Amorites that dwell in the hills', as we used to call the great host of semi-independent Rajas who ruled each his little territory in the hill-country. Mayurbhanj, Keonjhar, Dhenkanal and the rest of the Maharajas far away in their hill-fortresses deep in the western jungles got out their 'barbaric pearl and gold', and started with long trains of nondescript retainers in strange costumes, from complete suits of rusty armour, coats of mail, helmets of brass and cloaks of tiger-skin to a simple girdle of leaves round the loins. They made pompous public entries into Cuttack, their long processions headed by discordant music of horn and drum, and each vied with the other in the number of his retainers and the splendour of his own costume. In Cuttack itself Durbar tents, fireworks, illuminations, decorations and loyal addresses were being got ready. Fiddian and I arrived with our contingents in due course and began at once to co-operate actively with Macpherson, the Collector of Cuttack, in carrying out the arrangements. Suddenly a telegram arrived with the news that Lord Mayo had been stabbed by a convict when visiting Mount Harriet, one of the convict stations of the Andaman Islands, and was dead!

Ravenshaw, the Commissioner, with a large party of distinguished officials had gone down to False Point, the harbour of Orissa—the only one in those days—to receive the Viceroy. When it was signalled that the Viceroy's steamer was in sight the Commissioner steamed out to meet it. As it came nearer something strange in the appearance of the vessel attracted their attention, and through their glasses they made out the ensign half-mast high! On coming alongside they found that it was the companion steamer with some of the staff on board, the Viceroy's own steamer with his body and Lady Mayo had gone on to Calcutta. They then heard the sad news and were requested to hurry back to Cuttack and telegraph to Calcutta, so that the news might arrive before the steamer, which they did. All our grand preparations were stopped, the Kings returned to their hills and the great assemblage broke up amidst general grief and indignation. The assassin was an Afghan—of course—who had been sentenced to transportation for life for murder, as he thought unjustly, and had taken this opportunity of revenging himself. Lord Mayo was universally regretted. He was a tall, stately man of the most genial and affable manner, personally extremely popular, and officially an active, keen-witted, energetic ruler. It is needless to write more about this melancholy event; are not these things written in the chronicles of British India?

After this we settled down quietly in our sleepy hollow of Balasore and resumed the even tenor of our way. On the 13th October 1872 was born our fourth daughter and seventh child, Gertrude. The child was sickly at first and caused us much anxiety but eventually, owing to the care of her nurse, a strange old Irishwoman named Doran (she was widely known as 'Mother D.'), she grew up healthy and extremely pretty.

This year I wrote a Manual of the District of Balasore, its history, geography, land tenures, castes, industries and all sorts of other things. It cost me much time and labour, but for reasons which I shall mention hereafter it was never published. There *was*, however, published in this year the first volume of my *Comparative Grammar of the Modern Aryan Languages of India*. It was published by Trübner, and immediately taken up by Oriental philologists both in England and on the Continent. It was very favourably reviewed in English and German papers and adopted as a textbook in many universities. It won me considerable reputation and fame.

I also contributed articles regularly to the *Indian Observer*, *Indian Antiquary* and *Journal of the Bengal Asiatic Society*. Balasore was such a dull little place, and the few European officers there so stupid and uninteresting, that I was forced to keep myself constantly occupied at one thing or another to prevent myself from perishing from ennui. Long rides with my dear wife every morning, visits to the sea with boating and fishing, and reading such books as we could get were my chief amusements. My wife had her nursery and her garden, which was very lovely till the cyclone of this year swept it all away. She was a notable grower of roses and her garden was very much admired by our occasional visitors. Officials of various sorts passed through Balasore from time to time and enlivened our existence a little.

It came to an end very suddenly and unexpectedly by my being appointed in August 1873 to officiate as Commissioner of Orissa for three months while Ravenshaw went on leave. I visited Balasore once or twice afterwards, but our four years' residence there came to an end and we were very glad of it.

CHAPTER XVII

CUTTACK, 1873

ON arriving in Cuttack on the 12th August 1873 I took charge of the
office of Commissioner of the Orissa Division. This includes the three
districts of Balasore, Cuttack and Puri which are under direct British
rule, and seventeen petty Tributary States each ruled by its own Raja
under the general supervision of the Commissioner, who is also entitled
Superintendent of the Tributary States. These States all lie in the
tangled mass of hills, densely covered for the most part with virgin
forests, to the west of the settled districts.

Ravenshaw had taken three months' 'privilege' leave, as it is called,
and in order not to lose a single day he refused to sign the papers making
over charge to me till he was just about to go on board the steamer. This
necessitated my going down to False Point with him and his wife on
board one of the small Government steamers, and staying there twenty-
four hours while waiting for the British India Company's steamer from
Calcutta, which touched at False Point on her way to Madras, whither
Ravenshaw was bound. We had a merry time, as there was a large
party at False Point waiting for the steamer. At last the steamer from
Calcutta made its appearance, Ravenshaw departed and I was able to
start for Cuttack. My absence had been very inconvenient, not only
because work was accumulating there, but because our youngest child
Gertrude had been taken ill on the journey from Balasore, and I had
been obliged to leave my wife alone and in great anxiety about the child.
So as soon as I was free to return I started in the steam launch with
two other men who had also to get back to their work. We pushed on as
fast as the little vessel could carry us, and reached Cuttack early the next
morning. As we approached the landing place we saw old Wright, the
Sub-Judge, pacing up and down in an agitated manner with a very
white face. My heart sank, for I feared bad news about the baby. Bad
news it was, but of a different kind. As soon as we got within hearing,
he called out to us, 'Irvine is dead.' Irvine was the Collector, and we
had left him apparently in robust health three days before.

Ever since the terrible Orissa famine in 1866, the work of the large
and heavily-worked Cuttack Collectorate had fallen into confusion and
immense arrears of business had accumulated, which successive Collectors had toiled in vain to clear off. About a year before this time

217

Irvine had been appointed Collector, a clever young Irishman, but utterly unmethodical. He made matters worse by a groundless suspicion of all his native subordinates, which led him to try and do himself much work which they were quite competent to do, and for which he had not time. Thus the arrears accumulated worse than ever. Not content with working every day from ten to six in his office, he used to take home with him at night quantities of papers and would sit up till two or three o'clock in the morning working at them. On the day of my arrival in Cuttack, as I was driving to Ravenshaw's house with him, we met Irvine returning from office in a mail-phaeton, the back part of which was crammed full of large bags. These he said contained papers at which he was going to work after dinner. The result of this excessive overwork on the health of a stout, full-blooded man who required a great deal of exercise to keep him well, was fatal. One night when he had sat over his papers till nearly daybreak, he went to take a bath preparatory to snatching a few hours' sleep. In his bath he had an apoplectic stroke and was taken up senseless and died in a few hours after, never having recovered consciousness.

I thus found everything in confusion. I had my own work as Commissioner to learn, and the indescribable muddle in the Cuttack Collectorate on top of it. J. F. Stevens, the Joint Magistrate, though clever, was young and inexperienced and naturally very nervous at the great and novel responsibility thrown on him, for in the event of the Collector's death all the work of the district devolved on the Joint Magistrate, as the second in command. I had not been home an hour before he drove up, white and trembling, with a large quantity of poor Irvine's large bags full of papers in his dog-cart. All the previous day the Judge, whose duty it was to take charge of the property of deceased Europeans, had been sending him bags of papers which he had found in Irvine's house, littering all the rooms and thrown about in the wildest confusion. Stevens's only idea was to carry out a suggestion of Irvine's and set officers to work to sort, arrange and catalogue all these papers with a view to their being subsequently disposed of. But this seemed to me to be useless labour. The first thing to be done was to arrange for the charge of the district. It was essential to lose no time. I therefore telegraphed to the Government requesting that Stevens might at once be appointed to officiate as Collector. In a letter to Sir George Campbell I pointed out that much time would be lost by sending another officer from a distance. Stevens was rather afraid of undertaking so heavy a charge, though the promotion was great and unexpected, but on my promising to help him, he consented. His appointment came the same day by telegram, and the next morning he came to me early with his cargo of big bags but with a cheerful face. The bags were brought into my study and he then proceeded to unfold his notable scheme of having them catalogued and arranged.

'But,' said I, 'why this unnecessary labour? In the time it would take to make these long lists, the letters themselves could be answered.' He stared at me with lack-lustre eyes. 'How?' said he. 'Empty your bags on that table,' said I, 'and I will show you how.' The bags were emptied on to a large dining-table and as Graves, a very smart young police-officer, came in at the moment I pressed him also into the work. I seated them both before me, pencils in their hands. The first paper I opened required no answer. 'Write "file" on it,' and they wrote and Stevens put his initials. The effect of this order was that the paper would be placed by a clerk in the file to which it referred. As each letter or paper was opened, I read it, threw it to one or other of them, and dictated an order which they wrote. In this way we worked for some three hours, by which time quite half of the formidable mass had been disposed of. All Stevens had to do was to hand the papers to his Head Clerk who, in a few hours, having got orders on them, would be able to do what was required. So Stevens went away happy. Every day for some time I used to go for some hours to his office and work with him, and then go on to my own office and spend the rest of the day at my own work. Stevens, being a man of great clearness of mind and quick perception, soon learnt how to do the work and was able to dispense with my assistance. Being both Commissioner and Collector at the same time was rather hard work and I was not sorry when it was over.

But I had discovered one thing. The immense accumulation of arrears of work was due not merely to the disorder caused by the famine, nor to the unmethodical habits of the two last Collectors. It was due in a great degree to the slowness and dishonesty of the native ministerial staff. It would be impossible without going into technical details, which would not be intelligible to those who have not served in the Indian Civil Service, to explain the exact way in which these men act, and had acted in this case. The heads of the various departments were old men deeply rooted in old-fashioned ways and grooves, each of them had an army of dependants and filled all vacant posts with his relations. They all with one accord strenuously resisted improvements and changes of all sorts, and where they were unable to prevent their introduction, laboured hard and successfully to render them inoperative when introduced. A strong hand, an inflexible will, and rigid method and punctuality were required to restore order to this large and important district. As soon, therefore, as I had set my own work as Commissioner in order, and had allowed Stevens time to clear off his arrears, I held my official inspection of the Cuttack Collectorate. I made it as close and searching as I knew how, with the result that I discovered countless abuses, a total want of system, and an organized confederacy among the native officials to resist all change or improvement. In order to break the neck of the opposition I resolved on drastic measures, dismissed the heads of all the departments or compelled them to retire on pension, filling their places with younger men of more advanced views, some of whom I brought from my old district of Balasore. When Ravenshaw returned from leave after three months' absence, he found all the principal officials of Cuttack changed, all the work reorganized and absolutely no arrears! He rubbed his eyes with astonishment and was not at all pleased!

But throughout the business I had been in correspondence with Sir George and had obtained his approval to every step I had taken. Such a thorough reformation of a sleepy, neglected, mismanaged office was quite to his taste. He also fully approved of my introducing new blood into the office, and showed his approval by appointing me Collector of the Cuttack district and promoting me to the first grade of Collectors at a salary of Rs 2,250 a month.

During my short tenure of the Commissioner's office nothing very important occurred, and in November, on Ravenshaw's return, I took up my duties as Collector of Cuttack. We took a beautiful but rather uncomfortable house at Chauliàganj, a suburb of Cuttack, a broad, open plain near the river with a race-course, a canal, and a row of handsome houses in large compounds. It was the healthiest part of the station, though it had the inconvenience of lying rather a long way from the rest of the station and the Government offices. I had a drive of three miles to my cutchery. Here we lived for four years, perhaps on the whole the busiest, brightest and happiest period of my service in India. Not only was the sphere of my activity much enlarged, but the station in which we lived was a big one. There was a regiment of Madras Infantry with six or seven officers and their wives, about a dozen engineers of the Public Works Department, six or seven Members of the Civil Service, besides missionaries and merchants and men in other departments. Numerous officers stationed in outlying parts of the province were constantly coming in on business or pleasure, so that on special occasions we could assemble over a hundred Europeans of both sexes, a large number for an Indian station. Nor were they only numerous; they were, for the most part, cheerful, gay and sociable folk.

CUTTACK, 1873

Cut off as Cuttack was to a great extent from the rest of the world by defective means of communication, its residents had to rely on themselves and their neighbours for help, society and amusement. Sir William Grey, the Lieutenant-Governor, used to say that he could not get men to go to Cuttack, but once they had got there he could not get them to come away from it. Men did not like going there because it was so out of the way, but when they once got there they found it so pleasant they wished to stay.

Thomas Edward Ravenshaw, the Commissioner, was a little king in Orissa. He had his salute of eleven guns, his guards and elephants, and on state occasions appeared in uniform of dark blue covered with gold lace and embroidery, cocked hat and feather, and sword. He was a kindly, patriarchal sort of old man, grey-headed and stout and quite free from any official stiffness or haughtiness. I had no great respect for his abilities, nor had anyone else, but he had much experience and knew his Orissa and his Oriyas thoroughly. They loved him as much as they are capable of loving a European. His very slowness and muddling, hesitating ways commended themselves to the sluggish Oriya mind. They touched some answering string in their souls. He was one of those men, a not uncommon type in India, who live for their work alone. He had no literary tastes or cultivation, was as ill-informed about most things as English public school boys of those days usually were, and except for half an hour's pottering in his garden and an occasional holiday at his turning lathe, spent all his time sitting before a table covered with official papers, with a cheroot in his mouth and a pen in his hand. But he governed efficiently, if not brilliantly, a country somewhat larger than Wales, was a first-rate shot, and a good judge of a horse—an average, unpretentious English gentleman, in fact. My wife used to say that I led him by the nose, and I certainly did stir him up to doing many things which he would not have done of his own accord. But he was very easily led by the orthodox Hindu faction, which was very powerful in Orissa—of whom more anon.

This great city of Cuttack, the capital of a large and isolated province, was a curious study. So many little worlds lived side by side, understanding each other very imperfectly, disliking each other often very heartily, and yet all dwelling peaceably on the whole under the strong hand of British law and order. Its situation was peculiar and, in many respects, inconvenient. The Mahànadi, an immense river more than two miles broad, issues from the hills and divides into two great streams, which in their turn divide lower down into several others, so that all this part of Central Orissa is, in fact, the delta of the Mahanadi, a triangle, each of whose sides is about a hundred miles in length. At the apex of this triangle, which points to the west, lies the city. The site was in fact chosen for purposes of defence by the King of Orissa in the sixteenth century when his country was invaded by the Mahommedans. He left his former capital Chaudwàr (Chaudwàr = four gates), the ruins of which are still visible on the northern bank of the river, and pitched his 'camp' (in Sanskrit and Oriya, Kataka) between the two sheltering arms of the mighty river. Here he built a great fortress called Bàrobàti which still stands, though in ruins, and the rest of the apex was occupied by the houses of the townspeople.

The Marathas built a massive revetment, or wall of huge stones all round the two sides of the triangle which face the two rivers, and this lofty, reddish-grey wall with its bastions and ghats gives to the city, when seen from the south, the appearance of a fortified place. Of the two arms of the river, that which flows on the south of the city is called the Kàtjori. It is now dammed at its entrance by an 'anicut'. This is a strong wall of stone built right across the river, pounding up the water above it into an extensive lake, while the river-bed below is left a dry expanse of gleaming sand with a feeble thread of water trickling through it. In the rains, however, the river tops the dam and plunges in an enormous torrent through the bed below. The extent of its rise and the volume of the water may be judged from the fact that, while in the dry season the walls of the Maratha revetment tower sixty feet above the sand which stretches for more than a mile in width at its foot, in the rains the water laps the coping of the wall and covers the whole expanse of sand. Once or twice in recent times, in extraordinarily high floods, the water has even risen above the top of the wall and has only been prevented from bursting into the town below by the most strenuous exertions on the part of the engineers. A vast, turbid mass of water pours down the Kàtjori, bearing along whole forest trees torn from the banks higher up, which the townspeople amuse themselves by catching with an ingenious but simple contrivance. Two sticks, each a few inches long, are tied strongly in the shape of a cross, to which is fastened a coil of thin but very strong cord. They stand on the bank and hurl the cross, which flies through the air, unwinding the coil as it flies and, alighting on the floating tree, is entangled in its branches. Three or four men then haul on the cord, and so gradually pull the tree to shore, where it is cut up and sold for firewood. In this way the poorer townsfolk make a good deal of profit from the floods.

On the highest point of the revetment stands the Lal Bagh, the Commissioner's residence, a large and stately building in a park-like compound in which, in our time, a herd of spotted deer used to roam. A long avenue of tall trees with dense foliage (a species of Uvaria) led to the entrance gates, beyond which lay the native city.

The Collector's office (cutcherry) stood on the same revetment as the Lal Bagh, a little lower down. In its spacious, park-like grounds were numerous other public offices, including the College. The native city possessed no ancient or remarkable buildings. It was a large, busy place with many shops and some handsome streets, a market-place and a few old temples. To the north of it lay the lines of the Madras Regiment, a very wide, open plain used as a parade ground; lines of broad roads bordered by the houses of Europeans, a church, a Roman Catholic chapel, a Baptist chapel and finally the still imposing ruins of the old Fort of Bàrobàti, within whose enclosure was the station club, a racquet court and other buildings. The whole inhabited space between the two rivers was about five miles long by two broad, and for a long distance down-stream to the south-east were struggling suburbs— Jobra with its extensive workshops, Chauliaganj with a race-course and a row of pleasant, spacious villas in large compounds, in one of which we lived for four years.

It seems unnecessary to enter into a detailed account of the work I had to do in Cuttack. It did not very much differ from what has already been described in previous districts, though it was heavier and more varied. In fact the great charm of the work of Civil officers in India is its variety. One has no fear of getting wearied by a monotonous routine, or by perpetually hammering away at one unchanging task. In the course of one day's work one has a dozen or more different things to do, each presenting some new feature of interest, so that if one goes to bed very tired at night, it is not the depressing weariness of sameness or drudgery, but the healthy fatigue of keeping mind and body on the stretch with a multitude of ever-varying calls on one's attention, and the joy (than which I know no greater—and which I sigh for now in my unemployed old age) of feeling that one is working and ruling and making oneself useful in God's world. A brief outline of an ordinary day's work may be given once for all. We got up at five or thereabouts, drank a cup of tea while our horses were being brought, and went for a ride. If I had official work to do, I went alone, but mostly my wife and I went together. On our ride we met friends and rode with them, or stopped to talk and rode on. Returning about six-thirty we had our regular chota haziri in the veranda; our little girls, who had been for a ride on their ponies, played around us. Then we went round our beautiful garden and gave orders, or showed our roses and other plants to friends who dropped in. About seven the post came in and we read the paper, the *Englishman*—the leading journal in Bengal in those days—looked at our letters, discussed any matters requiring arrangement, and by eight I was settled in my study for two hours' work at my big book, my *Comparative Grammar*. At ten, bath and breakfast and off to cutcherry in my brougham, a drive of three miles, during which I read official letters or thought over the day's business. On reaching office about eleven, the first thing was to take the Faujdari or Magistrate's work. The public crowded into my large court-room and presented many petitions, each of which was read to me by a clerk and orders passed thereon. Most of them were plaints in criminal cases, which were made over to the various subordinate Magistrates for disposal. Then came the great police charge-book, in which were entered all the criminal cases sent up that day from the various police stations in the district—murders, robberies, burglaries, thefts and the like. Some of these cases I took myself, but the greater part of them was made over to the Joint Magistrate and others. On this followed a large number of miscellaneous petitions and reports about all sorts of things—ferries, cattle-pounds, jail matters, recovery of fines and forfeitures, arrangement of records; also punishments, rewards and promotions of officials and other matters. By the time all these things were disposed of it would be about twelve-thirty, and if I had no criminal cases to try—and I could but seldom find time to try any—the Magisterial officials were sent away to issue the orders I had passed and carry out those which it fell to them to do. Now followed interviews with the Head Clerks of each department—Magistrate's Office, Excise, Stamps, Treasury, Customs, Salt, Road Cess, Municipal, Education, Registration, Land Revenue. Each man brought those papers on which orders were required, took his orders and departed. Of course, the whole of them did not come every day, but only those who had something to report, or something which required orders. When they had gone I wrote replies to letters from the Commissioner, Board and other officials, and was usually a good deal hindered and interrupted by Deputy Collectors and other officers coming in to speak to me about this or that. Generally, however, by two o'clock the correspondence was finished. Whether it was or not, at two we had tiffin—and we wanted it. At this meal, served in a quiet room at the end of the terrace overlooking the broad river and the blue hills beyond, the Joint Magistrate, Stevens, and the District Superintendent of police joined me, and while we ate we talked shop and got through a good deal of business. At half past two I returned to my office and finished any correspondence that remained. At three the Collectorate officers came with a pile of reports and other business, some-times with a case to try. A little before four I called for petitions on the Collectorate side; these were not so numerous as those on the Magis-terial side, and while hearing them and passing orders on them, I was busy signing all the orders and letters I had issued during the day. By four o'clock the work was done and I went home. It was, of course, only by the utmost punctuality and strictness that so much work could be got through, but each clerk and official knew exactly what he had to do and at what hour he was to come to me for orders and reports. When once you establish a 'dastûr' (a custom or fixed routine) with natives they are all right, there is nothing they love so much as dastûr; they make themselves into machines and work admirably. There were never any arrears in the Cuttack office during the four years of my incumbency, and this was due not to any superior merit or cleverness on my part but simply to the introduction of a regular routine of work.

When I got home I had a cup of tea, and then received any native Rajas or other gentlemen. This was a tedious and tiresome business, but before six I had generally got rid of them and drove with my wife. We had a pretty Victoria and pair of grey Arabs. Our drive generally ended at the club in the Fort, where we met nearly everyone in the station, both men and women. Here there were sports of many kinds; some played lawn-tennis, others billiards or whist, others—mostly the chiefs—sat in the veranda round old Ravenshaw and talked—a good deal of 'shop' I fear—but many other things besides. About seven-thirty we drove home to dinner and were generally in bed and asleep soon after nine.

Then we had mornings at Jobra. Jobra was a suburb of Cuttack, a green, woody little village on the bank of the great river Mahanadi. Just above it the river was dammed by an anicut, a mighty wall of stone more than a mile in length, and at one end of it stood the great range of Canal workshops, under the management of George Faulkner. Faulkner was a man of a type perhaps little known in England, but far from uncommon in India; the Englishman to whom India has become a second mother-country, and who would be unhappy and totally mis-understood and out of place in England. Thoroughly English in man-ners and feelings, so much so that though he had been forty years in India he could not speak a dozen words of any Indian language, he had no wish to return to his native land, and though he spoke of it with pride and affection he preferred India as a place to live in.

A native of Manchester, bred up as a mechanical engineer in one of the big engineering works in Lancashire, he had come out to India at the age of twenty or thereabouts in the service of the Irrigation Company.[1] This company, formed for the purpose of making canals, had constructed several on the Godavery river in the Madras presidency, and had then extended its operations to Orissa where it had constructed three canals, of which I shall have much to say hereafter. Eventually the Company was dissolved and its works, plant and employees taken over by Government. Thus Faulkner and a number of others became Government servants.

In person he was a tall, stout, powerfully-built man with a ruddy face, a huge shock of flaxen hair turning white, and an immense white beard which hung down over his broad chest and floated all round his face. He looked like an old lion, a grand, jovial, coarse, hard-drinking old Viking, full of songs and jokes and highly improper stories. Utterly reckless and wild about money matters, always in debt, always full of wild schemes, and yet this rough old creature had the most exquisitely delicate taste as a designer, and the greatest skill and fineness of touch as an artisan. He painted, he carved, he moulded; he designed buildings, boats, bridges; he grew the most beautiful flowers, planned and laid out the most lovely gardens, and could use a chisel or any other tool as well as his best workman. He had four stalwart sons, three of whom were engineers and the fourth a doctor, all of them artists and skilful men with their hands. And the strange thing was that all these big, coarse, athletic men, father as well as sons, were fond of reading, read extensively and remembered what they read; had a fine taste in literature, loved their Ruskin and could quote and argue and talk admirably. The boys had, of course, been born in Madras and sent home to be educated. There were also three handsome daughters who had been educated partly in England, partly in Paris, and were very accomplished, speaking French in particular with a pure Parisian accent and playing and singing well. They were, in fact, a very interesting family and we became great friends with them all. Old Mrs Faulkner, the wife of the Viking, was as such men's wives generally are for some reason, a small, delicate, feeble-looking woman, very much better bred than her husband; but feeble as she looked, she had much determination and courage in her frail little body, and it was by her principally that their brilliant, reckless, rollicking family was kept going. She slaved for them and got them out of their scrapes and was always

[1] On second thoughts I am not sure of this. I think he came out to Madras in some other employ and joined the Irrigation Company later. But his yarns and reminiscences were, as usual with such men, apt to be a little confused, especially after dinner.

cheerful and helpful though she confessed to my wife that they were a sore burden to her.

Jobra was Faulkner's glory and the despair of the Public Works Department. Both by nature and by his irregular training Faulkner was quite incapable of red-tape or of following a decorous official routine. He was perpetually harrowing the souls of his official superiors and the Heads of the Department in Calcutta by doing the most unheard of and irregular things. He ruled Jobra in a way of his own, and could by no means be brought to understand or follow the official way of doing things. But he was tolerated because they could not well do without him. Among other things he was a most ingenious inventor, and if ever in the extensive and complicated canal works that were going on all over Cuttack district any hitch occurred, Faulkner was safe to invent some machine or device which solved the difficulty. His shutters for the sluices, his valves, screws, self-acting locks and other contrivances would have made the fortune of anyone else. He had a large number of Telugu artisans who had followed him from the Godavery. There were both men and women; the former were carpenters, smiths and the like, while the latter worked as coolies. Among these people, foreigners in Orissa crowded together in a small settlement near the workshops, there was at first much promiscuous intercourse and the chaplain complained to Faulkner, as a certain number of them were native Christians. So Faulkner assembled them all, Christians and heathens alike, and told them that he was not going to have any immorality in his works, and to stop it he ordered each man to select one woman as his wife. This being done he had the names entered in a book, made them a curious address in which scraps of the Church of England marriage service were mixed up, and then, to clench the matter, made each man pay one rupee. Then he solemnly informed them that they were all married! Of course they did not understand much of what he said as he spoke in English, and did not wait to have it all translated to them. But the ceremony and especially the payments were clear enough to them. It was indeed suggested to Faulkner that some, probably most, of them were married already, but he said that didn't matter. He gave them all a big feast, and spent the money they had paid in relieving widows and orphans among them. This strange plan answered admirably. Each man henceforth kept strictly to his so-called wife, and new-comers were made to come before Faulkner to be solemnly married and have their names entered in the big book. Immorality ceased and the little settlement became peaceful and orderly. If any man went away, he divorced his wife by the simple process of having his name scratched out of the book, and she was promptly married to someone else. A school was established for the children who were taken on to the works when old enough.

A morning's stroll through the long lines of workshops at Jobra was very interesting. The great Nasmyth's steam hammer would be made to beat a huge mass of red-hot iron, or crack a nut, other machines shaved iron like so much soap, or sawed big logs into planks in a few seconds. Then Faulkner would make the most beautiful ivory and ebony croquet mallets for the ladies, or exhibit his portfolios of lovely designs, his fretwork brackets and screens, stained-glass windows, designs in plaster or stone, a bewildering variety of beautiful things. He made for my wife two lovely screens of teak wood, perforated, which he had designed himself; I have them still. Many other things the old man made for us all, and he was always ready to put to rights anything in the way of machinery that went wrong in our houses. It used to be said with truth, 'Give old Faulkner a cheroot and a whisky peg[1] and there is nothing he cannot do.' Among other peculiarities of speech he totally ignored the letter 'h': saying, ' 'ead,' ' 'and,' ' 'igh,' ' 'eavy,' ' 'ot,' for 'head', 'hand', etc. He did not seem to be conscious of the omission. Some people said it was a characteristic of the Lancashire dialect. In other respects he spoke quite correct English.

[1] 'Peg'. This is an expression universal in India. It means a big tumbler of brandy or whisky and soda water. It does not seem to be known in England.

CHAPTER XVIII

CUTTACK, 1874

THE year 1874 passed happily and busily. In the cold weather we had many pleasant tours over new ground. The district is large and fertile and very populous. We enjoyed particularly the fine scenery and the spacious mango-groves where we pitched our tents. Under the influence of the scenery and the new places I took to my old amusement of water-colour painting again, stimulated also by other people in the station who sketched. I also worked hard at my *Comparative Grammar*.[1] Instigated moreover by the Civil Surgeon, Dr Stewart, an enthusiastic botanist, I took to that delightful science. On a large, sandy tract of land near one of the canals I laid out a public garden, which I stocked with many beautiful plants obtained from the Botanic Gardens at Calcutta. In it also I made a nursery of young trees which, when sufficiently grown, were planted by the sides of the public roads. In this way I made many avenues for miles along the roads. By this time—twenty-six years later—they must have grown into fine, shady trees and are, I hope, a blessing to the weary traveller.

The only incident of importance in this year was a famine in Bengal. Rice being the chief food of the Bengalis, there was great demand for it. At first the Government imported the rice from Burmah, but the people of Bengal for some reason did not like Burmese rice. To us Europeans all rice seems much the same, but to the Bengalis, who live entirely on it, great differences are perceptible in the various kinds. The Orissa peasantry recognize about one hundred and twenty kinds, each of which has its own name, and by much examination and comparison, aided by elaborate explanations by my native assistants, I was able to perceive many of the differences in size, shape, colour, and texture of the husked[2] rice. After the husk was removed, however, the difference was less perceptible.

The province of Orissa produces an immense quantity of rice, in fact it produces—or did in my time—nothing else, and the Cuttack and Balasore merchants do a very large business in exporting rice, chiefly

[1] I sent home the MS of the second volume in 1875.
[2] I should write 'the rice in the husk' or '*un*husked'. 'Husked' rice is a term generally applied to the grain after the husk has been removed by pounding. The unhusked rice is called 'paddy'.

to Madras. Many French ships, however, also come to False Point, the chief port of Orissa, for rice which they take to Mauritius, Bourbon and the adjacent islands for the use of the Indian coolies working on the sugar plantations. I made some very amusing acquaintances among the captains of these French ships—'capitaines au long cours' as they wrote themselves. But to return to the famine. Some Bengali merchants settled in Cuttack came to me and represented that the rice supplied to the famine districts by the Government was not liked by the people, and that there was a good opening for doing a trade in Orissa rice, which was of the same kind as that grown in Bengal. I therefore telegraphed to the Secretary to the Government and offered to send Orissa rice. My offer was accepted and I immediately gave out contracts to various firms for supplying rice. The amount tendered for was five lakhs of maunds or, in English weight, about 18,300 tons. The merchants offered to deliver the rice in Calcutta by their own vessels at a rate all included of two and a half rupees a maund or, in English money, about £125,000. The work began briskly; the merchants had begun to charter vessels and indeed had actually chartered several, and vast masses of rice were collected at the ports. Had they let us alone, in a month's time it would all have been safely delivered in Calcutta, but suddenly we were thrown into confusion by an order from the Government that we were not to ship the rice in private vessels, but were to wait for the steamers which the Government would send. I protested energetically and so did many of the contractors. We showed that this would involve heavy expense to the Government, as the merchants had already contracted to deliver the rice at their own cost. We knew also that the Government had not many steamers at its disposal and that there would be much delay. Our remonstrances, however, were unheeded. The rice lay for weeks on the jetties at the ports. The rainy season came on, and a good deal of it was damaged by wet before the slow process of carrying in three small steamers an amount sufficient to fill six or seven could be carried out. Owing to the delay and mismanagement of the Calcutta officials, not only was much of the rice damaged, but the cost of the undertaking eventually amounted to a total sum of Rs 1,523,373 as against Rs 1,250,000, a loss of about £27,000.[1]

No one at the time could understand the reason of this action on the part of Government. It was generally regarded as only one more in-

[1] Actual cost	Rs1,523,373
Cost by my plan	1,250,000
Loss	Rs273,373
Say	£27,000

stance of the reckless waste of public money in this famine by Sir Richard Temple, by whom the famine campaign was then being conducted. Some years afterwards, in 1881, I found out the secret. A man who did not know that it was I who had conducted the Orissa rice contract, told me as a good joke how he, in partnership with some others, chief of whom was a scoundrel called K—— (then an Assistant Secretary to the Government), had secured a contract from the Government for the supply of a large quantity of Burmah rice and how, before the contract was signed, they had been alarmed by the news that someone down in Orissa had offered to supply a very large quantity of rice at a cheaper rate, and that the famine officer in Calcutta, Toynbee, having served for many years in Orissa was trying to favour the Orissa merchants and induce Government to accept their offer. Then came the news that Toynbee had succeeded, principally owing to the dislike of Burmah rice by the Bengalis. K——, my informant said, took advantage of his position to suggest to Government that it would not be safe to rely upon the Orissa contractors sending the rice in their own vessels, as they would not be able to find vessels enough. He thus procured the issue of the order which had so much amazed us, and had no difficulty in taking care that the Government steamers were delayed till he and his partners had brought all their Burmah rice to Calcutta and disposed of it to Government. Of course, if it had been known that K—— as a Government official had any share in a private contract, he would have been severely punished, but he took good care that this should not be known. I received the thanks of the Government for my transaction of what turned out to be a difficult and onerous business. Mr K—— turned up again and mixed himself with my fortunes in a still more unpleasant manner some years later.

Now also Sir Richard Temple came into my life again, not to my advantage. I have told how he treated me at our first meeting in the Panjab, and from this it may be understood that my memories of him were not very agreeable. When the famine in Behar and Northern Bengal broke out in this year the Viceroy, Lord Northbrook, sent Temple to manage it. This was not only entirely unnecessary but was a grave slight on Sir George Campbell, who was not only thoroughly capable of doing all that was required, but had already, with characteristic energy, made all the needful arrangements. But the terrible famine in Orissa in 1866, with its excessive loss of life, was fresh in the memory of the Government of India. In Orissa the loss of life had been principally due to the great difficulty of getting food into the province, there being at that time few roads—and those bad—and no safe ports. Much, however, was due to the supineness of the Lieutenant-Governor of Bengal, Sir Cecil Beadon, and the wrong-headedness of Mr R. B. Chapman, Member of the Board of Revenue, both of whom underrated the necessities of the case. Lord Northbrook seems to have thought that Sir George Campbell was about to repeat this error in 1874, and Temple came down with orders to spare no expense in importing grain to feed the people. He carried out these orders to the letter, and beyond it. Though he had absolutely no previous acquaintance with Bengal, and was quite incompetent to form a judgment as to the quantity and nature of the relief that was likely to be required, he set aside the opinions of Sir George Campbell and the Collectors of the afflicted districts and followed his own unaided judgment. In his usual theatrical way he rode at the rate of fifty or sixty miles a day through the districts, forming, as he said, an opinion on the condition of the people and the state of the crops. What kind of opinion or what kind of observation could be formed by riding at a gallop along a road, no one could make out. The result was, however, that he would sit down at night after one of these wild scampers and write a vainglorious minute, in which he stated that he had that day fully examined such and such tracts, and had come to the conclusion that so many thousand maunds of grain (generally from three to four times as much as was really wanted) would be required to feed the people thereof. If any Collector were honest enough to object that a much smaller quantity would suffice, and to support his view by careful statistics collected by himself and assistants in a patient village to village and house to house inquiry, he was contemptuously told that he did not understand his business, and his name was put down in Temple's mental black book.

In disgust at this proceeding Campbell resigned, and Temple was made Lieutenant-Governor in April 1874, and the reign of trumpet-blowing (his own) began. The famine was relieved at the expense of some millions of pounds, and for a long time afterwards the Collectors were vainly endeavouring to dispose of the immense surplus quantities of grain which had been sent to their districts in defiance of their protests, and which the people did not want and would not buy. Much of it rotted away and was devoured by rats in the Government granaries. Several merchants and planters, both European and native, made their fortunes by taking contracts for the supply and carriage of this grain. The newspapers were full of complaints of this waste, of ridicule and satirical songs, but the great Temple abode in his accustomed halo of beatific self-admiration.

Meanwhile I was busy with improvements in the town of Cuttack.

The old market, a strange, ill-arranged mass of low, dark, stone vaults, had fallen into the hands of a close corporation of Koyals, as they were called. The word means 'weighers', and their function, under the native Governments, had been to weigh all grain brought to market. No sales could take place unless the grain was weighed by these men, who levied a small fee for the service and paid a fee to the native ruler for the appointment. They acquired power by degrees, as in India such middle-men always do, and presumed to regulate the market rates and prices and in many ways interfere with business, tyrannize over the traders, demand heavy payments on various pretexts and in many ways oppress and defraud the people. When I proposed to rebuild their market they objected and produced an ancient document granting them the pro-prietary right in the building. It was impossible to say whether this document was genuine or not (probably not,) but when I consulted the law-officers, I was advised that there was no legal means of contesting it, as through the carelessness of former Collectors the Koyals had been allowed to remain in possession long enough to establish a prescriptive right to the buildings, as well as to the exclusive exercise of their func-tions. This market was built against the outer side of the great wall surrounding the park in which the Lal Bagh—the Commissioner's resi-dence—stood. Attached to this ancient wall, and dating from the six-teenth century or earlier, there were several other half-ruined ancient buildings, empty and disused; strange, tall, gloomy structures of dark red stone. I at first thought of making use of these for an opposition market, but they were found to be too ruinous to be put into repair, and inconveniently shaped and situated. So I had to search elsewhere, and at length, at the eastern end of the town—the old market was at the western end—I found a large, neglected patch of ground grown over with jungle which was said to have been the site of the Maratha Gover-nor's law-courts. It was the property of the Government, so I could do what I liked with it. On clearing the jungle and digging up the soil the workmen came upon six or seven beautifully carved capitals of pillars, and by degrees unearthed the drums of the pillars themselves, together with numerous finely carved fragments of sandstone and great quan-tities of laterite blocks, which had evidently been used for building. With these materials I set to work and designed a handsome market, which was built on this site. It was of laterite, a lofty hall with chambers for warehousing grain, and in front a long, wide portico supported by the pillars above-mentioned which were duly pieced together. A little on one side we found a deep, ancient tank lined with laterite and adorned with carvings of gods, goddesses, men and animals. All this we restored,

cleaned out the tank, rebuilt the ghâts or steps and made a very handsome place of it. I put up an inscription over the front of the market-
house and opened it as a public market free from all interference of the
Koyals. In India one never remains long enough in any place to see the
fruits of one's work. I do not know whether the new market was suc-
cesssful or not. It began well and was doing well as long as I remained
in Cuttack.

Towards the close of the year we received information that the new
Lieutenant-Governor, Sir Richard Temple, was about to pay us a visit
of State, and great preparations were made for his reception. All the
Rajas of the Tributary States were summoned to meet him at Cuttack
as well as all the principal zemindars from all parts of Orissa. He came
to False Point in a Government steamer where Ravenshaw the Commissioner met him, and brought him and his suite up the canal in our
two steam-launches, the *Pioneer* and *Olga*. He was to land at Jobra, and
I arranged to have a handsome pavilion erected for the reception. Old
Faulkner and his son George undertook this work and performed it
with their usual skill and taste. With characteristic ingenuity they
constructed out of old posts, telegraph poles, odds and ends of old iron
and wood lying about the yards of the workshop, a graceful and spacious
pavilion roofed with tarpaulins and bits of sacking, old tent flies and
what not.

When finished it presented the appearance of a large hall with open
arches and a vaulted roof, the old posts and poles had been painted and
concealed by bright drapery and wreaths of foliage, the heterogeneous
substance of the roof was also hidden by sheets of white, red and blue
cloth festooned with wreaths of leaves and flowers. Long lines of
Chinese lanterns hung from end to end. The floor was covered with
scarlet cloth and rich carpets. Rows of chairs were set down both
sides and a broad pathway down the middle was fenced off by a light
railing. At one end some other steps went down to two large barges,
draped, wreathed and carpeted, where the landing was to take place.
At the other end a broad space was provided for the carriages, and beyond it the guard of honour from the Regiment. On both sides, both up
and down the river bank, were set tall Venetian masts with flags; the
masts were linked together by wreaths from which hung Chinese lanterns. As the arrival was to take place at night, it was considered advisable to light up the river bank as much as possible, so Faulkner placed
at intervals along the anicut small heaps of wood surrounding some
recondite chemical preparation known only to himself, which was to
burn with a peculiarly bright light. The salute caused us some difficulty.

A Lieutenant-Governor is entitled to a salute of fifteen guns, and there was not a gun in the place, except some old and useless cannon which had been sent to Jobra to be broken up and made into useful things such as hinges for lock-gates, but which were so honey-combed it would have been dangerous to fire them. But we managed it beautifully. We got some very large bamboos in lengths of four feet or so. These were filled with gunpowder, rammed tight and tightly plugged. Then they were lashed round with several layers of stout manilla and coir cables, a touch-hole was bored in one end and a slow fuse stuck in. Then the whole machine was half-buried in the sand of the river bank and fastened down by strong pegs. Fifteen of these were placed in a row a little above the pavilion, not too near lest there should be a stampede amongst the horses. A second similar battery was placed at Jagatpur, on the opposite side of the river where the canal joined it. The object of this was to let us know when they were coming.[1]

By six o'clock on the appointed evening all was ready. The pavilion was crowded with European officials and ladies, Rajas and big natives of sorts, gorgeous in cloth of gold and jewels. Outside were the long line of the native regiment and a bewildering mass of carriages of all sorts, police officers on horseback keeping order, and a vast sea of natives crowding every available foot of space. After a short period of waiting we heard the guns from Jagatpur, and suddenly, as if by enchantment, the whole river bank broke into a blaze. Faulkner had stationed men at every point with orders to light up as soon as they heard guns, and the order was carried out exactly. The people on the Lieutenant-Governor's steam-launch told us afterwards that the effect was beautiful, and all the more delightful because unexpected. I had not told Ravenshaw what we were going to do before he left for False Point. Beyond general instructions to have some sort of a reception he had given me no precise orders, nor had I contemplated any very great preparations. None of us liked Temple, nor did we feel inclined to put ourselves out for him. But the natives were eager to welcome their ruler on account of the position he held, not for himself, and they were anxious to show (like Todgers's) what Cuttack could do when it chose. The Faulkners also were delighted at having some artistic work to do, and so the thing grew. As the steamer emerged from the dark lock the party on board saw before them a wide lake—the river here is over a mile broad—on the further side of which lines and lines of lamps of all

[1] When the slow match catches the powder inside the whole thing explodes with a bang, quite as loud as a cannon. The tighter you tie them, and the more rope you put round, the louder is the noise. It can be heard several miles off.

colours were seen reflected in the water. All along the anicut, at equal distances, blazed piles of dazzling light, and in the centre the great pavilion, with its numerous Chinese lanterns, torches and flags made a bright spot in the darkness. They were enchanted and amazed.

Soon the great man and his suite arrived at the pier and on landing were received by me. I presented the members of the Municipality of Cuttack who read an address to which the Lieutenant-Governor responded.[1] The address was in the usual fulsome, turgid style. It expressed the deep and heart-felt joy of the people of Orissa at having their revered, beloved and longed-for ruler among them in the flesh, told how they had watched with bated breath and speechless admiration his brilliant management of the Bengal famine, and how profoundly they were impressed by the conviction that under a ruler who so deeply sympathized with his people and sacrificed himself so unsparingly for their sakes, the Lower Provinces of Bengal must now at last enter on a career of unexampled prosperity etc, etc. Your Bengali Babu can reel out this sort of stuff by the fathom from morn till dewy eve and then begin again.

Sir Richard Temple replied in the same style—he believed it all! no flattery was too gross for Dicky Temple! He admitted that he thought they were quite right in considering him the greatest man that had ever lived, and he quite understood how deeply interested they (and all mankind) must necessarily be in everything that concerned Him!!—and so on and so on. After which he went on a 'shake-hands' tour all round the pavilion. Then the troops presented arms, the guns fired, the people cheered and we all drove off in a long procession down three miles of streets all brilliantly illuminated, crowded with mobs who cheered frantically—they did not know why. Flags waved from every corner, rich rugs and clothes were hung from the balconies; torches, stars in oil-lamps, triumphal arches of bamboo and greenery across the streets, with coloured cloths bearing the word 'welcome' in several languages, met us at every turn, till at last, in the great square before the entrance gates of the Lal Bagh, a great crowd of wild pàiks[2] from the hills, in their strange garb, with their tiger-skins, birds' feathers, long, glittering spears and lighted torches, closed the scene.

The great man was immensely delighted at his unexpectedly grand

[1] I had taken the precaution of obtaining a copy of the address the day before, and had sent it by special messenger across country to Ravenshaw. It reached him at a point half-way up the canal and he at once handed it to Temple who was thus enabled to prepare a speech in reply to it.

[2] Pàiks are a sort of irregular police force, strange, wild creatures, a relic of old native rule.

reception. The pomp and pageantry, the shouting crowds, the illuminations, arches and procession gratified his inmost soul. He was so deeply touched that he even thanked me in a few curt words. He must have been moved to do that!!

The week which followed was a whirl. People who do not know India well imagine that a great deal of good is done by these State tours of Viceroys, Governors and Lieutenant-Governors. But my own experience leads me to doubt this. It may be that the local authorities succeed now and then in securing sanction to the execution of some work of great importance to their locality by showing the Governor the actual spot and proving to him by actual eyesight its necessity or usefulness. They are thus sometimes able to do, in half-an-hour's walk round a town or river bank, what they have been unable to achieve by months of writing to an unwilling or unintelligent Secretariat. But the idea that by a hurried tour—and all tours in so vast a country as India must be more or less hurried, because there is so much ground to be got over in a limited time—a Governor can make himself really acquainted with a province as big as England is a delusion. The place does not look itself to begin with, because it is dressed up for his reception and looks as unlike itself as a workman in his Sunday clothes. All the natural every-day dirt and misery is bundled out of sight. 'Eyewash', as it is called in India, prevails everywhere, even if everyone does not go to the length attributed by a well-known story to the Collector who had the trunks of the trees on all the station-roads whitewashed. So the great man does not see the real place, and unless he is an exceptionally keen-sighted man he takes his superficial, hastily-formed impressions for real knowledge, which does more harm than good. Ever afterwards he is prone to refuse sanction to proposals submitted by the local officers, or to contradict their assertions, because of some erroneous impression he has imbibed on his hasty tour. Often, too, when he has promised on-the-spot sanction to some project which has been shown and explained to him, he will withdraw that sanction on his return to Calcutta, because his secretaries have persuaded him that the local officers have hoodwinked, or at any rate, misinformed him.

If also we set against the problematical benefit of the great man's seeing things, or thinking he sees them, with his own eyes, the real and undoubted mischief he does by disorganizing the whole administration for a week or more, closing the courts, delaying the disposal of cases, putting a stop to business of all sorts, leading Municipalities and other public bodies to spend more money than they can afford in decorations, fireworks, illuminations and triumphal arches, it will be seen that the net gain for these tours is infinitesimal, if not absolutely nil.

It certainly was so in this case. Temple promised freely all sorts of things while at Cuttack, but refused to sanction them when he got back to Calcutta. He upset all our work and left us with heavy arrears on his departure, and the Cuttack Municipality with a considerable deficit in their accounts owing to the expenses of the reception. He was an extraordinarily active man, and we were in attendance on him daily from five in the morning till late at night. He went everywhere, up all the canals in the small local steamers to see all the locks, irrigation works and other things. On the steamer as we went along he made us all sit round a table on deck and answer innumerable questions, writing down the answers in a note-book. But as he would put the wrong questions to the wrong men—asking the Engineers questions about the land revenue, rents, rights of various classes in the soil—things which they knew nothing about—and asking Ravenshaw and me questions about cubic contents of reservoirs, discharge in gallons per second, working of various sluices, taps and machinery—things which we knew nothing about—and angrily stopping the right man when he attempted to answer—I fear the information he obtained was rather mixed. I think, too, he lost his note-book or left it behind in Cuttack. However, it did not much matter. It was always a weakness of his to think he knew all about everything, and in any case he would have been certain to believe and assert ever afterwards that he had visited Orissa and personally ascertained all about it, and in consequence override every suggestion or recommendation that did not agree with the strange jumble of confused recollections which he carried away with him.

Of course, there was a magnificent Durbar or State assemblage, at which all the Maharajas and Rajas of the Tributary States—'the Kings of the Amorites that dwell in the hills' as we called them—appeared in all their barbaric pearl and gold, with hosts of wild retainers in ancient, rusty coats of mail, tiger-skins, spears and jangling chains and ornaments. One man brought six hundred of these wild followers with him, and was very angry with me because I insisted on his sending three-quarters of them away again. I could not allow six hundred Highland caterans to stalk about my peaceful city of Cuttack armed with dirk and sword, swaggering and brawling and snatching anything they took a fancy to from the shops without paying for it. The police had a hard time of it to keep these light-fingered gentry in order.

Then we had big lunch and dinner parties every night, ending up with a grand ball and reception at the Lal Bagh the last night. The splendid suite of lofty rooms in this stately old palace were brilliantly lighted and decorated for the occasion. All the Europeans came, and to gratify the vanity and pomposity of Temple there was a 'reception' to begin with. On a sofa at the end of the furthest room, in his Windsor uniform, glittering with gold lace, star on breast, his suite in full uniform behind him, sat the great man, a positive miracle of ugliness. Lady after lady was brought up and presented, made her curtsy and passed on. Then the men followed one by one. It was like a levee or drawing-room at Court. Then the band struck up and the dancing began. At midnight there was a sumptuous supper in the long veranda. It was about one hundred feet long by twenty wide; the pillars were hung with wreaths and the spaces between them closed in with tent-flies (kanâts). After supper dancing was resumed and the great man retired to his rooms having, as he pompously announced, some official minutes to write! Many of the men, including myself, were no dancers and we remained in the supper-room smoking. We drew together round one end of the long table, called for more champagne, and installed old Faulkner in the Lieutenant-Governor's chair at the head. Songs were, of course, out of the question but, as we got merry, speeches began. Faulkner stood up and in a very amusing speech proposed my health as the future Lieutenant-Governor of Bengal. This was received with applause, and I then did a foolish thing, the consequence of which I suffered from all the remainder of my service—twenty years. I got up and returned thanks in the character of Lieutenant-Governor, parodying the reply which Temple had given on the night of his arrival to the address which the Municipality presented to him. I was perfectly sober—I do not think I was ever drunk in my life except once at Oxford. But of course I was excited, and the long pent-up feeling of disgust at the vanity and self-glorification of this windbag was irrepressible. I mimicked his manner, I satirized his past career, especially in respect to the famine; all sorts of smart things leapt to my lips. The audience roared with laughter and made so much noise that old Ravenshaw came in to see what we were up to. But one of the Lieutenant-Governor's staff—I will not mention the traitor's name—had been behind a curtain the whole time, and he at once went off and told Temple all I had said. One man who had seen this came and said to me, 'I suppose you will now take two years' furlough to England.' I said 'Why?' He laughed and went away. But as we drove home my wife told me all about it and I got a severe scolding from her.

Temple said nothing, but next morning he received me very sourly and was particularly disagreeable and offensive in his manner to me for the rest of his stay. I had written a Manual of the District of Balasore—

history, statistics, and so forth—district officers had been invited to write manuals of their districts—and I brought the MS to Temple at his request. He glanced at a few pages, found some expressions he disliked, scratched them out with his pencil, and turned on me savagely, saying I thought myself so very superior to everyone else but that the book would not do. He told me to take it back and re-write it in a way he described to me. I took it back, locked it in a drawer, and have it by me now. I never submitted it to the Government for acceptance again.

I learnt long afterwards that when he got back to Calcutta he told the story of my speech to his Chief Secretary, ending up with an expression of amazement, 'He actually mocked *Me*, mocked *Me*.' To think that anyone should dare to mock the great R. Temple!! From the same source I also learnt that he had written a very bad character against my name in the Black Book.[1] However, he sent us a letter after his departure thanking us for the grandeur of his reception, and adding that he considered the unanimous expression of loyalty and attachment to British rule a proof that the local officers did their work in such a way as to win the affection of the people.

Then he went away and left us to pick up the pieces and catch up the arrears of work, after which I went into camp for the usual cold weather tour.

It was, of course, very foolish of me to make that speech. I had, however, no idea that any of the aides-de-camp were listening. The man's self-satisfied air irritated us all, and me more than anyone as I had not forgotten the injustice he did me at the beginning of my career. I had reminded him of the incident the first night he was in Cuttack, as I sat by him at the dinner at Ravenshaw's. He asked in a lofty tone, 'What was *I* then?' I answered, 'Commissioner of Lahore.' He replied, 'Ah yes! I was Commissioner, I think, about that time,' as who should say, 'I have occupied so many distinguished posts in my time I really cannot recollect one more than another.' But my wife who was watching him keenly says she is sure from his manner and look that he remembered it perfectly.

I mention this visit of Temple's and the incident of the speech at greater length because I have always believed, and indeed have been told by many of my friends, that it was the real cause of my ill-success in the later part of my career. I had committed the old hereditary family crime of quarrelling with my official superior, selecting as usual for

[1] This is a book kept in the Bengal Secretariat in which the Lieutenant-Governors record their opinion of the characters of the officers. Whenever any officer obtains praise or incurs censure it is recorded in this book.

that purpose the most influential and popular of them. My grandfather with the Chancellor, Lord Eldon—my father with the Rector of
St James's, Bishop Jackson—I with Sir Richard Temple—and now I
hear that my eldest son David is quarrelling with his Colonel!

A little time before the Temple visit, my wife, one evening going
down the steps of the veranda to the carriage for the usual drive, slipped
and fell heavily. The result was a miscarriage; the child, a son, was
born dead, and she remained weak and suffering for some time. In
consequence of this she was unable to go with me into camp, and I went
by myself, being afterwards joined by Graves, the District Superintendent of police, and Atkinson, the Assistant Collector. I had a curious
and difficult task to perform.

Along the Mahanadi River some ten miles above Cuttack lay a large
estate called Dompara. It was about ten or twelve miles long by two
broad, and was for the most part low hills covered with dense forests,
though it had also considerable tracts of flat land along the river which
were fully cultivated. The owner of this estate, or 'kingdom' as he persisted in calling it, was a Raja. Now there were Rajas of three kinds in
Orissa. When the English first took the province in 1804 from the
Marathas, next to nothing was known about it. It was, however, soon
perceived that there was a broad strip of cultivated level land down the
middle called the Mughal bandi. This was cut up into the three districts of Balasore (north), Cuttack (centre), and Pooree (south), and
settled in the usual way. Such of the zemindars as were Rajas in this
territory paid land revenue assessed on their estates just like those in
other parts of Bengal. But along the sea coast was a dreary strip of
country consisting of large estates held by certain Rajas who claimed a
partial independence. There was hardly anything to assess in these
wastes, so they were allowed to hold their lands on payment of a *peshkash*, or tribute, a small, fixed sum which had no relation to assets or
income.

Similarly along the landward or western boundary of the three dis-
tricts was a string of estates held by persons who called themselves
Rajas, and who, on account of the wild and unproductive nature of their
estates at the time of the conquest, had been let off with a *peshkash*.
Dompara was one of these. Beyond them, stretching far away into the
Central Provinces, were the great Tributary States of which anon.

Poor little Dompara was a helpless fool, almost imbecile; unfortunately
for himself not quite so. If he could have been pronounced insane and
locked up he might perhaps have been cured in time, and meanwhile his estate would have been properly managed by the Collector.

But as it was, he was just foolish enough to do endless mischief, and not foolish enough to be put under restraint. He had fallen into the hands of a clever, wily, unscrupulous man whom he had appointed as his Dewan or Prime Minister. This man was oppressing the tenantry, enriching himself and keeping the Raja and his family miserably poor. A large body of the ryots came to me and begged me to interfere; the poor little Raja also came and implored me to save him from his Dewan, whom, of course, he might have dismissed with a stroke of his pen, but he feared him too much to do so.

I went to Dompara and pitched my tents in a lovely grove of dense trees by the river. Thither came a great crowd of the peasantry, the wily Dewan and his clerks and papers, and the feeble little Raja in a pitiful attempt at state, in an old, tawdry palanquin, a few ragged pàiks and drummers, himself in cloth of gold and Cashmere shawls, old, frayed, tarnished and moth-eaten. Then for some days we held long palavers and went into the whole affair thoroughly. The difficulty was that, although the Dewan was utterly untrustworthy, he was the only man in the place with a head on his shoulders. There were of course lots of capable men in Cuttack who would have been glad of the appointment, but the Dewan had a large following of devoted adherents as he had given leases of villages and farms to a crowd of his relations. With his intimate local knowledge and his numerous supporters, he had such a hold over the place that he would have rendered the position of any stranger whom I might introduce quite untenable. I had not the power of banishing him, and short of that nothing would have been of any use. So I revoked, in public meeting before the ryots, all the illegal and oppressive orders and arrangements he had made, issued a set of simple rules for management which I made known to the people, took away a number of farms from his adherents to whom he had illegally given them, bound him over to observe my rules in future, and after frightening his life almost out of him by awful threats of what I would do if he misbehaved in future, left him in his old situation as, I hoped, a wiser and a sadder man. It was a risky thing to do and I knew it, but it was the only course possible. The poor little Raja, however, was disappointed. After having for years blindly trusted the Dewan he had now taken a dislike to him, and with a weak mind like his, the dislike was as fierce and unreasonable as his former liking for him had been. I had a long talk with him in private. His huge and half-ruined palace, a mass of tumbledown brickwork overgrown with jungle and green with mildew, showing, however, traces of former elegance—a beautiful, carved gateway with great wooden doors half fallen from their rotting hinges—a mouldy temple with lovely statues all cracked and broken—was situated on a ridge half-way up a beautiful wooded hill amidst the remains of a spacious, lordly garden laid out by his father. Here, amongst roses choked with jungle, palms and tall trees matted with gorgeous flowering creepers, the poor idiot used to spend hours wandering up and down on a long, weed-covered pathway. I found him there, and pacing to and fro beside him I administered a severe lecture. I believe he profited by it for a time, and the affairs of Dompara went on fairly well as long as I could spare time to keep an eye on them. What happened after I left I do not know. One never does know in India. One can only do one's best while in a place and leave the future to one's successor, who as likely as not will take an entirely different view and upset all the arrangements one has made.

This, in fact, is one of the great problems of Indian administration, though it is one which people in England, and especially in Parliament, know nothing about though they talk so loud and lay down the law so very confidently. It cannot be too often repeated that the difficulty lies not in the laws and rules that are promulgated, but in getting them carried out. It is not always easy, I admit, to make a law which exactly meets the requirements of all the complicated systems of land revenue and other matters which occur. But the very greatest care is taken in making a law. Facts are collected with the most scrupulous and conscientious care, opinions are obtained from all those who know the subject (and from many who don't). The draft Bill is widely circulated for criticism and the criticisms carefully weighed, the Bill is then brought before Council, many eloquent and clever speeches are made, it is referred to a special Committee who cut and carve, add and strike out, argue for hours over every point and submit it as revised to Council again, where it is again speechified over and voted section by section. When it is finally passed the Governors, Secretaries, Councillors and Boards at headquarters sit down and fold their hands and say the affair is settled.

But it is not by any means settled. In fact the real difficulty now begins. This law so elaborately worded, these provisions the result of so much anxious deliberation, must now be enforced all over the country. The Act is printed and copies are sent to all the Collectors and other officers. Some of these are stupid, some are indolent and careless, some have been opposed to the measure all along and do not mean it to be a success. Then there is the vast mass of the native population who are affected by it. The native lawyers are as sharp as needles and very soon tear the heart out of it. This section may be made to work in one way, that section in another. Two sections may be shown to contradict each other, while most of them can be interpreted in more ways than one. The rural masses, of course, neither know nor understand a word of it. So then cases are instituted in the courts, and appealed and appealed till they reach the High Court. That august tribunal always considers itself the legally constituted interpreter of all laws, and proceeds to put an interpretation of its own on section after section. These interpretations are embodied in the decisions of the Court, and these decisions are printed and published as 'rulings'. So that before long there are two laws, the actual Statute as passed by the legislative body, and the mass of rulings thereon as pronounced by the judicial body. The lawyers are very proud of this; they call the former 'substantive law', and the latter 'adjective law', and very much prefer the latter, as their own creation. Now inasmuch as in arriving at their decision the judges carefully avoid taking into consideration the circumstances which led to the making of the law, and examine not what the legislature meant to lay down but what the words of the Act really import, it not infrequently happens that their decisions turn out to be the very opposite of what the law was intended to mean. Then a new law has to be passed to rectify the error. Divested of technical language such an 'amending act' is simply a confession of a blunder. It says virtually, 'whereas in a former Act we ruled that two and two make four, but from the wording of the Act it appears as if we had ruled that two and two make five, now we hereby alter that wording and substitute the two following words which make it plain that henceforth two and two shall make four and not five.' It *has* happened within my experience that the High Court has sat upon the 'amended Act' and observed that 'the law as now amended implies that two and two make six'!

But however carefully both the legislative and judicial bodies work at establishing the law, there remains always a great deal of weakness and uncertainty in carrying it out in the country.

The vast extent of country, the very various views, temperaments and mental acumen of the persons charged with administering it naturally lead to its efficiency being very different in different parts of the country, and being more or less impaired in all. More especially is every law of importance hindered in its working by frequent changes of the district officers. The Secretariat mind favours frequent changes. It considers that if a man is left too long in a district he 'gets into a groove'. This means that if a man stays long enough in a district to acquire a real insight into the condition and wants of the people, he is able to see the vanity of the fine theoretical cobwebs which the Secretariat mind is so

fond of spinning, and can administer inconvenient pricks to their wind-
bags and prove by his extensive local knowledge their emptiness. So
they like to have men new to the district who swallow all their nos-
trums. I shall mention later on one or two striking instances of this.

But to return from this long digression. After Dompara I visited
Pattia, a neighbouring estate, still more picturesque and wild, where the
Raja was more sensible but more extravagant. Here there were family
feuds. The Raja's mother had obtained a number of farms as her jointure,
and being like all Hindu widows entirely under the thumb of the Brahmins was exploiting her farms for the benefit of those gentry. The Raja
wanted money and was trying to take his mother's farms away from her.
Hence a row royal in the palace and indescribable confusion in the
villages, where the old Rani's men were going about collecting rent
and giving receipts in her name, and the Raja's men were doing the
same for him; the wretched ryots being thus made to pay twice over. This
matter was also settled, after endless talkee-talkee, by the old lady giving
up some of the farms and being definitely confirmed in peaceful possession of the rest, while in both classes the ryots had their rents fixed
and the double payments credited to future years. They could not be
refunded because the Raja had spent the money as fast as he got it!

As I am writing about Rajas I may as well mention here a visit which
we paid to another Raja, or rather Maharaja, somewhere about this
time. He was one of the Rajas on the sea-coast, whom I have mentioned
above, and claimed (rightly I believe) to be the lineal descendant and
sole representative of the ancient line of the native sovereigns of Orissa,
the old Gajapatis, who were descended from the sun or the moon, I
forget which. He lived at a small, dirty town called Al on one of the
lower channels of the Brahmani River, in a huge, rambling palace, half
ruinous, of course, surrounded by a moat and a thick belt of bamboos,
so as to be as unhealthy, mouldy and mildewed as possible. The little,
wizened old Maharaja received us in as much state as he could manage
and sent his eldest son with my wife, her English nurse and the children
into the Zenana to visit his queens. He took me through several tumbledown courtyards to a large brick platform on which stood, in rows, a lot
of children. This, he explained, was his school. I asked whose the children were, for they were all so well dressed that I could not suppose
they were children of the wretched inhabitants of the poverty-stricken
town. He looked at them and ran his finger down the lines and then
said, 'All these are my children—no, that one is the Prime Minister's
and that one is the Treasurer's—but all the rest are mine.' I counted—
there were seventy-five of them! I thought of the verse in Kings; 'Now

Ahab had seventy sons in Samaria . . .' Then we went and sat in a large, pillared portico overlooking a large tank surrounded by a lovely but badly-kept garden. Here we talked till my wife came out from her interview, when the Maharaja sent in to the palace to order his wives to clear out of the reception rooms so that he might show me round. The rooms were numerous, rather small and dark, but highly decorated. The walls of his own private sitting and sleeping rooms were covered with paintings which he told me he had done himself. They represented subjects so grossly indecent that I shuddered at the thought of my wife having seen them. Luckily, as it turned out, she had been so amused by the ladies that it had not occurred to her to look at the walls. Luckily also the drawing was so grotesque that no one not accustomed to native art would have been able to make out what was meant.[1] It seems that when taken into these apartments my wife and her party were met by a portly old lady perfectly smothered in jewellery and costly robes. The young prince introduced her as the Head Queen (Pàtràru), his mother. Then followed one woman after another all nearly as much bedizened who, he explained, were the subordinate queens. She counted between sixty and seventy of them. They all squatted on the floor in long rows and stared at her while she conversed, through the Prince as interpreter, with the Head Queen. The conversation was idle and banal, as usual, the only curious incident being that a rather poorly dressed girl threw herself at my wife's feet and poured out a string of words. This being interpreted was to the effect that she was the youngest queen and was only allowed silver ornaments and no silk garments or shawls, and she begged my wife to *order* the Maharaja to give her gold ornaments and silken robes like the others. She was at once ignominiously hustled away by the others and probably caught it hot afterwards. Then we took leave and returned to our camp. On making inquiries I learnt that there was an ancient custom, half religious and half traditional, by which the Maharajas of Al were required to marry a new wife every year on a certain festival. The present Maharaja, being nearly seventy and having begun life early, as they do in India, had by degrees amassed all these wives and had begotten all these children. What was to become of them all no one seemed to know or care. His estates were large but not very profitable, but living is cheap in India and the people generally seemed to think it was all right, so I suppose it was. He himself seemed very happy and rather proud of his large family.

[1] Indian scholars will understand when I say that they represented the sata-sangama-prakarah from the Koka-sastra.

CHAPTER XIX

CUTTACK, 1875–1877

WE had a Masonic Lodge in Cuttack, 'Lodge Star of Orissa'. It had a neat little building specially constructed for it and a fair attendance of members. Since belonging to 'Lodge Star of the East' in Calcutta under good Captain 'Enry 'Owe's guidance in 1858, I had not had any opportunity of belonging to a Lodge and had grown rather rusty. But at the earnest entreaty of Walker, Faulkner and others, I joined the Cuttack Lodge and in 1875–6 was made Master. The Lodge was a jovial, convivial institution. After work there was always a banquet, followed by much heavy drinking and singing of songs, at which old Faulkner presided gloriously. I was eventually obliged to retire from this Lodge because a large number of the penniless, loafing ne'er-do-wells, half-caste clerks, *déclassé* Europeans and the like who infest all large stations in India took to joining the Lodge, and then calling at my house incessantly to beg for help and for good appointments, pleading the sacred tie of Masonic brotherhood. This grew to be such an infliction that I was obliged, in self-defence, to withdraw from active participation in Masonry.

J. H. Walker, whom I ought to have mentioned before, was a leading member of our Cuttack society. He held the important post of Superintending Engineer, the Headship of the large and useful Irrigation Branch of the Public Works Department. Born at a place which he called 'Weendiwuls', but which on the map appeared as 'Windywalls', near Kelso, he was a typical lowland Scot, full of Border legends of Elliots and Armstrongs, a sturdy, determined, canny man with a strong literary and intellectual element in his mind, and an intense love of arguing on every conceivable subject. Many a happy day did I spend with him seated, cheroot in mouth, on one of the little steamers on some canal or river in the glowing sunshine, arguing and discussing on every imaginable topic. It was from him, or rather from a nickname of his,[1] that the station on False Point got its name.[2] When it was found

---

[1] He was familiarly known as 'Hookey Walker'. It may be necessary to explain to posterity that 'Hookey Walker', like 'Cheeks the Marine', 'Jim Crow' and other similar terms, was the name of some imaginary person popularly used by the street boys in the 'forties and 'fifties. He seems to have died out of the *gamin* memory now.

[2] False Point was so called because some forty miles to the north of it was

necessary to establish a port for central Orissa, Ravenshaw, Walker and Macpherson, the Collector, went down to False Point in one of the little steamers and with some difficulty found a suitable site for the Harbour-master and his Customs establishment. The site being uninhabited was also nameless, and they cast about for a name for it. Several were suggested and rejected. At last Macpherson said, 'Let us call it Hookey Tolah after old Hookey Walker.' The idea took and the place was solemnly named and a bottle of champagne was drunk by the company to christen it.[1] The native fishermen and boatmen who haunted those lonely swamps learnt the name readily and it was officially adopted, though of course the bigwigs in Calcutta had no idea of its derivation. Some years later the great W. W. Hunter in compiling his gazetteer found this name in use and, supposing it to be a native word, thought proper to write it according to the scientific method of spelling Indian names—Hukitolà!!

False Point and its history deserve some mention. It is a long, sandy spit at the mouth of the Mahanadi River. The current in the Bay of Bengal sweeps strongly northwards all along the Indian Coast. Consequently every big river that empties itself into the Bay is encumbered by a bar of sand trending ever northwards. Year after year this bar increases till the river breaks through, cutting it up into islands and forming a new mouth further north. In 1866, when the great and terrible famine occurred in Orissa, much of the suffering was due to the absence of any proper landing-place or port where ships could unload cargoes. All this coast is very deficient in harbours. Pooree is merely an open roadstead, where it is not always safe or possible to unload or load cargo and the mouths of the rivers had not then been properly developed. But the Engineers had long had their eyes on False Point and the Dhamra as possible ports, and soon after the famine work was over they began work on False Point. A canal had been made from Cuttack for some fifty miles to Marsaghai, a place on the main stream of the Mahanadi. Thence the route followed the river for some ten miles, and then turned off down a creek into an immense, shallow bay or backwater some three or four miles broad, surrounded by islands of soft mud in which grew dense thickets of mangrove, bamboo cane and long, creeping lianes.

Point Palmyras, at the mouth of the Brahmani River, a well-known landmark for vessels sailing up the Bay of Bengal. The point at the mouth of the Mahanadi was often mistaken for Point Palmyras and ships were wrecked in consequence. So it got to be known as the false Point Palmyras, and finally as False Point.

[1] The name was more native than they thought. For *hukki* is an Oriya word for a white-ants' nest and *tola* is a very common termination of names of villages in all parts of India. It means originally a 'market' from the root *tul*—'to weigh'.

Between this bay and the sea was a long, low island of sand, at the northern end of which was the entrance to the harbour, if it could be called a harbour. It consisted of those parts of the bay, principally close under the island, which were deep enough for ships of average draught, say, sixteen feet to twenty. On this island stood the Harbourmaster's house and offices with a cluster of huts for coolies, boatmen and the like. In the centre was a lofty structure surmounted by a flagstaff used as a look-out —this imposing settlement was Hookey Tolah. Close into the shore was anchored a huge Flat (as they are called), an immense, flat-bottomed cargo boat with rows of cabins built on both sides of its spacious deck, with kitchens, bathrooms and other conveniences. It was called the *Ghazipore* and was used as a sort of floating hotel for passengers waiting for the British India steamers which called once a week. There were also generally three or four French ships loading with rice for Mauritius and a good many native vessels in the same trade. Some two miles off, on an island somewhat more solid than the rest, stood a great stone lighthouse, built out of laterite stones taken from the Fort at Cuttack. It was in charge of a kind-hearted but low-bred Irish retired sea captain, Mr Geary (I used to tease my wife by calling him her cousin), who lived in that melancholy solitude with a wife and nine children. Around the lighthouse was an extensive grove of coconut palms which Captain Geary had planted. From the top of the lighthouse about sunset one could look down into the dense jungle that spread for miles, and frequently see tigers crawling across the open patches, on the look-out for Captain Geary's cows which he kept in a high-walled enclosure at night. Tigers had been known to leap over this wall and kill cattle—at least so he said, but sea captains are given to spinning yarns.[1] He added a little to his not too abundant means by selling butter to the ships in the harbour.

But *the* character of False Point was Captain Harris. He *was* False Point, and when he died False Point no longer seemed itself. He made it and fostered it and loved it. He was, like so many men in employ round the coast, an old skipper, who in his time had sailed the Indian seas from Suez and the Cape to Hong Kong and Batavia. The usual round, red-faced, loud-voiced skipper, clever with his hands, ready in any emergency, drinking like a fish, talkative and rather rough of speech, but a thoroughly good, useful, hard-working man, admirably suited for the post. Under him was a watchful, taciturn old sea-dog named Black, and these two lived alone at the melancholy station of

[1] I saw the tigers myself on one occasion, but the wall of the cattle-yard was about eight feet high. I will not say positively that a tiger could not leap so high, but I do not think he could leap out again with a full-grown cow in his jaws.

Hookey Tolah and spent their lives in trying to beautify and improve it.

My first introduction to Captain Harris was characteristic. It was on the occasion of my going to False Point with Ravenshaw when he went on leave. Our steamer arrived there at dusk, and anchored in the great, dreary lagoon. Not very far off was the flat *Ghazipore*, and on the deck under an awning sat a man at a table silhouetted against the dim light of a ship's lantern hung over his head. On the table was a water bottle and glass and under the table a small keg. With the regularity of a mechanical toy, the man stooped and turned the tap of the keg so that liquor ran into his glass, then he filled up the glass with water and drank it. After a short rest, during which he smoked a pipe, he repeated the process. We had just finished our dinner on the steamer, and as we smoked our cheroots we all sat on deck and watched with much amusement this solitary figure on the flat. Presently, out of the darkness a boat approached us, and a message was handed up to the effect that Captain Harris would like to see Mr Faulkner if he was on board. So old Faulkner went off in the boat. After a short time we saw him emerge from the darkness on to the deck of the flat where he took a chair opposite the solitary figure, and then *two* glasses were filled at the keg and regularly emptied. Perhaps they heard the roar of laughter from the steamer with which we greeted this new development, for a curtain was suddenly let down which hid them from our sight. Next morning Faulkner and Harris were up long before any of us—perhaps they sat up all night—went and had a dip in the sea and turned up at breakfast quite fresh and rosy.

But if he drank hard, he worked hard. Government in its usual way, having sanctioned the construction of a Port Office at False Point and appointed Harris and his staff, thought it had done all that was necessary and refused to sanction any further outlay. It was only by dint of very pressing representations often repeated that Ravenshaw was able after long delays to obtain a very small and utterly inadequate grant of money for the necessary buildings, jetties, buoys and other requisites. It was wonderful how much Harris did with his limited means. He had recourse sometimes to expedients which nothing but the stinginess of Government could have justified. Once, an old cargo boat sent down from the Calcutta Port Establishment, because it was too old to be of any use there, managed to get ashore in a storm. Harris immediately reported it as wrecked, and at once broke it up and used the timber and iron-work in his jetty and in flooring his office. The occurrence was duly reported to Government, and some months later a reply was received directing that the wreck should be sold by auction and the proceeds credited to the Customs Department. To this Harris was able to reply with perfect truth that she had gone to pieces, and that no remains of her could be found on the spot where she had been wrecked. He took advantage of the event to ask for a new cargo boat and a pinnace for his own use, and to our great surprise got them! A fine strong cargo boat and lovely green pinnace with handsome fittings and full supply of sailing and other gear arrived in a few days' time. She turned out to be a splendid and fast sailer and Harris spent almost all his time in her.

Some time after, meeting the head of the Customs department, I asked him why it was that there had been such difficulty in getting boats and other things for False Point at first, while they had responded so liberally to our request afterwards. He laughed and said that False Point being a new place was not down 'on the books' of the Department and no provision could consequently be made for it. The Government of India, a thousand miles off at Simla, had never heard of it and would not sanction any expenditure on it. But when once, with difficulty and after many explanations, they had grudgingly allowed some of the old and hardly usable stock to be sent there, the place got 'on to the books', and there was no difficulty in replacing anything that was worn out or lost by wreck, etc. 'I advise you,' he added, 'if you want anything for False Point, report something or other as worn out or lost and request that it may be replaced. You will get it at once, but it is no use asking for a new thing of a kind you have not had before:' I told this to Harris and he acted on it. He at once reported every old rusty bit of chain, every old anchor and worm-eaten plank about the place as worn out, and asked that they might be 'replaced'. By this means he before long got a very decent quantity of port requisites which he could not have got otherwise. Once, requiring a row-boat to take letters and messages to the Post and Telegraph Office (which by the wisdom of the Postal Department had been located some four miles off across the lagoon), he bought for three or four rupees a very rotten old fishing boat from some natives and entered it on his stock account. Then he used it to go to the Post Office for a week, accompanied by another boat lest it should sink and the rowers be drowned. When he thought he had used it enough, he managed that it should one fine day mysteriously sink. On which he indented for a new boat to 'replace' it, and got it too—a fine, strong English-built captain's gig with a sail and lots of first-class tackle.

In this way we gradually got all we wanted. The Government had to be treated like a child which does not know what is good for it. Eventually, owing to the unwearied energy of Harris, the place was thoroughly equipped with all the requirements of a port, but no one knew how he managed to do it with such small grants of money as we could wring out of the Government. He got no thanks; on the contrary he was always being blamed for any shortcomings, but like so many Englishmen in India he worked on cheerfully and even enthusiastically, doing his best for the place committed to his charge, not expecting praise or reward. A few years later he was drowned in his own bay, in sight of his beloved station, and his name is probably by this time quite forgotten. He was a common type. The British Empire in India is like one of those large coral islands in the Pacific built up by millions of tiny insects, age after age. Men admire the beauty of the land and profit by its fertility, but who thinks of the insects who built it up?

This reminds me of another death which occurred about this time. A bright, clever, promising boy named Atkinson, one of my Assistants, was stationed at Kendrapara, a subdivision some thirty miles from Cuttack. He had been distinguished at a Public School (Harrow or Rugby, I forget which) and at Oxford, had passed high for the Civil Service, and during the short time he served under me had shown signs of great ability and high promise. He had fallen in love with Florrie Faulkner, one of old Faulkner's pretty daughters, and had arranged with her that on his next visit to Cuttack he should ask her father's consent. Some festivity—ball or something of the kind such as we so frequently had—was to take place. I think it was on the occasion of the Queen's birthday, which we always made a public holiday with some celebrations. He asked me for leave to come in to Cuttack, which I granted. It was a blazing hot, sultry May day and he started early as usual and rode fast to get in before the heat began. At the very end of his ride, with the roofs and chimneys of Cuttack in sight, he had to cross the river which then was an expanse of dazzling sand about a mile broad, with a narrow stream of water trickling down the middle. The track across the sand was marked by deep ruts made by the cartwheels of the strings of carts that were constantly passing. This track wound up and down so as to cross the water at its shallowest, and Atkinson, anxious to get in, for the sun was already getting hot when he reached the river, seems to have tried to take a short cut. But the narrow thread of water was treacherous. Though in general not more than a foot or two deep, in places it formed deep pools, where some furious eddy during the rains had scooped out the sand. Right into one of these he rode. His horse in its mad plunging threw him off, struggled to the bank and galloped away, but he never rose again. The Faulkners had invited him to stay with them, and his servant had arrived with his luggage. They waited for him till one o'clock and then began to get anxious. Old Faulkner went to the door to look out and saw a policeman leading a riderless horse to the police lines. He stopped the man and recognized the horse as Atkinson's. The man said he had found the horse grazing by the road leading to the river, and was taking it, as unclaimed property, to the police station. When asked where the rider was, he stared after the manner of his kind and said he did not know. It had not occurred to him to consider the question. Faulkner came rushing over to my house which was close by, and I at once ordered out a strong body of police to go and search. On reaching the river bank the Inspector found numbers of men cutting grass for horses as usual. At that dry season the grass-cutters have to go long distances in search of green fodder and naturally seek it by the rivers. Questioned on the subject they all said cheerfully—Oh, yes! they had seen a sahib ride on to the sand from the other side and try to cross the river. They saw that he had left the track and was heading for a deep pool and they saw him fall off his horse, and they saw the horse come out without him and gallop away. 'Where was the Sahib?' They did not know, perhaps he was in the water. 'Did they not shout to warn him of his danger?' No, it was no affair of theirs. 'What did they do when they saw him fall?' They? They cut grass for their horses!![1] Also there was a Kanungo[2] riding on his pony with his servant following him. He saw the whole scene—and rode on to his work! He was quite close to the Sahib and saw he was riding into danger, but it was no affair of his. (I promptly dismissed that Kanungo from the Government Service, at which all the natives, official and non-official, were very much surprised —and asked what he had done to be punished.)

We dragged the pool and found the poor boy's body. He was quite dead. He was buried that evening and Florrie wept. She married another man a year after.

The charm of our life in Cuttack lay not only in the friendliness and sociability of the European residents, but also in its variety. Totally new and unexpected events were always occurring. About this time, for instance, occurred the wreck of the *Velleda*. She was a French ship from Nantes. I have mentioned in a former page the French ships that used to call at False Point. There were a good many of them. They took a cargo of wines and spirits and other things from French ports to Batavia,

---

[1] Cf *Charlotte having seen his body*
   Borne before her on a shutter
   Like a well-behaved young lady
   Went on cutting bread and butter.

[2] In India generally, an official who keeps registers of rent-payers. In Orissa, a native land-surveyor and estate-agent. An educated man who ought to have known better than the ignorant grass-cutters.

thence they came in ballast to False Point where they shipped rice for the Indian coolies working at Mauritius. At this latter place they shipped sugar for France, thus making a regular round. One day one of these ships, the *Velleda*, was driven ashore in a storm. The sagacious police, for some reason best known to themselves—the workings of a native policeman's mind are dark and tortuous and hard to understand —-arrested the captain and crew, and put a guard on the vessel as she lay on the beach at the mouth of the Dayà River. The latter precaution was wise and saved the vessel from being plundered. The Magistrate of Pooree, an eccentric person, Joseph Armstrong, telegraphed to me for orders[1] as to what he was to do with the men. In reply I instructed him to supply them with food and anything else they might require, and to get carts and send them to Cuttack at once. After a few days they arrived, a hungry, dirty, ragged, dishevelled party of about a dozen Frenchmen. We accommodated them in the Police Barracks, and gave them food and clothing and medical aid. The captain, named Semelin, was a merry, little, round Sancho Panza of a man and amused us very much while he remained at Cuttack.

But I had a dreadful task with him. Through all the terrors of the shipwreck he had kept his ship's papers and his 'Code Maritime', a little, fat, much-thumbed and dog-eared book, safe in a bag slung across him. These he now produced and read me many sections of the Code, declaring the steps he ought to take under the circumstances. First I had to record a *procès-verbal*, a very lengthy document reciting the whole story of the wreck and what led to it, including the depositions of the captain and the crew. Then I had to go through a long list of all the ship's gear, rigging, sails, cargo, and everything in fact except her hull. My French stood the test of the *procès-verbal* and the depositions pretty well, but when it came to such technicalities as ship's rigging and gear I was completely floored. So I sent for Tonnerre. He was a young Frenchman who had been appointed to the Bengal police and stationed at Cuttack, a charming, brilliant, high-spirited, clever young fellow. To my surprise he too was floored. He and Semelin, of course, chattered volubly together in their own language, but when it came to seafaring lingo he was as ignorant as I was. Eventually, with much gesticulating and pantomime between the two, aided by Spiers' dictionary, we got the list right and all the papers required by French law duly executed,

---

[1] He was not under my orders, but as the place of the shipwreck was on the boundary of our respective districts, and as he had no powers or experience in maritime matters, he threw the responsibility on to my shoulders, though it was his police who had arrested the men.

and sent off to the French Consul-General at Calcutta, who in due course sent down a request to sell the ship and remit the money to him for transmission to the owners in France. This was done; a rich merchant in Cuttack bought her as she lay and broke her up and made a good deal, I was told, by selling the timbers and other things. Semelin being part-owner kept his share of the money, and the rest was sent to the Consul. But he had on board a small stock of provisions for his own use, and these he got up from the coast (it was about fifty miles from Cuttack that the vessel was wrecked) and offered them for sale. Needless to say they were eagerly bought up—champagne, Sauterne, Burgundy wines, and the most delicious preserved fruits, fish, cheese and other provisions. My wife laid in a good stock and we fully enjoyed them. They were very cheap too. Then poor little Sancho Panza Semelin fell ill, and the doctor said he had better be sent to Calcutta, where he would find a French doctor who could understand him. His disease was some internal ailment of an obscure nature. So I shipped him and his crew off to Calcutta, whence, as I was informed, they shipped on board various French vessels and so got home. Poor Semelin, however, died in the hospital at Calcutta, and I received a touching letter of thanks from the Consul-General for my kindness to him.

These French skippers entitled themselves 'capitaine au long cours', but Tonnerre called them 'vieux ours maritimes', old sea-bears. I always found them very amusing and I enjoyed talking French to them. False Point was a dreary place for them to lie at. No town, no drinking places, no amusements of any sort—only a great shallow lagoon, half of it bare, glistening mud at low water, bounded on all sides but one by low, swampy, mangrove jungle. On one occasion Ravenshaw and Walker and I were down there in the *Pioneer*, and Toppino, one of these captains, came to see us. Our table was being laid for breakfast on deck, and among other things there was a bowl full of fresh limes. Toppino's eyes glistened. 'Ah! vous avez des limons, des limons!' he cried. Knowing how good limes and other fruit are for sailors after a long voyage we let him fill his pockets. He went away rejoicing, and shortly after he sent us two bottles of claret, grown he assured us, on his own estate near Bordeaux, and known as *Gros Bonnet*; also a tin of delicious truffled sausages. When I got back to Cuttack, I ransacked the bazaar for fresh fruit and vegetables, and sent him down a boat-load of pumpkins, plantains, limes and such things as we could get. He wrote me a most gushingly grateful letter. The *Gros Bonnet*, when we drank it, turned out to be a very fine delicate wine of the Médoc type.

During the cold weather of this year I paid a visit to a curious place,

Udayagiri, i.e. the Sunrise Mountain. It lies between two of the great rivers of the delta of the Mahanadi, and is so called because it is the furthest spur to the eastward of the Orissa ranges. It is an isolated rocky peak of no great height with a mosque on the summit, small, modern and ugly. But in a great cleft nearly a mile long on the eastern face, Faulkner, who was with me on this occasion, and I found a strange place. At the head of the ravine we saw what looked like images, so we started to explore. The ravine was covered with a jungle of low, thorny bushes, but on setting coolies to work to clear this off, we first came upon a deep well of the kind called Bàoli, a large, circular hole lined with stone masonry descends for about fifty feet. In one side of this wall is an archway, and a broad flight of stone steps leading down from another archway at the top. At the bottom of the steps is a platform of stone, in the middle of which is the mouth of the well. It was full of water and apparently very deep. On the sides of the wall going down the steps were rudely carved numerous names, apparently of pilgrims, in an archaic character, the so-called Kutila, which has not been used since about the ninth or tenth century. The inscriptions must thus be more than a thousand years old. Our coolies were half afraid of venturing into the gorge as it has the reputation of being haunted. It was only by liberal payment we could induce them to go on. Beyond the well was a pathway flagged with stone, and on either side, for the most part over-turned and lying under the bushes, were great quantities of statues of Buddha of stone. These were of all sizes from a few inches to four feet high. We counted some hundreds of them. At the end of the pathway which was more than half a mile long and ascended gradually, we came upon a beautiful gateway of stone, the lintel and sideposts of which were covered by delicately-carved groups of figures illustrating events in the various Jâtakas or former births of Buddha. Looking through this gateway we were startled to see, deep in the gloom of dense, overhanging trees, a colossal seated Buddha in the usual attitude of meditation. The image was buried up to the waist in débris and soil, but the huge upper half stood up so high that a tall man standing on the palm of its right hand could only just touch its shoulder.

The whole place had evidently in ancient times been a Buddhist monastery and place of pilgrimage. Here, as everywhere in Orissa, the noses of all the images had been broken off. It was the custom of the Mahommedans thus to disfigure all the statues of gods and others they found in any part of India. The local legend says that at the sound of the kettle-drums of Kàlapahàr[1] all the noses of the gods in Orissa fell off.

[1] Kàlapahàr was the first Musulman invader of Orissa, A.D. 1570.

I thought some at least of these carvings worthy of preservation. The colossal Buddha was too big to move, but Faulkner sent for boats and derrick and managed to remove the lovely gateway and half a dozen of the best statues, which he set up for me in the Public Garden which I had made close to the canal in Chauliaganj, the suburb of Cuttack city in which most of the Civil officials live. I presume they are there still. I should have been unwilling to disturb the ancient shrine on Udaya-giri, but the images were lying neglected and buried under jungle and soil, the place was somewhat inaccessible and the Public Garden at Cuttack was a central situation where these rare and beautiful objects could be seen and studied as well as preserved. Therefore I acquitted myself of the charge of vandalism. I wrote a long and minute account of the place with copious illustrations, which was published in the *Journal* of the Bengal Asiatic Society.[1]

Orissa is full of ancient temples, forts and statues. Many of these I visited, sketched, and wrote articles about for the Asiatic Society during the nine years I spent in that old-world province, now (or at least then) the home of the most bigoted, Brahmin-ridden Hindus in all India. But it would take up too much room to describe them in detail; besides—are they not written in the *Journal* of the Asiatic Society of Bengal?

The year 1876 passed without any very memorable event. The work was incessant, varied, interesting, and I found time also for my linguistic studies. The third volume of my *Comparative Grammar* occupied most part of my spare time.

On the 24th April 1876 was born my youngest child. I was reading at that time a novel in the *Revue des Deux Mondes*, the heroine of which was named Angèle, so I had the child christened Angela. As Tonnerre said, 'C'est un nom très gentil,' but the child herself, when she grew up, disliked it. It is perhaps an unusual name in England. My wife suffered a good deal over this her last confinement, and I was told she required a run home. Moreover, certain things had fallen out badly with regard to my three boys who were with my brother Pearson at Corfe, near Taunton, and there was urgent need for one of us to go home and put things right. So by degrees the conviction grew on us that my wife must go home. My financial position would not allow of my going, and as Sir Richard Temple was about to leave Bengal I hoped that my prospects would improve. Ravenshaw talked of taking leave, and under a new Lieutenant-Governor I might have a chance of succeeding him. It would not do for me to be absent at such a time, even if I had been

[1] See *Journal*, Asiatic Society of Bengal, vol. xliv, p. 19, 1875.

able to afford it. So during the cold weather of 1876–7 I made my arrangements. The little girls were also, the elder of them at any rate, getting to an age when they could no longer stay in India. All things combined to force us to separate. We felt it very keenly. We had never been parted for more than a few days at a time for eighteen years. But it had to be done for my wife's health and for the sake of the children.

But my preparations and our sorrows were, as was so often the case with officials, interrupted by a great public event. On the 1st January 1877 Lord Lytton, the Viceroy, held a magnificent Assembly at Delhi, at which all the great feudatory nobles, princes and territorial magnates attended in great pomp and splendour, with gay clothing, masses of diamonds and jewels, elephants and horses with gilded and jewelled trappings and all the brilliancy that can be imagined. The Viceroy was attended by quantities of troops, councillors, heads of departments and others, not to omit a vast cloud of newspaper reporters and globe-trotters. There with solemn state Queen Victoria was proclaimed Empress of India.

In every part of India it was ordered that there should be a similar ceremony at the local capital. Cuttack, of course, was not going to be behindhand. So I was ordered to construct a tent big enough to hold all the people, great and small, who were to be invited. So we set to work and erected a big pavilion on the plain in front of the Fort. It was made of poles and a roof of canvas, covered with red, blue and white calico, and wreathed in wreaths of green leaves and palm branches. Large numbers of flags waved from the top. Inside was a dais and rows of chairs for the notables. The floor was covered with thick carpets, with a strip of scarlet cloth up the centre. Behind the dais was a gallery for the ladies. The Regiment supplied a guard of honour. Ravenshaw, in his blue and gold Windsor uniform, the Colonel in scarlet and gold, and this humble writer in plain morning dress sat on the dais, and a brilliant line of native Maharajas, Rajas and zemindars blazing with jewels sat on one side, while on the other were all the European officials and be-hind, on both sides, a large crowd of natives.

Then the Queen's proclamation was read, first in English, then in Oriya, and a Royal Salute (or something as near as we could get) was fired. The native chiefs arose one by one and were led before the Com-missioner to salute and be saluted. Then the servants went round with silver scent sprinklers and silver trays with betel nut in little packets, and every chief was duly sprinkled with attar of roses and presented with a packet of betel. Then the ceremony ended and all departed. The 'Kings of the Amorites who dwell in the hills' marched away surrounded by a small army of followers—we were obliged to limit each king to 100 followers, which gave some offence; Moyurbhanj had brought 600 with him—and a band discoursing barbaric, discordant music.

In the evening a social meeting was held in the same pavilion where the chief European officials and their wives met and did their best to be civil to the native chiefs, while nâch girls danced before them and sang native songs through their noses. This lasted till long past midnight when they all departed apparently well-pleased.

As soon as this business was over and we had picked up the pieces I went off to Calcutta with my wife and children—five girls—and saw them off on the steamer for England. Even at this distance of time I can recall the intense grief of that moment—I cannot dwell on it. A few days later I returned by sea to my empty home.

It was some compensation to me that a few weeks later Ravenshaw was appointed to officiate on the Board of Revenue, and I was appointed to act in his place as Commissioner of the Orissa Division. This promotion involved an increase of pay amounting to about £800 a year, making my total salary in round numbers £3,000 a year. But I had heavy debts to pay and the expense of a wife and eight children in England. The cost of the education of my three sons now began to weigh heavily. They had cost me up to that time £100 a year each, but they were now to cost a good deal more. In a very short time they began to cost close upon £200 a year each. As Commissioner I was obliged to entertain a good deal, and was expected to subscribe more than others to all kinds of objects. So my income did not do more than meet the demands upon me.

The promotion, however, did me good by presenting to me a great variety of new kinds of work. In addition to the three districts of Balasore, Cuttack and Pooree, the Collectors of which were now under my orders, I was *ex-officio* Superintendent of the Tributary States; in other words a sort of bear-leader to seventeen petty chieftains living in the hill country on the west of Orissa. I have not said much about these people as far as I remember, and a brief account of them may perhaps be interesting.

When the English conquered Orissa in 1803 with two regiments of native troops from Madras, the Marathas fled westwards through the hill country back to their own land. Our knowledge of the geography of Orissa was at that time so slight that Colonel Harcourt, who commanded the little force, did not venture to follow them. This did not much matter as they were caught by Sir Arthur Wellesley at Assaye, where they arrived in time to share in the crushing defeat of their nation. In the course, however, of his inquiries Colonel Harcourt and the Chief Commissioner, Mr Melvill, learnt of the existence of a number of independent or semi-independent chieftains, each ruling a small tract of territory in those wild hills. Not understanding the status of those men, and assuming them to be far more powerful than they really were, Harcourt and Melvill executed on behalf of the British Government treaties of alliance with each of them, by virtue of which they were to be confirmed in their possessions on payment of a *peshkash*, or small annual tribute. One cannot read without a smile in these treaties a solemn promise on the part of each of these microscopic potentates not to wage war against the British Government—as though a gnat should promise not to fight an elephant. In later times, when we knew all about these people, it was seen what a mistake we had made in treating them as independent potentates. A careful study of the records and documents subsequently discovered proved beyond a doubt that those hill chiefs had been from the earliest times feudal vassals of the Kings of Orissa, under whom they held their land chiefly on the tenure of military service. This they themselves now frankly admit. They say we knew this all along, and everyone in Orissa knew it, but if Colonel Harcourt was good enough to grant us the position of independent rulers it was not our business to undeceive him. In spite of their treaties they willingly consented to be treated as vassals, provided their *peshkash* or tribute were not increased. They were then placed under the general management of the Commissioner of Orissa who was ordered, as Superintendent, to control them, guide them, elevate them and so forth.

At the same time he was not given any power over them. The Government, by the treaties, had cut itself off from exercising any power, and so could not delegate to the Commisioner what it did not possess itself. He was directed to keep them in the paths of virtue by his 'moral influence'. Here was a strange problem, and it is wonderful how it was solved. It is typical of the way we have managed to rule India. First a minute of instructions was drawn up and issued by the Government of India. The chiefs were not asked whether they approved of these rules or not. They were merely told that these rules would be enforced in future. How they were to be enforced was not stated, but by this time we had learnt how petty and powerless the chiefs were, and they had learnt how overwhelmingly powerful we were, so there was no necessity to enter into the question of how obedience was to be enforced. But the 'how' was illustrated by events which happened shortly after the promulgation of the rules. The Rajas of Angul and Bànki, two of these chiefs, after a long course of gross tyranny and oppression of their subjects refused to obey the British Government. Angul even went so far as to get up a small armed force for the purpose of rebellion. Whereupon a handful of Sepoys was sent to Angul, the Raja was seized and deposited in the Cuttack jail where he soon afterwards died, having, I learn, shown unmistakable signs of insanity. The territory of Angul was annexed and governed thenceforth by a British official. A similar fate befell Bànki, which was also annexed.

With these object lessons before them the other chiefs have ever since been perfectly submissive.

The system in force in 1877 when I took charge was as follows. The Rajas were allowed the general administration of their territories, but any of their subjects who felt himself aggrieved by any act of his Raja might appeal to the Commissioner, who asked for an explanation from the Raja, and finally decided what ought to be done and communicated his decision to the Raja. If the Raja had refused to obey, no one exactly knew what would have happened. But it was tacitly understood that he would not refuse and, as a matter of fact, he knew better than to do so. This is what is called 'moral influence'. When backed by bayonets it is a great power. Moreover each Raja had a minister. This is a very ancient native institution. Far back in dim antiquity, in the most ancient books of the sacred Hindu law, the institution of the Mantri[1] or Brahmin minister beside the Raja is found, and terrible are the spiritual punishments denounced against a Raja who refuses to follow the guidance of his Mantri. Ravenshaw and his predecessors had in a great number of cases induced the Rajas to appoint as Mantri persons of their own choosing, and by selecting men who were natives of British territory and had in many instances served in our courts and offices, they secured a partisan at every Raja's Court, and one, moreover, who could be relied on to keep his Raja straight. The power of sentencing men to death was withdrawn from the Chiefs, because it was found that their ideas on this subject were not in accordance with modern views. For instance, being all rigid Hindus by religion—though several of them were of non-Aryan or aboriginal descent—they considered the killing of a cow a heinous offence and one punishable by death. In several places also the practice of human sacrifices was still in force. All murder cases therefore had to be tried by the Commissioner, and if a sentence of hanging were pronounced it had to be sent up to Government to be confirmed.

[1] Oddly enough the Portuguese got hold of this word and applied it to the counsellors of the Emperor of China in the form Mandarin! The Persian word 'Dewan' is now ordinarily applied to designate the Mantri, even by Hindu Rajas.

A curious instance of the survival of human sacrifice occurred in Keonjhar, one of the largest of these petty states. It had been from ancient times the custom that the Raja, at a particular stage of the very long and intricate ceremony of coronation, should have a man brought before him, should draw his sword and slay the man. A grant of rent-free land was then given to the man's heirs as compensation. But on the first occasion of the accession of a Raja to the throne of Keonjhar after the issue of the rules above-mentioned, the Commissioner, who was present at the ceremony, forbade this part of it. Much discontent on the part of the young Raja and all his family and court was caused, but of course the Commissioner stood firm. After long discussion it was arranged that the man should be brought before the Raja as usual, the Raja was then to draw his sword and make a cut at the man, who was to fall down as if dead, and to be at once carried off by the attendants. He was then to disappear from the Raja's territory, and to be carefully on his guard never thereafter to approach the Raja or be seen by him. He was in fact to be reckoned as dead. This compromise satisfied, or seemed to satisfy, all concerned.

There were in all seventeen of these Rajas; their territories varied in extent. Those of Moyurbhanj (sometimes erroneously written Mohurbhunge) and Keonjhar in the north of Orissa were very extensive, perhaps about 3,000 square miles in extent. Dhenkanàl in the centre was about 2,000. The rest were much smaller. One or two of them in fact, such as Baramba and Tigaria, consisted of only about two dozen villages. In each, however, there was a large fortified residence (called a Garh = Fort) for the Raja, and from this cause they were collectively known as the Gurhjàt, i.e. the Forts.

I had not been long in charge before a case occurred in one of these Gurhjàt. The Raja of Daspalà, one of the worst of the lot, took a fancy to a married woman, the wife of one of his subjects. He had her brought into his zenana, and when the husband complained he was banished from the ten square miles or so which constituted the Kingdom of Daspalà, and threatened with death if he returned. So he wandered away homeless. His house and all it contained were confiscated by the Raja's retainers. But in his wanderings the wretched man came across people who were not afraid of His Majesty of Daspalà, and advised him to return and boldly claim his wife and property, and if they were not given up to him to go to Cuttack and complain to the Barà Sahib. So he plucked up courage and went to Daspalà. But as soon as he appeared he was arrested by the Raja's orders, taken into the Garh, stripped and branded all over the body with red-hot irons. He fainted, and his insensible body was cast out on the sandy bank of the river. At night, however, some of his relations came secretly, put him into a boat and carried him to Cuttack where he was received into the hospital and healed. Then he came to me with his story, and showed his back and thighs covered with long black streaks where he had been branded.

This was a more outrageous case than ordinary. I therefore took strong measures. I deposed the Raja and sent the order for his deposition by the Superintendent of police, Poole, with a guard of native police. Poole was instructed to tell the Raja that if he made the least opposition to the police, I should send the regiment of Sepoys from Cuttack. The Raja was a little insolent, but finally assured Mr Poole that his accuser was lying, and that he would go into Cuttack and explain the matter to me. Meanwhile the man's witnesses had been sent for, and on the Raja's arrival I tried the case in the usual way. The Raja's guilt was clearly proved and also the complicity of his minister and officials. I sent up a trustworthy man to conduct the administration and dismissed the Dewan and chief officials. In the course of the trial it came out that the Raja's rule had for some time past been scandalously tyrannous as well as corrupt. I therefore detained him in Cuttack and reported the case to Government, recommending that the Raja should be deposed and the administration carried on by a British officer until the Raja's son, a minor, should come of age and assume the management. I gave the past history of the man, showed how repeatedly his bad conduct had been noticed by my predecessors, and how he had persistently disregarded their remonstrances. The general disorder, mismanagement and wretched condition of his subjects resulting from his oppression were also pointed out. The Raja was in great terror. He was a big, black, bloated, unwholesome-looking beast, and his fear made him look even worse than nature intended. He came to my house, flung himself at my feet, tore off his turban and tried to place my foot on his head, and wailed and howled so that I was obliged to have him removed by my attendants. In his terror he released the woman, sent her back to her husband adorned with jewels, sent him a big bag of money and a deed, duly signed and sealed, conferring on him a large piece of land rent-free for ever.

The Government were inclined to follow my advice, but doubted whether they had power actually to depose the man. I did not think they had myself, but the temporary deposal effected my object just as well as a permanent one. Ravenshaw, being in Calcutta, was consulted and gave his opinion against deposition, though admitting that the wretch deserved condign punishment. Eventually it was ordered that the Raja should not be actually deposed, but that he should for a time be suspended from the administration of his State, which was to remain in the hands of the man sent by me. The Raja got a very severe scolding, which he did not mind in the least, and was threatened that *next time* he would be deposed and probably imprisoned.

With many of these Rajas threats and admonitions were useless, because they had not the wits to understand what was expected of them. They were wild, jungly, uncivilized creatures, mere savages in fact. Others were more intelligent and educated. Much good was done by the Superintendent's tours. He went round every year and inspected the Raja's Court and offices, blaming or praising as the case might be, indicating improvements and so on. By this means a rough sort of administration, quite as civilized as the people were fitted for, was maintained, and the mistake was avoided of trying to govern on principles of the highest cultivation a primitive people living in the forests, many of whom wore no clothing but the leaves of trees, and lived on roots and such game as they could shoot with their rude bows and arrows.

I gained much insight into the habits and manners of the Gurhjat people by an incident which occurred this year. The Maharaja of Dhenkanàl was one of the richest of the Gurhjat chiefs. His territory was the third in extent, and though a good deal of it was covered with forests, there was a large extent of cultivation and the people were prosperous under his rule. He had built himself a large and imposing palace in European style—he supposed it to be a facsimile of the Commissioner's residence, the Lal Bagh, at Cuttack. The sanitation of his town of Dhenkanàl was well attended to and he had built and maintained a hospital, a school and a guest house. He was an immense man weighing twenty-two stone —but big as he was he was a keen sportsman, and used to be carried into the forest to shoot tigers in a vast octagonal sort of couch or chair on poles borne by twenty-four men. For some years he had been a sufferer from some internal disease, and to ease his pain he indulged in the national habit of taking opium in pills. Stewart, the doctor at Cuttack, had been trying to reduce the amount of opium that he took, and had instructed him, when an attack of pain from his internal disease came on, to take some medicine (I forget what) instead of morphia. One night the Maharaja woke up in pain, and finding none of the drug recommended by Stewart in his room, sent a man down to the hospital for some. The native doctor in charge—a Bengali—woken up in the middle of the night, went sleepily with a lamp to his dispensing room, took down what he thought was the proper bottle, measured out a sufficient quantity and sent it up to the Palace. The Maharaja took it, and then discovered by the taste that it was the wrong stuff! He began to be very ill and in fearful pain. Mounted messengers were sent off at once to Stewart in Cuttack (fifty miles off) to beg him to come at once. Stewart packed up his stomach-pump, got on his horse and rode off. He arrived in time, though the poor old Raja's limbs were getting blue and livid. By applying the proper remedies he was brought round at last. Stewart then asked to see the bottle and discovered that it was a poison.[1] He at once started off to the dispensary to question the native doctor, but on arriving there found that he had disappeared! When the news that the Raja had been poisoned reached the dispensary, the timid Bengali, knowing that he was the cause of the accident, was panic-stricken. He rushed out of the building into the darkness, and was never seen again. A hue and cry was raised, detectives were employed, inquiries were made in all directions, even in his native place in Bengal, but that native doctor was never found. The people of Dhenkanàl unanimously believe that he wandered into the jungle which lies dense all round their little town, and was killed and eaten by the tigers and other wild beasts which abound there. This is highly probable, and to look for a dead man's bones in the jungle would be to search for a needle in a bundle of hay. All we could say was that he had disappeared.

The Maharaja recovered for the moment, but the shock to his health was serious. He did not long survive it, dying some two or three months later. He left only one son, a minor, and his State therefore was taken charge of by Government in the same way as Court of Wards management. I had to go there and inquire into everything, from the finances and Courts of Justice to the Palace cooking-pots; and to arrange a scheme for the future management of the State, and the maintenance of the deceased Maharaja's family, and the education and care of the minor.

Had this been an ordinary zemindari, the task would have been easy enough, and such as I had done often before. But in the first place we had no legal right at all to interfere in a Tributary (as it was called) and quasi-independent State, and secondly the wishes and feelings and superstitions and pride and crazes of all kinds of the Royal Family, as

[1] The stuff the Raja ought to have taken was 'hydro'—something, and the stuff which the native doctor sent him was 'hydro'—something else and a deadly poison. In examining the bottles on the dispensary shelves afterwards, Stewart found several bottles of 'hydro' this and 'hydro' that close to one another, so arranged that only the word 'hydro' on the label was visible, the rest of the label being hidden by the neighbouring bottle. It was a pure mistake and the native doctor need not have been so frightened about it. But then he was a Bengali, and Bengalis are the funkiest race in the world.

well as of the population of the State, had to be considered. Financially
Dhenkanàl was highly prosperous, the revenues though not large were
respectable, the late Maharaja had been a prudent and moderate man
and an excellent administrator; his only extravagance consisted in lavish
(but not reckless) generosity to all around him. But the very excellencies of his character caused a difficulty. He had had a long reign and
had so endeared himself to his people that they could not endure to see
any of his arrangements altered in the least. Every suggestion for improvement was met by the most determined opposition.

Ultimately I concluded to leave well alone, not thinking that it was
judicious to insist on mere technical improvements at the risk of
wounding the laudable, if mistaken, feelings of the people.

As to the family, they did not count. There was, at the back of the
Palace, it is true, a large, gloomy building surrounding a big courtyard
in which I was told there were some sixty-odd females composing the
late Prince's harem. But it was matter of common notoriety that the
state of his health had prevented him for many years past from fre-
quenting the society of his wives, and I was told by the Palace servants
that he never even visited the harem.

It further appeared that it was customary among these Orissa princes
when a Raja died to disperse his harem, and to allow the ladies to go
away and marry again—provided only that they had not borne any
children to the deceased. Those who had, had to remain and were entitled to maintenance for their lifetime. As there was only one child, the
minor, it was feasible to make a considerable clearance of the gloomy
building. A large reduction was also made in the Palace servants, whose
name was Legion. The system of payment and employment of these
was curious. For every post there were two tenants, two head footmen,
two head cooks (Brahmins). On asking the reason of this I learnt that
all the servants without exception were paid, not in cash, but by grants
of rent-free land, and it was necessary to have two men for each post
so that one might be away tilling the land while the other was on duty
at the Palace. They took it in turn like Lords-in-Waiting to the Queen.
Even the twenty-four men whose duty it was to carry the Raja in his
big travelling couch were in reality forty-eight—half of whom were on
duty at a time while the other half were away farming their lands. A
strange system but, as no one got any money, it was not expensive.
Land was plentiful enough in those sparsely peopled jungles.

After a stay of some days busily engaged in settling and arranging
everything, I returned to Cuttack. I find in one of my letters to Elliot,
written immediately after my return home, a description of this journey.

I copy it here, as it is a good instance of the difficulties of travelling during the rains in some parts of India. The whole distance was only about fifty miles.

'Cuttack. August 31. 1877.

'Left Dhankanàl at seven last night, and only just got too far to go back when down it came—heavy rain like hail—thunder and lightning walloping all round. The bearers don't wear much clothes, and they seemed not to like it on their skins. However, just as they were giving in up came the Jemadar with a lantern in his hand, which he informed me he had snatched up from the Raja's own room on seeing the rain. It was a wonderful affair with panes of red and blue glass which shed a ghastly light on the thick forest on either hand. This amazing little man who is a Pachima[1] or up-country man (quite a title of honour down here), is a small ex-sowar Musulman and consists of a pair of extensive boots, a sword, a medal and a voice. By dint of calling the bearers alternately "beta" and "betich—"[2] and much shrieking and galloping to and fro he induced them to go on. At last we came to a nullah, nothing at all usually, but now a deep, roaring torrent. There was nothing to be done but to put the pàlki down and send back to Dhenkanàl for an elephant. As I sat boxed up, smoking a pipe amidst the warfare of the elements, with the shivering bearers crouching under the trees, smoking one cigar of mine among them and the rain rattling down on the pàlki roof, and one small, cold thread of wet slowly creeping under one thigh from a crack in the door, it occurred to me that my lines on Dhenkanàl in my last letter did not quite hit off the correct pronunciation of the word. Bawl does *not* rhyme with Dhenkanàl. It occurred to me that the language of "our lively neighbours" (as the newspapers say) would hit off the sound better.

So I improvised this:

> *Je suis parti de Dhenkanàl*
> *Par un chemin très-inégal*
> *Un gros orage tropical*
> *Versait son torrent pluviale*
> *Et tout autour de Dhenkanàl*
> *Hurlaient les loups at les chacals.*
> *Les sentiers de Dhenkanàl*

[1] Pachima means a man from the North-Western Provinces. They are much looked up to for their superior valour by the unwarlike Bengalees and Oriyas. 'Ex-sowar' means that he had formerly been a trooper in a Cavalry Regiment.

[2] Beta = son and 'betich—' (I do not give it in full) a peculiarly obscene term of abuse very common among natives.

Mènent à la foret virginale
Dont les bocages fleuris exhalent
Un parfum très-original.

(There is a lot more, but this may suffice—the page is torn off.) 'After this arrove two elephants. The bigger of the two really a fine beast, a mighty tusker full ten feet high. They hoisted my pàlki bodily on to his back, crosswise, the two poles almost touching the trees. I mounted the lesser beast. It was one of those weird Rembrandt pictures one sees occasionally. Figure to yourself a narrow road shaded by tall trees and bordered by dense jungle. Crossing it a very black nasty-looking nullah with steep sides altogether uncanny and dangerous looking. Moonlight, but very sickly and fitful owing to the heavy, slow-moving clouds. In front in the rift between the trees, a big elephant looking double his size in the strange, uncertain light with a pàlki towering higher still; behind, a confused glare of torches and crowds of dusky men crossing the nullah in batches on the other elephant. Can't you see the scene? Its weird effects of light and shade, great black masses with points of light here and there and the mysterious, sickly moonlight over all. If in addition you had your feet wet, as well as half your right leg, were rather sleepy and shaken to pieces, were anxious about the safety of your office-box on the head of a naked savage fording the stream with water up to his armpits, and were in addition aware of some ten nullahs, all unbridged, plus the vast Mahanadi between you and Cuttack, you would be in a position to appreciate all the ghastly grandeur of the scene. Fortunately I had a brandy-flask with me and partook thereof, also thanks to the in-defatigable Jemadar, his boots and his voice, we passed unscathed through all the perils of the road and at dawn reached the Mahanadi where lay the *Pioneer*. A table on deck with shining tablecloth, eggs, toast, tea, and other necessaries greeted me there, and I was safe at home by eight o'clock.'

Another serious case which occurred this year arose from the misconduct of the highest native prince in Orissa. It was extremely difficult to deal with owing to the exalted rank and peculiarly sacred position of the culprit, who though in reality a silly, debauched, half-witted boy, was regarded by the Hindus of Orissa as a living embodiment of their great god Jagannath. The ancient Kingdom of Orissa had been ruled by a long succession of dynasties till the Mahommedan conquest in the sixteenth century. When that cataclysm took place, the sovereign, fleeing from his capital of Cuttack, took refuge in the difficult hill country to the south-west, where he and his successors maintained a precarious semi-independent position at Khurda until the days of British rule. Their vicissitudes and family history are too varied and complicated to be here related. It may suffice to say that the British Government, in accordance with its invariable practice of recognizing all just claims, allowed the Raja of Khurda as we called him—the King of Orissa as the people considered him—to enjoy the revenues of several very large and fertile pargannahs (= counties), partly for his own maintenance, and partly for the support of the celebrated temple of Jagannath at Pooree, the well-known place of pilgrimage. This temple was founded by a King of Orissa in the twelfth century, and subsequent kings had protected it, given it large endowments, and held it as their chief glory to be reckoned among the servants of the god. On the day of the great festival when Jagannath rides abroad in his Car, the King sweeps the steps in front of the temple with a golden broom.

It was found necessary to remove the King from his mountain retreat at Khurda, to place the administration of his estates in the hands of Government officials, who merely handed over to him the revenues they collected, and to settle him and his family in a large and handsome palace in the town of Pooree close to the temple, of which he was still the recognized and acknowledged guardian and chief manager. Certain duties were imposed upon him in this capacity, chief among which was that of keeping order among the vast crowds of pilgrims who flocked every year to the festivals, especially to the crowning solemnity of all, the Car Festival. On this occasion it was his duty to enrol a large number of special constables to prevent overcrowding and admit the pilgrims to the temple in order. He was also bound to arrange with the numerous priests within the vast enclosure of the temple as to the times and order of celebration of the various pujas or sacrifices, so that the pilgrims might be able to attend them and perform their religious ceremonies without hindrance or confusion. The task was a difficult one owing to the immense crowds, generally about a million people, men and women, who assembled on those occasions; also on account of the intricacy of the ceremonies which each pilgrim had to perform, and more than all on account of the shameless rapacity of the temple priests, who levied fees from the pilgrims at every stage of the proceedings and sometimes stopped the ceremonies until they were paid, thus causing extreme confusion among the crowds who were pressing in with frantic shouts and every kind of extravagant enthusiasm.

The interior of the temple was cut up into numerous courtyards divided by high stone walls pierced by narrow doorways. In each court were two or three shrines. The pilgrims had to visit each of these in succession, and as they could not find their way through this labyrinth unaided there was a large number of official guides or parihàris, each of whom took charge of a batch of pilgrims and piloted them through courtyard after courtyard, till they finally reached the shrine of the great Jagannath, worshipped there and were sent away through a side door. No European and no native in European dress might enter the temple, but to keep order inside and see that all the arrangements were properly carried out, a native Deputy Magistrate dressed in native costume of simple waist-cloth and scarf (dhoti and chadar), bare-headed, bare-footed, was allowed to enter and remain in the temple till all the pilgrims had passed through. At every shrine the parihàris demanded a fee from the pilgrims and refused to let them pass till it was paid. It was the Deputy Magistrate's very difficult duty to insist on the pilgrims being allowed to pass without being too severely fleeced. Outside the temple, in addition to the Maharaja's special constables, the Magistrate and District Superintendent of police collected a large force of police. The approach to the Lion Gate, the entrance to the temple, was barricaded with strong posts fixed firmly in the ground forming a narrow lane, so that the pilgrims had to form a *queue*, and enter one by one. These precautions sufficed in ordinary years, and no accidents had occurred for a long time past. It is a vulgar error to suppose that people throw themselves under the wheels of Jagannath's Car and are crushed to death. Such an event never happens, and if it ever did happen in former times—which is strenuously denied by the priests—it must have been from some leper or other diseased wretch suddenly breaking through the cordon, and flinging himself before the Car so suddenly that those who drew it could not stop it before it had passed over the body of the suppliant. But so averse is the spirit of Vishnu worship[1] from the shedding of blood, that if such an event had ever happened it would have been regarded as a serious calamity, and the ceremonial unpurity thereby caused would have had to be expiated by many costly sacrifices.

In the present day the road down which the Car passes is fenced on both sides, and a continuous line of police guards the whole route—about a mile in length. Moreover the front of the Car is armed with a powerful 'cow-catcher' such as are used on railway engines, which would effectually prevent any body of man or animal being crushed under the wheels.

I have never been able to discover how this extraordinary error about the Car of Jagannath arose.

[1] Jagannath means Lord of the World. It is a name of Krishna, the well-known incarnation of the god Vishnu.

CUTTACK, 1875–1877

But to return to my narrative. In the year 1877 there occurred, according to the calculations of the Brahmin astrologers of Benares, a conjunction of stars which only happens once in a hundred or more years. The year in which such a conjunction happens is specially sacred and those who make the pilgrimage to the shrine of Jagannath reap special benefits. In such a year, therefore, an unusually large concourse of pilgrims might be expected. The Benares Pandits wrote to the Maharaja to inform him, so that he might make extra preparations. The Maharaja, however, consulted the Pooree astrologers and they asserted that the Benares men were wrong, and that no such conjunction of planets would take place that year. It was in vain that some sensible men represented to the silly boy that all northern India believed in the Brahmins of Benares and would be guided by them, so that whether they were right or wrong the announcement which they made of a specially holy year was sure to be widely believed, and the rush of pilgrims would be immense. He obstinately stuck to the opinion of his Pooree astrologers and refused to make any preparations beyond the ordinary.

When the time came, an unprecedented large number of pilgrims arrived and terrible confusion ensued. Joseph Armstrong, the Magistrate, with as large a force of police as he could muster, sat on his horse all night before the Lion Gate keeping back the great surging multitude who filled the broad, open space as far as the eye could reach, all eagerly pressing into the temple. At midnight a new day would begin and the religious merit of visiting the god would be over. All day they had been crowding in, but at nightfall there were still thousands eagerly pressing forward ere it was too late. Half a dozen times Armstrong sent messengers to the Raja for help. But though the boy had a large number of guards in the palace he refused to send any of them, alleging that he required them all for his own protection, which was nonsense as no one even dreamt of attacking him. Nor would he come out and address the crowd, a step which would have had great effect owing to the veneration with which his person was regarded. He had already caused great confusion by delaying earlier in the day to send to the Head Priest permission to begin certain sacrifices. This he did because at that moment an enormously wealthy merchant was with him, who offered a large sum for the privilege of being the first to enter the temple, which ensures certain special spiritual benefits. The Maharaja and the merchant could not agree as to the sum to be paid for this privilege, and while they were haggling the worship was delayed. This made the crowd still more impatient. At last, towards midnight, the crowd grew

271

unmanageable. The District Superintendent of police was thrown from his horse and badly trampled upon. Armstrong only saved himself by freely using a stout blackthorn cudgel which he had brought from his native Antrim. The mass of men and women stormed the barrier and rushed into the entrance hall of the temple. Thence they had to go by a narrow passage into the first court. The parihàris in fear shut the door and a crowd jammed into the dark, closed passage. Then someone from within shouted a command to open the door. It was opened and the pent-up crowd, thrust forward by those behind, poured itself into the court. The foremost pilgrims were thrown down, trampled upon and killed. The frightened parihàris seeing blood flowing, fled shrieking that men had been killed. The rumour spread through all the temple courts. The doorkeepers at the Lion Gate, men specially selected for their great strength—eight stalwart Brahmins—by a mighty effort thrust back the crowd and banged the great doors together.

The Brahmin cooks who had just finished cooking the sacred food for the god, hearing the cry that blood had been shed in the temple, at once threw all the food away as defiled, and standing on the top of the walls near their cook rooms, shouted to the crowd below that all was over—the temple was defiled—the pilgrimage was useless—the festival was at an end.

A wail of disappointment and despair went up from the vast crowd, and it was a very difficult matter to induce them to go away. It was daylight before this was accomplished and the Deputy Magistrate could get out of the temple to tell Armstrong exactly what had happened. Six men, I think, had been crushed to death at one door and one or two others in other places, and nearly a million people had journeyed hundreds of miles for nothing, the sacred precincts had been defiled by blood, costly expiatory rites would be necessary—and all this because a half imbecile boy would not do his duty. When they went to tell him of the accident, he was so drunk he could not understand what was said to him.

As soon as the news of this catastrophe reached me, I reported it to Government and at once started for Pooree to inquire into the matter. I held a long and careful investigation in which I was well supported by the High Priest, a genial, highly educated old man. He rivalled the old Maharaja of Dhenkanàl in size and boasted that he was ten or fifteen pounds heavier. He was furious with the Maharaja of Pooree for his mismanagement. The temple priests, however, perjured themselves freely; though they had suffered from the accident and knew that it was the Maharaja's fault, their traditional veneration for the 'Walking Vishnu' led them to lie their best to screen him. From the boy himself I could get nothing but incoherent mumblings.

The result of the inquiry was to establish his guilt. It was difficult to know how to punish him. We could not well take from him his hereditary functions in connexion with the temple. No living Hindu would have dared to usurp his place. Eventually the Viceroy deprived him of his title of Maharaja, and ordered that he was to be called Raja merely. This, of course, did not affect him in the least. It could not matter to him or to the people of Orissa what a handful of foreigners might choose to call him. To himself and his people he would always remain their liege lord and an incarnation of Vishnu.

Nemesis overtook him, however, soon after. Being displeased with an old fakir who visited him at Pooree, he ordered him to be put to the torture in a particularly brutal fashion and then thrown over the palace wall into a lane behind. The police patrol passing by the head of the lane at night heard groans, and by the light of their bull's-eyes discovered the old man nearly dead. They carried him to the hospital where he lingered long enough to make a dying deposition to a Magistrate. The Maharaja was arrested, tried and sentenced to imprisonment for life. He is now, if still alive, at the convict prison on the Andaman Islands. Immense excitement was aroused all over Orissa and crowds assembled round the Judge's court every day during the trial. The boy was smuggled away at night with a strong guard to the steamer. No actual outbreak occurred, though the authorities fully expected it and had taken their measures accordingly. But the Oriyas are too timid for actual *émeutes*. The Maharaja had a son who was placed in charge of the Court of Wards, and has probably by this time succeeded to his father's rank and position.

After this I went for a tour along the beautiful shores of the Chilka Lake, and spent some time at Khurda working hard at the settlement of the revenue and rent arrangements of the estate. It is a wild, romantic, hilly country inhabited by a strangely backward old-world race. I regretted I had no time to stay longer among them and study their quaint customs and old traditions. I had, however, time to visit the Buddhist monastery at Khandagiri, which consists of ranges of caves hollowed out of the red sandstone rock and beautifully carved. I also visited the far-famed rock of Dhauli whereon is still to be seen the long inscription carved by order of King Asoka, the great propagator of Buddhism, in A.D. 240. The inscription has often been copied and translated, the letters are still, after the lapse of two thousand years, quite clear and legible. A few miles off stands the majestic temple of Siva at Bhuvaneswar.

The creed of Siva displaced Buddhism, only to be displaced in its turn by the now all-prevalent cult of Vishnu, whose temple at Pooree attracts yearly a thousand times as many votaries as the grander but neglected Bhuvaneswar.

I next paid a visit to my old district of Balasore, where the good folk received me very cordially. They illuminated the town and station, had fireworks, 'nâches' and feastings. This made my successor rather jealous, and he had the bad taste to refuse to take part in the rejoicings.

In November my dear wife came back, bringing our two youngest children, Gertrude aged five and Angela aged two; also an English nurse, a Dorsetshire girl, Emma Gale. Much to my disgust, moreover, Ravenshaw came back also a few days later. We had hoped that he would not return, and I had rather set my heart on being made permanent Commissioner of Orissa—*sed dis aliter visum.* Sir Ashley Eden, the Lieutenant-Governor who had succeeded Temple, thought that I had been too long in Orissa, and at the beginning of 1878 transferred me as Commissioner and Judge to Chittagong.

I was bitterly disappointed at leaving Orissa, to which I had grown very much attached, and I feared Chittagong which had an evil reputation for unhealthiness. But of course there was no help for it. We sold most of our furniture, packed up the rest, and on the 14th February 1878 left Orissa after a residence there of nine years.

CHAPTER XX

CHITTAGONG, 1878–1879

AMONG my letters to Elliot I find one which gives the account of our voyage to Chittagong far more vividly than I could write it now from memory after the lapse of twenty-two years. I will, therefore, insert it here. It is dated 27 February 1878.

'Arrove this morning and found your letter. Where did I leave off, and how shall I begin the long and varied tale of our wanderings and vicissitudes? Breaking up our beautiful house and garden was *too* heart-rending. It was so stately and handsome with all the new things my wife had brought from home. However we packed away, and sold our furniture. Then came the last day—the parting at Jobra Ghât. There was a very large crowd to see us off, both of natives and Europeans. Many cried—we were all very much affected and I felt very much like crying myself. My wife wept copiously, and so we steamed away with waving of hats and handkerchiefs till we were out of sight. We were delayed four days at False Point by the steamer being late and in consequence only had three days in Calcutta, one of which was Sunday, so there was much running to and fro, much to do and very little time to do it in. We put up with old Stalkartt at Goosery near Howrah. He is hospitality incarnate, and his big house on the riverside is always full of people who come and go, and stay for as long as they like, call for what they want and make themselves quite at home. I called on the Lieutenant-Governor who was very savage and nasty on account of his Canal scheme. Of which more anon. On Sunday evening after a royal dinner at Stalkartt's we got into his barge—*Beaulieu* they call it—and were rowed down the river to our steamer. Both shores are now lighted with gas, as is also the Howrah bridge. Floating down the silent, dark river under the stars was like Venice. Between the rows of black shipping and the lights on shore the effect was very striking. Presently we came to the *Calcutta*, brilliantly lighted, out in the middle of the river, scrambled on board and into our cabins where we went to sleep. When we woke next morning we were dropping down the river past Garden Reach, and soon were under full steam and away. . . . For two days we steamed across the Bay of Bengal. On Wednesday morning I was on deck with the first streak of dawn and found we were at anchor in a jobbing sea. As it got light, behold on our starboard bow a long, low line of coast, densely wooded, with a broken outline of low hills in the distance; away to the north a large fleet of native craft bearing down upon us from the Sundarbans, and all round us a noisy crowd of naked boatmen in sampans.[1] When the sun rose we weighed anchor and stood in for a wide river up which we steamed some three or four miles. It was very wide, very winding and very muddy—low hills on both sides and the densest vegetation—the loveliest palmery—imaginable. Suddenly, at the turn of a corner, a mass of English, French and Yankee ships—long lines of godowns on piles—a jetty—a flagstaff—roofs peeping over the trees—fringe of palm above them, and above that again a lot of curious little hills each with a crown of tall casuarina trees and a bungalow. In the extreme distance, faintly seen through the haze, the blue mountains of Burmah—*voilà* Chittagong.'

The Chittagong Division is the easternmost corner of Bengal and lies on the eastern or Burmese side of the Bay. A very large proportion of the population are Mughs, a race akin to the Burmese. Another, and perhaps larger, section consists of Bengali Musulmans, the most quarrelsome, litigious, vindictive race in India. Many of them are bold and skilful sailors and supply the crews of most of the steamers and sailing vessels in the Indian waters. The town of Chittagong owes its importance as a sea-port originally to the Portuguese, who settled there in the fifteenth century and made it the headquarters of their trade and the favourite hiding place of the piratical gangs which, under Gonsalvez and other half-caste Portuguese ruffians, infested the Bay of Bengal and were formidable opponents of the Moghul Empire. It is still a sink of iniquity, full of the scum of various nations: Bengalis, Hindu and Musulman, Mughs, Portuguese, and others. It is deadly unhealthy, isolated from the rest of India, and the work is not only heavy but of a peculiarly troublesome and intricate kind. The dirt, the noxious vermin, and the smells are unique. 'Chittagong the Loathsome' we called it. But perhaps I had better describe it more in detail.

The district of Chittagong is a long, narrow strip bounded on the west by the Bay of Bengal, on the east by a tangled network of low, densely-wooded hills. It is not more than thirty miles wide and over one hundred miles in length. Several large rivers issue from the hills and fall into the Bay. On the largest of these, the Karnaphuli, about five miles from its mouth, lies the town of Chittagong. This consists of a loosely arranged network of streets along the river, and up a creek, the old Porto Grande of the Portuguese. Here there is a large Roman Catholic cathe-

[1] A 'sampan' is a very curious kind of boat, a long, low, canoe-shaped affair splitting into two at the stern. It is practically unupsettable.

dral and bishop's residence of masonry, round which cluster the houses of the Portuguese, built of mat and thatch, and raised, as are all the houses in these parts, on stout piles, thus leaving under the house an open space some three feet high, which is a receptacle for garbage and refuse of all kinds. Large warehouses belonging to the English, French and native merchants line the bank of the river, and the rest of the space is occupied by the huts of the native (principally Musulman) population, with one or two large, handsome brick mosques. The whole of this quarter is shrouded in rich vegetation, palms, plantains, mangoes and other trees bound together by huge tropical creepers and thick undergrowth, amidst which gleam pools of black and stagnant water. This low-lying tract is bounded on the north by a spur of the hills, cut up into a number of small, conical hills by ravines. On each of these hills is a European house surrounded by casuarina trees, the slopes covered with wild turmeric plants. There are also large courthouses and public offices, a big Protestant church, schools and post office. From these sandy hills gush out here and there springs of fresh water, jealously fenced and guarded, which supply the inhabitants with drinking-water. From these hilltops the eye ranges landwards over a rich, fertile plain bounded in the distance by beautiful blue hills. The scenery is everywhere enchantingly lovely. I have never seen so lovely a place to look at, nor one so loathsome to live in. There was postal communication by land with Calcutta daily, but for parcels and goods of all descriptions and for entering the place or leaving it, we were dependent on a fortnightly steamer from Calcutta.

Here is another scrap from one of my letters to Elliot: 'As we sit here in a veranda hung with orchids in bloom we look down on masses of palms and other trees, and on little specks of men and carts crawling far below—the great white river full of ships beyond, and over the long line of trees we can see the faint blue line of the sea. The scenery of this place is perfectly lovely, roads running in deep gorges between wooded hills, no end to the palms and little sparkling waterfalls. But alas! the things which our feeble human nature requires for its comfort are very bad. Servants get very high wages, and are the most awful scum that you could dream of in a nightmare. The houses swarm with vermin and are dilapidated beyond belief.'

On the low sandhills which intersected the plain in all directions were extensive tea gardens. The tea-plant flourishes here and yields a tea finer, in my opinion, than any other district of India—Ceylon had not started tea in those days. There were consequently many European tea-planters, chiefly English and Scotch, a rough, rowdy bachelor lot.

There was also a small colony of Frenchmen, headed by a funny, little, old, parched pea of a man, M. de Termes, 'Agent Consulaire de la France', as he styled himself, with a pleasant wife and daughter.

In the hills to the east of Chittagong lived a curious population of semi-Burmese tribes—Mughs, Chakmas and others. This tract had been formed into a non-regulation district called the 'Chittagong Hill Tracts', with a Deputy Commissioner, Major Evans Gordon, a charming, pleasant, courteous, brilliant young fellow, who thoroughly understood the wild, primitive people he had to govern. He had a small military force under him for the defence of the frontier. For across the frontier lived a congeries of still wilder tribes known generally as Lushais, but locally divided into Howlongs, Syloos, Shendoos and other barbaric designations. These all were much addicted to raiding and the military force was kept at Rangàmati, the capital of the Hill Tracts, to overawe them. Gordon was assisted by an Assistant, one Jarbo; a Superintendent of police, Crouch, and an old Portuguese, Inspector Rosario.

We were supremely unhappy at Chittagong. In fact we spent there two of the most miserable years of our existence. The contrast to Cuttack where we had been so happy, was cruel. Sir Ashley Eden, the Lieutenant-Governor, was unfriendly to me and put junior men into good appointments over my head. The pay of the appointment of Commissioner and Judge of Chittagong was less by some £350 a year than that of other Commissionerships, though, as everyone said, a man ought to have been paid higher, and not lower, for having to live in such a place. And it was a terrible burden to have the work of Judge, work of which I had no previous experience, added to the already very heavy work of Commissioner.[1] The two posts were, in fact, incompatible. The work of one interfered with that of the other. If I devoted time to the administrative work of Commissioner, I got into trouble with the High

[1] The amalgamation of the two posts was one of Sir George Campbell's eccentric steps. Wishing to obtain funds for raising the salaries of Collectors, he provided a portion by doubling up the two Chittagong posts, though everyone who had a voice in the matter pointed out the objections. Finally, after being a serious hindrance to public business and a source of constant friction between Government and the High Court, the arrangement came to a hopeless deadlock. When the general revenue settlement of the greater part of the district took place, the zemindars had by law a right to sue Government in the Civil Courts if dissatisfied with their assessment. It thus became impossible that the man who, as Commissioner, was chiefly responsible for the assessment should, as Judge, sit to decide appeals against it. The legal profession and the general public raised such an outcry against this state of things that the unnatural combination had to be dissolved after lasting about seven years (1873–80).

Court for neglecting my judicial work as Judge, and vice versa. The arrangement was an unworkable one. Fortunately circumstances arose (though after my time) which compelled the Government to sever the two posts and appoint a separate officer as Judge.

But it is now time to narrate the events of our new life in some sort of chronological order. We had hardly been a week in the place, and were still in all the confusion of unpacking and settling in a new house, when Sir Ashley Eden arrived in his steamer with all his staff on a tour of inspection. Great men in office do not stop to think how much trouble they cause. Being new to the place I was, of course, quite unable to explain anything about the work and, indeed, hardly knew my way from one office to another. My predecessor had departed, and the Collector was an idle fellow who took no sort of interest in his work, so I fear the Lieutenant-Governor did not get such an insight into affairs as he would have done had he timed his visit better. Serve him right! He only stayed some three days and then, much to our joy, departed.

An incident, trifling in itself, may be mentioned as indicative of the petty pride and jealousy which the French always display towards the English. As usual, triumphal arches were erected to welcome the Lieutenant-Governor and all the public buildings had flags, all the ships both English and foreign in the harbour were also decorated. Only the flagstaff at the French Consul's office remained bare. As we stood on the jetty to receive the great man, whose vessel was already in sight coming up the river, the Collector of Customs pointed this out to me. I at once sent an officer to ask M. de Termes, with my compliments, why he did not fly his flag. He replied that he would not do so, so long as the insult to the 'drapeau français' was kept up. Our messenger returned with this answer and pointed to the Government Customs brig which was dressed with flags from stem to stern. We then noticed that the topmost flag on the mainmast was an ordinary signalling flag, while in the second place, just below it, was a French tricolour! To put the French flag lower than any other was, in M. de Termes's opinion, an insult. We laughed, but I at once ordered the flags to be changed and the French flag to be put above the other. It did not take many minutes to make the change, and as soon as it was done M. de Termes, who was watching through his glass from the window of his office, at once hoisted both the Union Jack and the tricolour together with a perfect rag-fair of other flags! It was only just in time, for a few minutes after the Lieutenant-Governor's steamer rounded the point. I must do de Termes the justice to say that he told me afterwards that he himself cared nothing about the matter, and thought it childish to make a fuss about what was evidently a mere accident; but he was surrounded by Frenchmen, any one of whom might, and probably would, have reported the circumstance to Paris, and the result would have been that he would have lost his appointment!! For a good many years after the Franco-Prussian War the French were very touchy about their dignity. I experienced evidence of this at a later time when I was at Hoogly, as will be related in its place.

The natives had put up mottoes in English and Bengali over the public buildings and triumphal arches. These mostly consisted of 'Welcome', but over the Public Hospital some wag had put up the line which Dante read over the gate of Hell—or rather the English translation of it—'Abandon hope, all ye who enter here!' This gave much amusement to Sir Ashley, and much offence to the Inspector-General of Hospitals who accompanied him.

Now I fell into Noàbàd. But before I explain the significance of this terrible word, I must tell of our visit to the Hill Tracts. Some difficulties had arisen with a gentleman called the Bohmong (Burmese boh = head; mong = chief) of the Mughs, and I had to go and settle matters. I took my wife and children for the sake of the change. We started in the *Chaffinch*, a pretty little steamer kept by Government for the Commissioner's use with a flat attached, all extremely clean and comfortable. The distance to Rangamati is about eighty miles by river. The first fifteen miles or so are through the plains, and the scenery though rich and green is monotonous. Then you come to the hills, and the river, broad, rapid and deep, swirls in eddies of dark green water round the base of sandstone cliffs, topped and tufted with palm, mango, bamboo and other trees all laced with giant creepers gorgeously coloured. In one place a whole rock face fifty or sixty feet high is one blaze of red, another is a blaze of yellow; a little further on, an immense Beaumontia with its great white trumpet-shaped flowers covers half the hillside. Every ledge and cranny is full of orchids, grasses and ferns, and the foot of the cliffs, just where the waves plash, is covered with a thick velvety carpet of vivid emerald moss. Then you pass the mouth of a long, narrow valley running up and up till it ends in grey, misty distance. Here and there on a hilltop in a clearing a small cluster of Mugh huts built on piles, and sturdy Mugh women in scarlet petticoats and blue jackets crawling up the steep hillside with water jars on their heads.

Rangamati is (or was in 1878) a small place on a plateau surrounded on three sides by the river, about 300 feet above the water, chosen by us on account of its impregnability. It consists of a small native bazaar, the lines and parade-ground of the Regiment, and some six or seven roomy bungalows on piles, with walls of mats and thatched roofs. Major Gordon and Mr Crouch met me at the landing-place in full uniform. The Regiment presented arms, and from a cliff over our heads a salute of eleven guns was fired. It seems I was *ex officio* Agent to the Viceroy for the Eastern Frontier and so entitled to a salute. Then we all had a steep climb up to the Circuit House, a large, comfortable building.

The next day the Mong, the Bohmong, and the Chakma Raja with a large concourse of followers arrived to pay their respects to the Mong Gri (= Great Chief, i.e. Commissioner). It is the custom for a Chief to feed his subjects when they visit him. So there was a big shamiàna[1] pitched, with carpets for the Europeans, and about two o'clock we all went there and took our seats, the Chiefs on one side and the Europeans on the other. Then the whole multitude came up before me one by one and saluted by going down on all fours and touching the ground with their foreheads. They are all Mongolian in type, short, broad figures with the regular Chinaman's features, slanting pig's eyes, flat, broad nose and high cheekbones. Most of them carried a cheroot about ten inches long through a hole in the lobe of their huge ears, the women had large Beaumontia or orchid flowers behind their ears or in the knot of their hair. Then they all sat down in rows, and neat little stools of plaited bamboo with a plantain leaf carefully folded on the top were placed before each person. Cups made of a length of bamboo cut off slanting were given to us, and a man came round and filled them with rum and water from an earthen jar. Then we all drank. This, it seems, is an indispensable preliminary, after which the plantain leaves were unfolded and revealed a mess of eggs, rice, fowl, chillies, etc., all very nicely cooked. The Mughs are celebrated for their cookery. We ate a little, whereupon all the Mughs fell to, and for the space of two hours men, women and children continued uninterruptedly eating, drinking rum and water, laughing, shouting and joking. Men with huge earthen pots moved among the crowd, filling the plantain leaves afresh from time to time as fast as they were emptied. It was amazing how much they ate and drank. After this, bundles of cheroots were handed round and we all smoked. The women, who were adorned with gold ear-rings and necklaces, gathered round my wife and the children and examined them curiously. Baby Angela was handed round and kissed by them all. Then they took to making up little parcels of betel nut and pàn and giving them to us. They seemed rather surprised that we did not chew

[1] Shamiàna, a large flat-roofed tent open at the sides, used for public ceremonies, official receptions and the like.

them as they did. Meanwhile there was more rum going round and the jokes and laughter began getting rather wild, so we closed the entertainment by rising and departing. Later in the afternoon, when the Chiefs had slept off their feast, we had a meeting at which we got through a great deal of business, and the day wound up with a magic lantern which delighted them all excessively. Government makes us an allowance for the purpose of giving these feasts, without which no business could be done amongst the Mughs.

We were engaged on a very difficult, in fact an almost impossible, task with these Mughs. The tangled maze of hills in which they live is densely wooded and contains a great deal of valuable timber. It had been placed under the charge of the Forest Department. A department of any kind in India always assumes that the world exists solely for the use of itself, and considers that anything that interferes with the working of the department ought to be removed. It was undoubtedly true that the Mughs and other hill tribes used their native forests very wastefully. Their system of agriculture, called *jhūm*, consists in setting the forest on fire and burning down a whole hillside. In the space so cleared they sow their crops, the rich virgin soil bears abundantly, and the ashes of the burnt forest are excellent manure. They continue to cultivate the same spot for a few years when they find its fertility decreases, whereupon they go away and burn down a fresh place. In former times the incessant wars between the tribes kept down the population, and they were not numerous enough seriously to affect the growth of the forest. Trees grew again in the deserted '*jhūm*', and by the time—perhaps forty years—people wanted to burn that particular hillside again there was a thick growth of trees and jungle on it. But when the Pax Britannica was extended to those wilds and intertribal warfare ceased, the population increased so much that if not checked they would soon have burnt every bit of forest off the hills. Dr. Schlich, the Head of the Forest Department, calmly proposed that the whole Mugh and Chakma population should be removed from their native hills! He did not say where they were to go to. He merely said, in the true departmental spirit, 'These people destroy the trees, therefore let them be sent away.' Of course, the district officers and the Commissioner strongly opposed this view. The Commissioner[1] even went so far as to say that if trees and Mughs could not live together, he thought it would do less harm if the trees were removed, which caused Dr Schlich to foam at the mouth and utter bad words. Finally some wise man observed that it was not so much the Mughs themselves as their practice of 'jhūming'

[1] My predecessor, not me.

that did harm, and he suggested that they should be taught to till the soil by ploughing like the Bengalis. In the *jhūm* method no plough is used; they make holes in the ground with a sharp stick burnt hard at the end, and drop the seed in. No Mugh was ever known to use the plough. Sir Ashley Eden, however, caught at this suggestion and we were ordered to induce or compel the Mughs to give up their *jhūms* and take to ploughed fields instead. With his usual bullying injustice, he intimated that if we did not succeed he should consider that it was because we did not try, or because we were incompetent idiots. So of course we had to try to do what we knew beforehand would be utterly impossible. The Mughs declared that it was a well-known fact that if they took to ploughing their race would die out. Their women were particularly vehement on this point, more so even than the men. They are by nature an extremely cheerful race, very idle, careless and merry, but on this point they grew stern, sulky and melancholy. There seems to be something congenial to their light-hearted, easy-going nature in their method of cultivation. Burning down a whole hillside, dibbling in some seed almost anyhow in the ground, and then sitting smoking and laughing till the crop grows and ripens is a proceeding that somehow seems made for them and they for it. It is altogether a different thing from the laborious ploughing of the soil, harrowing, sowing, weeding, watering and all the rest of it which occupies the melancholy quarrelsome, anxious Bengali. These children of nature will not even reap their own crops. Every year the steamers of the British India Company carry from Bengal to Chittagong, Akyab and Rangoon thousands of Bengali labourers, who go to earn good wages for two or three months by cutting and garnering the crops, while the lazy Mugh proprietors sit in their verandas smoking their long, rank cheroots and cutting jokes at the hard-working Bengalis. And now we were ordered to turn the Mughs into ploughers and reapers! The way we did it was this. Among the Mughs live a curious people called Chakmàs who, though Mongolian by origin and Buddhist by religion, have adopted many customs and ceremonies from Hinduism and Islam. They have a Raja. In my time the Raja bore the Hindu name of Harishchandra, but his father had a Mahomedan name. They are not so averse to the plough as the pure Mughs, so we found a flattish piece of land in the Chakma Territory which we hired, and then let it out to some Mughs who nobly sacrificed themselves for the good of their race (being also handsomely paid for so doing), and undertook to plough it and raise a crop of rice from it. But we represented to the Government that ploughing, like all other arts, requires to be learnt, so we got permission to engage

283

a few Bengalis to teach the Mughs. When I visited the spot with Gordon, we found the Bengalis laboriously ploughing and sowing in the swampy land, and the Mughs, whom they were supposed to be teaching, sitting happily on a rising ground with their backs to the Bengalis, smoking and joking together! When we called them they came forward quite cheerfully and, in answer to our questions, said, 'Oh yes! we are learning very well. It is very easy. We quite understand. Soon we shall be able to hold the plough ourselves.' But I never heard of the experiment getting beyond this. It afforded, however, material for a good long paragraph in our annual report, and that was all that apparently was wanted. We had done as we were told, we had started the experiment, and must leave it to time to prove whether it would be successful or not. So long as I was in the Chittagong Division, it got no further than Bengalis ploughing and Mughs looking on and cracking jokes.

Noàbàd now claimed much of my time. I despair of making it intelligible, nor would it be interesting if I could. Roughly and briefly, it was a vast mass of petty estates covering the greater part of the Chittagong district which, owing to certain circumstances, were the property of Government. The 'settlement' of these estates (that is to say measurement, classification of kinds of soil, rates of rent, rights of certain tenants, and assessment of the rents which they were to pay) was being made. It had to be made every thirty years. As usual in Bengal, there were such extraordinary intricacies and complications of conflicting rights, so many different kinds of tenants, so much uncertainty and dispute about boundaries, rates, status, privileges—disputes about everything that was disputable—that it was enough to drive one mad. Everything that could be litigated about was eagerly litigated by these, the most litigious people in the world. It was well said of them by Sir Henry Ricketts, an experienced administrator who knew them well, that every Chittagonian was born with a 'stamped paper'[1] in his hand, and as soon as he could walk went to a lawyer and got him to put a case in court for him. A brilliant, active, keen-witted little Scotchman named Fasson was Settlement Officer and was half-killing himself over the business, and of course I had to guide and advise him. It was an odious business and cost us many a sleepless night and many a day's hard work. Indeed

[1] A stamp revenue is raised in India by requiring all law papers and many classes of legal and commercial documents to be executed on paper bearing a Government stamp and only sold at Government offices. Petitions, i.e. the document by which a law suit is originated, are required to be written on 'stamped paper', of value corresponding to the amount of the sum sued for. Stamped paper for petty suits is sold for a few pence and eagerly bought up by the litigious peasantry.

the work at Chittagong was very much harder than in Orissa, and it was thankless, uninteresting and irritating. One could not help feeling that two-thirds of it might have been avoided, if only the hungry, vicious, venomous little black Musulmans would show a more conciliatory and reasonable spirit. But this Noàbàd business had been going on ever since the beginning of the century, when one Jay Naràyan, an intriguing employee of Warren Hastings, had by underhand means obtained possession of vast tracts of land in this district.[1] His frauds were eventually discovered, and the lands resumed by Government. They were at that time newly reclaimed from the all-pervading jungles, hence the name, 'no àbàd = newly settled'. But there were tracts still belonging to the estate of Jay Naràyan, lands which he had obtained lawfully, and these were managed separately by an Englishman named Sandys.

It was a relief now and then to tear oneself away from the dry details of sterile Noàbàd litigation, get into the steamer *Chaffinch* with wife and children, and go for an hour's trip to the mouth of the river. The little blow of fresh sea air and salt water picked us up. My brother Harry was at this time in charge of the Subdivision of Cox's Bazaar, some hundred miles to the south of Chittagong. He had a charming little schooner, the *Firefly*, in which he used to come up the coast to visit us now and then. We went to Cox's Bazaar later in the year. This miserable year 1878! I was extremely wretched. I detested Chittagong the Loathsome and everything in any way connected with it. I longed for and regretted Orissa. I disliked the work, the place, the people. It seemed to me an evil, malignant place and people. Its very beauty is an evil beauty—a *beauté du diable*. The people in the Hill Tracts were amusing, and that was the only part of the Division I liked. But they were always up to something. In July I had to look after them again. This time it was the Lushais beyond the frontier. But as the so-called frontier was merely an imaginary line running along the top of a range of hills, which had been quite arbitrarily fixed by Sir Richard Temple, it was not wonderful that the Lushais paid no attention to it. Temple's idea was that on the British side of this line British law was to prevail, but how was a Lushai to understand that? Now it happened that the Chief of one branch of the Lushai nation fell sick, and when his friends, according to their custom, asked him who had bewitched him, he

---

[1] He would for instance get a grant of 100 acres and on the strength thereof take possession of 1,000, driving out any inhabitants there might be by virtue of the grant. As they were also mostly squatters whose rights were as vague as his own they were unable to resist him.

mentioned a neighbour with whom he had had a quarrel These people believe that all kinds of sickness are caused by witchcraft, and that a man when at the point of death is able to know who bewitched him. As soon as the dying Chief had mentioned the name of the witch, it became the duty of his son or other near relative to find the witch and kill him or her. The Chief's son, on his father's death, sought out the man who had bewitched him and killed him. In doing so he thought he was performing a sacred duty and so did all his tribe.

But, unfortunately for him, the spot where he met and killed the man was on the British side of the newly-drawn frontier line, and was therefore technically within British territory, so the poor Lushai boy was arrested and tried for murder, found guilty and sentenced to a long term of imprisonment. My predecessor and all the local officers protested strongly, but Temple wrote some of his usual bombastic nonsense about making the Lushais respect the sacredness of British territory, and insisted on the sentence being carried out. The prisoner, a child of the forest who had lived all his life in the open air, sickened and died in a few weeks of the confinement. The Lushais all naturally said we had killed him, and were very troublesome and hostile for a long time in consequence. But Captain Lewin, the Deputy Commissioner, and his successor, Evans Gordon, managed them with great tact—treating them with a mixture of firmness and good-nature, like the big children that they were, and gradually acquired great influence over them. Their habit of raiding the Mugh country was almost entirely suppressed, but the Hill Regiment had to patrol the boundary very strictly to prevent the Bengali traders of Chittagong selling guns and ammunition to them. They amused themselves by raiding in other directions—for raid somewhere they must—'It was their nature to.'

In August 1878 the Pui Shendus, incited thereto by the Haulongs, made a raid on the Khweymi tribe of Arracan, our neighbours to the south, and carried off, among other things, the wife and four children of Lahauk, Chief of the Khweymis. This was done to avenge the Haulongs for a previous raid made on them by Lahauk and his people. The Shendu Chief, Saipoiya, sold the captives to the Sailoos for two old tower muskets, and the Sailoos carried them off to the village of their Chief, Johwatà, beyond the Kainsa Thoung or Blue Mountains in Burmah. It must be remembered that in 1878 Burmah was still an independent kingdom, ruled over by King Theebaw, with whom it would have been useless to open negotiations for the return of the captives, partly because Theebaw had no real power or influence over the Lushais, and partly because he would not have helped us if he had. So Gordon brought Lahauk and Soiya, a chief of the Hlongthya Haulongs, with their followers down to Chittagong to see me about it. Of course I had to give them a dinner. They got through two goats, six fowls, a pile of rice, twelve bottles of rum, one hundred cheroots, and pàn sopari (betel nut) uncounted. Then they sent word that they were ready for a palaver. So they were led into my big hall where we discussed matters. It took some time, because I spoke in English, which Gordon translated into Mughi and the Mugh interpreter again into Lushai. Finally, however, the matter was arranged. Soiya arranged—for a consideration—to get the captives restored, and did so in due course. Then when the business was over, they asked to see my house. So I took them into the drawing-room where my wife and some other ladies were seated. The savages behaved very well. They bowed respectfully to the ladies and were very much surprised to be told that they were women. It seems that they thought that they were only some other kind of European men. Lahauk had never seen an Englishwoman, and asked the interpreter a number of curious questions. I saw Gordon grinning in the background, and I did not wonder when he repeated the questions to me afterwards. They were very interested in the pictures on the walls, the china ornaments on the tables and chiffoniers, the table laid for dinner, but especially at the blaze of light given by the numerous kerosene oil lamps about the rooms. But they were very subdued, and I was afterwards told that they were rather frightened at all the splendour of our simple English house. They thought some of the things were magic.

If a complete contrast to the savage Lushais were wanted, it could easily be found in the Portuguese of Chittagong town. Few, if any of them, were of pure Portuguese blood; they were mostly descended from the intercourse between the old piratical Portuguese and Mugh female slaves, and though they bore grand Portuguese names such as Pereira, Teixeira, da Silva, da Sousa, Almeida, their features were often purely Mongolian. A frowsy, worthless, debauched lot they were. I asked their priest once—he was an Italian, a new arrival from Europe—what he thought of his flock. He smiled and uttered one word—'bestie'. He himself was a well-educated Benedictine, far too good for such a flock. Proud, lazy and immoral they all were. The men dressed in a white calico shirt, white trousers and a crimson sash round the waist; the women in a cotton gown with black mantilla and a parasol of some vivid colour. Down in the native town, close along the river bank, they kept shops where they sold bad liquor to the sailors, and the back rooms were kept for immoral purposes by the women. Brawls were frequent, and the two English constables, with a native force of police, had enough to do to keep the peace in those unsavoury slums. The Roman Catholic Bishop, a Dutchman, and the priest above mentioned, laboured among them but with scanty results. In the rains these low-lying parts of the town were mostly under water, and cholera as well as a very bad type of malarious fever were endemic. The rain in Chittagong was phenomenal; to quote myself again (from a letter to Elliot in August 1878): 'You up-country fellows never see rain like we have here. It begins early in the morning before daybreak on the first of the month, and when you go to bed at ten o'clock on the 31st it is still drizzling on in the same remorseless way. Your boots grow a crop of mould every night. My beloved books, the only things that keep me going, are losing their bindings, and curling up into limp masses of pulp. The green mould crops out all over the damp, unwholesome walls, rank weeds grow all up the hillsides, and the rain carves out great gutters ending in a 'moraine' of muddy, fetid slush at the bottom. Whatsoever things are loathsome, whatsoever things are slimy, whatsoever things are stinking, sickening, ghastly, oozy, decaying and decayed, morbiferous, faeculent, miasmatic, malarious, and repulsive—these things abound. And over everything steadily, slowly, pitilessly, drenchingly, comes down by night and by day the dull, deadly rain like a pall covering the flaccid corpse of the soil. This is not an attempt at fine writing though it looks like it—I am too low in spirits for that! It is only an effort to put on paper the impression made on me as I sit in my veranda looking out at the sodden landscape below me.'

I was called back to Rangamati again in September by a fresh row among the Lushais. Lalbura, a Sailoo Chief, and Poiboi, Chief of the Shendus, had attacked Vanhoiya the Haulong and were said to have killed fifteen of his men, and Vanhoiya had been detected in an attempt to smuggle some rifles and gunpowder across near the frontier post of Demagri by means of some Bengali traders, who went up there to buy rubber which the Lushais collect in their forests. Fortunately Crouch, the police officer, had managed to recover the guns and ammunition. Poiboi and Lalbura had retired into the depths of the jungle, but Vanhoiya had been detained for me to see him. He came to the Circuit House to see me on my arrival, but there was only one sitting-room, and there was a difficulty in admitting him as my wife and some other ladies were there, and Vanhoiya wore no clothes *at all*. A scarlet blanket was offered him but he refused to wear it. Eventually a compromise was arrived at. Two men walked in front of him holding up the blanket till he reached a chair into which he was pushed, and when he was seated the two retainers held the blanket before him all the while, so that only his head and hands were visible. In this position he harangued volubly and the interpreter translated. He swallowed a wineglassful of neat brandy and held out his glass for more, but Gordon ignored this and began to talk at him vigorously. He was a splendid animal—tall, muscular and active, with a keen, bright eye and a lordly demeanour. When we had finished our discussion and arrived at a satisfactory conclusion he rose to retire, and the blanket was then held behind him as he retreated. Though he would not wear it, he condescended to accept it as a present, as also a large glass tumbler which he took a fancy to.

When we got back to Chittagong a case of a very different nature called for my attention. Among other things I found I was *ex officio* 'Chief Customs Authority', and had the powers of a Judge of the Court of Admiralty under some Act of Parliament. In this totally new capacity I was now called upon to try the captain of an English ship, the *Ocean Belle*, for running his ship ashore at the mouth of the Chittagong River. Mr Warden, the Collector of Customs and Harbourmaster, was *ex officio* Public Prosecutor in such cases, and after instituting the case in my court, he informed me that it was my duty to inspect the vessel as she lay, also to appoint two of the captains of merchant ships lying in the port as assessors at the trial. So I arranged to go. It would be a pleasant little jaunt for me and my family. My wife as usual looked after the provisions. In this she was helped unexpectedly by receiving the following notice from the local butcher. I copy it literally:

'Shake Kadir Ali and Shake Lutpoo begs to inform the following gentlemens that they will kill two very gram-fed sheeps much more Fatt and very Bigg than muton clubs ditto.' The last part was the unkindest cut of all, for my wife managed the station mutton club and was not a little proud of the excellence of her sheep.

However, she laid in a supply of the very Bigg gram-fed sheeps and other provisions, and a party of us all went off in my steamer with the flat attached. Here is what happened (from a letter to Elliot). 'I am not myself nautical, but Mr W. Warden is—in fact he is so much so that he has the earache in his starboard ear, and he belays his dog-cart, slacks her off, and fetches her up a point in the wind when he is driving. As we steamed out through the lines of big sailing-ships loading with jute for Dundee, I derived much pleasure from my nautical subordinate's criticisms on the ships. The *Prince Oscar*, a four-masted vessel whose huge hull towered high above us, had, I found, not slipped his braces (I think it was), or he had when he oughtn't to, and did you ever see a fellow to hamper his yards (or something to that effect) like the *Latona*—but lor' bless your 'eart, the way these 'ere merchantmen do

things—— Ah! you should have seen the *Celerity*—they knew 'ow to
sail a ship in the old Injen Navy—I believe yer—— When I was in the
old Injen Navy—— (then followed a yarn which lasted for about six
miles down the river—I didn't catch it all, as I was looking at the
scenery.) Warden's enemies say he was only a purser's clerk and doesn't
know one rope from another. At any rate he has laid in a fine stock of
nautical phrases, and if he uses then *à tort et à travers*—I don't know any
better. So we got to the inner buoys, where the visible land leaves off in a
wide river mouth some three miles across. Right in front of us, a black
dot on the blazing, glittering surface of the sea, was the pilot cutter with
a huge ensign as big as herself, and a little way off the *Ocean Belle*, a big
three-masted ship lying outside the fairway, apparently a long way from
land, but in reality on a soft bed of mud into which she was rapidly
working herself a hole. From my dense ignorance of marine affairs I
had always supposed that when a ship grounded she stuck fast, but here
was the *Ocean Belle* heeling over from one side to the other in a slow,
sickly way, and as the side nearest to us came up, we saw torrents of
muddy water pouring out of what I thought were her portholes. But
I found that, "bless yer, she ain't got no ports she ain't, that's 'er scuppers." (*N.B.* It afterwards turned out that it wasn't her scuppers—but
let that pass.) On her forecastle (anglice foksl) were a lot of frowzy
English sailors lolling with their legs over the taffrail (I think it is), with
bare feet and throats burnt a deep red, and greasy shirts. They didn't
seem to mind the sun, they only had straw hats and light caps made of
grease and tobacco juice on their heads. In the "waist" (see how nautical
I am) a gang of coolies were hauling out her cargo, and two or three very
powerful negroes were apparently directing them. This they did by sitting on a barrel and spitting. There was such an eddy round her that the
steamer could not get near, so we went in the jolly boat, and climbed
up over the side by ropes at that part where the ropes come down from
the mast. I forget what they call it, something about chains or shrouds,
I think, but I was getting a little mixed by this time. I know it was all
over tar and filth. On deck the scene was beastly. Her cargo was earth-
oil (a coarse kind of petroleum) and kutch, and the stink was ——!
All the hatches were open and the barrels had got loose, the oil had
come out and got mixed with the bilge water (I *know* that is right). The
result you can imagine. The gentleman in command, whose official
title is Cap'n (one syllable) had gone ashore to see the agents—and as
we subsequently found, had no intention of returning. The mate was
a very hazy young fellow, lounging on the (what *did* they call it?—It
isn't binnacle, or capstan, or davits, or guys, or cat-heads, or dead-eyes

—I heard all these separately). It is a sort of projecting cornice with a brass rail, where you go up from the middle of the ship to the poop— have I made myself clear? He, too, was spitting. A very fat and wise-looking duck sat beside him and used its wings occasionally when the slope of the deck got too acute.

'I tried to look very grave as befits a C.C.A. (Chief Customs Authority) but it is very hard to do so when you can, with difficulty, keep your feet owing to the ship's deck assuming a different slope every minute, and you are afraid to lay hold of anything because it is covered with tar or other beastliness. The mate was very cheery and stated that if the Cap'n didn't come off soon, he and the crew were going to take to their boats and go ashore. Warden said that would be deserting, which did not seem to affect him much. He said he wasn't going down along with her, and invited us to see how she was "hogged". Warden saw it (or said he saw it —I didn't). When Warden observed that the water was pouring out of her scuppers, the mate replied, "Scuppers be ——d, it's 'er seams." Then I did manage to observe that the planks of her sides were started. "Started," said the mate, "lor' bless yer, yer might put yer 'ead in the 'oles, look yere and yere," and he pointed to some alarmingly big gaps. Then it occurred to W. Warden that he hadn't sent down his something, to which the mate replied that he had sent down his royals, and would send down something else as soon as the Cap'n came back. Then they got into depths far beyond me, so I exercised myself in looking official under difficulties by holding on to a brass rail which was fortunately clean. I was glad, however, when Mr Warden, who I must say kept his balance beautifully and was sublimely nautical to the last, and didn't *look* as if he felt at all sea-sick, came up to me and reported that he had completed his inspection. I declined to go below and tap at planks in the dark—*I* was superior to the weakness of pretending I understood anything about it, so I gracefully replied that I would reserve my opinion till I received his written report. At this point the deck got quite too unhorizontal so we got into the jolly boat. I don't quite know how, except that the sailors caught hold of me by the legs as I was dangling from some shrouds, or chains, or things tarry, whatever they are called. We got back to our party on the steamer and had a sumptuous lunch as we steamed back up the river.'

Subsequently I sat with two nautical assessors to try the captain. I thought he had run his ship ashore to defraud the underwriters—a thing very often done; and I strongly suspect the assessors thought so too, but the matter was so involved in technicalities that it was hard for a landsman to decide, so I took the advice of the assessors and only found

him guilty of unskilful navigation and suspended his certificate for six
months. This was my first and last experience of the duties of a Judge
of the Admiralty Court.

Life was so disagreeable in the Station of Chittagong owing to the un-
congenial society that we were always getting away from it when we
could. The officials were not very pleasant. Chittagong, being very unhealthy, was regarded as a penal station, and all the worst men in the
Services were sent there. It was, as I was afterwards told, felt as a great
shame by men of my own Service that I, who had always had a good,
not to say a high, reputation in the Service, should have been sent to a
penal settlement by Eden out of personal spite. In addition to the officials there were some merchants and tea-planters, rough, rowdy bachelors, hardly fit society for ladies or gentlemen, and all disposed to be
hostile or at least unpleasant to officials. As soon as the *Ocean Belle* case
was over, we went for a visit to Cox's Bazaar, the subdivision to the
south on the borders of Burmah. I take the description of our trip from
one of my letters to Elliot written in (I think) November 1878.

'Cox's Bazaar is a subdivision of Chittagong, about one hundred and
twenty miles to the south of this. It is a Mugh town founded by a mistaken person, one Captain Cox, in 1793 or thereabouts, when we were
fighting the Burmese. The long-defunct Cox, being a person of small
discrimination (he probably wore a pigtail and powder and a stiff black
stock and highly-padded red coat, tight breeches and Hessian boots. He
drank "brandy pawnee" and said, "demme" and " 'fore Gad, sir!"),
could find no better place in which to settle the Mughs that fled from
the oppression of the Arakanese[1] than a pestiferous swamp on the banks
of a stinking little creek, with slimy, muddy banks carefully shut out
from the sea by a high, sandy ridge. However, the place flourished. My
brother Harry was in charge of it for four years, and only kept himself
alive by taking cruises in the Bay in the *Firefly*. Vile, foul, penetrating,
body- and soul-destroying as are the stinks of Chittagong, they are
nothing to Cox's Bazaar. There the people live in bamboo huts on piles,
and the natural filth of humanity accumulates in the space under the
houses. Their principal food is fish kept (on purpose) until it is putrid.
It is called Nya-pe and is accounted a great delicacy. You can nose a
Mugh to windward a mile off. They are, however, very jolly, always
laughing, with cheroots a yard long in their mouths. They apparently

[1] The kingdom of Arakan, capital Akyab, comprised the northern part of
Burmah, lying along the coast of the Bay of Bengal and divided from the rest of
Burmah by a high mountain range, the Yuma Doung. It became British territory
in 1826.

never do any work. The dirty, little, wizened Bengalis do all the work and appear to fleece the Mughs, who live by fishing when they do anything.'

They wear gorgeous, bright silk handkerchiefs round their heads—emerald green with scarlet flowers, orange with purple flowers, etc.—made, of course, in Manchester—a jacket of bright blue or yellow or red and a dhoti of some equally glaring colour. The women wear a bright red bodice tied tight over the breasts and under the arms, leaving the shoulders bare, and a bright coloured petticoat. Seldom anything on their heads but a flower or two out of the hedge. The scenery was very picturesque. My brother's house stood close to the sea shore, looking on to a long stretch of shining sand, then low, abruptly wooded cliffs and far away to the south a long blue point (Elephant Point) running well out to sea. The waves were rolling in with crests of foam, breaking on the sand ridge and tossing up columns of spray against a few scattered rocks. To the north a group of beautifully wooded islands, between which and the coast lay our way to Chittagong. Moheshkhal, the largest of these, gives its name to the channel.

We had quite a surfeit of fish there—oysters, prawns, pomphret, sole and skate, all fresh caught. The journey both there and back was through a fresh breeze and a slightly rough sea, but as we were all good sailors we enjoyed it very much.

Christmas passed quietly. A large number of very rough-looking English, Scotch and Irish tea-planters came in from outlying gardens and played a cricket match, after which they had a big supper and great quantities of drink, and singing. Next morning they departed to their jungles again with bad headaches, but asserting that they had had a very jolly time of it!

On New Year's Day 1879 I received some poetry from an old native gentleman, one Ram Kinu Dutt, widely known as the poet of Chittagong. His Baboo friends admired his poetry very much. One fantastic person went so far as to call him the 'Byron of Bengal'. He had such a full confidence in his own powers that he used to send long poems to the Viceroy and other high officials. As these great men good-naturedly used to write and thank him for his beautiful verses, he was confirmed in his high opinion of them. He had been a member of the subordinate medical service, a very useful class of men who are placed in charge of hospitals in various places. After many years' service he retired on a pension, and passed his old age cheerfully in one of the most malarious corners of his native Chittagong, composing what he was pleased to consider as English poetry.

The poems he sent me on this occasion were written in a beautiful copperplate hand on large sheets of paper, with an elaborately drawn and coloured border which it must have taken him a long time to do. The following are the only scraps of his immortal work which I can now find. As he had all his poetry printed for him by a friendly Bengali printer, posterity will not be deprived of them. I copy *literatim* and *verbatim*.

Old Year!

Sir (*me*—not the old year).

> *Our friend old year gasping his last*
> *Neither he tastes supper nor break-fast,*
> *Not inclines sago, not a drop of tea,*
> *Never feels well even in the land or sea;*
> *His declining health now never gives him hopes,*
> *Shudders at the face, and senselessly mopes.*

(then follow about a hundred lines ending with):

> *He is sorry for a look about Cabul prepotency*
> *Is to assume the beauty of a decadency[1]—Adieu!*
>
> R.K.D.

Then followed a much longer piece in red ink (a sign of joy) celebrating Christmas. I have preserved only the last verse.

> *Reciprocal amusement and the receptions*
> *Hospitably pass on amongst citizens.*
> *Alas! for many who weary of care,*
> *Nought in the future but dread and despair.*
> *Alas! for the widows and fatherless child,*
> *And for the poor the happiness never smiled,*
> *They are awfully undermine with fresh fear,*
> *I wish you—'happy new year—a happy new year!'*
> *Your most obedient and devoted servant*
>
> Ram Kinoo Dutt

It was too long to copy entirely, but here and there occurred verses of peculiar beauty, such as these from the second stanza:

> *Ladies being desired to caress favourably,*
> *Pass from hand to hand in the assembly;*
> *What a sweetest their address—'dear, dear, dear.*
> *I wish you happy new year—a happy new year!'*

[1] This apparently refers to the events occurring in Afghanistan at that time, but the poet's precise meaning is not very clear.

He also wrote a long poem beginning:

Set not your heart upon a desideratum
Oh for an ultimatum, oh for an ultimatum!

What he meant was not quite clear. When I last saw him he had composed a poem in several thousand lines on the Franco-Prussian War which he asked me to read. Unfortunately I had not leisure for such a stupendous task.

During the cold weather of 1878–9 there was, of course, the usual amount of inspection tours to be made. These were almost entirely performed in the steamer. In fact, travelling by land is difficult, if not impossible, to any great extent in Eastern Bengal. The whole country is one vast network of rivers, most of them deep, broad tidal streams. The native population for the most part go about in boats. Small 'dug-out' canoes, fashioned by hollowing out the stem of a big tree, are the usual means of conveyance. Where there are not rivers there are swamps, and enough earth to build a house upon, however small, is only obtainable by digging a big hole and piling up the loose, sandy soil therefrom into a platform, into which bamboo poles are planted to serve as supports for the thatch and matting of which the house is built. Then there are innumerable narrow, winding creeks through which the water of the swamps overflows into the rivers. These are crossed by slight bridges of bamboo. A few poles are planted on each bank and one or two in the bed of the creek. Each pair of poles crosses X fashion, and bamboos are put across from pair to pair resting in the joining point of the X. The natives with their naked feet easily cross the frail structures, but it is a difficult task for a European with boots on to get across a 'sangha' as they are called. Your horse had to swim or wade, and the mud was soft and slimy; moreover there were generally alligators about, so it was not altogether pleasant. Nor was it pleasant to travel, as some men had to do, in a dug-out, sitting in a cramped posture for hours together, afraid to move lest the canoe should upset, through a gorge between lofty hills clothed with dense vegetation of bamboo and creepers, shutting out air and light and producing a stifling heat in which swarms of stinging insects luxuriated. One place there was called Bandarban, a stockade in the Hill Tracts on a ridge where the jungle had been cleared and a few huts built and surrounded by a palisade. The Lushais had been in the habit of raiding down the valley of the Sangu River which flowed at the foot of this ridge. It could only be got at by the river. A small force of Gurkhas with one English officer held this post. No food was procurable in that wilderness; all their provisions had to be brought from Chittagong, a distance of sixty or seventy miles up the winding Sangu through stifling, fever-haunted gorges. The young Lieutenant (Carnac) who commanded in this dismal spot, after enduring loneliness and bad food for some months, was attacked by the deadly fever of those parts. They put him in a dug-out and brought him down the Sangu as fast as they could, but he had to spend a night and a day on the awful river. It was not surprising that he was carried into our house at Chittagong delirious. My good wife nursed him carefully and I put him on the first British India steamer that called, as soon as he was fit to be moved, and just managed to save his life. So rapidly fatal was the Chittagong fever that I had special permission from Government to send away any officer who fell ill without waiting for the usual leave order. This fever always attacked the head, producing violent delirium.

Fortunately for me I was not often compelled to go into such places. As Judge I had to inspect the Munsifis every year, and they were in out-of-the-way places. But I took this duty rather lightly. I had an additional Judge—a sort of coadjutor—to whom I freely and undisguisedly left as much of the judicial work as I could, and he did not mind taking a trip to inspect a Munsifi now and then. These inspections were rather a farce. Munsif in Bengal is the title of a Judge of the lowest grade, who has power to try civil suits of small value and simple nature. In every district there are four or five of these petty courts dotted about all over the country, so as to bring justice close to everyone's door—a much-valued boon in a land where litigation is the principal amusement and joy of all men. Chittagong, the litigious district *par excellence* of all Bengal, supported twelve such courts! One there was picturesquely perched on a hill by the side of the Chittagong River, some twenty miles above the town. It was a small, square building with mat walls and a thatched roof, containing one centre room furnished with bench for the Judge, witness-box and seats for the 'local bar' (as the pleaders love to call themselves) and side rooms for the clerks and records. I took my seat on a chair by the side of the Munsif, a smart young Bengali gentleman who had recently taken the degree of B.L. (Bachelor of Law) at the Calcutta University, and after a short career as a pleader had been promoted to the Bench. It was my duty to hear a case tried and report to the High Court whether it was tried properly or not. Of course the Munsif and his 'bar' were well aware of this, and being born actors, like all natives, they got up a beautiful case for my edification. Such strict adherence to legal forms and technicalities, such very scrupulously correct procedure, such smart and searching cross-examination of witnesses, such very learned and eloquent speeches by the pleaders, with such masses of quotations from, and references to, the most recondite authorities, quite overwhelmed me. The Munsif and one of the pleaders had an argument on a point of law, in which they discharged themselves of all the legal knowledge they had crammed for their last examination, and finally the Munsif delivered judgement in a long and weighty decision, which would not have been too profound had the matter in dispute been of the value of many thousands of rupees, instead of, as I learnt on inquiry, only two rupees four annas! Of course, the knowledge that all this display had been got up specially for my benefit and had been carefully rehearsed beforehand, added to the enjoyment. I expressed my obligations in suitable language, and we parted on the best of terms.

About this time I had, as Judge, to try a curious case about the granting of probate of a will, which presents the characteristic features of the half-caste Portuguese society of Chittagong so vividly that it may be worth while to record it. The names are, of course, fictitious, as the actual persons are still alive, and well known in Bengal. A man, whom I will call Wallace (he actually bore a very famous Scotch name, though how he came by it is a mystery to me), a very black half-caste, had been a Deputy Collector for thirty-odd years and had amassed, in ways that it would be better not to inquire into too closely, a considerable fortune. This he invested in the purchase of two flourishing and remunerative tea-gardens in the Chittagong district. These he left to his son, who was a minor, on the condition that he supported the rest of the family, consisting of old Wallace's widow and two or three children. He appointed a brother Deputy Collector, an old half-caste like himself whom I will call Masson, as Executor and general supervisor of the property, enjoining his son in his will to obey Masson's instructions and to be guided by him in all things. Wallace died some years before the case came on. The widow and children trusted everything to Masson, who managed the estates and allowed them a sufficient though not very bountiful maintenance. What he did with all the money no one ever knew, because his accounts, when produced, were utterly incomprehensible. Intentionally so, the other side said, and probably they were not far wrong. Matters went on in this way for some years. Masson induced the widow to leave her comfortable bungalow at the tea-garden, and remove to a mouldy, dilapidated house in the Portuguese quarter at Chittagong, on the pretence that as his official duties detained him in the town he could look after them better there. His real motive, of course, was to have a free hand at the tea-garden without the family seeing what he was up to. The two eldest children meanwhile attained their majority.

The eldest, a girl, Edith, a very handsome brunette, speedily went to the bad, and after a period of promiscuous intercourse with both native and Portuguese roués of sorts (she also boasted of having bestowed her favours on nearly all the Europeans in the Station!) she became the mistress of one Fraser, an unprincipled Scotch adventurer who had obtained by various means a good deal of property in the district, including a tea-garden adjacent to Wallace's. Fraser kept his eye on Masson and managed to find out all he did, but he held his tongue, biding his time. To cover his liaison with Edith Wallace, he married her to a Portuguese sailor, Pereira, whom he immediately sent away on business to Akyab. Edith, now Mrs Pereira, lived in her husband's house, where she received visits from Fraser, and, as she afterwards confessed, in his absence from anyone else who took her fancy. Pereira was, of course, paid to keep away, and his absence was facilitated by his having the misfortune to sign another gentleman's name instead of his own, which led to his being confined in the Akyab jail for two years. But he had left behind him a brother, one Washington Pereira, a little black monkey with strongly marked Mugh features, who acted as spy on all the rest in the interest of his brother, and also, as it subsequently turned out, of Edith, who, though she took her pleasure with all and sundry, had no idea of letting either Fraser or Masson or anyone else cheat her out of her share of the property. Washington, who was half a Mugh, was, of course, on intimate terms with all the Mugh and Bengali employees on the tea-garden. The son, Henry Wallace, a sickly youth, plunged into the same sort of dissipation as his sister, plus heavy drinking and gambling. Masson furnished him with money for his pleasures, taking care to take receipts from him for every rupee, and compelling the weak-minded boy to keep the matter secret from his mother and sister. When the youth came of age, Masson made over to him the tea-gardens under his father's will, to hold for himself and family, but at the same time he presented him with such a formidable bill for expenses incurred by Masson in the management of the tea-gardens that the youth was easily persuaded to sign two documents, one mortgaging the gardens to Masson for repayment of the expenses, and another appointing him manager of all his property. During the minority Masson had borrowed considerable sums on the security of the gardens, and Henry Wallace was induced to sign documents whereby he made himself responsible for all these sums. Fraser and Edith were made aware of all these doings through Washington and other spies; indeed Fraser privately bought up all or nearly all the debts and held them in the name of a native clerk of his own.

Then came the crisis. Henry Wallace fell ill. 'Drink and the Devil' had done for him. He had a complication of diseases and he had the frail constitution of the Portuguese half-caste. Masson grew alarmed and lost no time in inducing Henry to make a will. He sat by the boy's bed and suggested this and that disposition of the property, and wrote the particulars down as the boy agreed to them. He then took the paper home to write out a fair copy and, having done so, sent it by two native clerks to Henry to sign. Henry, they say, signed it, but instead of return-ing it to Masson called for an envelope, had the will sealed up and put it under his pillow, strictly enjoining his native servants, who waited con-stantly by his bedside, to allow no one to remove it. When his relations heard that he was ill and likely to die, they came over to his house to watch for his last moments. The scene, as depicted by an eye-witness, was horrible. In one room was Edith with one or two male companions, drinking and playing cards and quarrelling; in another the old mother weeping and praying and telling her beads with the priest and some nuns, who, however, were not allowed to visit the wretched boy, 'for fear,' Edith said, 'of frightening him.' In a small inner room, with no furniture but a small cot and some pots and pans, surrounded by a crowd of frightened native servants, lay the unhappy Henry. He had pneumonia, some nameless disease in a virulent form, together with threatenings of delirium tremens. Half-raving, half-crying with pain and fear, attended only by an ignorant native physician, denied the services of a priest, which to him as a Roman Catholic was a necessity, he lin-gered a few hours and then died. No sooner was he dead than there was a rush of all his relatives to the bed to get hold of the will. But the will was gone!!

The servants declared they knew nothing about it, and no amount of search resulted in its being found. Masson, then acting on a section of a certain law, produced the rough copy and applied to me to grant him probate on that. Edith opposed, and (Fraser, of course, paying the ex-penses) got down a barrister from Calcutta to fight her case. Should no will be found she and her mother and sister were the heirs.

The case attracted great attention and my court was crowded for the three long days it lasted. We had Masson in the witness-box for a day. He was a loose, flabby, dark man, and by the end of the day the Counsel for the objectors had reduced him to a pitiable condition. The rough copy, when read in court, commenced by stating that the testator had obeyed his father's wishes and entrusted Masson with the management of the estates, that Masson had discharged his duties faithfully and intelligently, but that owing to bad seasons there had been heavy losses which Masson had made good out of his own pocket, besides paying large sums for the maintenance of the family. Consequently the testator was heavily indebted to him. Then followed a long specification of mortgages and other transactions, and the document wound up by leaving the whole of the testator's property to Masson. In court Masson swore that the fair copy of the will now lost was an exact copy of the draft, that it had not been suggested by him, but was the spontaneous expression of the testator's will. Under a very rigid cross-examination, a cruel system of peculation, lies and treachery was revealed as practised by Masson during a long term of years. There had not been heavy losses on the gardens, but large profits, all of which, apparently, Masson had pocketed. Edith also gave evidence. She was a tall, very handsome woman with a beautiful olive complexion, bold, bright back eyes, a sumptuous figure and a *vultus nimium lubricus aspici*. Washington also gave evidence. It would take too long to detail all the base intrigues, the almost animal sensuality, the total absence of any moral sense in the whole of these people. Ultimately I refused probate, and declared Masson what the law calls an executor *de son tort*, which made him responsible for all the income of the estate since he had charge, and also liable to criminal proceedings for malversation. Edith then proceeded to claim the estate, when her wily lover, Fraser, stepped in and produced proof that he held all the mortgages and bonds. He thus obtained possession of the estate and worked the gardens to his own profit for some years. Unfortunately the Wallaces were too poor to carry on legal proceedings against Masson, so he escaped. But he had received so severe a shock that he soon afterwards died. Fraser also died very suddenly a few years later. In his will he left all the gardens and the rest of the Wallace estate to Edith, who by this time was living with her husband, Pereira, on his release from the Akyab jail. When I last heard of her she was living in some state at Chittagong, going to Mass regularly, and universally respected! The common belief in Chittagong was that the will was stolen by Washington Pereira with the connivance of Wallace's servants, and by him handed to Edith who destroyed it. Edith acquiesced in Fraser's foreclosing the mortages and taking the estates, partly because she could not help it, partly because she hoped to wheedle them out of him eventually. In this she succeeded and he supported her handsomely as long as he lived.

EPILOGUE

JOHN BEAMES, who was my grandfather, called this book *The Story of My Life*, but did not live to finish his tale. He retired from India in 1893 and lived in Somerset, at first near Taunton and later at Clevedon, where he died in May 1902, at the comparatively early age of sixty-five. In his Preface he has explained how and why he came to write these pages, which were never intended for publication but to amuse himself and his family and to occupy his leisure. He has described himself as an 'ordinary average Englishman' living in the reign of Queen Victoria, for he was born on the day Queen Victoria came to the throne and died only a year after the close of her reign.

The first five chapters describe his early life in England and the remainder his career in India, from his arrival in Calcutta in March 1858 as one of the last batch of cadets appointed by the East India Company until the close of his time at Chittagong in 1879. The narrative breaks off quite suddenly on the last page of the great leather-bound volume in which he recorded the story in his neat, flowing hand, with hardly an addition or an erasure throughout its hundreds of pages. The reader may wonder why the narrative was left unfinished, or not at least brought down to the point when he retired from India. The main reason is that he was busy with other writing during his retirement and died before he had time to complete his manuscript. In the Preface he explains that he began the story in Cuttack in 1875, and that after continuing at intervals for a few years he broke off till after his retirement. Then in 1896 he started re-writing it from the beginning when living at Bishop's Hull, near Taunton, but in the middle of Chapter XVII of the original manuscript there is a head-note 'Clevedon, near Bristol, August 1900'. From this it appears that he had again laid aside the manuscript for some time and took it up again after he had moved to Clevedon. There follow some three and a half fairly long chapters, and as he was then also busy with an (unfinished) *Historical Geography of India* and a translation from the Turki of Babar's Memoirs, it is apparent that the completion of his memoirs was prevented by other writing and by his early death in May 1902.

Perhaps another reason is that, like the sundial, he preferred to record only his happy hours. The latter part of his time in India was spent mainly alone, with his wife and family in England for most of the time, and in addition to this separation his closing years were clouded by a disappointment in his official career, which is mentioned below.

In case the reader is interested in John Beames's later career, the following biographical details are added. These have been gathered partly from a brief note left by him, giving merely the dates between 1880 and 1899 of the half-dozen or so principal events of each year, and partly from the recollections of my mother, his youngest daughter, Angela, whose birth in Cuttack in 1876 is mentioned in the narrative. As, however, she was taken home to England from Chittagong at the age of three, and only saw her father once, when he was on short leave in England before he retired, her knowledge of the latter part of his career in India is of necessity somewhat restricted and lacking in detail. She herself returned to India in 1896 after her marriage to my father (who was also in the Indian Civil Service) and did not return to England till 1900 when I was about a year old, so that she did not see much of her father before he died.

In the note referred to above he has described the period of eighteen months spent in Chittagong as one of 'continual misery', and he certainly has some hard things to say about the climate and people of that place, which he seems to have disliked intensely after his nine happy years in Orissa. However, in September 1879 he took two months' leave in Calcutta and Mussoorie, while his wife and younger children went home to England. On return to duty he spent the next year or two as Collector of Hooghly, near Calcutta, and in 1881 became Commissioner of Burdwan, living at Chinsura in Bengal proper. For the next four years he continued at Chinsura, mainly alone, as my grandmother had to remain mostly in England with his large family of eight children.

During this period there is not much of interest in his notes, which mainly concern tours in his division and other official work, interspersed with occasional visits from the Lieutenant-Governor of Bengal. There was even a visit from the Viceroy, Lord Ripon, with whom he notes that he had 'tiffin in the train at Burdwan' in December 1882. The next year he went to Bareilly in the North-West Provinces (later the United Provinces, now Uttar Pradesh) to meet his eldest son David, who had come out with a commission in the Indian Army and whom he had not seen for fifteen years. His second son, Frederick, had also about this time passed into the Indian Civil Service, and was spending the usual probationary period at the University learning Indian languages, law, etc. But in 1884 there was a bitter disappointment when Frederick failed to pass his final examination and was thus unable to follow his father in a career in India.

EPILOGUE

In 1885, when the old Maharaja of Burdwan died, John Beames moved his headquarters from Chinsura to Burdwan, probably to enable him to deal more easily with the series of intrigues which arose over the succession to the title and estates. These occupied his attention for several months, during which it was even suspected that an attempt was made by one of the interested parties to poison him. He was ill for some time during the summer, but seems to have recovered by the time his wife returned from England in November, bringing with her their eldest daughter Margaret, who was then seventeen. Christmas and the winter of 1885–6 were a gay time, and he notes that his old friend Elliot came to stay with him in Calcutta, and that there were 'nothing but balls and parties' during January and February.

That year passed uneventfully at Burdwan, but early in 1887 there occurred an incident which affected the remainder of his official life. This was when he was asked to give evidence before a public commission in Calcutta inquiring into Indian education, a subject on which he held strong, but what would now be considered reactionary, views. Little material is available of the details of this episode beyond the fact that he was very unwilling to give evidence in a public inquiry of this kind, but was assured that he need have no hesitation in expressing his opinions. His reluctance in this matter is not easy to reconcile with his more usual habit of speaking his mind with alarming frankness whenever his convictions so impelled him, but, as it turned out, his premonitions on this occasion were justified. Students of Indian history will remember that this was the period of the Ilbert Bill controversy, a measure which aroused much heated feeling throughout India, particularly in Calcutta. Though the Education Commission was not in any way concerned with the matters dealt with by the Ilbert Bill, John Beames's reluctance to give public evidence on a controversial subject at that time is perhaps understandable. Whatever he said to the Commission must have been in character, but in the brief notes he left there is only the significant entry dated 22 February 1887: 'Gave evidence before Public Service Commission and cut my own throat without being aware of it.' A month later he was promoted to the Board of Revenue, then the highest administrative post below the Lieutenant-Governor in the province—an indication that the Bengal Government at least did not disapprove of the views he had expressed.

In April, however, there was a violent attack on him in an Indian-owned daily newspaper of Calcutta, followed by a second similar attack in June, the sequel to which is noted by him laconically on 14 July: 'Removed from the Board by order of the Government of India.' This is followed by another entry immediately afterwards: 'July 20th—Letter promising reappointment.' He has left no further record of this incident, and one can only surmise that his evidence before the Commission displeased the local politicians of that time, and that as a sop to the ensuing political agitation he was demoted by the Government of India—not, be it noted, by the Government of Bengal, who wrote to him promising reappointment.

In August 1887, however, he reverted as Commissioner of Bhagalpur, where he remained for nearly two years, until in April 1889 he returned to Calcutta and again acted for some months on the Board of Revenue. Thereafter he remained in Calcutta, mostly as a Commissioner, but with occasional periods of special duty drafting Government Bills on revenue matters and as president of the Police Commission. He returned to England for six months during the summer of 1891—only the second home leave in thirty-five years' service—but came back to Calcutta in November, and spent his last eighteen months there as Commissioner of the Presidency division, before he finally retired in March 1893. Thus ended his official career, of which the last few years were embittered by the Education Commission episode, rendered perhaps more difficult to bear by the loneliness and separation from his wife and family, which at one time or another affected the lives of all who served in India. It is no part of such a biographical note as this to criticize, but it must be evident to all who read this narrative that John Beames was a man of strong personal opinions, and by temperament unable to suffer gladly those official superiors with whose views he did not agree—a pre-requisite for advancement then, as now. Like his grandfather, 'Cross Beames, Q.C.', whom he has described in an early chapter, he had a hasty temper and a caustic tongue, which made him enemies among those senior officials who did not relish his outspoken and often ill-timed comments. His brushes with Sir Richard Temple at various stages of his career are an example of this, and are described with a diverting *naïveté* which shows that he only half-realized the inevitable results of exercising his wit at the expense of Lieutenant-Governors, however pompous and irritating. But then, as Philip Mason remarks in his book, *The Rulers of India*, referred to below, John Beames 'did not really care for Lieutenant-Governors as a class'. It may well be that the unhappy episode of 1887 and its consequences induced in him a reluctance to continue his narrative to the end, and that, even if he had lived, he might have felt an aversion from recalling to his memory, by setting them down in writing, the events which cast a shadow over the last years of his long and otherwise happy service.

A point which does not fully appear from his story is that in his time John Beames attained some eminence in the philological world. He mentions now and again his interest in languages, the winning of two gold medals for Persian early in his career, and the publication during his time in India of his *Comparative Grammar of the Modern Aryan Languages of India**. This was published in three volumes between 1872 and 1879, and was preceded by his *Outlines of Indian Philology* in 1867, which was described as 'the first attempt to prepare a scientific general account of all the languages then known to be spoken in India', and which, though now, of course, largely out of date, has recently been translated into Urdu in Lucknow. He was a fellow both of the Royal Asiatic Society of Great Britain and of the Asiatic Society of Bengal, and contributed numerous articles to the Journals of both these learned bodies and to the Indian Antiquary. His *Grammar of the Bengali Language*, published in 1891, was still a textbook as late as 1922 for I.C.S. probationers posted to that province. A colleague and contemporary, Sir George Grierson, author of *A Linguistic Survey of India*, wrote of his *Comparative Grammar*:

'It is difficult to decide which to admire most in this Grammar, the learning displayed, or the clearness with which the results of that learning are put forth. . . . He had a trenchant pen, and could wield it with effect when he considered it to be necessary, but the numerous references in his *magnum opus* to the opinions of other scholars showed that he possessed a double portion of the spirit of Saraswati [the Hindu goddess of learning]—a just confidence in his own great store of learning, and an ungrudging recognition of the discoveries made by other students in the same line of research as that in which he had an acknowledged claim to be recognized as one of the first authorities.'

In addition to his interests in Oriental languages, particularly Persian and Sanskrit, he had a working knowledge of German, French, Italian and some other European languages. To anyone who has served in India, it must be a matter of astonishment that he was able to find time from his official duties, which were heavy and continuous, to delve so deeply into linguistic studies.

My father retired in 1916 after thirty years' service in India, spent mainly in the United Provinces, and after a gap of six years I followed him in the same province till 1947. The family connexion with the ser-

---

*This great work was still in print as recently as 1981, more than a century after its first appearance.

vice thus lasted for some ninety years—by no means unique or even un-usual, but a long time nevertheless. It was not till after leaving India that I came across my grandfather's memoirs among old family papers in my mother's possession. A few years later Philip Mason, an old friend and colleague in India, asked for the loan of material of this nature for a book he was then writing on the history of the Indian Civil Service, and I was delighted to lend him the manuscript, of which he made considerable use. Extracts have therefore already appeared in the two volumes of *The Men Who Ruled India*, and I am glad to take this opportunity of acknowledging my gratitude to him, for without his advice and encouragement this book would not now have been pub-lished.

Lastly, my thanks are also due to Dr Mahadeva Prasad Saha of Cal-cutta, Secretary of the Asiatic Society of Bengal, who, though previously unknown to me, has taken great trouble in searching out and sending me details (too numerous to quote here) of the many papers on philo-logical and antiquarian subjects contributed by my grandfather during his time in India to the Journal of that Society.

CHRISTOPHER COOKE.

Great Missenden, 1960.

INDEX

Adams, Major Robert Roy 97–103

Agra 93, 127

Aitchison, Dr 116–18

Al, Maharaja of 245–6

Alabaster, Chaloner 87–8

Allahabad 79, 85, 88, 93, 127

Ambala 94, 111, 119–23

Andaman Islands 156, 215

Angul, Raja of 260–1

Armstrong, Joseph 254, 271

Arrah 127–8, 131

Asiatic Society of Bengal 216, 257, 305–6

Atkinson, Mr 252–3

Auckland, Lord 69

Balasore 186, 190–216, 220, 241, 274

Baldwin, Mr 170–4, 183

Balramgarhi 199, 206–7

Bani 117

Banki, Raja of 261

Bashley Lodge 21–3, 37–40, 49–54, 60, 71–2, 160, 189

Bayley, Sir Steuart 127, 129–31

Beadon, Sir Cecil 151, 252

Beames, Ellen (*née* Geary) 57, 71, 73, 105, 109–12, 116, 122, 133, 164, 175, 185, 187, 215–16, 241, 246, 275, 289

Beames, Harry 17, 37, 50–3, 71, 150–1, 178, 184, 186, 285

Beames, Uncle John 18, 23, 39–40, 50, 51

Beames, Pearson 27, 29, 38, 49, 51–5, 58, 70–1, 131, 133, 150, 175, 257

Beames, Susannah Amelia (*née* Dewsnap) 24–9, 188

Beames, Rev. Thomas 18, 19, 20, 22, 23, 25, 27–8, 35–6, 38, 48, 53–4, 72, 73, 150, 159–60

Beames, Willie 29, 50, 51, 53, 58, 72

Benares 89, 93, 127, 271

Bernard, Charles Edward 75, 116, 124, 201–2

Bettiah, Maharaja of 172, 181–3

Bhagalpur 152, 304

Bhutan campaign, 1864–5 159–164, 169

Bhuvaneshwar, temple of 273–4

Bignold, Frank 200–1

Birch, Lulu 88–91

Birch, Gen. Sir Richard 88–90

Blunt, Rev. Henry, and Jasper 31, 33, 34, 37

Bond, Capt. Alfred 192

Bond, Mrs Bridget 193

le Breton, Dean William 30

Buckley, Rev. J. 63, 67

Buddhists 127, 165–7, 273–4, 283

Bulandshahr 93, 95, 108, 109, 127

Burdwan, Maharaja of 186, 302–303

Busk, Col 120

Calcott, Dr 22

Calcutta 9, 10, 78–91, 128, 186, 206, 215, 217, 237–8, 259, 275, 277, 302–4

Cameron, Emma 29, 31, 34, 38

308

INDEX

INDEX

Previously published by

ELAND BOOKS

A VISIT TO DON OTAVIO

SYBILLE BEDFORD
A Mexican Journey

I am convinced that, once this wonderful book becomes better known, it will seem incredible that it could ever have gone out of print.
Bruce Chatwin, Vogue

This book can be recommended as vastly enjoyable. Here is a book radiant with comedy and colour.
Raymond Mortimer, Sunday Times

Perceptive, lively, aware of the significance of trifles, and a fine writer. Applied to a beautiful, various, and still inscrutable country, these talents yield a singularly delightful result.
The Times

This book has that ageless quality which is what most people mean when they describe a book as classical. From the moment that the train leaves New York...it is certain that this journey will be rewarding. When one finally leaves Mrs Bedford on the point of departure, it is with the double regret of leaving Mexico and her company, and one cannot say more than that.
Elizabeth Jane Howard

Malicious, friendly, entertaining and witty.
Evening Standard

This edition is not for sale in the USA

ELAND BOOKS
specialise in the literature of travel.
If you wish to receive details of forthcoming publications,
please send your address to
Eland Books, 53 Eland Road, London SW11 5JX

Previously published by

ELAND BOOKS

VIVA MEXICO!

CHARLES MACOMB FLANDRAU

A traveller's account of life in Mexico

With a new preface by Nicholas Shakespeare

His lightness of touch is deceiving, for one reads *Viva Mexico!* under the impression that one is only being amused, but comes to realise in the end that Mr Flandrau has presented a truer, more graphic and comprehensive picture of the Mexican character than could be obtained from a shelful of more serious and scientific tomes.
New York Times

The best book I have come upon which attempts the alluring but difficult task of introducing the tricks and manners of one country to the people of another.
Alexander Woollcott

The most enchanting, as well as extremely funny book on Mexico... I wish it were reprinted.
Sybille Bedford

His impressions are deep, sympathetic and judicious. In addition, he is a marvellous writer, with something of Mark Twain's high spirits and Henry James's suavity...as witty as he is observant.
Geoffrey Smith, Country Life

ELAND BOOKS
specialise in the literature of travel.
If you wish to receive details of forthcoming publications,
please send your address to
Eland Books, 53 Eland Road, London SW11 5JX

Previously published by

ELAND BOOKS

TRAVELS WITH MYSELF AND ANOTHER

MARTHA GELLHORN

Must surely be ranked as one of the funniest travel books of our time — second only to *A Short Walk in the Hindu Kush* ... It doesn't matter whether this author is experiencing marrow-freezing misadventures in war-ravaged China, or driving a Landrover through East African game-parks, or conversing with hippies in Israel, or spending a week in a Moscow Intourist Hotel. Martha Gellhorn's reactions are what count and one enjoys equally her blistering scorn of humbug, her hilarious eccentricities, her unsentimental compassion.
Dervla Murphy, Irish Times

Spun with a fine blend of irony and epigram. She is incapable of writing a dull sentence.
The Times

Miss Gellhorn has a novelist's eye, a flair for black comedy and a short fuse...there is not a boring word in her humane and often funny book.
The New York Times

Among the funniest and best written books I have ever read.
Byron Rogers, Evening Standard

ELAND BOOKS
specialise in the literature of travel.
If you wish to receive details of forthcoming publications,
please send your address to
Eland Books, 53 Eland Road, London SW11 5JX

Previously published by

ELAND BOOKS

MOROCCO
THAT WAS

WALTER HARRIS

With a new preface by Patrick Thursfield

Both moving and hilariously satirical.
Gavin Maxwell, Lords of the Atlas

Many interesting sidelights on the customs and
characters of the Moors...intimate knowledge of the
courts, its language and customs...thorough understanding of the Moorish character.
New York Times

No Englishman knows Morocco better than Mr W.
B. Harris and his new book...is most entertaining.
Spectator (1921)

The author's great love of Morocco and of the Moors
is only matched by his infectious zest for life... thanks
to his observant eye and a gift for felicitously turned
phrases, the books of Walter Harris can claim to rank
as literature.
Rom Landau, Moroccan Journal (1957)

His pages bring back the vanished days of the unfet-
tered Sultanate in all their dark splendour; a mingling
of magnificence with squalor, culture with barbarism,
refined cruelty with naive humour that reads like a
dream of the Arabian Nights.
The Times

ELAND BOOKS
specialise in the literature of travel.
If you wish to receive details of forthcoming publications,
please send your address to
Eland Books, 53 Eland Road, London SW11 5JX

FAR AWAY
AND LONG AGO

W. H. HUDSON
A Childhood in Argentina

With a new preface by Nicholas Shakespeare

One cannot tell how this fellow gets his effects; he writes as the grass grows.
It is as if some very fine and gentle spirit were whispering to him the sentences he puts down on the paper. A privileged being

Joseph Conrad

Hudson's work is a vision of natural beauty and of human life as it might be, quickened and sweetened by the sun and the wind and the rain, and by fellowship with all other forms of life...a very great writer... the most valuable our age has possessed.

John Galsworthy

And there was no one – no writer – who did not acknowledge without question that this composed giant was the greatest living writer of English.
Far Away and Long Ago is the most self-revelatory of all his books.

Ford Madox Ford

Completely riveting and should be read by everyone.
Auberon Waugh

ELAND BOOKS
specialise in the literature of travel.
If you wish to receive details of forthcoming publications,
please send your address to
Eland Books, 53 Eland Road, London SW11 5JX

Previously published by

ELAND BOOKS

A DRAGON APPARENT
NORMAN LEWIS
Travels in Cambodia, Laos and Vietnam

A book which should take its place in the permanent
literature of the Far East.
Economist

One of the most absorbing travel books I have read
for a very long time...the great charm of the work is
its literary vividness. Nothing he describes is dull.
Peter Quennell, Daily Mail

One of the best post-war travel books and, in retro-
spect, the most heartrending.
The Observer

Apart from the *Quiet American,* which is of course a
novel, the best book on Vietnam remains *A Dragon
Apparent.*
Richard West, Spectator (1978)

One of the most elegant, witty, immensely readable,
touching and tragic books I've ever read.
Edward Blishen, Radio 4

ELAND BOOKS
specialise in the literature of travel.
If you wish to receive details of forthcoming publications,
please send your address to
Eland Books, 53 Eland Road, London SW11 5JX

Previously published by

ELAND BOOKS

THE CHANGING SKY

NORMAN LEWIS

Travels of a Novelist

He really goes in deep like a sharp polished knife. I have never travelled in my armchair so fast, variously and well.
V.S. Pritchett, New Statesman

He has compressed into these always entertaining and sophisticated sketches material that a duller man would have hoarded for half a dozen books.
The Times

A delightful, instructive, serious and funny book. Norman Lewis has the oblique poetry of a Firbank, the eye of a lynx.
Anthony Carson, The Observer

ELAND BOOKS
specialise in the literature of travel.
If you wish to receive details of forthcoming publications,
please send your address to
Eland Books, 53 Eland Road, London SW11 5JX

Previously published by

ELAND BOOKS

GOLDEN EARTH

NORMAN LEWIS

Travels in Burma

Mr Lewis can make even a lorry interesting.
Cyril Connolly, Sunday Times

Very funny . . . a really delightful book.
Maurice Collis, Observer

Norman Lewis remains the best travel writer alive.
Auberon Waugh, Business Traveller

The reader may find enormous pleasure here
without knowing the country.
Honor Tracy, New Statesman

The brilliance of the Burmese scene is paralleled by
the brilliance of the prose.
Guy Ramsey, Daily Telegraph

ELAND BOOKS
specialise in the literature of travel.
If you wish to receive details of forthcoming publications,
please send your address to
Eland Books, 53 Eland Road, London SW11 5JX

Previously published by

ELAND BOOKS

NAPLES '44

NORMAN LEWIS

As unique an experience for the reader as it must have been a unique experience for the writer.
Graham Greene

Uncommonly well written, entertaining despite its depressing content, and quite remarkably evocative.
Philip Toynbee, Observer

His ten novels and five non-fiction works place him in the front rank of contemporary English writers ... here is a book of gripping fascination in its flow of bizarre anecdote and character sketch; and it is much more than that.
J. W. Lambert, Sunday Times

A wonderful book.
Richard West, Spectator

Sensitive, ironic and intelligent.
Paul Fussell, The New Republic

One goes on reading page after page as if eating cherries.
Luigi Barzini, New York Review of Books

This edition is not for sale in the USA

ELAND BOOKS
specialise in the literature of travel.
If you wish to receive details of forthcoming publications,
please send your address to
Eland Books, 53 Eland Road, London SW11 5JX

A YEAR IN
MARRAKESH

PETER MAYNE

A notable book, for the author is exceptional both in his literary talent and his outlook. His easy economical style seizes, with no sense of effort, the essence of people, situations and places... Mr Mayne is that rare thing, a natural writer ... no less exceptional is his humour.
Few Westerners have written about Islam with so little nonsense and such understanding.
Times Literary Supplement

He has contrived in a deceptively simple prose to disseminate in the air of an English November the spicy odours of North Africa; he has turned, for an hour, smog to shimmering sunlight. He has woven a texture of extraordinary charm.
Daily Telegraph

Mr Mayne's book gives us the 'strange elation' that good writing always creates. It is a good book, an interesting book, and one that I warmly recommend.
Harold Nicolson, Observer

ELAND BOOKS
specialise in the literature of travel.
If you wish to receive details of forthcoming publications,
please send your address to
Eland Books, 53 Eland Road, London SW11 5JX

Previously published by

ELAND BOOKS

KENYA DIARY (1902–1906)
RICHARD MEINERTZHAGEN

With a new preface by Elspeth Huxley

This bracing if often bloodthirsty tale is an invaluable chronicle both for the serious historian of East Africa and for the curious safari-going passer-by with an alert sense of history . . . a splendid republication.
Times Literary Supplement

This book is of great interest and should not be missed
New Statesman

The overall impact hits harder than, say, Hemingway because the author's reactions to any situation are never less than utterly instinctive, and hence honest, and because his scientific interest in animals transcends the trophy-hunting. A black mamba travels, we learn, at 7 mph. He timed it with a stopwatch while it was chasing one of his bearers.
Hugh Seymour-Davies, Country Life

Anybody at all interested in the evolution of Kenya or the workings of 'colonialism' would do well to read this diary.
William Plomer, Listener

ELAND BOOKS
specialise in the literature of travel.
If you wish to receive details of forthcoming publications,
please send your address to
Eland Books, 53 Eland Road, London SW11 5JX

Previously published by

ELAND BOOKS

JOURNEYS OF A
GERMAN IN ENGLAND

CARL PHILIP MORITZ

A walking-tour of England in 1782

With a new preface by Reginald Nettel

The extraordinary thing about the book is that the writing is so fresh that you are startled when a stage-coach appears. A young man is addressing himself to you across two centuries. And there is a lovely comedy underlying it.
Byron Rogers, Evening Standard

This account of his travels has a clarity and freshness quite unsurpassed by any contemporary descriptions.
Iain Hamilton, Illustrated London News

A most amusing book...a variety of small scenes which might come out of Hogarth...Moritz in London, dodging the rotten oranges flung about the pit of the Haymarket Theatre, Moritz in the pleasure gardens of Vauxhall and Ranelagh, Moritz in Parliament or roving the London streets is an excellent companion. We note, with sorrow, that nearly two centuries ago, British coffee was already appalling.
Alan Pryce-Jones, New York Herald Tribune

ELAND BOOKS
specialise in the literature of travel.
If you wish to receive details of forthcoming publications,
please send your address to
Eland Books, 53 Eland Road, London SW11 5JX

Previously published by

ELAND BOOKS

TRAVELS INTO THE INTERIOR OF AFRICA

MUNGO PARK

With a new preface by Jeremy Swift

Famous triumphs of exploration have rarely engendered outstanding books. *Travels into the Interior of Africa*, which has remained a classic since its first publication in 1799, is a remarkable exception.

It was a wonder that he survived so long, and a still greater one that his diaries could have been preserved . . . what amazing reading they make today!
Roy Kerridge, Tatler

The enthusiasm and understanding which informs Park's writing is irresistible.
Frances Dickenson, Time Out

One of the greatest and most respected explorers the world has known, a man of infinite courage and lofty principles, and one who dearly loved the black African.
E. W. Bovill, the Niger Explored

Told with a charm and naivety in themselves sufficient to captivate the most fastidious reader...modesty and truthfulness peep from every sentence...for actual hardships undergone, for dangers faced, and difficulties overcome, together with an exhibition of virtues which make a man great in the rude battle of life, Mungo Park stands without a rival.
Joseph Thomson, author of Through Masailand

ELAND BOOKS
specialise in the literature of travel.
If you wish to receive details of forthcoming publications,
please send your address to
Eland Books, 53 Eland Road, London SW11 5JX